Design for **Information**

First published in the United States of America in 2013 by
Rockport Publishers, a member of
Quarto Publishing Group USA Inc.
100 Cummings Center
Suite 406-L
Beverly, Massachusetts 01915-6101
Telephone: (978) 282-9590
Fax: (978) 283-2742
www.rockpub.com
Visit RockPaperInk.com to share your opinions, creations,
and passion for design.

10 9 8 7 6 5

ISBN: 978-1-59253-806-5

Digital edition published in 2013
eISBN: 978-1-61058-948-2

Library of Congress Cataloging-in-Publication Data available

Design: Isabel Meirelles
Cover Image: "Wind Map" by Fernanda Viégas and
Martin Wattenberg

Printed in China

Design for Information

An introduction to the histories, theories, and best practices behind effective information visualizations

Isabel Meirelles

Rockport Publishers
100 Cummings Center, Suite 406L
Beverly, MA 01915

rockpub.com • rockpaperink.com

CONTENTS

6 INTRODUCTION

16 CHAPTER 1:
HIERARCHICAL STRUCTURES: TREES

46 CHAPTER 2:
RELATIONAL STRUCTURES: NETWORKS

82 CHAPTER 3:
TEMPORAL STRUCTURES: TIMELINES AND FLOWS

114 CHAPTER 4:
SPATIAL STRUCTURES: MAPS

158 CHAPTER 5:
SPATIO-TEMPORAL STRUCTURES

184 CHAPTER 6:
TEXTUAL STRUCTURES

204 APPENDIX: DATA TYPES
206 NOTES
210 BIBLIOGRAPHY
214 CONTRIBUTORS
218 INDEX
223 ACKNOWLEDGMENTS
224 ABOUT THE AUTHOR

INTRODUCTION

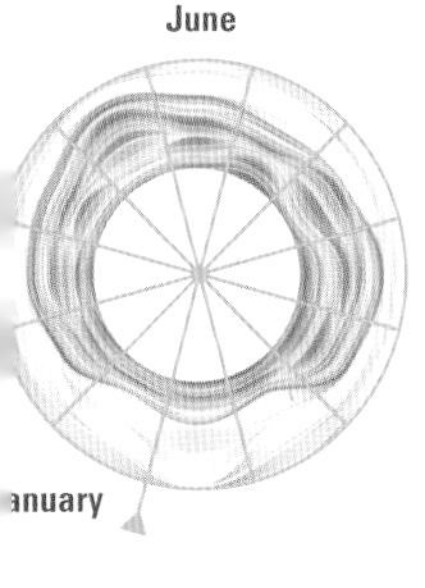

Fernanda Viégas and Martin Wattenberg, U.S.: "Flickr Flow," 2009.

The circular flow of colors represents the Boston Common over time, with summer at the top, and time proceeding clockwise. After collecting photographs of the park at Flickr, Viégas and Wattenberg applied their own algorithm to calculate the relative proportions of different colors seen in the photos taken in each month of the year. The final output is a visual experiment whose materials are color and time.

INTRODUCTION

Design for Information offers an integrative approach to learning basic methods and graphical principles for the visual presentation of information. The book surveys current visualizations that are analyzed for their content (information) as well as for their methods of presentation and design strategies (design). The objective is to provide readers with critical and analytical tools that can benefit the design process of visualizing data.

Chapters are organized around a main visualization that, working as a sounding board, provides the context for scrutinizing information design principles. The selection criteria considered visualizations that are representative of relevant graphical methods and, most important, can serve as a platform for discussions on the histories, theories, and best practices in the field. The selections represent a fraction of effective visualizations that we encounter in this burgeoning field, offering the reader an opportunity to extend the study to solutions in other fields of practice.

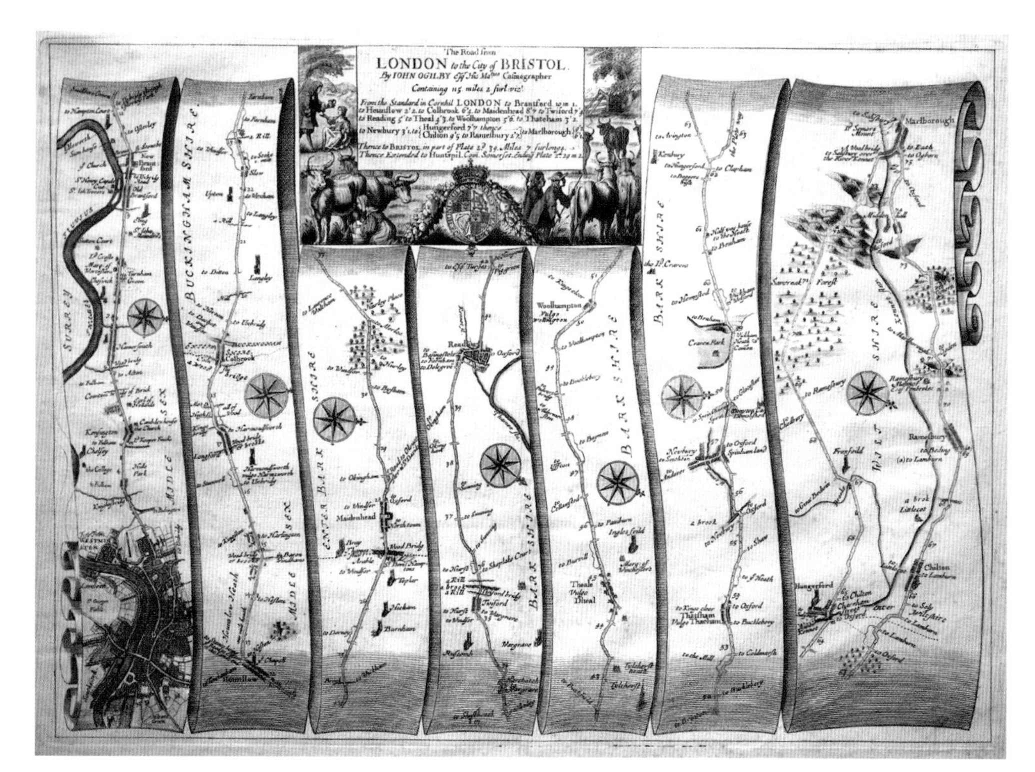

John Ogilby, U.K.: The Road from London to the City of Bristol, 1675.

This map was published in the *Britannia,* which is considered the first national road-atlas in Europe. The atlas presents over 100 folio-sized route maps in England and Wales. Michael Dover explains, "The maps, of seventy-five major roads and cross-roads, totalling 7,500 miles (12,500 kilometers), were presented in a continuous strip-form and, uniquely, on a uniform scale at 1 inch (2.5 cm) to a mile (1.6 kilometers). Of the hundred sheets of roads, most depicted a distance of about 70 miles (112 kilometers) on one sheet. The road is shown as a series of parallel strips. The surveyors noted whether the roads were enclosed by walls or hedges, or open, local landmarks, inns, bridges, (with a note on the material of construction), fords and sometimes cultivation in the countryside on either side of the road."[3]

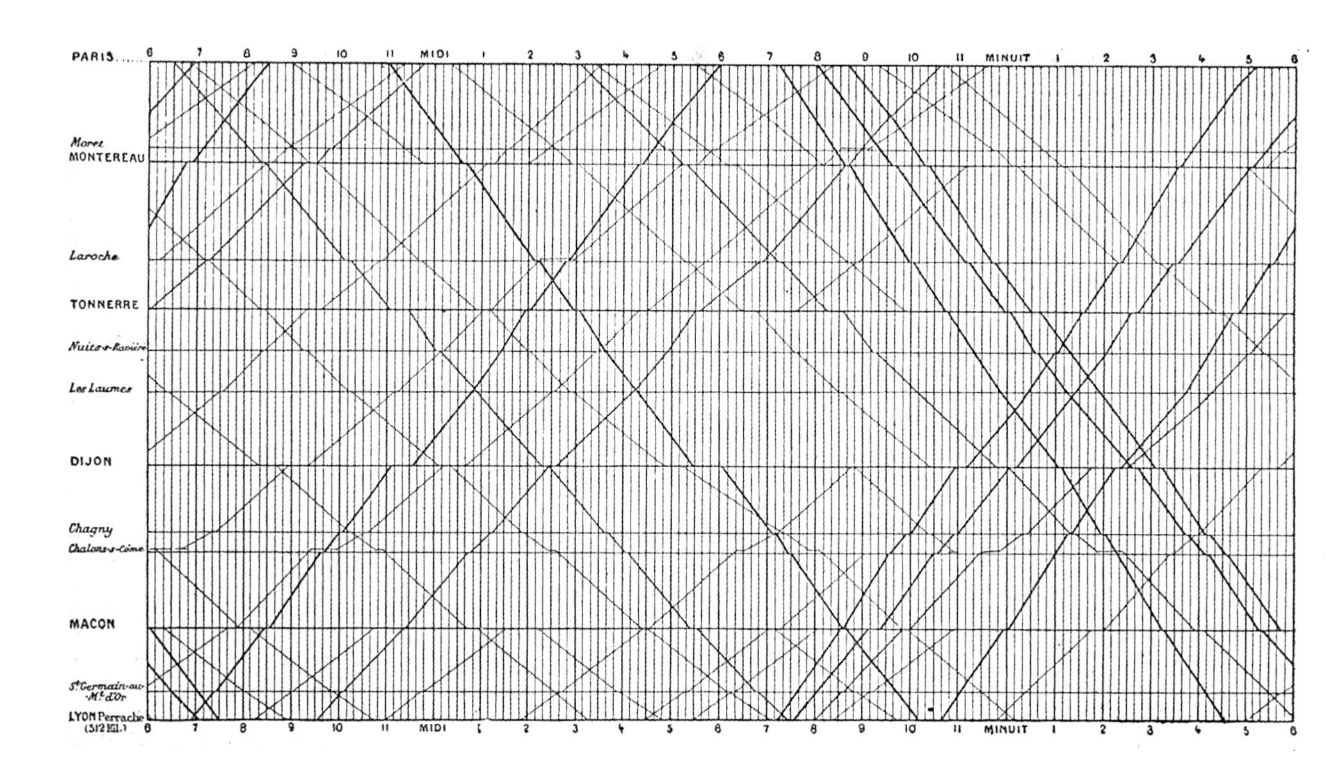

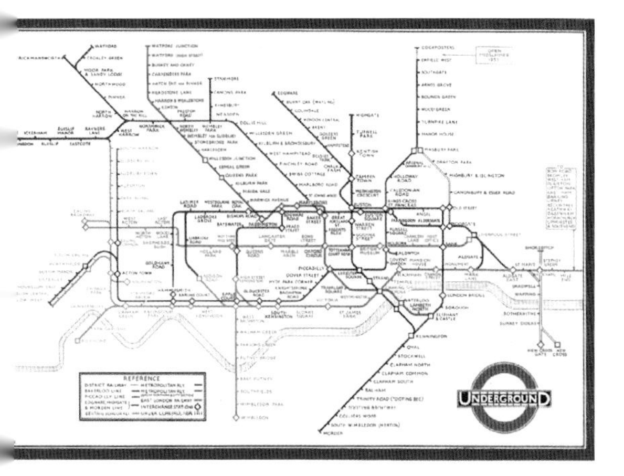

Harry Beck, U.K.: London Tube Map, 1933.

The method devised by Beck has been used all over the world to communicate subway systems. Note the use of only two angles to represent all lines as well as the equidistance between stations.

Etienne-Jules Marey, France: Paris–Lyon Train Schedule, 1885.

The graphic uses a method attributed to the French engineer Ibry, in which lines represent distances traveled in relation to the time taken to traverse them. At a glance, we learn several levels of information, from the micro level of a specific line and time in which trains stop at a particular city, to a macro-level comparison between speeds of trains in both directions, to and from Paris.

I firmly believe that a full understanding of how others have solved (design) problems enables one to successfully develop a set of skills that may be deliberately accessed for use in expert and productive ways.

SKILLS

Representing multidimensional information structures in a two-dimensional visual display is not trivial. The design process requires both analytical and visual/spatial methods of reasoning. Graphic design in general, and information design in particular, depend upon cognitive processes and visual perception for both its creation (encoding) and its use (decoding). If the decoding process fails, the visualization fails.

Understanding the constraints and capabilities of cognition and visual perception is essential to the way we visualize information. From cartography to computational methods, from statistics to visual perception, skills are examined in the context of the selected visualizations.

My goal is to bridge the technical requirements with the design aspects of visualizations, with an emphasis on the latter. To this end, I bring established scientific theories to clarify and enhance how we organize and encode information, including suggested readings and sources for further investigation. It is my hope that this book will help broaden the dialogue and reduce the gap between two communities—designers and scientists—and foster problem-solving skills in designing for information.

Although this book targets design students, it can be helpful to students in other disciplines involved with visualizing information, such as those in the (digital) humanities and in most of the sciences. This book encourages three different levels of knowledge acquisition: theoretical, historical, and practical, with guidelines for the construction of visualizations. Ultimately, this book promotes visual literacy while developing a practical design lexicon in the context of visualization of information.

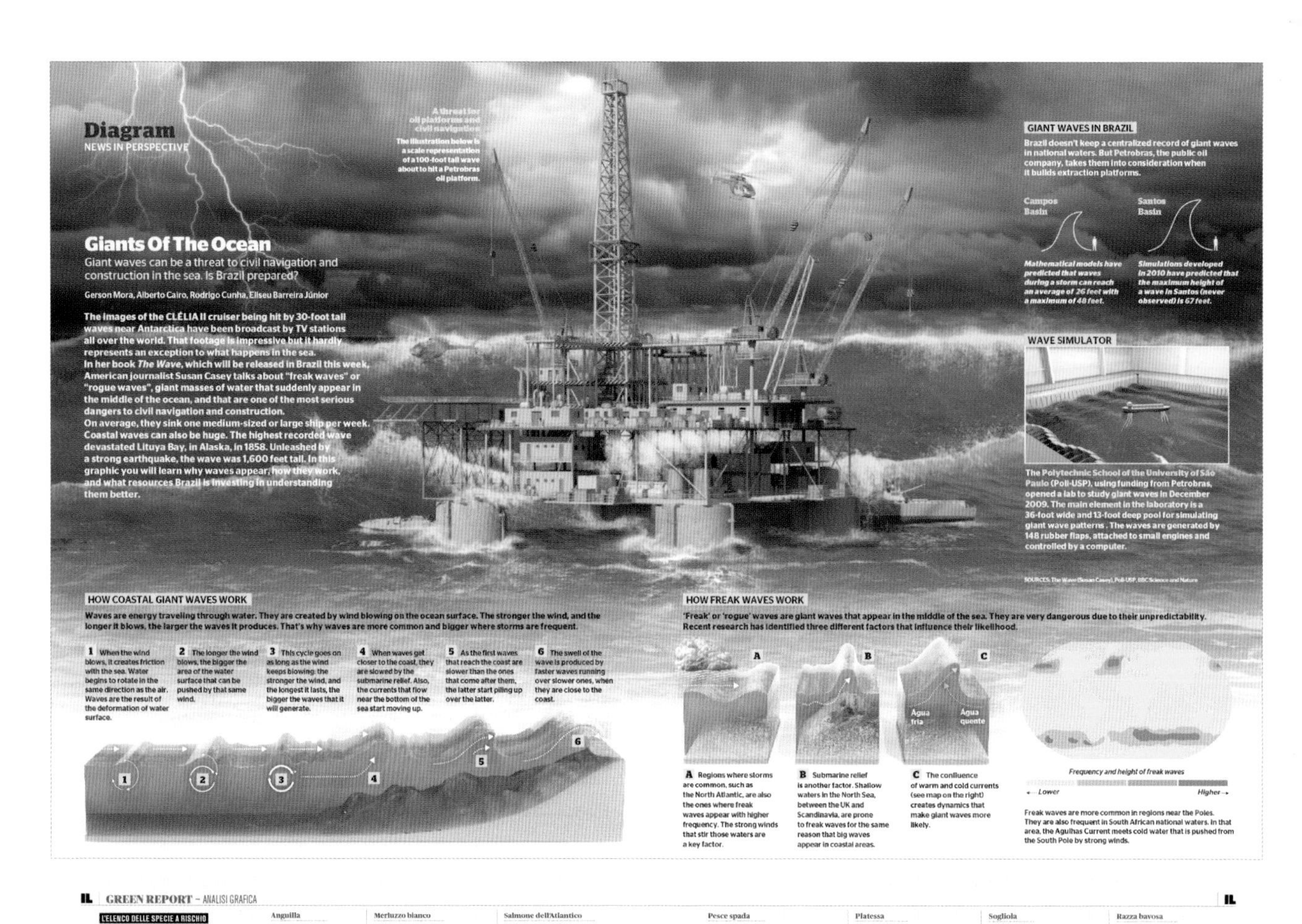
Diagram
NEWS IN PERSPECTIVE
A threat for oil platforms and civil navigation
The illustration below is a scale representation of a 100-foot tall wave about to hit a Petrobras oil platform.
Giants Of The Ocean
Giant waves can be a threat to civil navigation and construction in the sea. Is Brazil prepared?
Gerson Mora, Alberto Cairo, Rodrigo Cunha, Eliseu Barreira Júnior
The images of the CLÉLIA II cruiser being hit by 30-foot tall waves near Antarctica have been broadcast by TV stations all over the world. That footage is impressive but it hardly represents an exception to what happens in the sea.
In her book The Wave, which will be released in Brazil this week, American journalist Susan Casey talks about "freak waves" or "rogue waves", giant masses of water that suddenly appear in the middle of the ocean, and that are one of the most serious dangers to civil navigation and construction.
On average, they sink one medium-sized or large ship per week. Coastal waves can also be huge. The highest recorded wave devastated Lituya Bay, in Alaska, in 1858. Unleashed by a strong earthquake, the wave was 1,600 feet tall. In this graphic you will learn why waves appear, how they work, and what resources Brazil is investing in understanding them better.
GIANT WAVES IN BRAZIL
Brazil doesn't keep a centralized record of giant waves in national waters. But Petrobras, the public oil company, takes them into consideration when it builds extraction platforms.
Campos Basin
Mathematical models have predicted that waves during a storm can reach an average of 26 feet with a maximum of 48 feet.
Santos Basin
Simulations developed in 2010 have predicted that the maximum height of a wave in Santos (never observed) is 67 feet.
WAVE SIMULATOR
The Polytechnic School of the University of São Paulo (Poli-USP), using funding from Petrobras, opened a lab to study giant waves in December 2009. The main element in the laboratory is a 36-foot wide and 13-foot deep pool for simulating giant wave patterns. The waves are generated by 148 rubber flaps, attached to small engines and controlled by a computer.
SOURCES: The Wave (Susan Casey), Poli-USP, BBC Science and Nature
HOW COASTAL GIANT WAVES WORK
Waves are energy traveling through water. They are created by wind blowing on the ocean surface. The stronger the wind, and the longer it blows, the larger the waves it produces. That's why waves are more common and bigger where storms are frequent.
1 When the wind blows, it creates friction with the sea. Water begins to rotate in the same direction as the air. Waves are the result of the deformation of water surface.
2 The longer the wind blows, the bigger the area of the water surface that can be pushed by that same wind.
3 This cycle goes on as long as the wind keeps blowing: the stronger the wind, and the longest it lasts, the bigger the waves that it will generate.
4 When waves get closer to the coast, they are slowed by the submarine relief. Also, the currents that flow near the bottom of the sea start moving up.
5 As the first waves that reach the coast are slower than the ones that come after them, the latter start piling up over the latter.
6 The swell of the wave is produced by faster waves running over slower ones, when they are close to the coast.
HOW FREAK WAVES WORK
'Freak' or 'rogue' waves are giant waves that appear in the middle of the sea. They are very dangerous due to their unpredictability. Recent research has identified three different factors that influence their likelihood.
Agua fria
Agua quente
A Regions where storms are common, such as the North Atlantic, are also the ones where freak waves appear with higher frequency. The strong winds that stir those waters are a key factor.
B Submarine relief is another factor. Shallow waters in the North Sea, between the UK and Scandinavia, are prone to freak waves for the same reason that big waves appear in coastal areas.
C The confluence of warm and cold currents (see map on the right) creates dynamics that make giant waves more likely.
Frequency and height of freak waves
Lower
Higher
Freak waves are more common in regions near the Poles. They are also frequent in South African national waters. In that area, the Agulhas Current meets cold water that is pushed from the South Pole by strong winds.

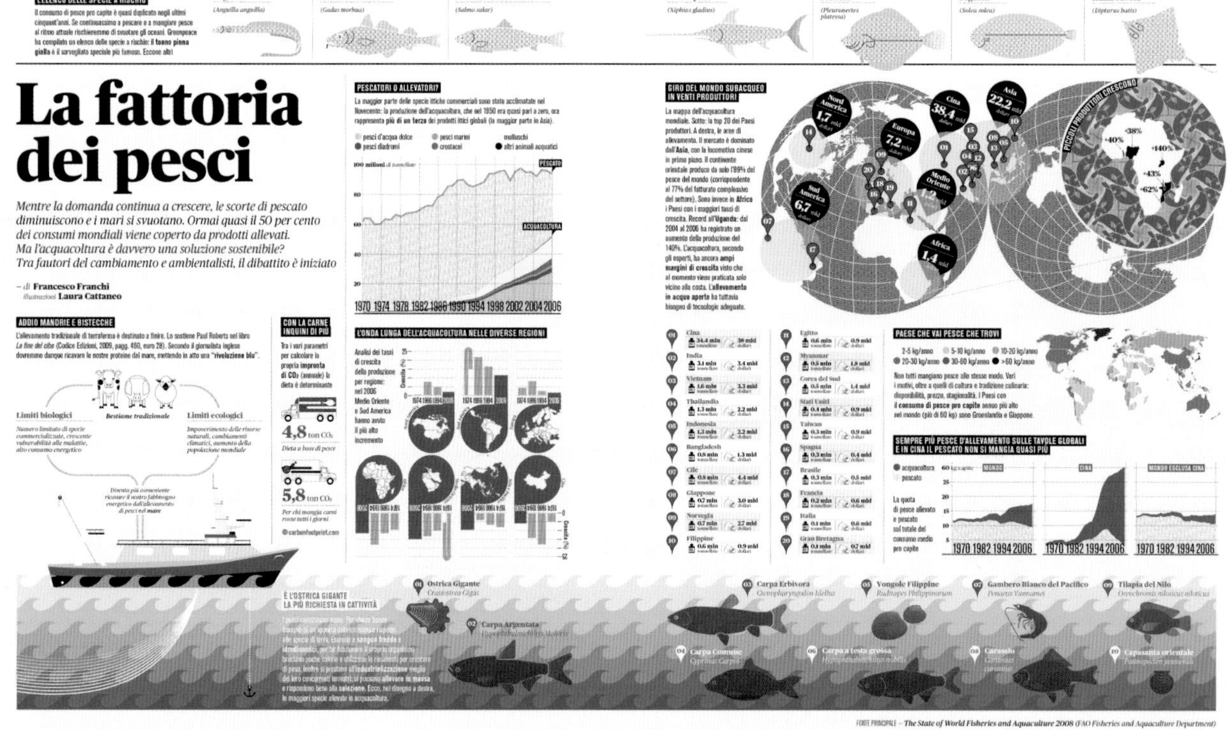
IL GREEN REPORT – ANALISI GRAFICA
L'ELENCO DELLE SPECIE A RISCHIO
Anguilla
Merluzzo bianco
Salmone dell'Atlantico
Pesce spada
(Xiphias gladius)
Platessa
Sogliola
(Solea solea)
Razza bavosa
(Dipturus batis)
La fattoria dei pesci
Mentre la domanda continua a crescere, le scorte di pescato diminuiscono e i mari si svuotano. Ormai quasi il 50 per cento dei consumi mondiali viene coperto da prodotti allevati. Ma l'acquacoltura è davvero una soluzione sostenibile? Tra fautori del cambiamento e ambientalisti, il dibattito è iniziato
– di Francesco Franchi
illustrazioni Laura Cattaneo
ADDIO MANDRIE E BISTECCHE
Limiti biologici
Bestiame tradizionale
Limiti ecologici
CON LA CARNE INQUINI DI PIÙ
4,8 ton CO₂
5,8 ton CO₂
PESCATORI O ALLEVATORI?
PESCATO
ACQUACOLTURA
1970 1974 1978 1982 1986 1990 1994 1998 2002 2004 2006
L'ONDA LUNGA DELL'ACQUACOLTURA NELLE DIVERSE REGIONI
GIRO DEL MONDO SUBACQUEO IN VENTI PRODUTTORI
PICCOLI PRODUTTORI CRESCONO
PAESE CHE VAI PESCE CHE TROVI
SEMPRE PIÙ PESCE D'ALLEVAMENTO SULLE TAVOLE GLOBALI E IN CINA IL PESCATO NON SI MANGIA QUASI PIÙ
MONDO
CINA
MONDO ESCLUSA CINA
È L'OSTRICA GIGANTE LA PIÙ RICHIESTA IN CATTIVITÀ
Ostrica Gigante
Carpa Argentata
Carpa Comune
Carpa Erbivora
Carpa a testa grossa
Vongole Filippine
Carassio
Gambero Bianco del Pacifico
Tilapia del Nilo
Capasanta orientale
22 % sul totale mondiale è la produzione asiatica di pesce in acquacoltura, Cina esclusa
FONTE PRINCIPALE – The State of World Fisheries and Aquaculture 2008 (FAO Fisheries and Aquaculture Department)
23

Gerson Mora, Alberto Cairo, Rodrigo Cunha, and Eliseu Barreira, Brazil: Infographic on "Giant Waves," 2010.

The magazine spread describes the phenomena of giant waves, from their formation to how they affect offshore oil platforms. Translated from Portuguese from the original infographic published in *Revista Época*.

Francesco Franchi (art director) and Laura Cattaneo (illustration), Italy: "Green Report and Global Report," 2009

The infographic describes the state of world fisheries and aquaculture. In *IL–Intelligence in Lifestyle*, Number 11 (Settembre 2009): 22–23.

A FEW DEFINITIONS

The graphic design community mostly uses two terms for the visual displays of information: **infographics** and **information design**. In a nutshell, infographics stand for visual displays in which graphics (illustrations, symbols, maps, diagrams, etc) together with verbal language communicate information that would not be possible otherwise. Infographics can range from early scientific illustrations of the human body to modern representations of how the brain functions, from early route maps and train schedules to the emblematic London subway map. Journalism as well as technical and pedagogical books employ established practices that traditionally have used infographics to explain complex information and tell stories. From the familiar weather map to visual explanations of natural phenomena and recent facts, infographics help us better understand the news around us.

Information design, on the other hand, is broadly used to describe communication design practices in which the main purpose is to inform, in contrast to persuasive approaches more commonly used in practices such as advertising. Infographics is one of the possible outputs within the large information design discipline. Other possible outputs involve the design of systems, which can be exemplified by information systems, wayfinding systems, and visualizations of statistical data. All examples share the common objective of revealing patterns and relationships not known or not so easily deduced without the aid of the visual representation of information. Traditionally, infographics and design of systems were static visual displays. With the advances and accessibility of technology, we currently see an expanding practice in interactive and dynamic visual displays for information.

Bureau Mijksenaar, Netherlands: Digital interactive wayfinding system for Amsterdam RAI, 2010.

Amsterdam RAI is an exhibition and convention center with 500 events, 12,500 exhibitors, and 2 million visitors a year. Because of the changing character of the center (type of event, exhibition size, entrances in use, facilities), Mijksenaar developed a digital interactive wayfinding system with customized information about current events and facilities. RAI Live combines event and exhibition signage with the possibility to give every exhibition its own character (look and feel) and show content (advertising, promotion, and infotainment). This exhibition signage can be altered and placed as desired according to the actual demands of the exhibitors.

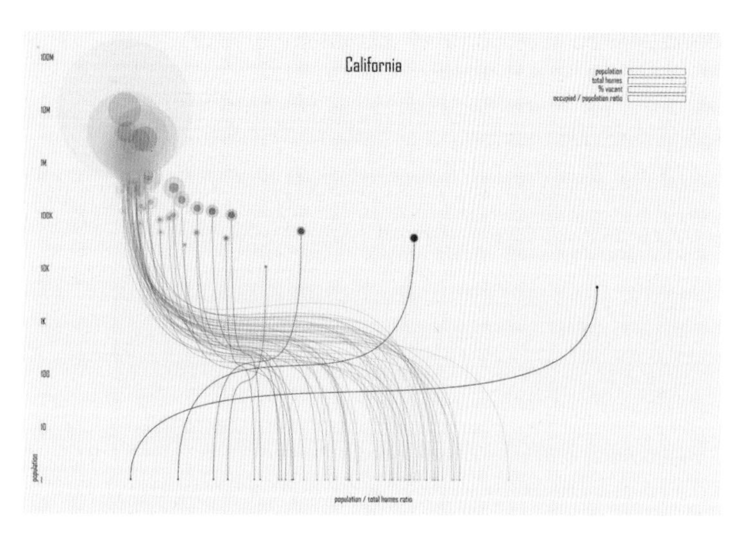
California
population
total homes
% vacant
occupied / population ratio
100M
10M
1M
100K
10K
1K
100
10
1
population
population / total homes ratio

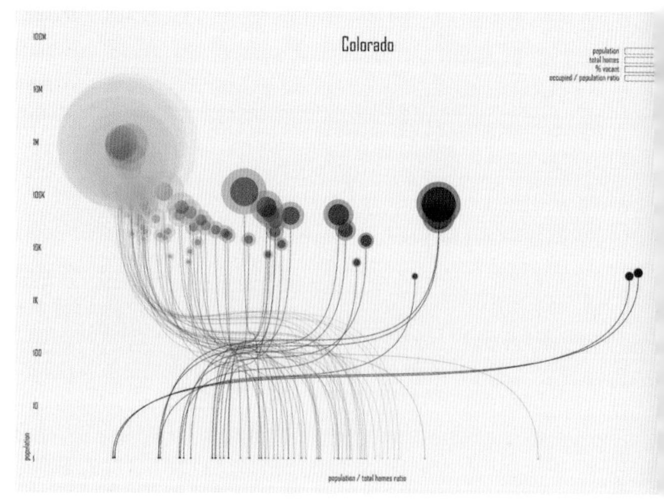
Colorado
population
total homes
% vacant
occupied / population ratio
100M
10M
1M
100K
10K
1K
100
10
1
population
population / total homes ratio

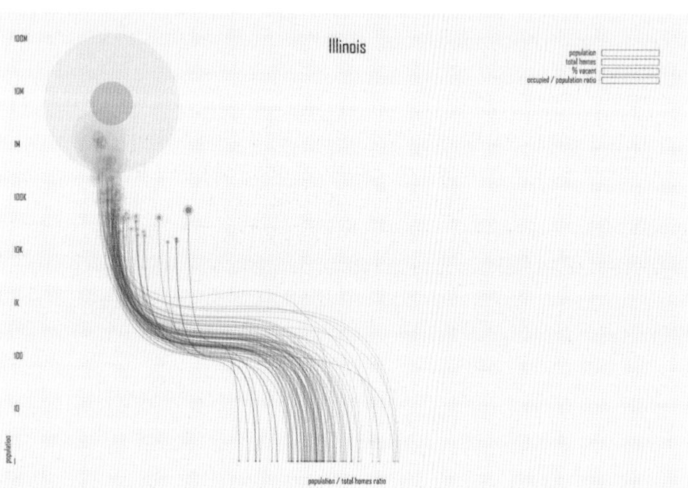
Illinois
population
total homes
% vacant
occupied / population ratio
100M
10M
1M
100K
10K
1K
100
10
1
population
population / total homes ratio

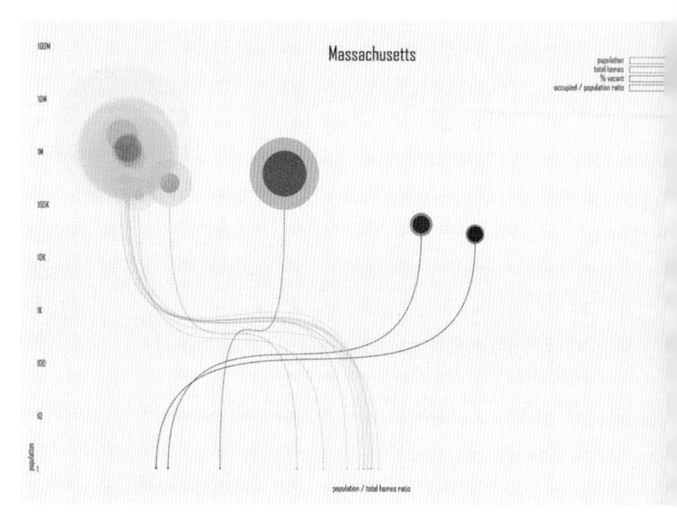
Massachusetts
population
total homes
% vacant
occupied / population ratio
100M
10M
1M
100K
10K
1K
100
10
1
population
population / total homes ratio

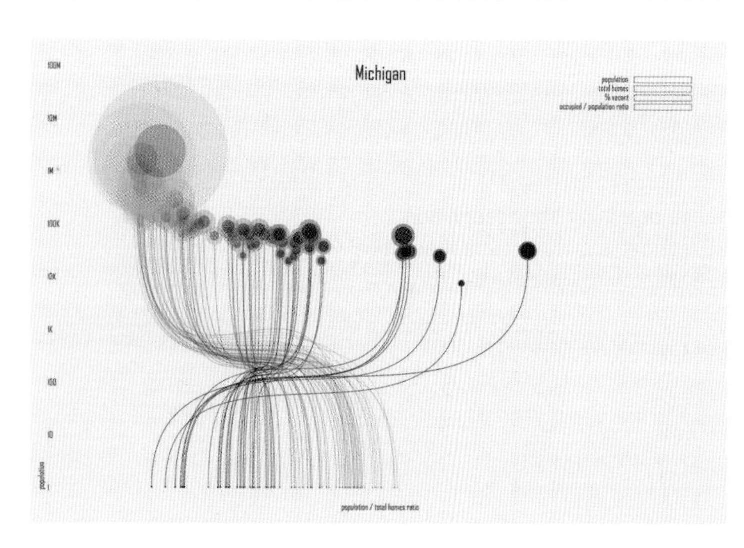
Michigan
population
total homes
% vacant
occupied / population ratio
100M
10M
1M
100K
10K
1K
100
10
1
population
population / total homes ratio

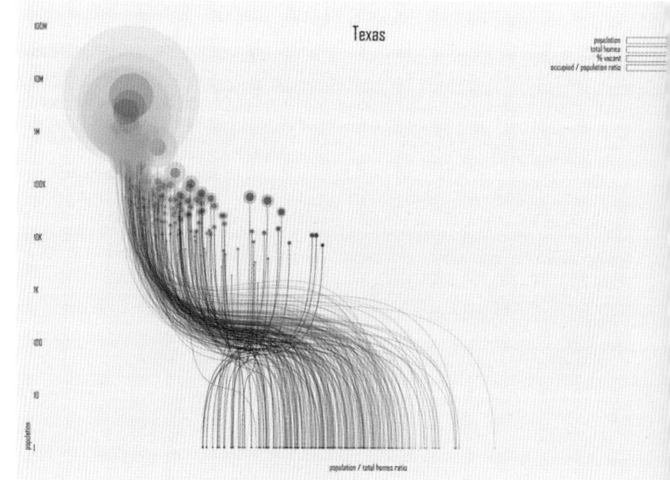
Texas
population
total homes
% vacant
occupied / population ratio
100M
10M
1M
100K
10K
1K
100
10
1
population
population / total homes ratio

Data visualization and **information visualization** are terms often found within the scientific community to refer to "the use of computer-supported, interactive, visual representations of abstract data to amplify cognition," according to *Readings in Information Visualization: Using Vision to Think* by Card et al.[1]

Independent of the term, the analytical methods, the media, and the source field of knowledge, I use information design and information visualization interchangeably in this book. The focus is on visual displays in which graphical approaches play a central role in communicating information in a meaningful way. Information visualizations are ubiquitous and critically important to understanding several fields today. With the omnipresent access to large amounts of data, computational techniques have become integral to the burgeoning practice of visualizing data. This book briefly introduces the programming languages, techniques, and algorithms used in the selected visualizations, and points to additional resources for further study.

DESIGNING FOR INFORMATION

Another point of discussion between the design and the scientific communities relates to the purpose of visualizations, whether they serve as a means to communicate stories and research findings or as a platform for data manipulation and exploration. The selected visualizations cover both functions, and rather than dwelling on the distinctions, the projects are examined in relation to how they help produce knowledge.

Visual displays of information can be considered cognitive artifacts, in that they can complement and strengthen our mental abilities.[2] I examine the visualizations in relation to the cognitive principles underlying them, which can be a combination of the following:

- to record information;
- to convey meaning;
- to increase working memory;
- to facilitate search;
- to facilitate discovery;
- to support perceptual inference;
- to enhance detection and recognition;
- to provide models of actual and theoretical worlds;
- to provide manipulation of data.

Jan Willem Tulp, Netherlands: "Ghost Counties," 2011

This project, by Tulp, a Dutch information visualizer, won the visualization challenge organized by visualizing.org and Eyeo Festival: "Create an interactive portrait of America by visualizing the 2010 Census data." "Ghost Counties" was developed using Processing environment and plots data for all counties in the United States by state. Each circle stands for a county, where the size of the outer circle represents the total number of homes and the size of the inner circle represents the number of vacant homes. The visualization uses a scatterplot technique with a double *x*-axis. The first *x*-axis represents the number of vacant homes per population, which is then connected with curved lines to the second *x*-axis, which shows the population-to-home ratio. In most cases, the second *x*-axis is the inverse of the first *x*-axis, but not always. The *y*-axis measures the population size. The number of vacant homes is color coded by a blue-red sequence, where blue represents few vacancies and red represents many vacancies. Interaction with the bubbles brings additional statistics at the top right corner. The visualization reveals some interesting insights, such as counties that have more homes than people or counties that have more than 50 percent vacant homes.

http://tulpinteractive.com/projects/ghostcounties

Mark Newman, U.S.: "Presidential Election Cartogram," 2012.

The 2012 presidential election cartogram shows county-level election results, where the sizes of counties are rescaled according to their population. The map uses not just the two party colors, red (Republican) and blue (Democrat), but also shades of purple in between to indicate percentages of votes. The result is a country more evenly divided politically. Mark Newman, Center for the Study of Complex Systems at the University of Michigan, used the diffusion method of Gastner and Newman to make this cartogram.

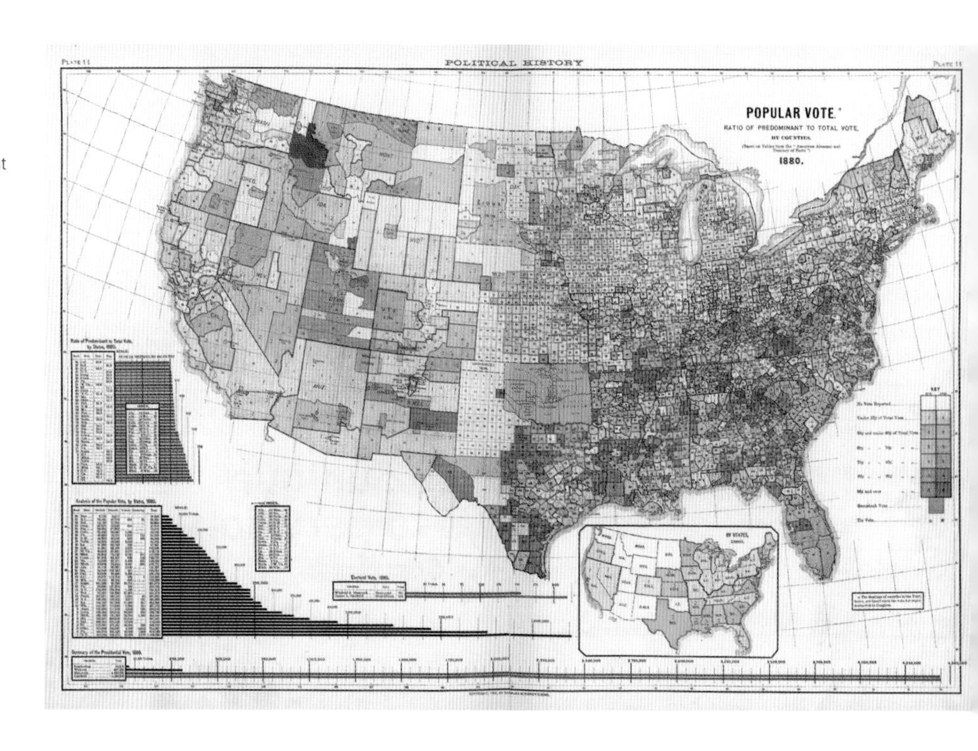

Fletcher W. Hewes and Henry Gannett, U.S.: *Statistical Atlas of the United States*, 1883.

This map in Scribner's *Statistical Atlas of the United States* shows the popular vote in 1880 mapped according to the ratio of predominant to total vote by counties.

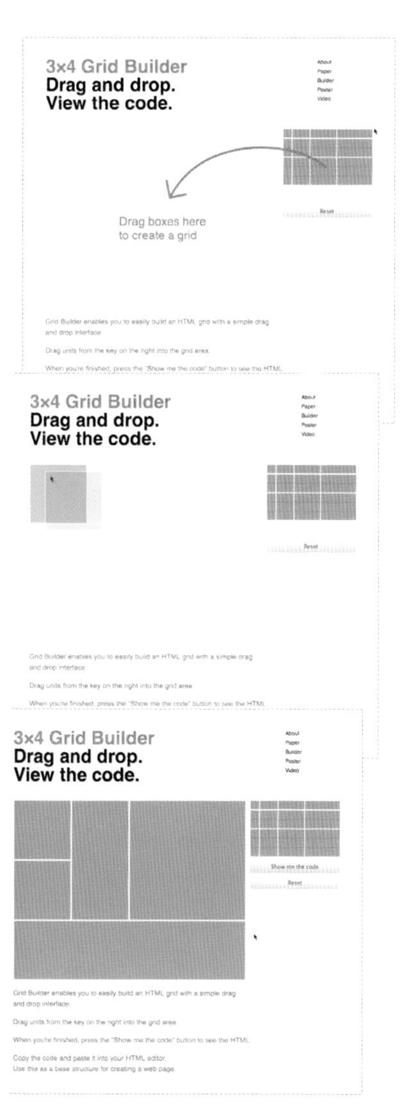

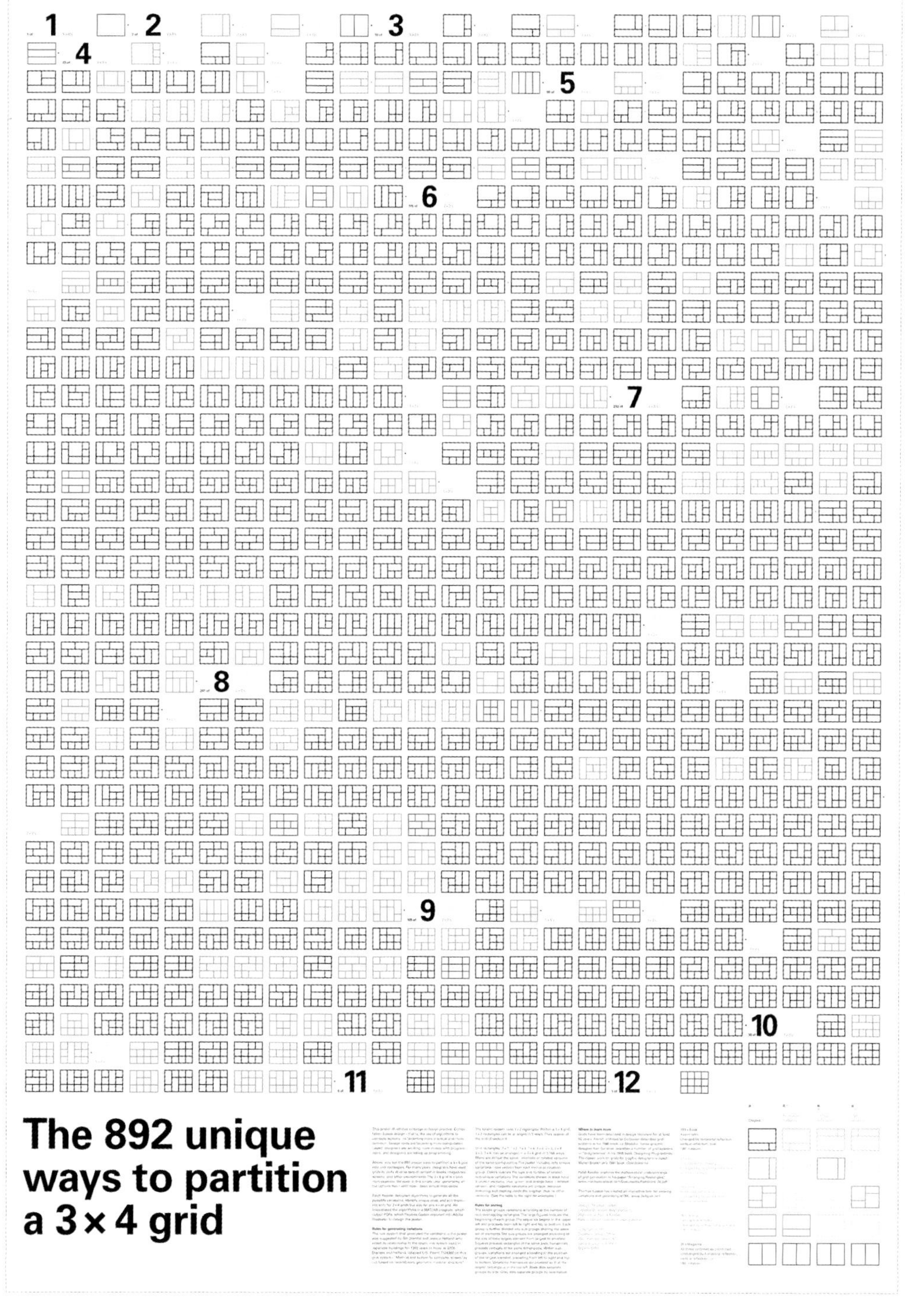

Hugh Dubberly (creative direction), Thomas Gaskin (design), and Patrick Kessler (algorithms) Patent belongs to William Drenttel and Jessica Helfand, U.S.: "3 x 4 Grid," 2011.

The poster presents the 892 unique ways to partition a 3 × 4 grid into unit rectangles. The website introduces a grid builder that allows anyone to build an HTML grid with a drag-and-drop interface. The project "illustrates a change in design practice. Computation-based design—that is, the use of algorithms to compute options—is becoming more practical and more common. Design tools are becoming more computation-based; designers are working more closely with programmers; and designers are taking up programming."[4]

www.3x4grid.com

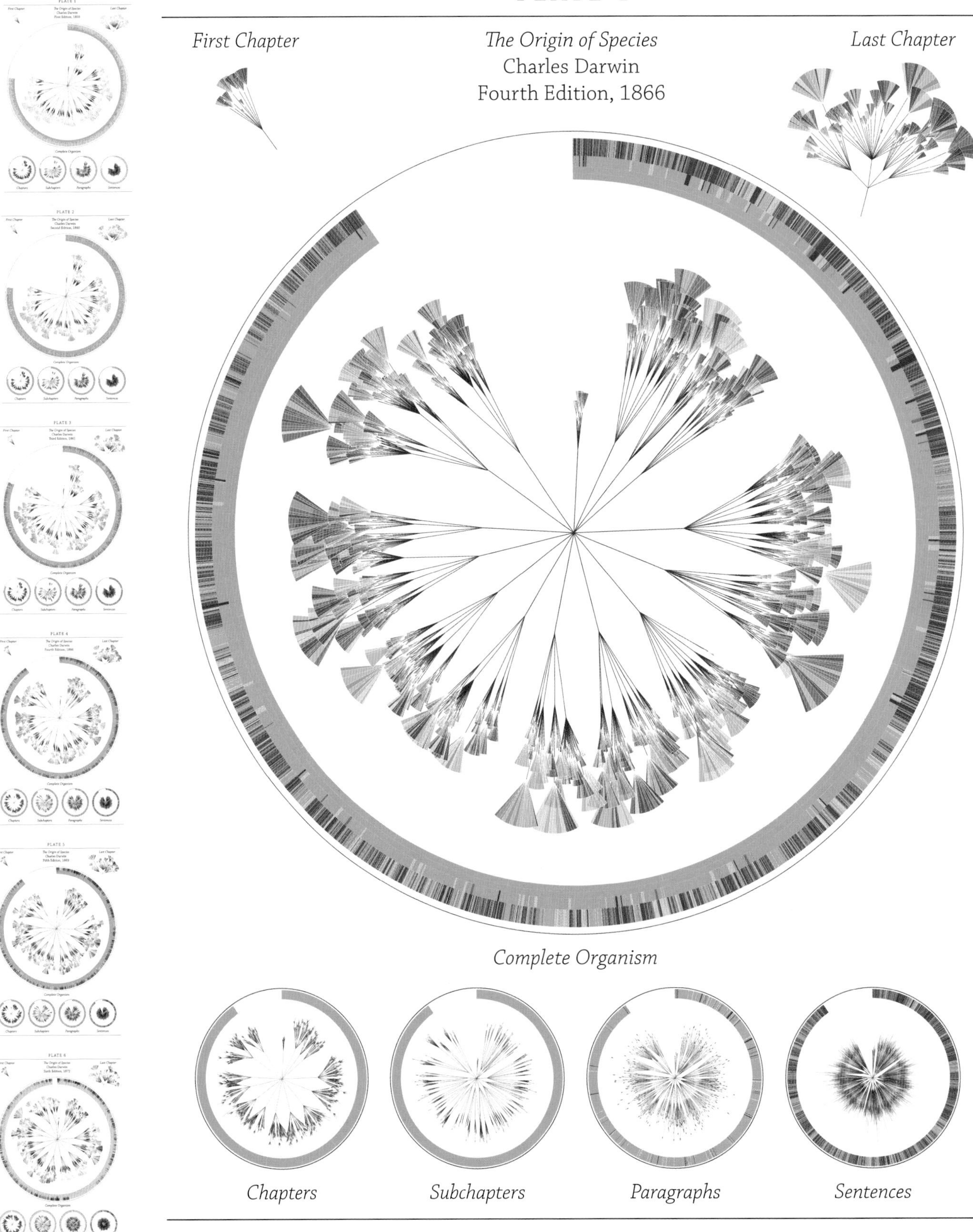
PLATE 4
First Chapter
The Origin of Species
Charles Darwin
Fourth Edition, 1866
Last Chapter
Complete Organism
Chapters
Subchapters
Paragraphs
Sentences
(En)tangled Word Bank
Greg McInerny & Stefanie Posavec

CHAPTER 1

HIERARCHICAL STRUCTURES: TREES

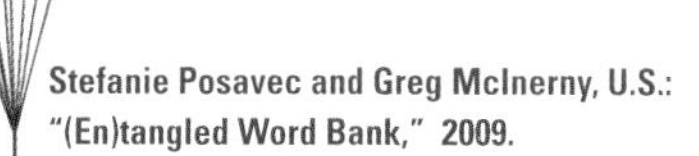

Stefanie Posavec and Greg McInerny, U.S.: "(En)tangled Word Bank," 2009.

The series of diagrams represents changes in the six editions of Charles Darwin's *On the Origin of Species*. Chapters are divided into subchapters, subchapters into paragraph "leaves," and, finally, small wedge-shaped "leaflets" stand for sentences. Each sentence is colored in blue if it survives to the next edition, and in orange if it is deleted.

In a nutshell, hierarchical systems are ordered sets where elements and/or subsets are organized in a given relationship to one another, both among themselves and within the whole. Relationships vary according to the field domain and type of system, but, in general, we can describe them by the properties of elements and the laws that govern them (e.g., how they are shared and/or related).

In the seminal article "The Architecture of Complexity," Herbert A. Simon contends that complexity often takes the form of hierarchy and, as such, hierarchy "is one of the central structural schemes that the architect of complexity uses."[1] Examples of hierarchical representations abound in the social and natural sciences throughout time up to today. According to Chen, "Visualizing hierarchies is one of the most mature and active branches in information visualization."[2]

REPRESENTATION

Looking at hierarchical structures over time, it becomes apparent that ordered datasets are represented visually in two basic graphical forms, which sometimes are also combined: stacked and nested schemes.

In stacked schemes, the elements are arranged in a directional relationship to one another: vertically, horizontally, or centrally (superior/inferior, center/periphery). In many instances, lines connect the elements in the set. Lines are one-dimensional visual elements described by their length and also provide directionality. Different geometries have been used to display stacked schemes, especially with recent computational models such as cone trees and hyperbolic views, for example.[3]

Elements in nested schemes are positioned within containers assembled according to their interdependency and subordination. The container, often a two-dimensional plane, provides the grouping

CARTESIAN SYSTEMS

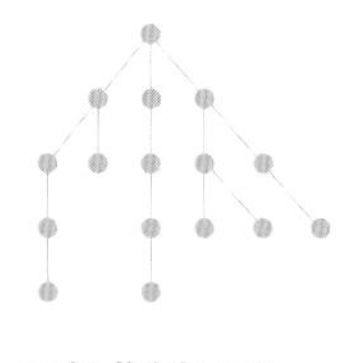

node–link layout

dendogram

indented layout

cone-tree

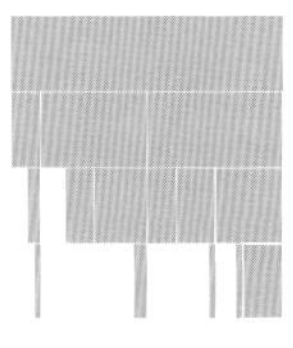

icicle tree

treemap

POLAR SYSTEMS

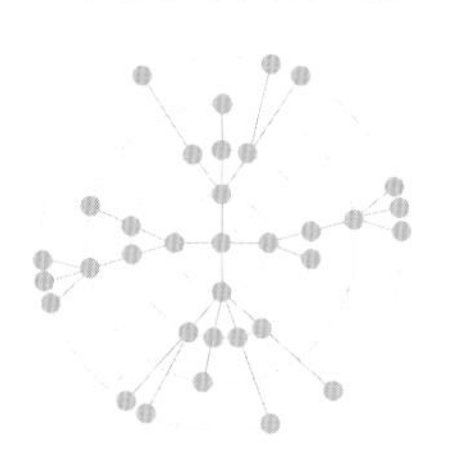

node–link radial layout

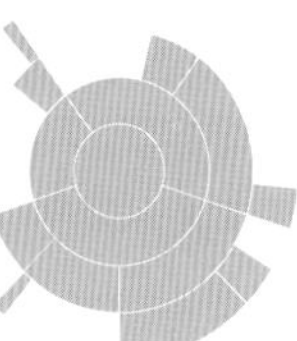

radial icicle or sunburst

OTHER GEOMETRIES

3D hyperbolic tree

vonoroi treemap

The table provides a summary of hierarchical structures used in diverse fields over time. With the increasing accessibility of data in the digital age, and the need to represent trees with huge amounts of leaves, methods are constantly being devised to solve readability issues of hierarchical representations in the constrained spatial computer screens. Most methods use interactivity to enhance navigating between macro and micro scales of trees with large depth and breadth. For example, degree of interest trees use "focus + context" strategies to interactively navigate large trees by allowing filtering of nodes to display or collapse, as well as semantic zooming. These and other approaches for navigating large trees with text are investigated in chapter 6, Textual Structures.

and association of elements. Known examples are Venn diagrams and treemaps.[4] The latter is examined in closer detail at the end of this chapter.

VISUAL HIERARCHIES

It might sound like a tautology, but to effectively visualize hierarchical systems we need a well-defined hierarchical visual encoding system. In the art and design fields, we refer to hierarchy of visual elements mostly in relation to emphasis and attention, for example, as a means to help the eyes follow a certain direction or purpose. It is common to find the term *contrast* rather than *hierarchy* in art and design literature. Dondis in his seminal *A Primer of Visual Literacy* considers contrast as the prime visual technique: "In the process of visual articulation, contrast is a vital force in creating a coherent whole. In all of art, contrast is a powerful tool of expression, the means for intensification of meaning and, therefore, of simplification of communication."[5]

Whatever the term—visual hierarchy or contrast—to further understand the implication of how we visually encode data, it is necessary to first briefly examine how our visual perception and cognitive systems work.

SPATIAL ENCODING

We process spatial properties (position and size) separately from object properties (such as shape, color, texture, etc).[6] Furthermore, position in space and time has a dominant role in perceptual organization, as well as in memory.

It is perhaps no coincidence that the ancient "art of memory" relied on spatial information for augmenting long-term memory.[7] Although the method called mainly for the creation of internal representations to enhance memorization and recollection, it is worth referring to its basic procedures here. The rules varied throughout its history, but, overall, the method proposes the use of an ordered sequence of *loci* as placeholders for concepts and of "active" visual images to stand for subject matters. It is quite fascinating how much these "invisible" mnemonic devices share with external data representations: an artificial and ordered system made out of visual elements, properties, and spatial relations.

Proximity

Proximity describes the tendency to group visual elements that are near one another into a perceptual unit. For example, we perceive the same six elements below as forming different groups:

||||||	= 1 group	= *word*
||| |||	= 2 groups	= *two words*

Proximity relates to locational characteristics and is essential to how elements are spatially associated, whether intentionally or not. Note how easily we detect groups and how we tend to make sense of the perceived patterns in the image above with randomly generated sets of dots.

The difference between the images above is that one is rotated 90 degrees in relation to the other. Otherwise, they are identical. Note how we perceive rows in the first one and columns in the second. The space between dots makes us perceive the dots grouped as linear units in the horizontal or vertical direction.

In visual displays, it is crucial that we locate information that is conceptually related spatially close together. Spatial proximity will facilitate the detection and search for associated data.

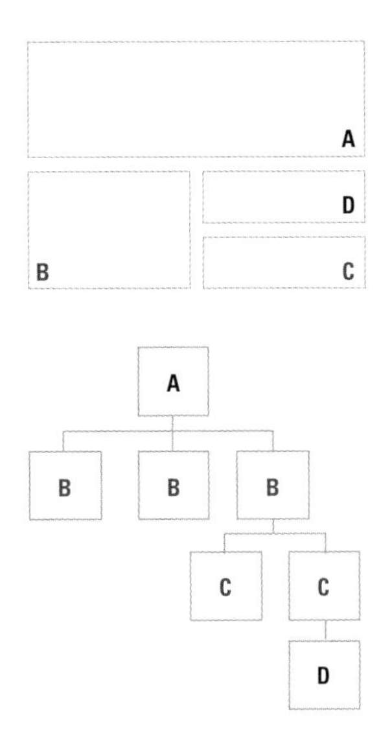

In visual representations, the use of space is always schematic, independent of whether depictions of elements are direct or metaphorical. Spatial encoding is central to how we construct visualizations, in that the geometric properties and spatial relations in the representation—the topology—will stand for properties and relationships in the source domain. For example, in representations of physical data, graphical proximity represents proximity in physical space. The distance between A and D in the plan corresponds (in a given scale) to the physical distance between these places in real space.

In representations of abstract domains, graphical proximity corresponds to conceptual proximity, such as a shared property. For example, in an organizational diagram, distance in graphical space represents distance in the hierarchical structure of an organization. Graphical space is mapping the source domain of power and not the physical space, such that two people (A and D) might have adjacent offices in the real world, and be at opposite poles in the organizational diagram.

Most examples in this chapter visualize abstract domains, whereas spatial datasets are mostly examined in chapter 4. Because abstract domains mostly don't provide visual cues, assigning visual encoding to abstract data is a crucial step leading to robust and reliable visualizations.

Research on the cognitive operations a person executes in the process of reading a graph yields interesting results that contribute to the critical issue of finding the best spatio-visual representation to abstract data. Pinker examined these operations in relation to quantitative graphs and found that "people create schemas for specific types of graphs using a *general graph schema*, embodying their knowledge of what graphs are for and how they are interpreted in general."[8] He suggests that the theory can be extended to representations of qualitative information, where again, the reader would use schemas to mediate between perception and memory. Efficiency would be provided to the extent that the schema allows for correspondences between conceptual information and visual attributes, and insofar as the visual attributes are encoded reliably. In other words, to what extent do the visual schema and visual attributes stand for the structure and variables in the source domain? What is the likelihood of nonspatial content that is encoded spatially being readily recognizable and understood?

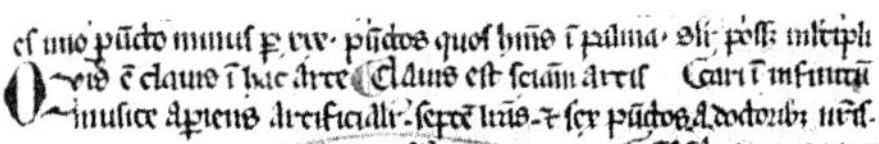

Guido of Arezzo, Italy: "Hand of Guido," 1274.

This was a popular medieval music theory mnemonic device created by eleventh-century musical scholar Guido of Arezzo, hence the name. The one pictured here is taken from a manuscript written in 1274. Murdoch explains, "[It] is unique in its inclusion of a human, one of whose magnified hands provides the 'diagram.' In addition to the foregoing letter notation, it represents the 20-note sequence in two other manners: first, numerically as puncti (often abbreviated as a mere 'p') with accompanying Roman numerals; second, by solmization, that is, by syllables ut-re-mi-fa-sol-la, a system invented by Guido himself, the symbols themselves being the initial syllables of a familiar hymn to St. John."[13] The solmization appears both in the hand as well as in the outer circumference.

VISUAL PERCEPTION AND COGNITION

Although information in visual displays is available to us simultaneously, our visual systems extract features separately and over stages: from early vision processes, mostly precognitive, and dominated by bottom-up processes; to higher levels of processing, in which outputs from previous stages are combined with previous knowledge and knowledge structures. Ware proposes a three-stage model of perception:[9]

Stage 1: Rapid parallel processing to extract basic features;

Stage 2: Slow serial processing for extraction of patterns and structures;

Stage 3: Sequential goal-oriented processing with information reduced to a few objects and held in working visual memory to form the basis for visual thinking.

Preattentive processing happens very fast (usually in fewer than 10 milliseconds), and simultaneously (in parallel) for the purpose of rapid extraction of basic visual features (Stage 1). Preattentive features are processed prior to conscious attention, and refer to detection of what we commonly call "at a glance." Designers can use preattentive features to enhance detection of relevant information in visualizations, because the marks will literally *pop out.*

To illustrate the relevance of preattentive features in visual tasks, I borrow and expand on Ware's example provided by the four numerical images showing the same sequence of numbers. Imagine that we have to discover the total number of occurrences of 3.[10] In the top image, we would have to scan each number sequentially until we found our "target." In the other images, preattentive features help us perform the task faster and more efficiently by rapidly identifying the target and scanning only the relevant marks.

18596746321475030608030504090
70502769843010215346748950213
06057204020503090845064201040
70204070835061305080239245798

18596746321475030608030504090
70502769843010215346748950213
06057204020503090845064201040
70204070835061305080239245798

18596746321475030608030504090
70502769843010215346748950213
06057204020503090845064201040
70204070835061305080239245798

18596746321475030608030504090
70502769843010215346748950213
06057204020503090845064201040
70204070835061305080239245798

The examples use the same numbers but with different encoding for the number 3. In which one is it easier to detect the target "3" in the midst of the distractors?

THREE-STAGE MODEL OF PERCEPTUAL PROCESSING

A schematic overview of the simplified information-processing model of human visual perception proposed by Collin Ware.[14]

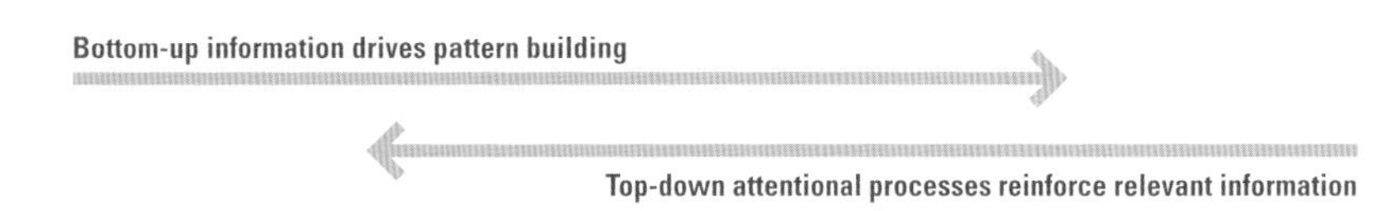

STAGE 1

Billions of neurons work in parallel to extract millions of **features** that are processed rapidly and simultaneously, such as color, texture, orientation, and so on.

STAGE 2

Patterns are extracted serially and slowly, such as regions of the same color, and regions of the same texture. The pattern-finding process leads to two pathways: object perception, and locomotion and action.

STAGE 3

At the highest level of perception, we are able to hold between one and three **objects** at any instance in our working visual memory. Patterns that provide answers to the visual query construct the objects in conjunction with information stored in our long-term memory and that are related to the task at hand.

INTEGRAL AND SEPARABLE DIMENSIONS

Visual dimensions can be perceived holistically (integral dimensions) or independently (separable dimensions).

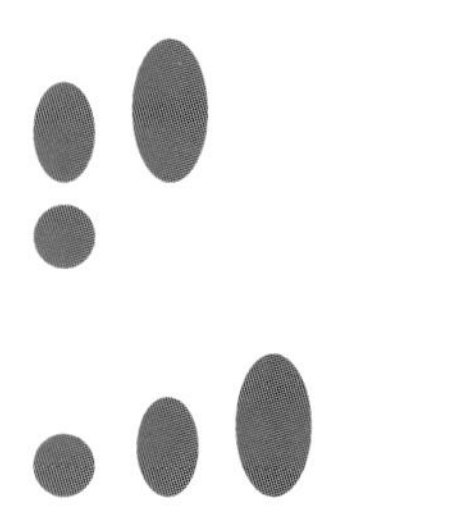

The height and width of the ellipses create an integral perception of shape: the ellipses appear more similar to each other than to the circle, though it has the same diameter as the ellipse right above it.

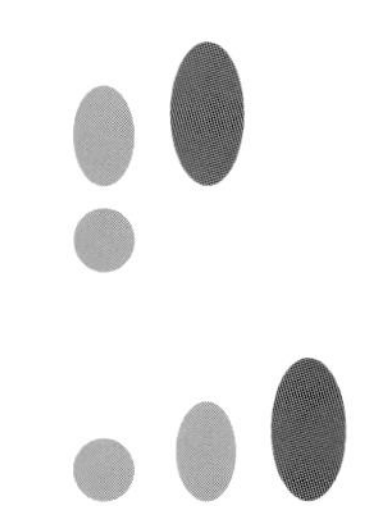

Shape and color are separable dimensions, and the ellipse and circle with the same color are perceived as more similar than the two ellipses.[15]

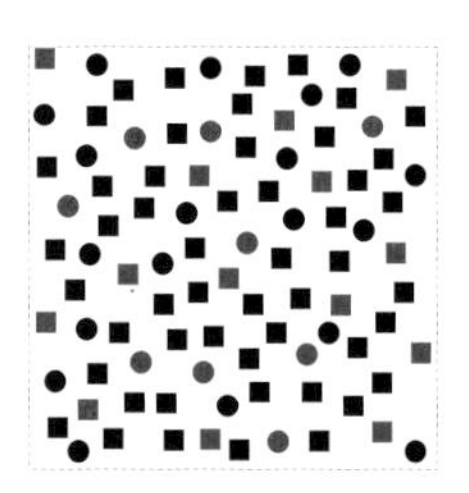

CONJUNCTION SEARCHES

Elements in which features have been combined are not easily found, especially if surrounded by other elements with shared features. For example, searching for red squares in this image is not as easy as finding just red elements or only squared ones, because the surrounding elements have common features to those in our task: (black) squares and red (circles). Ware explains that these types of searches are called "conjunction searches" and are generally not preattentive and happen slowly.[16]

In this case, the visual properties of color hue (red), intensity or color value (gray/black), and line weight (bold) help us perform the task, because they are preattentively processed.

Preattentive features can increase the performance of the following tasks: target detection, boundary detection, region tracking, and counting and estimation. A series of features has been identified as preattentively processed, and they can be organized by form, color, motion, and spatial position. Sixteen preattentive features are illustrated on the table to the right, showing features for lines and planes.

There are, however, factors that might impair the detection of preattentive-designed symbols, such as the number and variety (degree of differentiation) of distractors in the representation and whether they stand for targets or nontargets (distractors).

Preattentive properties are not perceived equally. Studies in psychology have shown that our visual systems favor certain visual features over others (read more on the Similarity principle on page 51). The hierarchy depends on other features present in the visualization, such as color saturation and the degree of distinctness from surrounding marks.

Effective visualizations make intentional use of the preattentive features in the representation of graphical marks. The objective is to support perceptual inference and to enhance detection and recognition. This requires experimentation, as well as testing so as to check whether the target audience can easily perform the required tasks.

It is through discrimination (same-different dichotomy) in early vision that elements and patterns are detected and ordered (Stage 2). Patterns are central to how visual information is structured and organized. The Gestalt psychologists proposed a series of principles—known as the Gestalt laws—describing the way we detect patterns and how individual units are integrated into a coherent percept: Proximity, Similarity, Common Fate, Good Continuation, Closure, Simplicity, Familiarity, and Segregation between Figure and Ground.[11] Principles are explained in boxes throughout this book.

The Gestalt laws can be used as design principles for effective ways of enhancing pattern detection and perceptual inferences. For Wertheimer (1959), the Gestalt principles are effective not only in enhancing perceptual inferences but also in facilitating problem-solving and thinking processes.[12] He explains that the mechanisms of grouping, reorganizing, centering, etc, facilitate the understanding of the structural requirements of problems, allowing problems to be viewed as integrated and coherent wholes.

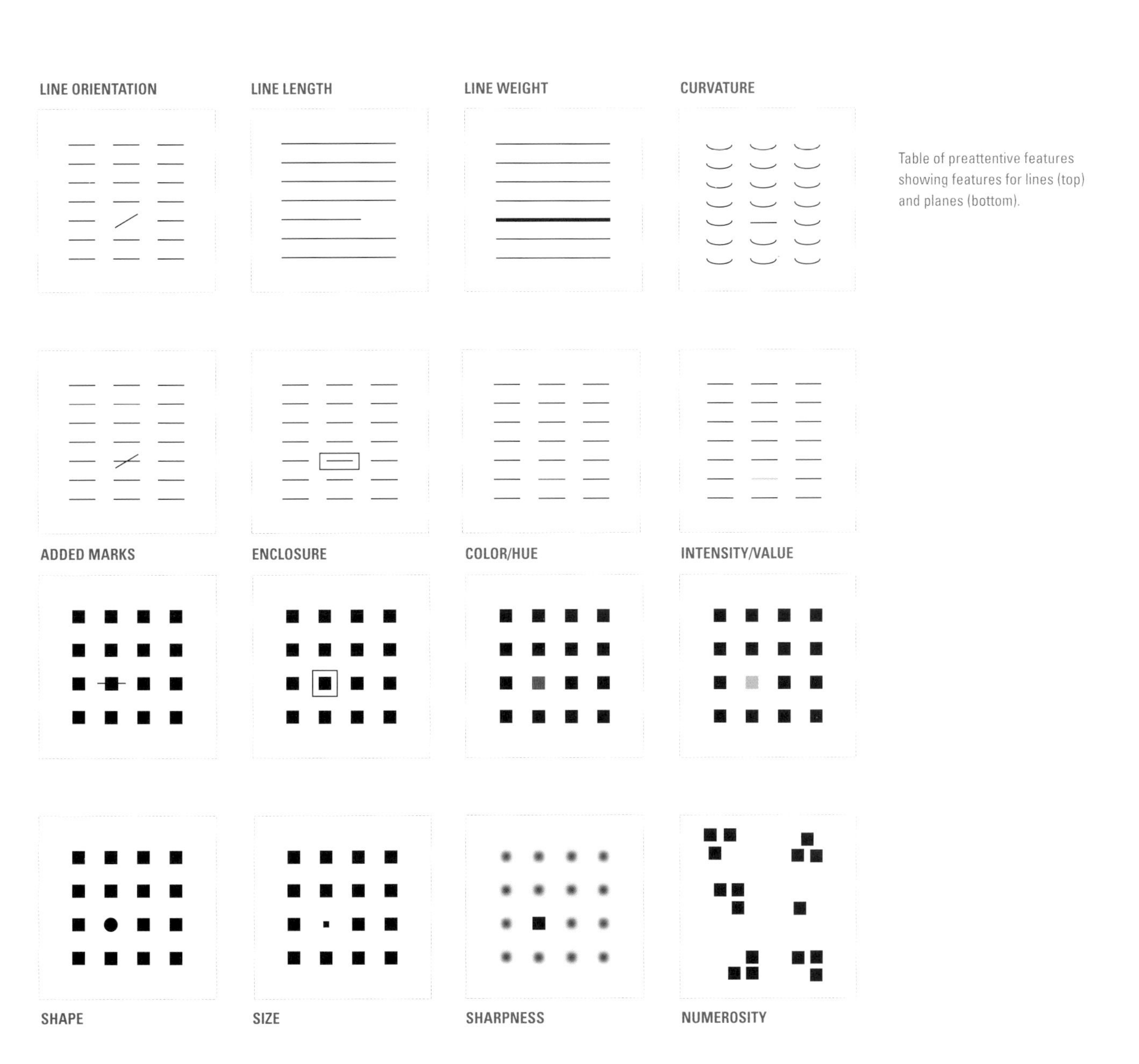

Table of preattentive features showing features for lines (top) and planes (bottom).

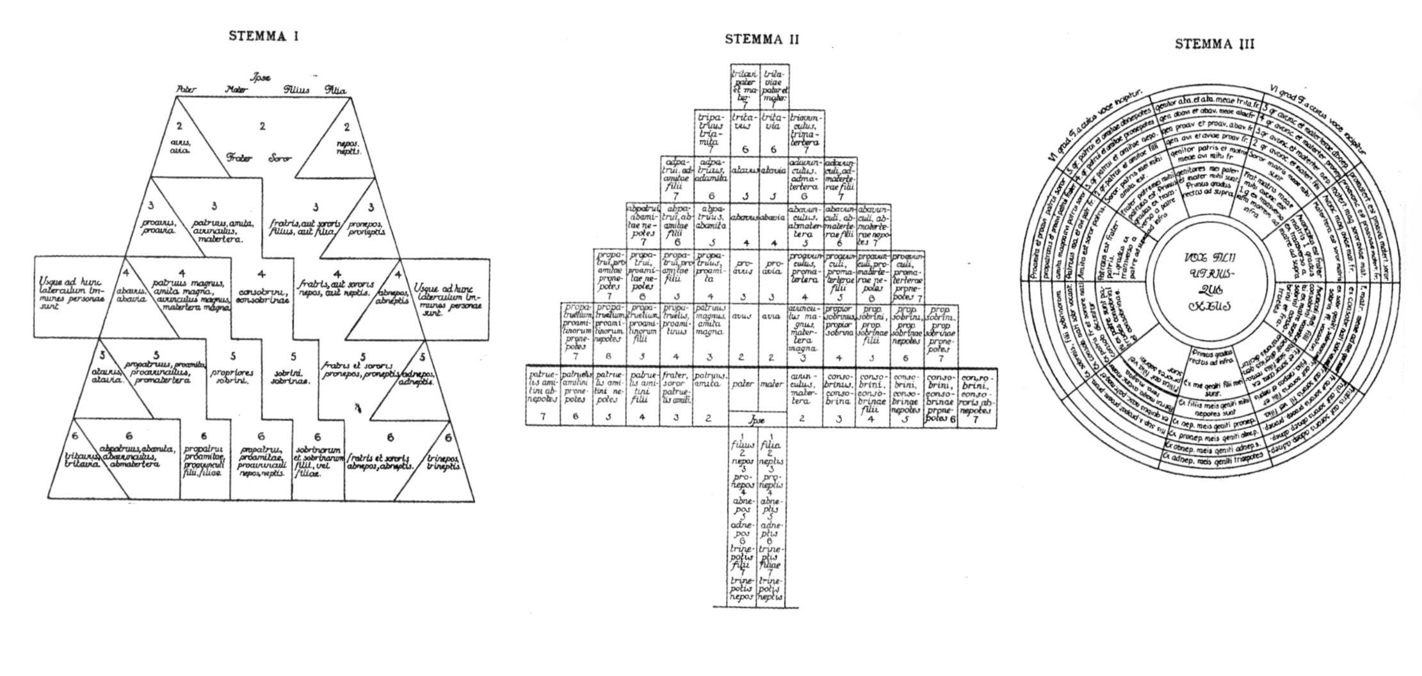

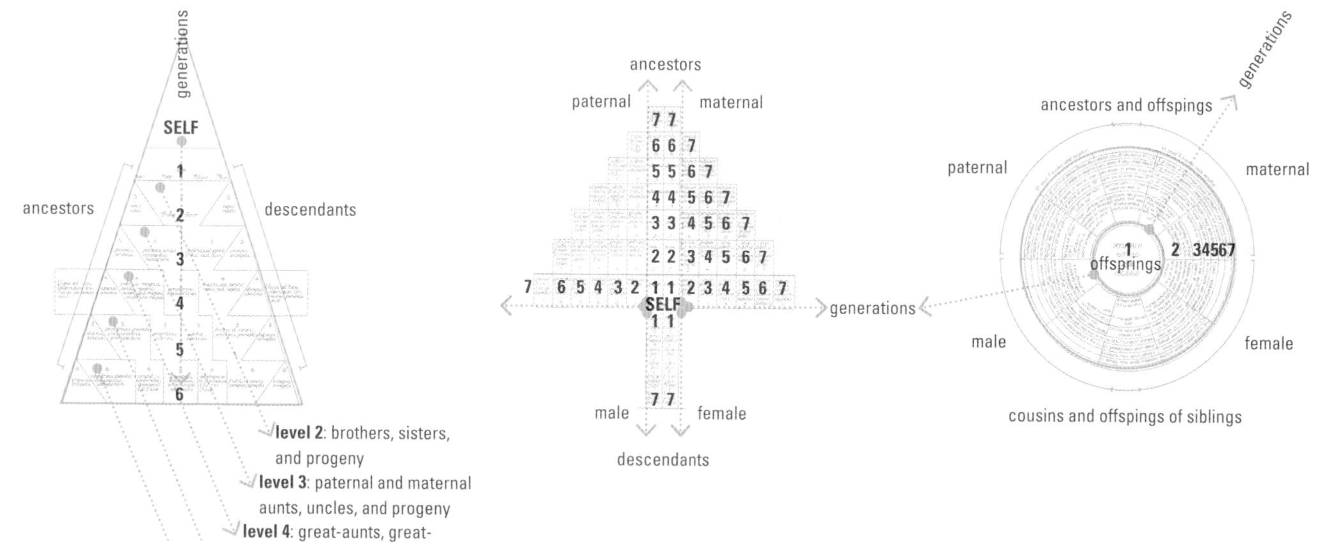

Bishop Isidore of Seville: "Consanguinity Trees," I, II, III, Seventh century.

Murdoch explains that one of the earliest uses of trees to illustrate a point in written text was genealogical, of which the first two diagrams are considered among the earliest instances.[17] The third option is a *rota*, a circular diagram.[18] All three consanguinity schemas appeared in the seventh-century Bishop Isidore of Seville's medieval encyclopedia *Liber Etymologiarum sieve originum*, book *XX*.

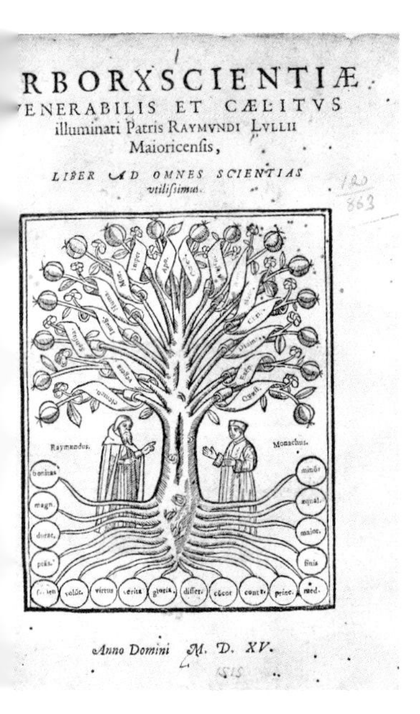

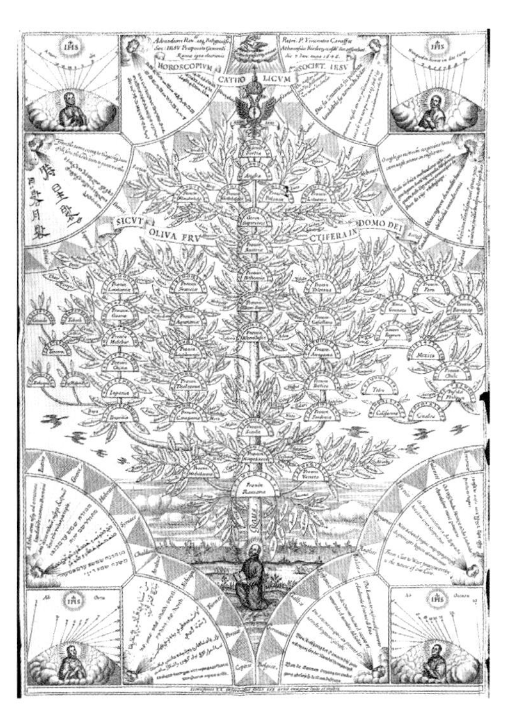

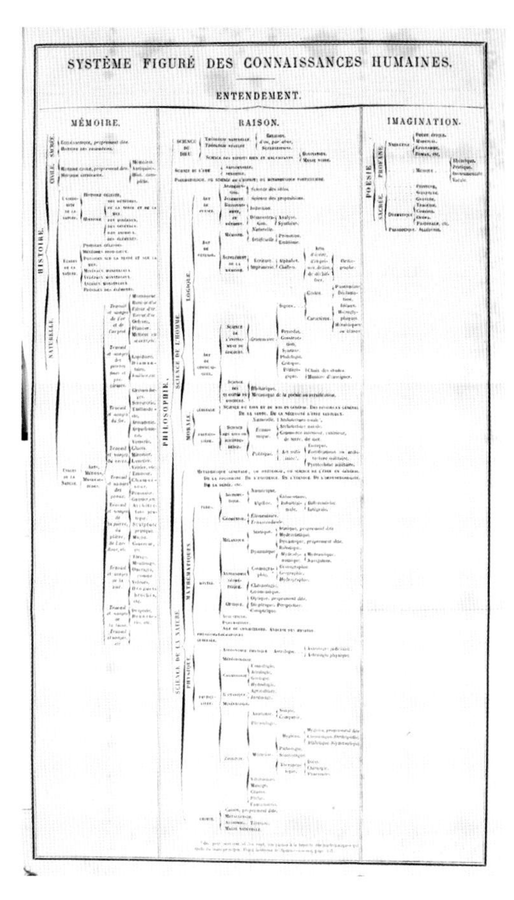

Hierarchy: *A body of persons or things ranked in grades, orders, or classes, one above another; spec. in Natural Science and Logic, a system or series of terms of successive rank (as classes, orders, genera, species, etc.), used in classification.*

Oxford English Dictionary

Ramon Llull: "Tree of Knowledge," 1515.

The diagram was published n the title page of *Arbor Scientiæ Venerabilis et Cælitvs*.

Athanasius Kircher: "Universal Horoscope of the Society of Jesus," 1646.

The diagram uses a composite sundial in the form of an olive tree with the base representing Rome. It appeared in *Ars Magna Lucis et Umbrae*, page 553.

Denis Diderot: Table of "Figurative System of Human Knowledge," 1751.

The system was published in *Oeuvres Complètes* (1876), tome XIII, between pages 164–165, edited by J. Assézat, Garnier, Paris.

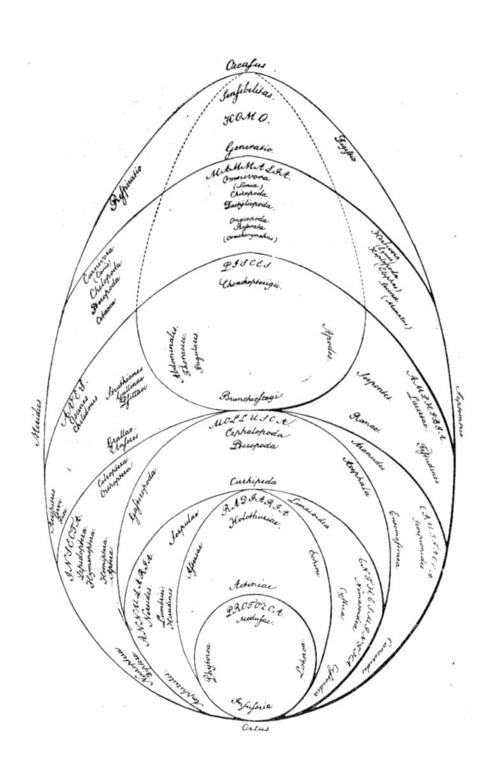

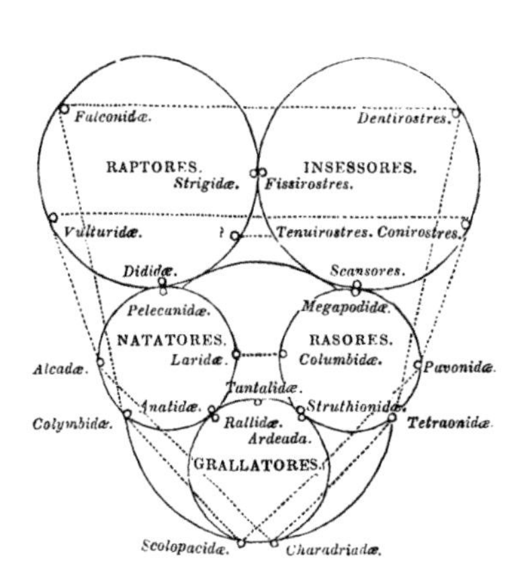

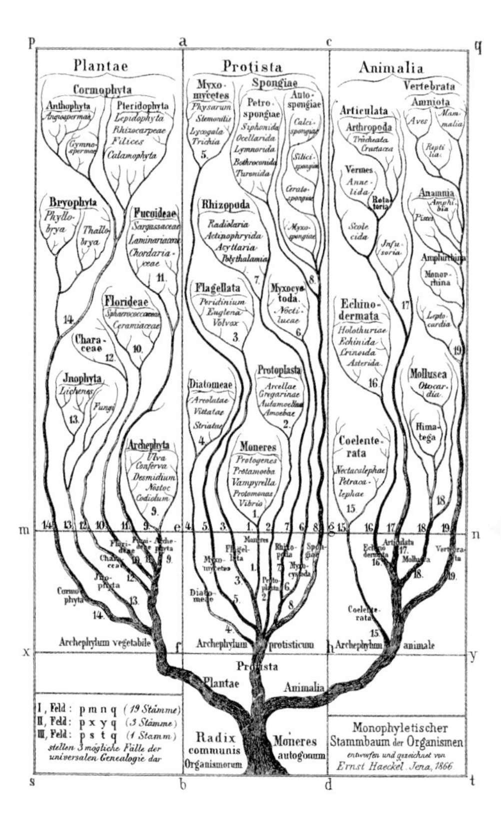

By a hierarchic system, *or hierarchy, I mean a system that is composed of interrelated subsystems each of the latter being in turn, hierarchic in structure until we reach some lowest level of elementary subsystem. In most systems in nature it is somewhat arbitrary as to where we leave off the partitioning and what subsystems we take as elementary.*

Herbert A. Simon

Georg August Goldfuss: "System of Animals" in *Über de Entwicklungsstufen des Thieres* (*On Animal Development*), 1817.

The nested diagram represents a linear progression from single-cell animals at the bottom to humans at the top. Pietsch suggests that this unique egg-shaped diagram might have been "meant to invoke an analogy between egg and the birth and progression of life."[19]

William Swainson: "Five Natural Orders of Birds" in *Natural History of Birds*, 1837.

A proponent of general classification based on quinarianism, Swainson represented in the diagram the orders as circles, each containing five families. The dotted lines indicate relationships of analogy. Pietsch draws attention to the bottom part of the diagram in which the three lower orders are enclosed in a larger circle, standing for closer affinities.[20]

Ernst Haeckel: "Monophyletic Family Tree of Organisms" in the first edition of *Generelle Morphologie der Organismen* (*General Morphology of Organisms*), 1866.

This branching diagram is considered the earliest one published by Haeckel.[21] It shows the three kingdoms of life: unicellular organisms (*Protista*) and multicellular organisms—animals (*Animalia*) and plants (*Plantae*).

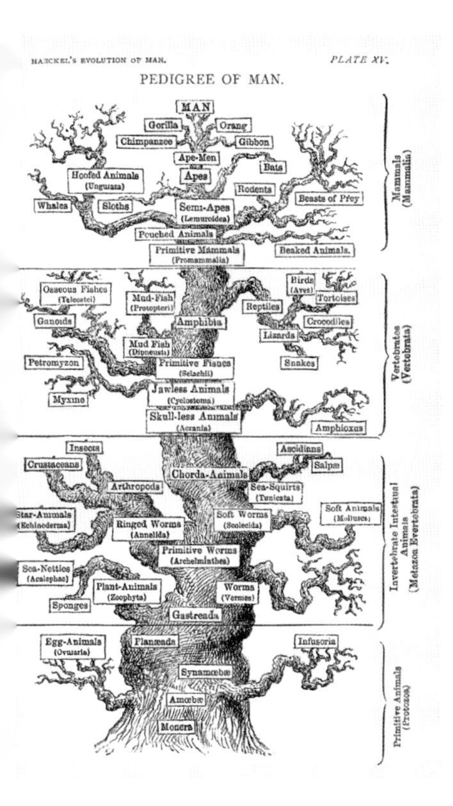

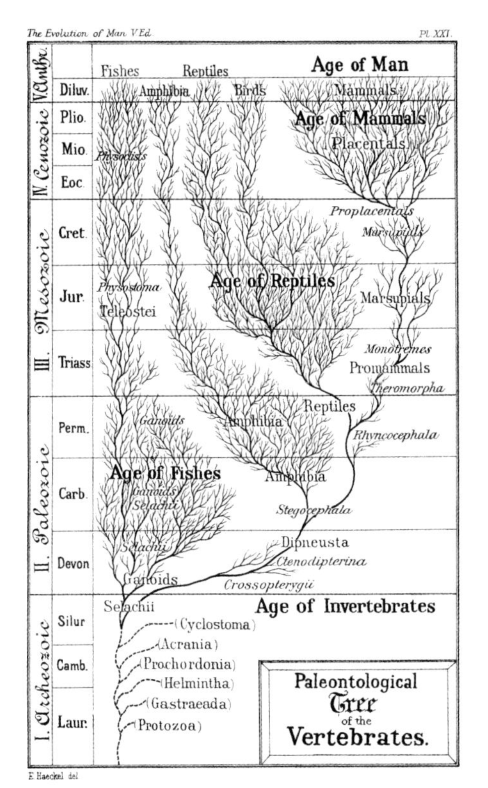

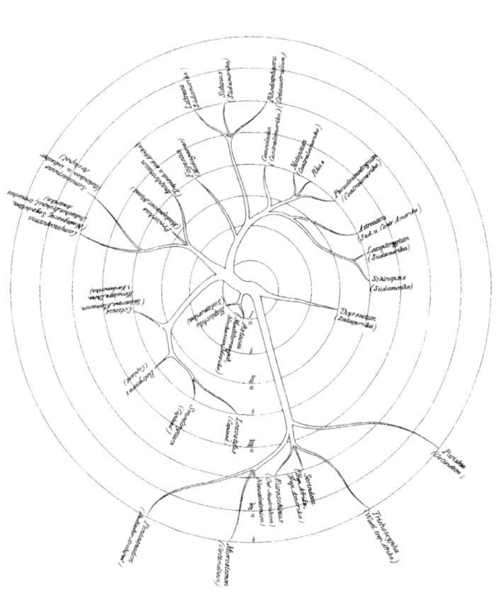

Ernst Haeckel: "Family Tree of Man," 1879.

The well-known oak "Family Tree of Man" was published in the first edition of *Anthropogenie oder Entwickelungsgeschichte des Menschen* (*The Evolution of Man*).

Ernst Haeckel: "Paleontological Tree of Vertebrates," c1879.

This diagram shows the evolutionary history of species.

Heinrich Gustav Adolf Engler: Top-down view of "Tree of Relationships of Plants of the Cashew Family Anacardiacae," 1881.

Pietsch explains that the "concentric circles, each corresponding to a morphological feature, provide a measure of relative divergence from a common ancestor. The idea of a tree is further demonstrated by the gradual narrowing of the branches toward their tips."[22]

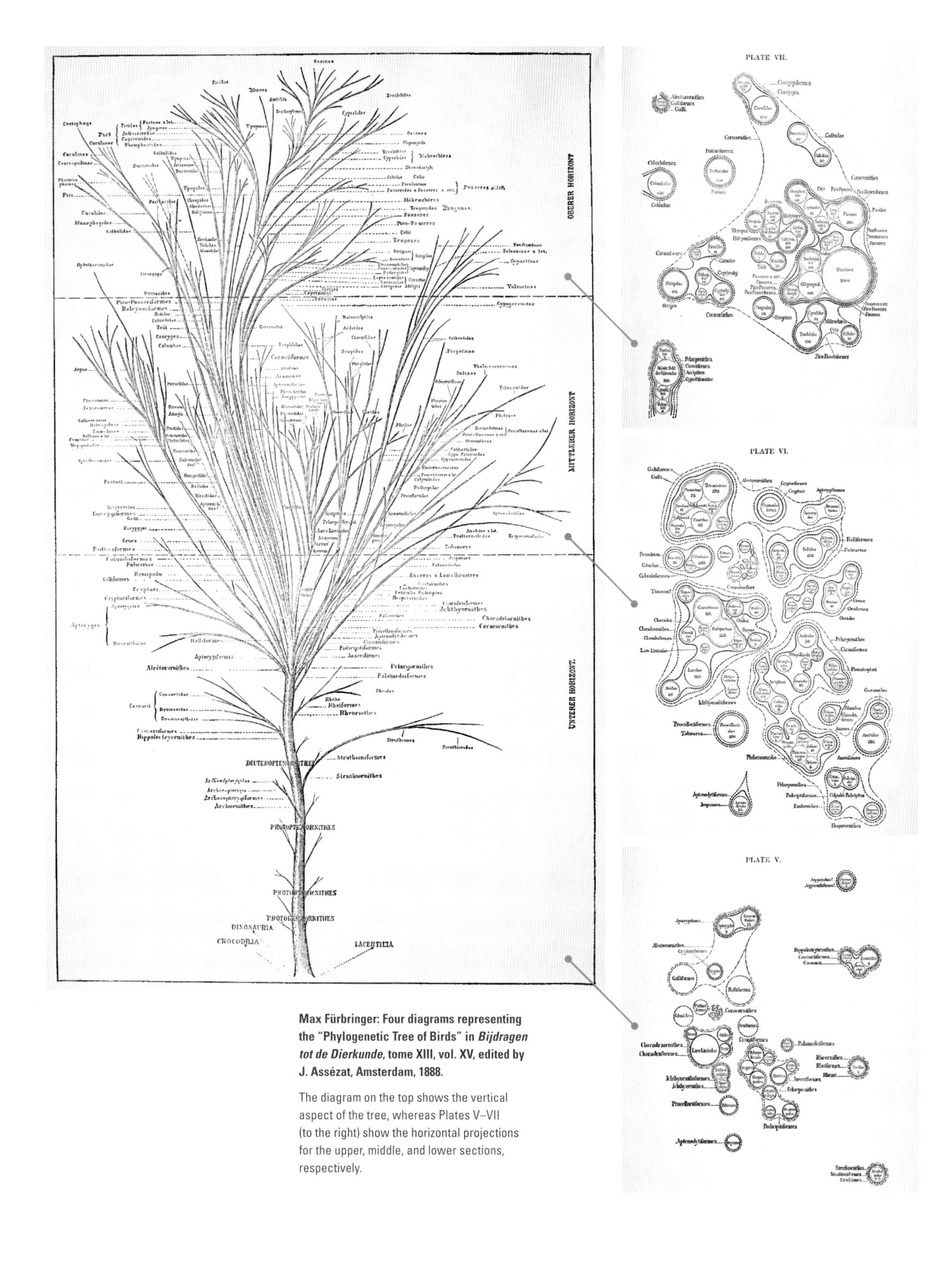

Max Fürbringer: Four diagrams representing the "Phylogenetic Tree of Birds" in *Bijdragen tot de Dierkunde*, tome XIII, vol. XV, edited by J. Assézat, Amsterdam, 1888.

The diagram on the top shows the vertical aspect of the tree, whereas Plates V–VII (to the right) show the horizontal projections for the upper, middle, and lower sections, respectively.

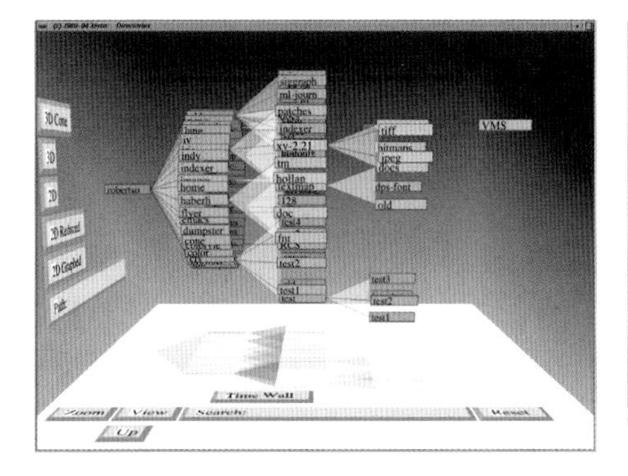

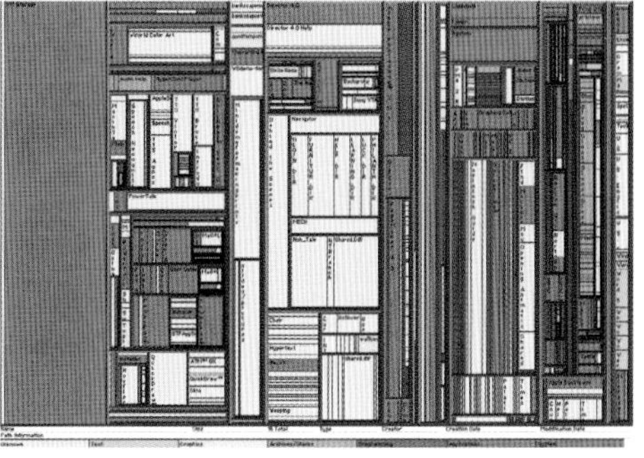

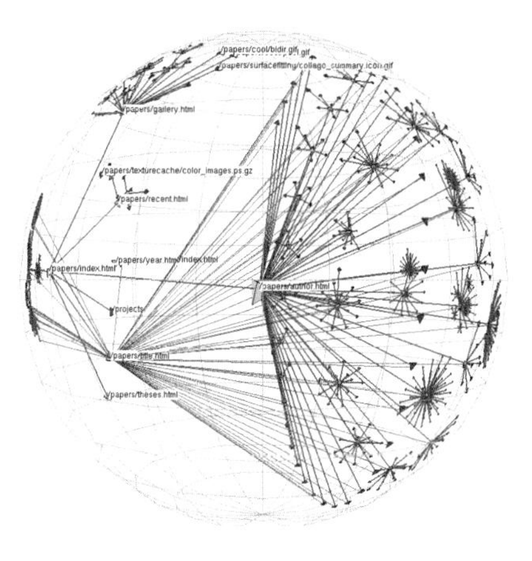

With increased access to large amounts of data, several new problems have arisen related to managing, accessing, and manipulating large information spaces within the constraints of computer screens. It is interesting to note that the orientation of diagrams, which mainly was vertical due to configurations of the book page, now, in the digital age, is mostly horizontal, because it better fits the aspect ratio of computer screens.

George Robertson, Jock D. Mackinlay, and Stuart Card at Xerox Palo Alto Research Center, U.S.: Snapshot of the "Cone Tree" visualization technique, 1991.

The method explored early technologies for 3-D visualization and interactive animation to structure hierarchical systems using cones: Each node is the apex of a cone, and the children are drawn around the base of the associated cone. Robertson and colleagues explain, "The hierarchy is presented in 3-D to maximize effective use of available screen space and enable visualization of the whole structure. Interactive animation is used to shift some of the user's cognitive load to the human perceptual system."[23]

Brian Johnson and Ben Shneiderman at the Human-Computer Interaction Laboratory[24] University of Maryland, U.S.: Snapshot of the "TreeViz" interface that uses a treemap to represent files in a computer, 1993.

Shneiderman originally devised the treemap technique in 1991 and he contends that "treemaps are a convenient representation that has unmatched utility for certain tasks. The capacity to see tens of thousands of nodes in a fixed space and find large areas or duplicate directories is very powerful."[25] The treemap technique is further examined in the case study that follows.

Tamara Munzner, U.S. : Snapshot of the "3-D Hyperbolic Tree," 1998.

Munzner devised and implemented the 3-D Hyperbolic Tree technique to navigate large datasets with the objective of reducing visual cluster and supporting dynamic exploration. Tamara explains that the layout in three-dimensional hyperbolic space allows for focus on a point of interest while providing enough context.[26]

CASE STUDY

TREEMAPS

SmartMoney Map of the Market

www.smartmoney.com/marketmap

The SmartMoney website describes its *Map of the Market* as "a powerful new tool for spotting investment trends and opportunities." The application represents information that is not inherently visible: stock market values. Data are structured by the value of market capitalization of public traded companies organized by sectors with updated information on capital gains and losses.

The visualization provides information on a large number of companies in a very small space: more than 530 stocks are grouped by sectors and updated every 15 minutes inside a rectangular shape of approximately 800 X 500 pixels. The display affords different levels of perceptual inferences, the most relevant being the discovery of patterns at the macro level. The application provides ways to interact with and examine data for specific periods of time in addition to other analytical tools and graphs.

Companies are organized by sectors (e.g., Financial, Technology, Communication) and arranged spatially as groups. Groups are separated by an outline that is easily detected by the line quality, which is thicker than other lines. The perceptual principle of closure facilitates the segregation between sectors in addition to the principle of simplicity affording easy detection of the groups.

Rectangular shapes representing individual companies populate each sector group. Companies are organized into two scales of order: market capitalization and price performance. The sizes of rectangles represent the market capitalization of individual companies. The color scheme encodes the stock price performances. Overall patterns in the data can be inferred easily by color detection and differentiations in the spectrum. The result is that, at a glance, we are able to spot areas showing gains and their related categorical industries.

THE BIRTH OF TREEMAPS

In 1990, Ben Shneiderman faced the problem of having a full hard disk and needing to find the files that were taking up most of the space. As an alternative to the analytical tools available at the time, mostly using tree structures, Shneiderman and his students at the Maryland Human-Computer Interaction Lab devised a method for visualizing the hierarchy of files using a space-filling technique called *treemap*. The name provides a good description of what the technique accomplishes: it uses all available space in a given shape to display hierarchical data.[27]

Treemap visualizations are space-efficient displays of large structured datasets: contiguous shapes are organized according to their hierarchy or categorization.

ALGORITHM

Novel algorithms have extended the treemap technique by proposing different layout methods for the partition of hierarchical data. The algorithm devised by Wattenberg generates a layout where the partitions have reasonable aspect ratios and are optimized by neighbor similarity. In other words, partitions are as close to squares as possible. This facilitates comparison of areas by positioning companies with similar price histories near each other.[28]

The popularity of the *SmartMoney Map of the Market*, which became one of the most trafficked sections of the site according to Wattenberg, gave rise to a broad use of the treemap technique in different domains. Treemaps are now considered to be one of the most often used techniques for visualizing large sets of hierarchical or categorical data. Furthermore, the technique has become a standard tool for visualizing financial data.

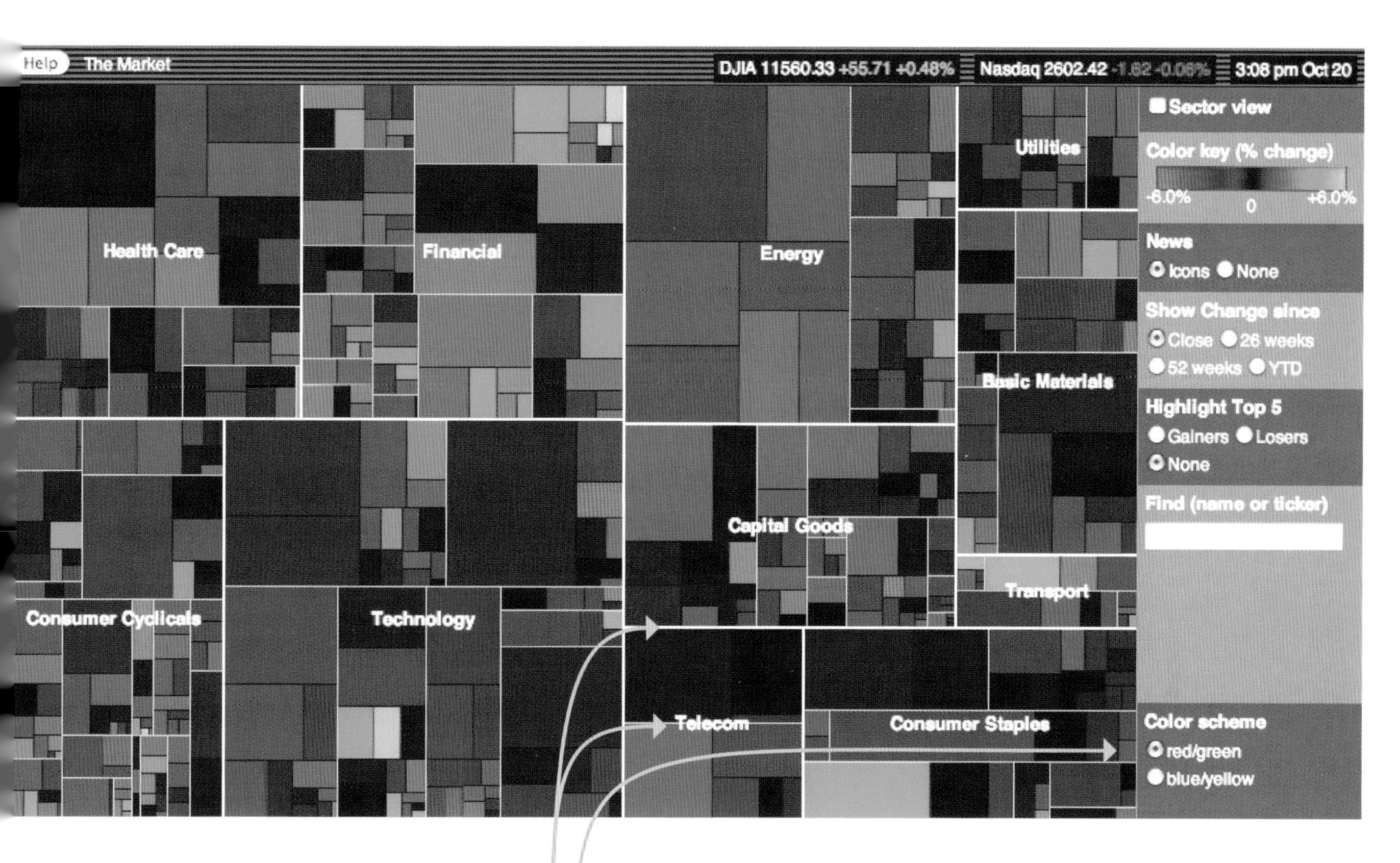

AUTHOR	Martin Wattenberg
COMPANY	SmartMoney.com
COUNTRY	United States
DATE	1998
MEDIUM	Online, real-time interactive application
DOMAIN	Finance
TASK	To provide an overview of stock market performance with detection of trends at given periods of time
STRUCTURE	The visualization uses the treemap technique. The algorithm devised by Wattenberg renders the internal divisions closer to squared shapes, resulting in a more legible and easier to interact with interface.

DATA TYPE AND VISUAL ENCODING

Categorical:	Sectors
Encoding:	Spatial positioning (grouping) and line weight
Temporal:	Invariant period of time
Encoding:	Text (enabled by selection)
Quantitative:	Market capitalization
Encoding:	Area size
Quantitative:	Price performance as percentages
Encoding:	Color scheme

CONCEPTUAL MODEL

Lakoff's theories on metaphor and categorization describe how basic-level and image-schematic concepts structure our experience of space and are used metaphorically to structure other concepts.[29]

The *container* and the *part–whole* image schemas play a central role in the *SmartMoney Map of the Market* tool. These two image schemas are meaningful because they structure our direct experience, and in particular, our bodily experience. We experience ourselves as entities, as containers with a bounded surface and an in-out orientation. Lakoff explains that we tend to project this view onto other physical objects, events, and actions and to conceptualize them as entities and most often as containers.[30] The result is an act of quantification, in that we are defining territories—bounded areas—that can be quantified in terms of the amount they contain. We also experience our bodies as wholes with parts.

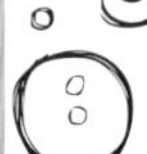

The structural elements of a container schema are interior, boundary, and exterior. Containers are the most appropriate schemas to structure categories.[31]

The structural elements of a part–whole schema are a whole, parts, and a configuration. The configuration is a crucial structuring factor in the part–whole schema. Considering that the parts can exist without constituting a whole, it is the configuration that makes it an image schema.

In the *SmartMoney Map of the Market*, enclosed rectangular shapes hierarchically represent quantitative data: sectors (containers) are each populated by subdivisions (sub-containers), which are divided into companies (sub-sub-containers). In all levels, we find part-whole schemas.

ARTIFACTS

Two artifacts that use similar fitting mechanisms as the treemap technique come to mind: nesting dolls and Tetris, the ubiquitous computer game from the 1980s. Coincidentally, both have Russian origins.

LEVEL 1:
Sectors

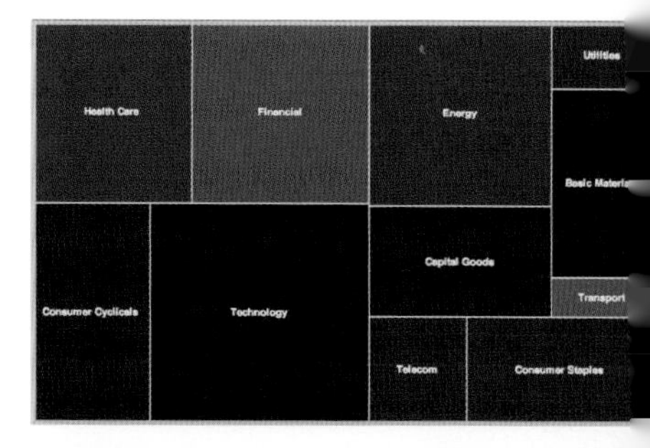

LEVEL 2:
Subdivisions of sectors

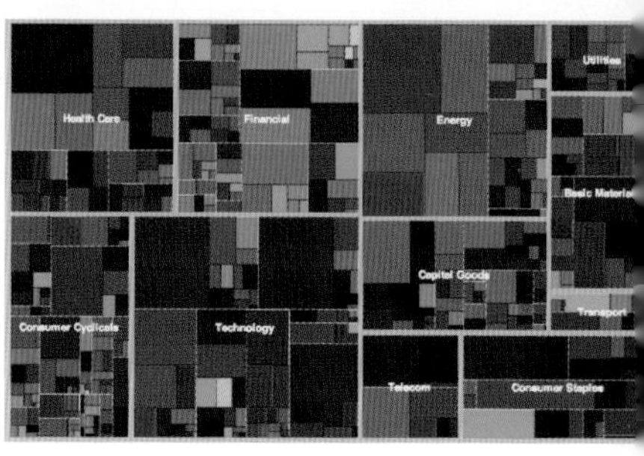

LEVEL 3:
Companies

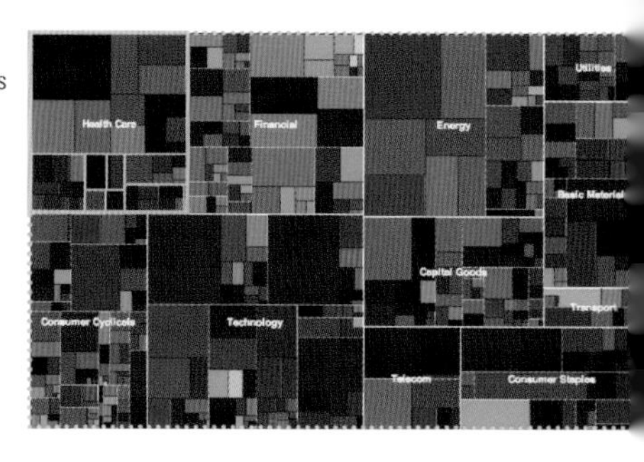

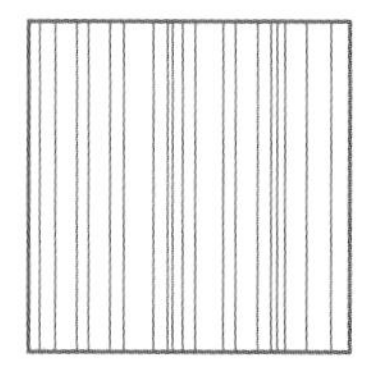

slice-and-dice

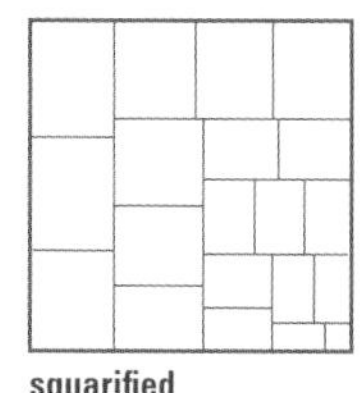

squarified

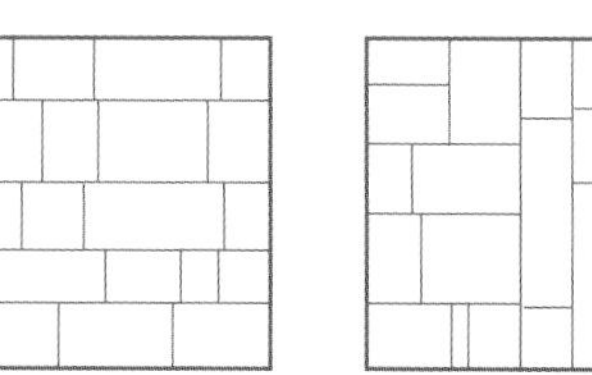

strip treemap

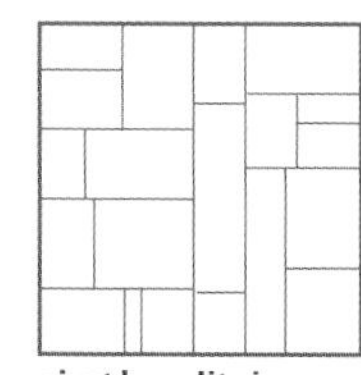

pivot by split size

Martin Wattenberg and Ben Bederson, from the Human-Computer Interaction Lab at the University of Maryland, designed an applet titled Dynamic Treemap Layout Comparison. As the title suggests, the tool allows comparison between the four most common layout methods for the partition of treemaps. The diagrams to the left were redrawn after their tool.[38]

www.cs.umd.edu/hcil/treemap-history/java_algorithms/LayoutApplet.html

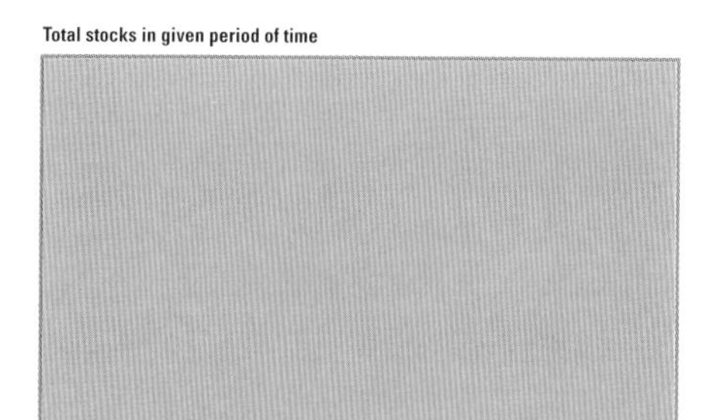

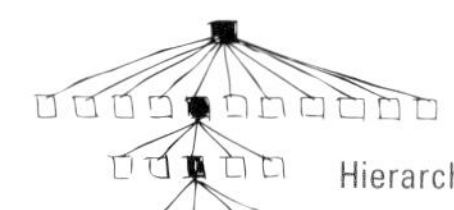

Hierarchical node–link diagrams are not effective for visualizing large datasets, as the tree structure for the data highlighted in the screenshots on the left attempt to show. In the diagram, sectors are organized by market capitalization, from larger to smaller areas. Rectangles that were rotated to facilitate area comparison have their original orientation displayed with dotted outlines. In comparison, the treemap technique as seen in the *SmartMoney Map of the Market* presents hierarchical data in a very condensed and effective way.

Technology Energy Financial Health Care Consumer Cyclicals Basic Materials Capital Goods Consumer Staples Telecom Utilities Transport

Pharmaceutics Medical Products Biotech-nology Health Insurance Hospital Management Specialized Services

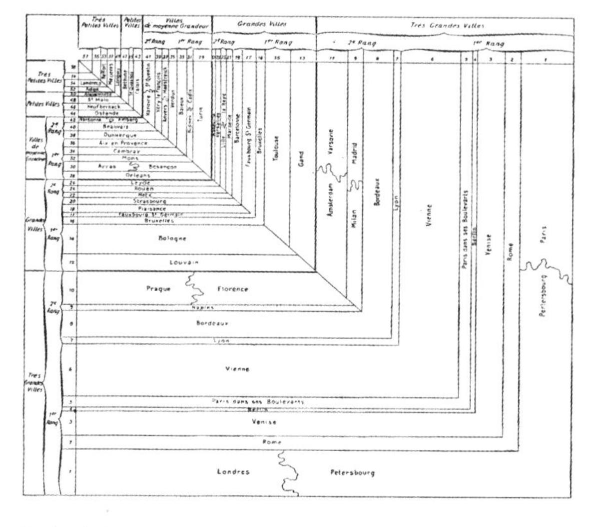

Charles de Fourcroy, France:
***"Tableau Poléometrique,"* 1782.**

Jacques Bertin considers this one of the earliest representations of proportional data.[39] The method uses variation in area sizes to compare quantities by superimposing squares. Each city is represented by a square with the size proportional to its land area. Cities are organized by size, and the smallest cities are represented by a half square. This can be noted on the top left, where we see a diagonal line.

Closure

The closure principle of perception describes our tendency to see bounded visual elements as wholes and to unite contours. Even when bounded elements overlap, there is a tendency—influenced by the principle of good continuation—to separate units and apply closure to defining units. It is as if the mind "fills" the missing parts and "closes" the visual element. For example, we tend to perceive the four lines below as a square.

When we perceive data representations such as Venn diagrams, for example, we make use of the closure principle to extract information. The closure principle plays a significant role in distinguishing the sectors and the levels of hierarchy in the *SmartMoney Map of the Market*. Each sector, or container, has a clear boundary represented by thicker and lighter lines.

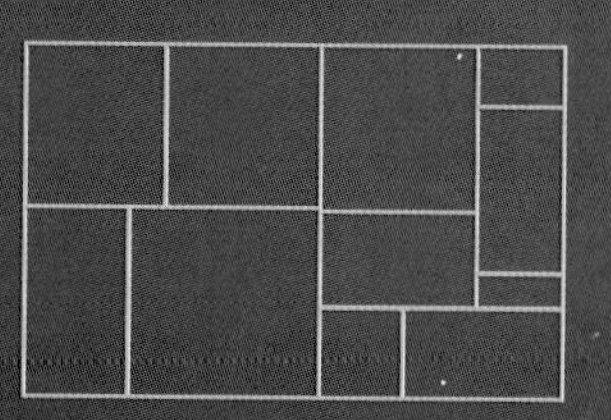

AREA SIZES

The area sizes of rectangles encode the market capitalization of companies within the hierarchical wholes. Because we are not good at making comparisons between area sizes due to constraints in our perception processes, our impressions of sizes are impaired. In most cases, we can say that a shape is larger or smaller than another, but hardly ever with any precision. It gets harder when comparing rectangles of different aspect ratios, or orientations. For example, which is the largest: Basic Materials or Capital Goods? And it is often a struggle when comparing shapes with different colors, because colors affect how we perceive area sizes. Visual perception studies indicate that we tend to perceive lighter areas as larger than darker ones (see box on page 145).[32] Our perception of color is also not absolute, such that surrounding colors often influence our impressions.

We can still get an overall sense of proportions in the *SmartMoney Map of the Market*, despite the fact that comparisons of absolute quantities are compromised. Precise amounts are provided on demand and displayed on an extra window positioned adjacent to the selected company when we mouse over its shape. Recall that the main goal of the visualization is to provide patterns to help inform investment decisions. Thus, the stock performance is the main variable to be watched, which is encoded by color.

PROPORTIONS

The external (and larger) container of the *SmartMoney Map of the Market* has a fixed size, around 500 X 800 pixels, and represents the topmost level selected. When we initiate the application, the container represents the entire map of the market with more than 530 companies. In this view, the subcontainers provide information about sectors, and their sizes are relative to the aggregated market capitalization of their innermost divisions, the companies. When we select to view a sector—say, Health Care—the external container now represents the total value for that sector, and the subsectors and related companies have their sizes changed according to the proportions to this new whole. Once again, if we select a subsector, Pharmaceuticals, inner partitions change accordingly.

Given that we interact with the partitions in the *SmartMoney Map of the Market*, it is relatively easy to understand changes in meaning for what the shapes stand for: At every level, the larger container represents the whole. In other words, the external container always stands for 100 percent of its parts.

However, attention should be paid when comparing treemap visualizations in static media, because most often they will represent different total amounts. Although such displays may do a good job communicating differences in their compositions, the comparisons of the amounts are hindered.

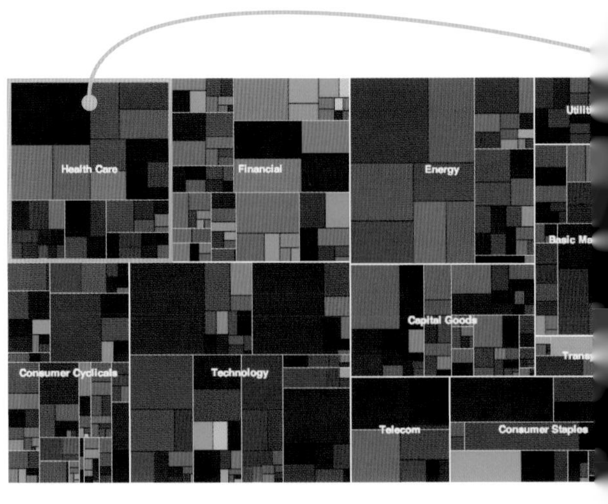

All sectors = 100%

The external container of treemaps stands for the total amount of the top-most level selected, independent of their absolute numbers.

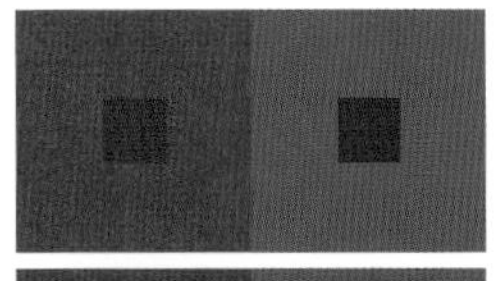

The surrounding colors affect our perception of area sizes as well as our impression of the colors themselves. The inner squares are identical but perceived differently due to background colors

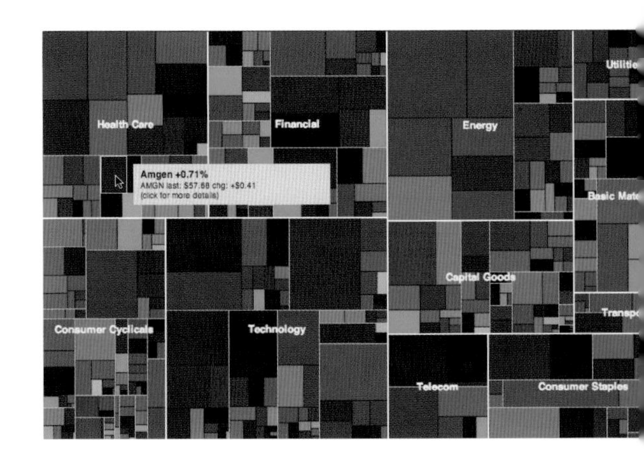

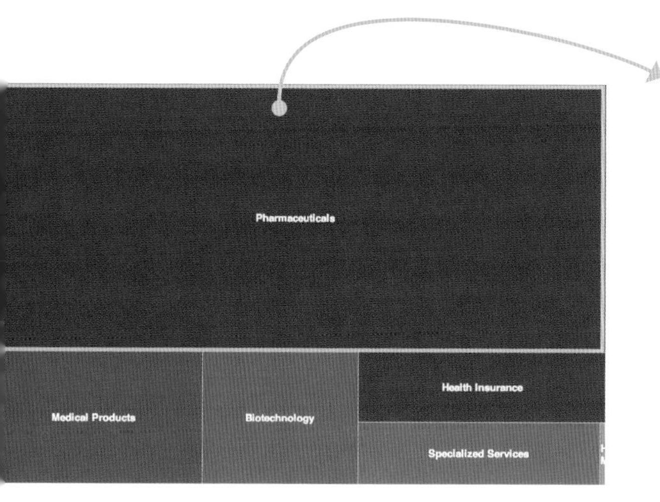

Health Care sector = 100%

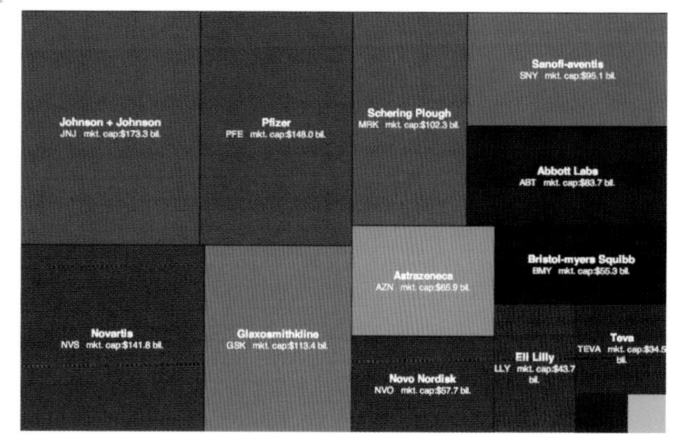

Pharmaceuticals subsector = 100%

COMPARISON OF GRAPHICAL REPRESENTATIONS OF QUANTITIES:

Diagram and descriptions are based and expand on the original explanation by Otto Neurath, *Isotype* (1933).

Squares (or Other Area Comparison)

We can say that: 2 is larger than 1
B is greater than A

But we cannot say by how much. Representing quantities only by area size provides an impression of magnitude, which might suffice for macro-scale views.

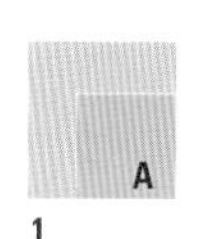

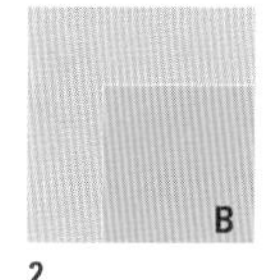

Pie Charts

We can say that: 2 is larger than 1 in area
A is 3/5 of 1
B is 6/10 of 2

But we cannot say by how much. Pie charts are good at providing relative quantities to a whole insofar as there are not many partitions. Comparison between edges is problematic, as explained on page 36.

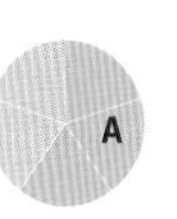

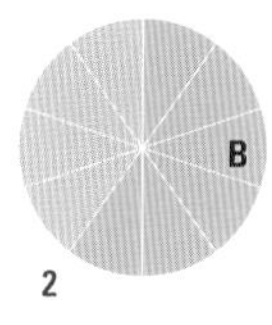

Groups of Geometric Units

We can say that: 2 is twice as large as 1
A is 3/5 of 1
B is 6/10 of 1
A is 1/2 of B

This format provides measurable comparisons between units and groups. It is recommended that units be grouped into meaningful amounts to facilitate counting. Decimal groups are the most commonly used.

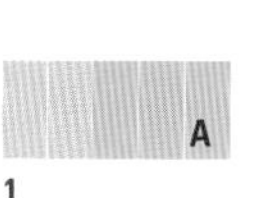

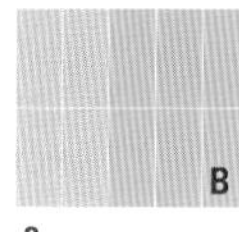

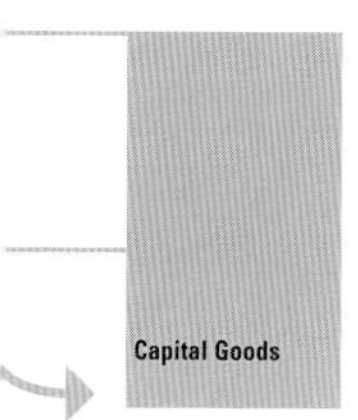

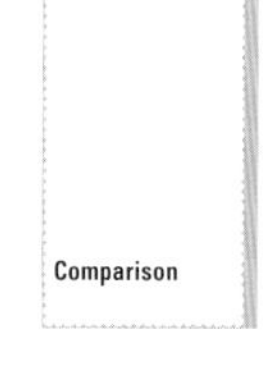

It is hard to compute areas with different aspect ratios and orientations. By flipping the rectangle for Capital Goods and comparing it to the one for Basic Materials, we see that the first is slightly larger.

Groups of Signs

We can say that: 2 is twice as large as 1
the number of women is 3/5 of 1
the number of men is 4/10 of 2
the number of women in 1 is 1/2 the number of women in 2

Scale of Signs

We should not represent quantitative information using the area of icons, nor should we use the height of signs to represent quantities. In other words, when using signs to represent quantitative information, assign each a numeric unit and a semantic meaning.

PIE CHARTS

Our visual system tends to distort the dimensions of area sizes. This factor affects the efficiency of displays representing proportions to a whole and that use area size to encode quantitative data.[33]

A familiar example is the pie chart, which is considered one the most used displays of quantitative data currently, especially in mass media and business publications. Pie charts convey general information about proportions of a whole, but we cannot infer absolute amounts from the perception of the wedges. Kosslyn explains that "about one-fourth of graph readers apparently focus on relative areas of wedges when they read such [pie] graphs—which means that they will systematically underestimate the sizes of larger wedges."[34] Furthermore, when it comes to presenting proportions among many entities, pie charts are inefficient, because it becomes almost impossible to compare and judge segments. It is often recommended that pie charts have not more than five or six wedges.[35]

The pie chart as a graphical invention is attributed to William Playfair, who devised and published a series of statistical graphs in the late eighteenth and beginning of the nineteenth century. The first known version of a pie chart was published in his notable *Statistical Breviary.*

COLOR SCHEMES

The variable of color encodes the price performance. There are two color schemes available: red-green and yellow-blue, which coincide with two of three of an individual's color channels, with the third one being black-white (or luminance).

The default color scheme ranges from bright green—showing that stock price is up—to bright red—representing the opposite, that price is down. The midpoint on the scale is black, representing no loss or gain (zero value). The shades of green and red represent the gradations in price performance since the previous market close.

The red-green scheme uses the metaphor of green "to go" and red "to stop, danger," accepted universally as a color convention. Take for example traffic lights, which are well understood all over the world. Convention apart, the two colors are very distinct from each other and afford easy discrimination.

The second color scheme is not an aesthetic device; rather, it offers an option for people with color-perception deficiencies and represents the information on a blue to yellow scale. Ten percent of the male population and 1 percent of the female population suffer from some form of color-perception deficiency. The most common form of color blindness relates to the inability to distinguish red from green, while almost everyone can distinguish colors in black to white as well as yellow to blue dimensions. Ware explains that color-blind people can still detect these sequences, including green to blue and red to blue.[36]

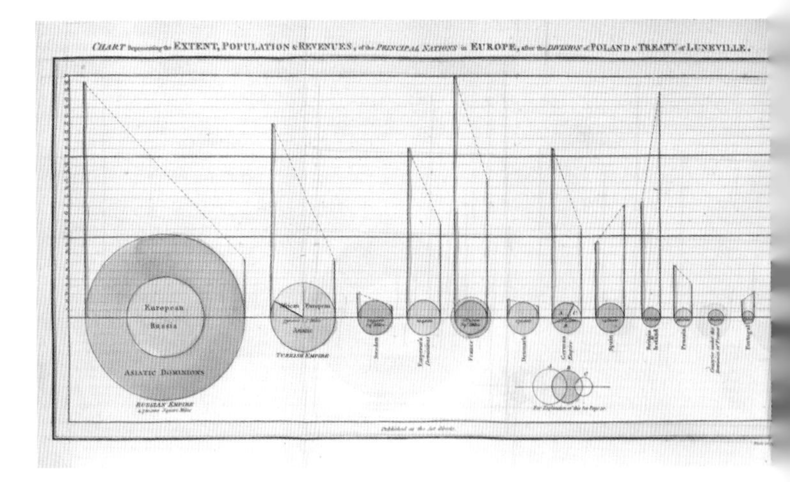

Spence and Wainer attribute William Playfair as the first person to use pie and circle diagrams to represent statistical data: "Playfair was a capable and inventive adapter of ideas from other domains, and his adaptation of logic diagrams to portray and compare empirical data was ingenious."[40] The graphic compares the extent, population, and revenues in European countries in 1801. The area of circles stands for the land area, the length of the left line (for each country) represents the population, and the length of the right line represents the revenues. Both lines share the same scale of millions, the latter in pounds sterling. Playfair used two methods to show subdivisions in the countries: inner circle (as in the Russian Empire) and sectors (as in the Turkish and German Empires). The latter is considered to be the first use of pie charts to display empirical proportions as well as to distinguish fractions by the use of colors. Playfair is also know to have invented the line graph and the bar graph, both having appeared in the *Commercial and Political Atlas* of 1786 (see page 93), in addition to the circle graph and pie diagram published in his 1801 *Statistical Breviary.*

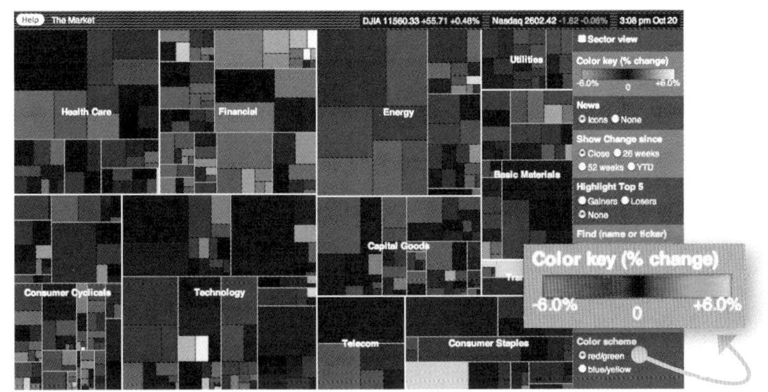

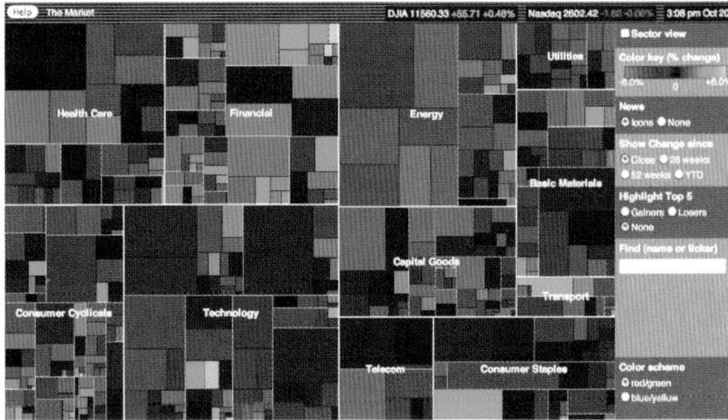

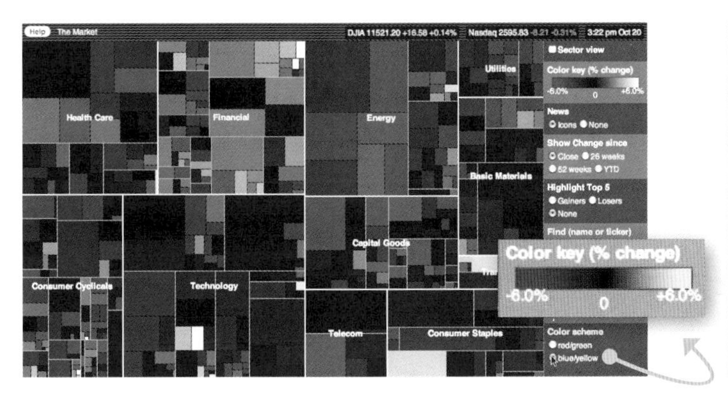

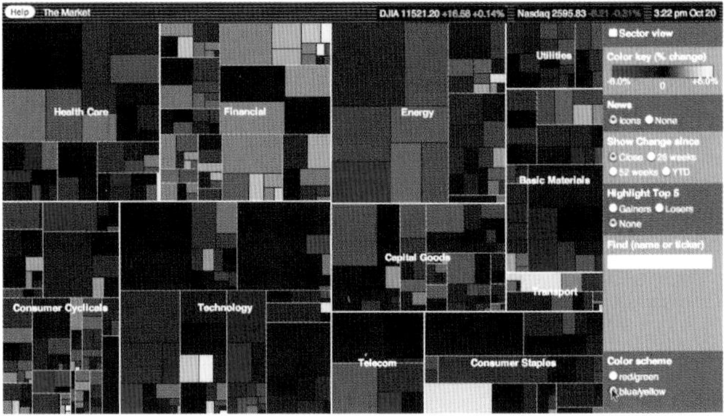

Comparison of the two color schemes available in the *Smart Money Map of the Market* against their grayscale representations.

The luminance channel is better at conveying detail, shape, and motion information than the chromatic channels are. We are unable to perceive differences that are purely chromatic. As such, the luminance channel plays a crucial role when designing for conveying information.[37]

Considering the dominance of tonal values in our perception, it would be beneficial to check color schemes against their grayscale representations. For example, it is possible to check that both color schemes for the *SmartMoney Map of the Market* when viewed in grayscale keep the distinction between the shades. This is not to say that information should be encoded on grayscale; rather, close attention should be paid to luminance illusions as described previously (see box on page 145).

On a side note, it is interesting how intuitively we perceive monochromatic representations, such as when we see black-and-white photos and films. The lack of colors (or hues) doesn't affect our understanding of images; rather, quite often we fill the images with colors from our imagination and memories. For more on the perception of colors, see pages 146–147.

SEVEN COLOR SEQUENCES AFTER COLIN WARE[41]:

Sequences in bold will be perceived by people suffering from color blindness.

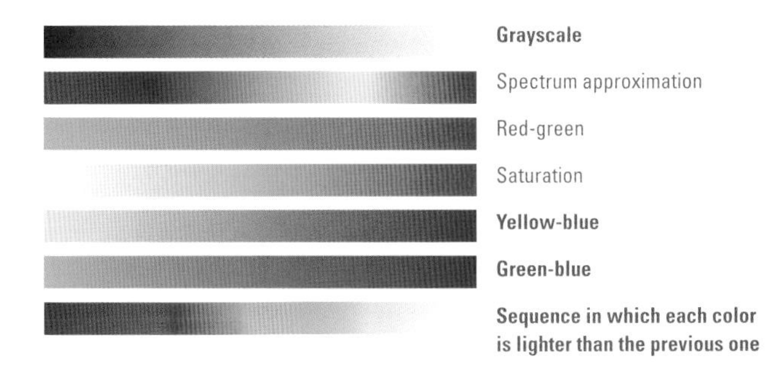

AUTHOR Marcos Weskamp (concept, design, frontend and backend coding) and Dan Albritton (backend coding)

COUNTRY United States

DATE 2004

MEDIUM Online, real-time interactive application

URL http://newsmap.jp

DOMAIN News coverage aggregated by Google News API

TASK To provide an overview of online news stories and reveal underlying patterns in news reporting around the world

STRUCTURE The visualization uses the treemap technique. The algorithm renders the inner-division shapes closer to rectangles, facilitating readability of text.

DATA TYPE AND VISUAL ENCODING

Categorical: News segments
Encoding: Color hues and spatial grouping
Categorical: Countries
Encoding: Label and enabled by selection
Temporal: News age: how old the news is
Encoding: Color value
Quantitative: Number of related stories
Encoding: Area size
Nominal: Title of news story
Encoding: Type size relative to the quantitative data

ERICAS

s pruebas
édicas a Chávez
agnostican un
ncer más
resivo
Ven positivo anuncio de las FARC de fin de secuestros
Correa perdona a "El Universo"
Garzón, libre de cargos por investigar franquismo
sonoro éxito de
he artist'
Chivas, bajo la lupa holandesa
WikiLeaks publica e-mails de Stratfor
Los Oscar consiguen la segunda mayor audiencia desde 2007

a estrena
stitución entre
icas internacionales
epresión
Silencio absoluto en La Habana sobre operación de Hugo Chávez
Embajador de Ecuador en Venezuela critica medios de su país
Stratfor: "una CIA privada"
El honor del presidente
Segundo joven muerto tras tiroteo en escuela de Ohio, EE.UU.
Los sobornos son parte de la vida cotidiana en la Rusia de Putin
s FARC liberarán a
rehenes en un
es y en varias fases
Baltasar Garzón, absuelto por investigar los crímenes del ...
Dos hermanos logran sobrevivir a los accidentes de Costa Cruceros
Costa Allegra es remolcado hacia Seychelles
mito de origen del
scar, en la era digital
El padre de Lucas renovó su reclamo de justicia
o que el
Oscar nos
dejó
La silenciosa lección que nos dejó "El artista"
El Parlamento alemán aprobó el paquete de ayuda a Grecia

EUROPE

Feyenoord beboet Fernandez
Van Wijk toch per direct weg
FC Eindhoven verliest van Sparta Rotterdam
Ook romanschrijvers liepen mee in VUmc
Joan Rivers kraakt Angelina Jolie af
Impopulaire interlands van baan
Van Der Vaart geeft titelstrijd op
'Seksrel in Wassenaar leidt tot onderzoek'
Opnieuw cruiseschip van rederij Costa op drift
Minder omzet en winst TomTom
Chronologie Royal Hospicering

Oscars : les Américains déçus par cette «nuit soporifique»
Dakar : Abdoulaye Wade et Macky Sall au second tour
Guide Michelin: les lauréats étoiles de l'année 2012
Football : les Bleus vont-ils dans la bonne direction ?
Syrie : les journalistes occidentaux en sécurité au Liban
PSA céderait 5% de son capital à GM
MWC 2012 : Nokia lance son Lumia 900 en Europe

Correa perdona a "El Universo"
Tiroteo en secundaria de EU deja un muerto
Costa Allegra y Costa Concordia: dos hermanos en dos siniestros ...
Jean Dujardin: «Para mí no es una película muda»
Los sobornos son parte de la vida cotidiana en la Rusia de Putin
#34;El Chapo#34; caerá como Osama: EU
Las cinco claves de Michigan y Arizona
La gala del cine mejora la audiencia pero no supera a los Grammy
Madrid, única región que cumple el déficit; Castilla La Mancha, la ...
Víctimas del franquismo piden investigar los crímenes tras la ...
Guardiola podría estallar contra los árbitros en breve
Marc se hace 'estrella'
La prueba del '9' para la selección española

Der doppelte Friedrich ärgert Angela Merkel
Vereiteltes Attentat "Geschenk" für Kandidat Putin
Solidarstreik der Fluglotsen Lufthansa will einstweilige Verfügung beantragen
Wieder 135 Tote in Syrien - Sanktionen in Kraft
USA Schießerei in Highschool - mindestens ein Todesopfer
Westerwelle für EU-Kandidatenstatus für Serbien
"Costa Allegra": Zweites Costa-Schiff treibt nach Brand auf hoher See
Im Elend der Städte
Glocks neuer Marussia fällt durch den Crashtest
Jean Dujardin und Meryl Streep: Sieger der Herzen

Romney and Santorum in key test in Michigan and Arizona
Ohio shooting: second victim 'brain dead'
Alleged Ohio gunman rarely spoke about 'trouble' at home
Russia election: Putin shrugs off 'assassination plot'
Men killed by the dozen, women and children missing in besieged Syrian city
Crippled liner being towed to Seychelles
Red Cross quit Homs as evacuation talks fail
Costa cruise liner adrift in Indian Ocean six weeks after Concordia disaster
Iran Calls Nuclear Arms Production a 'Great Sin'
Wouah! The French Cheer as One for the Oscar-Winning 'Artist'
Charlotte Church And Family Settle For £600000 In Phone Hacking Case

Romney hits Santorum on economic credentials
Santorum admits using robocalls in Michigan primary campaign
US keeps withdrawal timeline despite Koran row
Classes canceled in Ohio community hit by school shooting
The London-based Russians who oppose Vladimir Putin
Aides: Yemen's Saleh to Seek Ethiopia Exile
UK photographer 'evacuated from Syria to Lebanon'
Italian cruise ship adrift off Seychelles taken in tow
Matt Kenseth wins bizarre Daytona 500

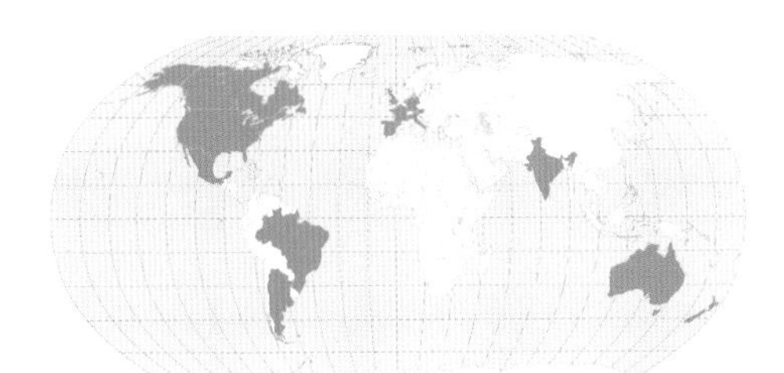

Canada
United States
Mexico
Brazil
Argentina

United Kingdom
Netherlands
France
Spain

Germany
Austria
Italy

India
Australia
New Zealand

The interactive application *Newsmap* displays news stories aggregated by Google News API using a treemap algorithm. Marcos Weskamp designed *Newsmap* with the objective to "demonstrate visually the relationships between data and the unseen patterns in news media."[42] The application shows stories for fifteen countries in their original languages. Stories are categorized into seven segments: World, National, Business, Technology, Sports, Entertainment, and Health, and are easily detected by different color hues. Color hues are effective for encoding categorical data.

This page shows screenshots taken within seconds of each other for all fifteen countries offered in the tool. The images were captured on February 28, 2012, a day after the Oscar ceremonies in the United States. It is revealing how countries cover the news in diverse ways, both in relation to proportions dedicated to specific news segments, as well as to individual stories. For example, all countries have covered both the Oscars and the GOP race in the United States, but not equally: Canada seems to have attended more to the political issues of its neighbor than did the United States, which dedicated more attention to the Oscars. Overall, it is contrasting the coverage of world news between the two countries. The tool allows many interesting comparisons and readings of how we differ culturally around the globe. For example, we can see that sports plays a larger role in Italy, whereas in Brazil we see the predominance of the national news.

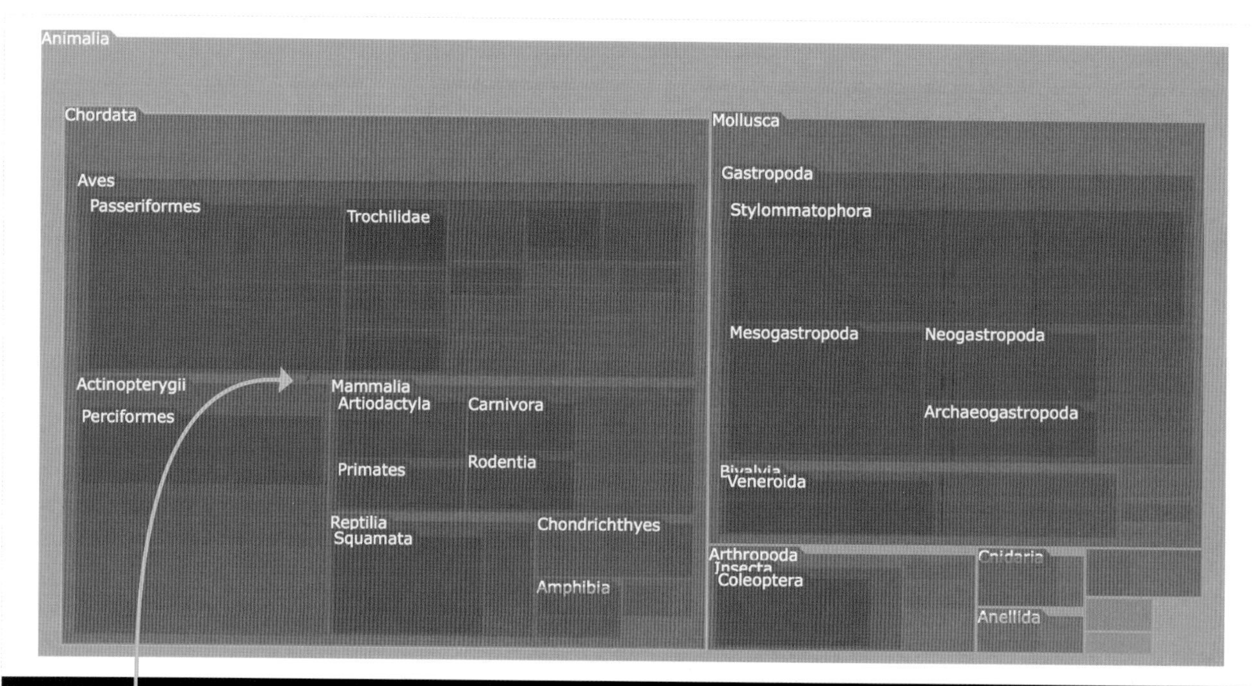

AUTHOR Bestiario
COUNTRY Spain/Portugal
DATE 2010
MEDIUM Online interactive application
URL http://arbre.bioexplora.cat
DOMAIN Biological records
TASK To provide access to 150 years of biological records collected around the world by the Natural Science Museum of Barcelona
STRUCTURE The project uses a treemap structure to display hierarchical biological data.

DATA TYPE AND VISUAL ENCODING
Categorical: Taxonomy (classification of organisms)
Encoding: Spatial positioning (grouping)
Quantitative: Amount of species within each *phyla* (taxonomic category)
Encoding: Area size
Qualitative: Divisions of the classification
Encoding: Colors of rectangles. A different color is used for each of the eight divisions of the Animalia kingdom

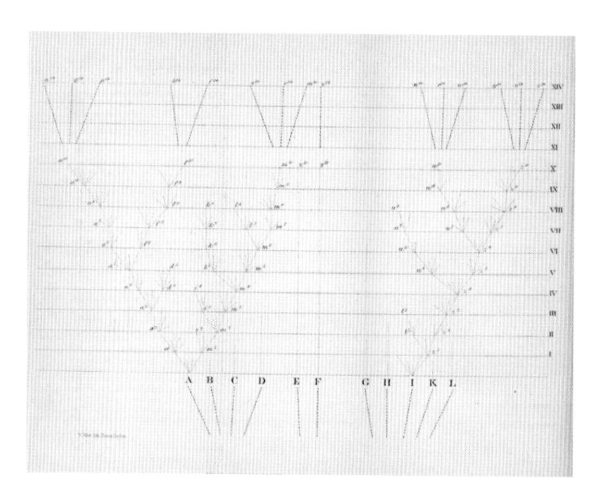

William West: The single illustration in Charles Darwin's first edition of *On the Origin of Species*, 1859.

This diagram demonstrates "how the degree of similarities between a number of varieties and species is explained by descent from common ancestors."[43]

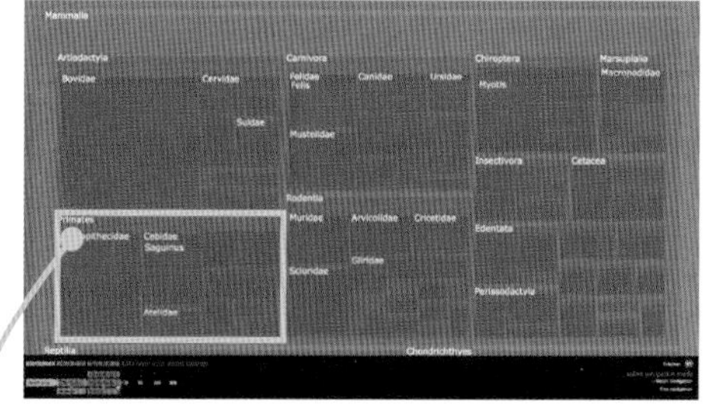

The heat map visualization allows access to the collection of the Natural Science Museum of Barcelona both by selecting geographical areas in order to learn about species with provenance in those locations and by selecting species from the list of records.

http://mapa.bioexplora.cat

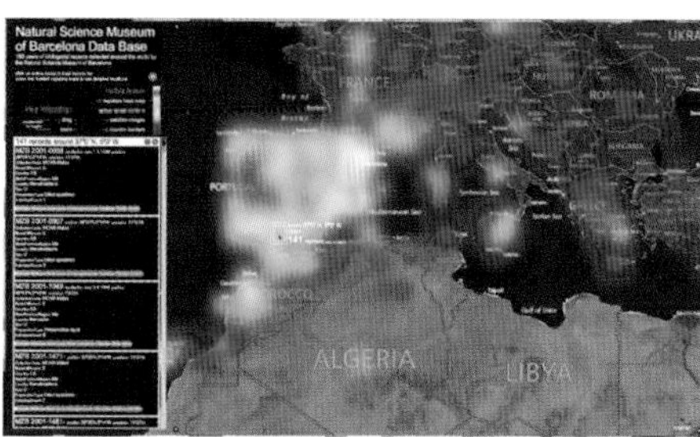

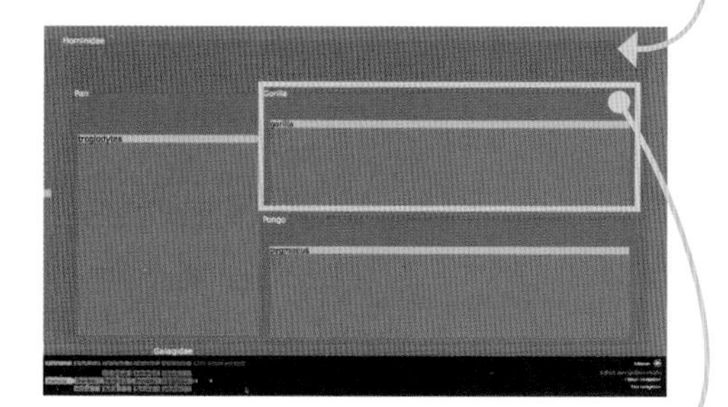

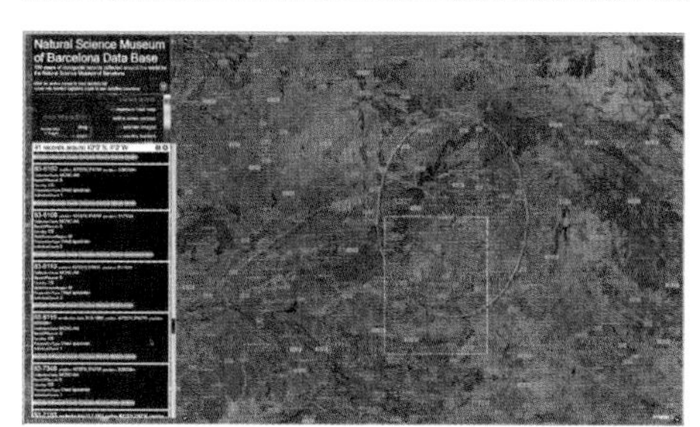

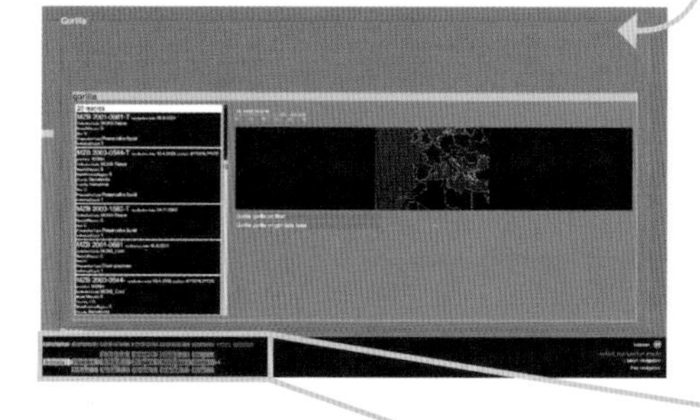

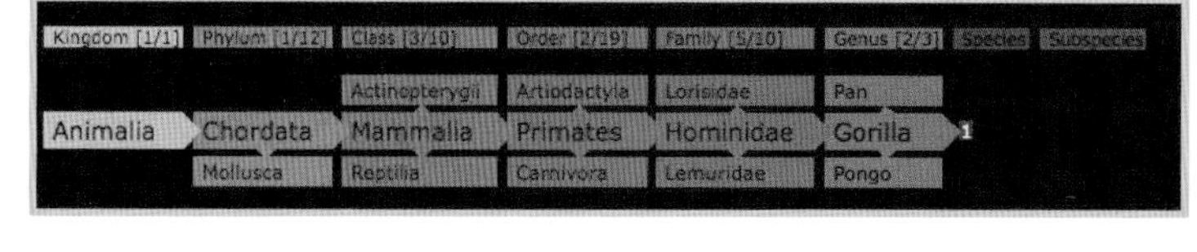

Regardless of whether one chooses to navigate data in space or using the taxonomy system, the output includes both types of information. The bottom image is an inset that shows the map with location of the related active record, similarly to the screenshots of the map interface, where the taxonomy information is included for each record on the list.

In 2010, Bestiario designed two visualizations that are used as interfaces to explore the collection of the Natural Science Museum of Barcelona. One is a treemap interface with data organized by taxonomy (on the left). The other provides geographical access to the same data, which can be viewed on the right.

The database contains more than 50,000 records and is continuously updated as new data are entered into the collection. The records belong to places all over the world, with higher density on the Iberian Peninsula and western Mediterranean Sea. This is particularly visible when one navigates geographically.

In both interfaces, data are structured following the Darwin Core standard, developed by the Global Biodiversity Information Facility (GBIF), for which the museum is one of the information providers.

The use of a zoomable treemap structure is easily used by the museum's general audience, especially considering that the "tree of life" metaphor is strongly associated with evolutionary theories, even though it predates them.

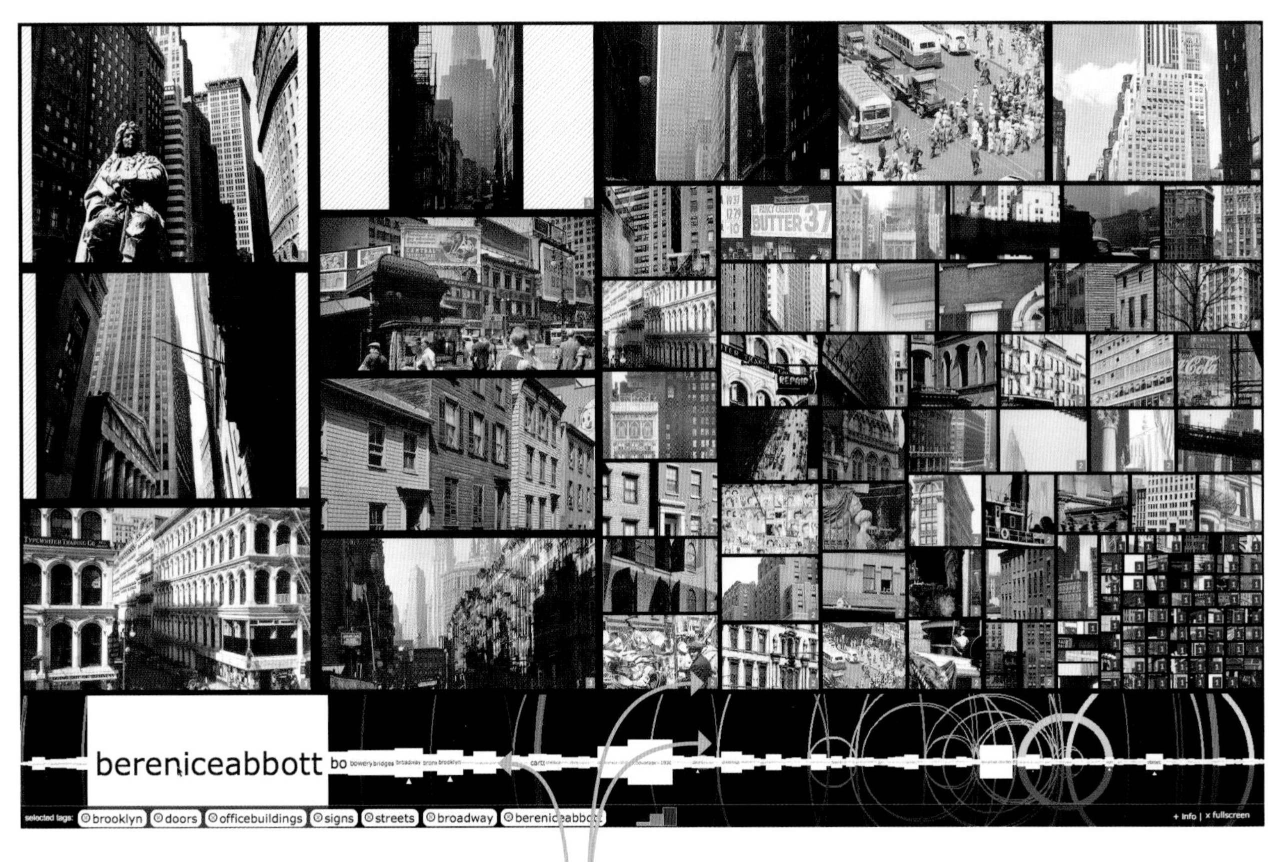

AUTHOR	Bestiario
COUNTRY	Spain/Portugal
DATE	2010
MEDIUM	Online interactive application
URL	http://bestiario.org/research/tessera/changingnewyork
DOMAIN	Data visualization
TASK	To provide a means to explore large image collections
STRUCTURE	The project uses a squarified algorithm for the display of images, and a tag structure for the navigation of categories.

DATA TYPE AND VISUAL ENCODING

Categorical:	Semantic tags
Encoding:	Label inside white rectangle, organized alphabetically
Quantitative:	Amount of images within category
Encoding:	Area size of white rectangles at the bottom navigation
Quantitative:	Amount of semantic connections between tags
Encoding:	Colored rectangles on bottom right corner of images indicating exact number of shared tags within given selection. Also encoded by the image size, which is relative to the quantitative data. The thickness of colored arcs (at the bottom navigation) indicates the number of connections.

When *Tessera* is first opened, fifty images are shown with approximate sizes. When a project has been selected, it is positioned on the top right corner, with the most related images organized according to the quantity of shared tags, which can be checked by the small colored rectangles with numbers.

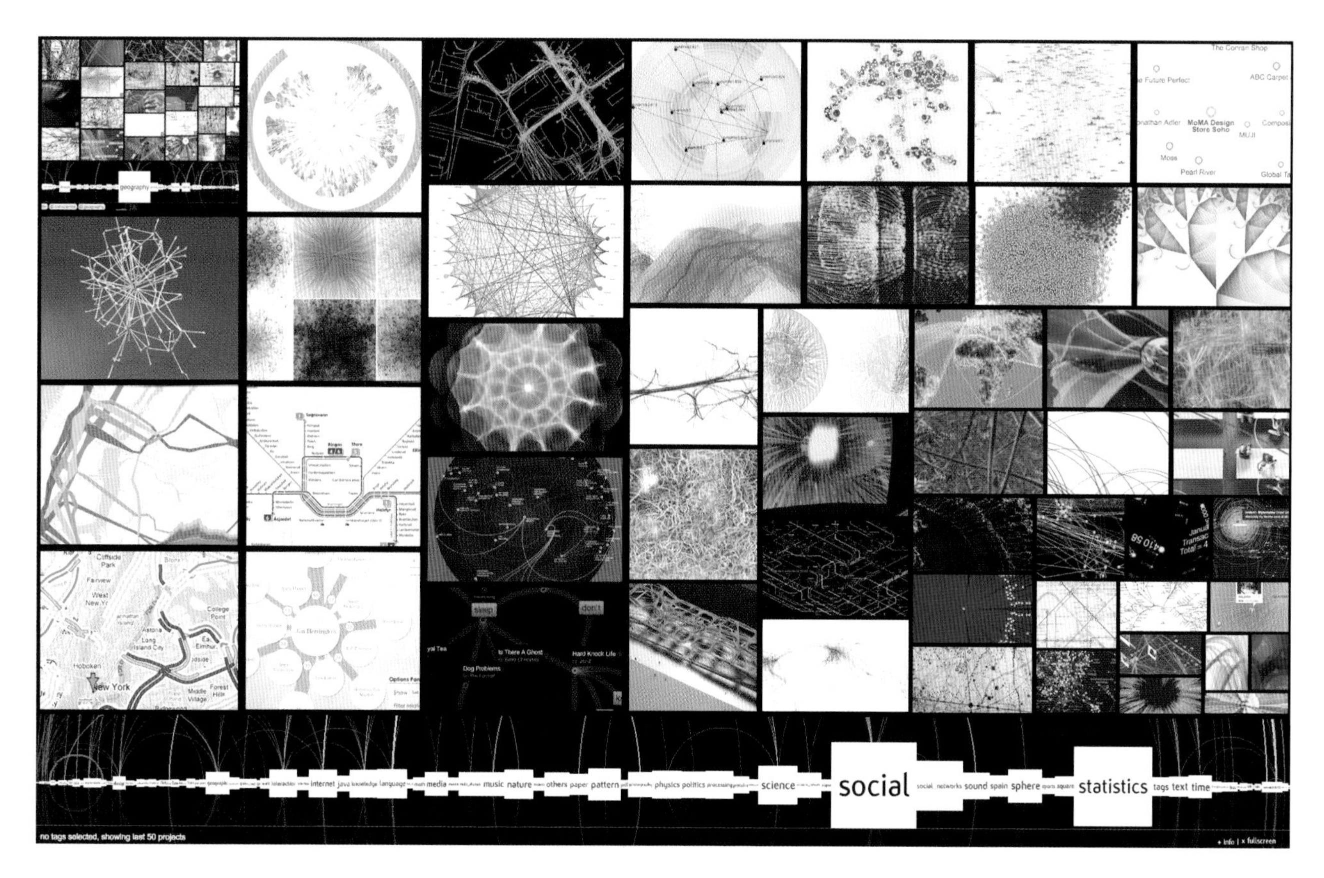

Tessera is based on a 2009 project titled "ReMap," which displays projects from the website VisualComplexity.com, a collection of visualizations curated by designer Manuel Lima.

http://bestiario.org/research/remap

Tessera is a prototype designed by Bestiario for the display and exploration of large image collections using a quadrification visualization method. The version of *Tessera* reproduced here displays the New York Public Library's Flickr photo stream "Changing New York, 1935–1938, Berenice Abbott."

Users can navigate the photographic collection using *Tessera* in two ways:

1. By category: Clicking on a category tag at the bottom navigation reconfigures the image structure to represent projects within the category (or combined categories) selected. Category tags are assigned using a semantic engine by Bestiario.
2. By project: Directly clicking on the project's thumbnail reconfigures the structure to display related visualizations.

Access to large amounts of data, including visual data such as photos and videos, has increased exponentially in recent years. The need for applications that will enable both archiving and accessing datasets in a meaningful way is unprecedented. *Tessera* is an attempt to solve the problem of image collections. It proposes a structure based on semantic navigation while visualizing the hidden meta-data connections.

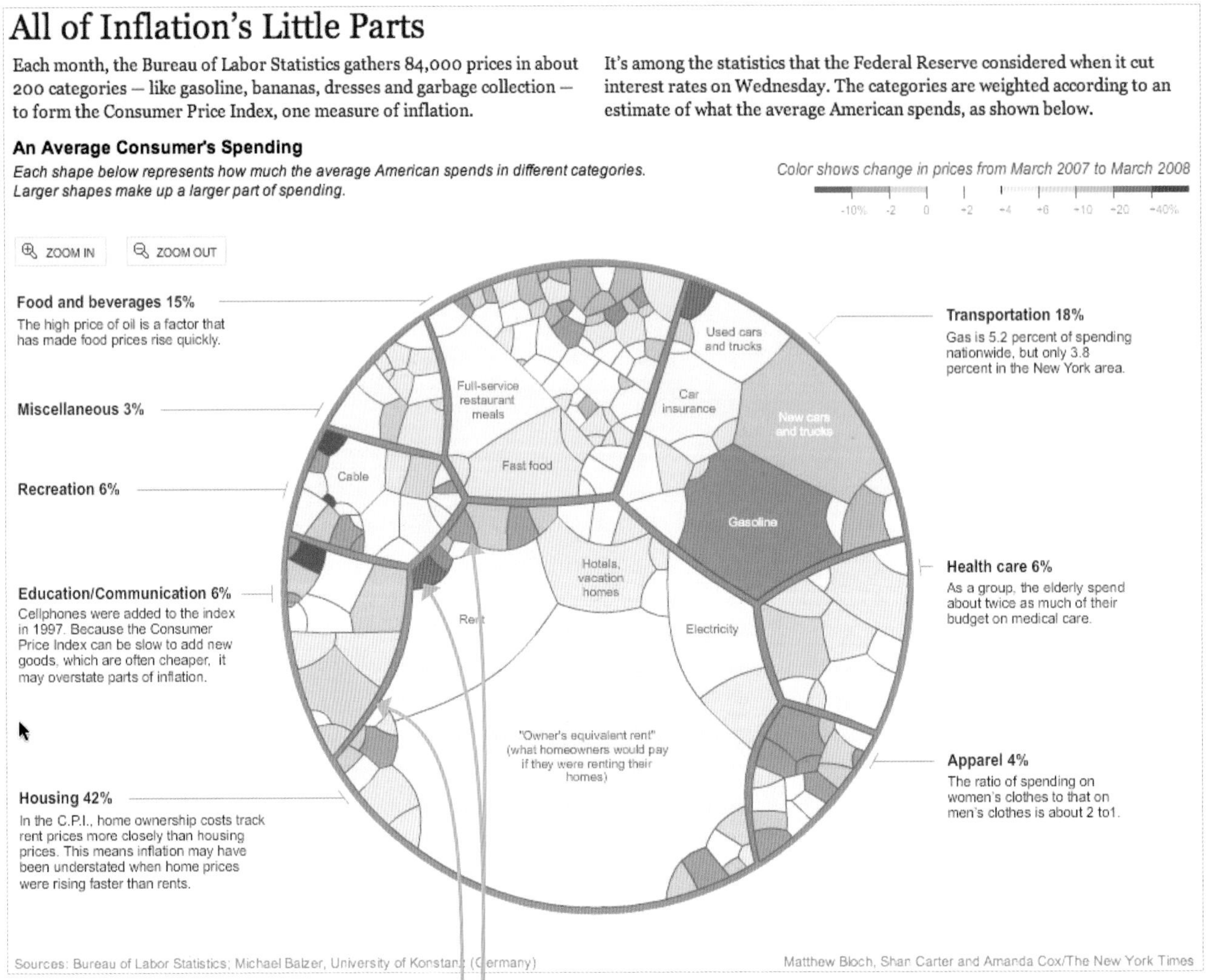

All of Inflation's Little Parts

Each month, the Bureau of Labor Statistics gathers 84,000 prices in about 200 categories – like gasoline, bananas, dresses and garbage collection – to form the Consumer Price Index, one measure of inflation. It's among the statistics that the Federal Reserve considered when it cut interest rates on Wednesday. The categories are weighted according to an estimate of what the average American spends, as shown below.

An Average Consumer's Spending

Each shape below represents how much the average American spends in different categories. Larger shapes make up a larger part of spending.

Color shows change in prices from March 2007 to March 2008

-10% -2 0 +2 +4 +6 +10 +20 +40%

ZOOM IN ZOOM OUT

Food and beverages 15%
The high price of oil is a factor that has made food prices rise quickly.

Miscellaneous 3%

Recreation 6%

Education/Communication 6%
Cellphones were added to the index in 1997. Because the Consumer Price Index can be slow to add new goods, which are often cheaper, it may overstate parts of inflation.

Housing 42%
In the C.P.I., home ownership costs track rent prices more closely than housing prices. This means inflation may have been understated when home prices were rising faster than rents.

Transportation 18%
Gas is 5.2 percent of spending nationwide, but only 3.8 percent in the New York area.

Health care 6%
As a group, the elderly spend about twice as much of their budget on medical care.

Apparel 4%
The ratio of spending on women's clothes to that on men's clothes is about 2 to1.

Used cars and trucks
Car insurance
New cars and trucks
Gasoline
Full-service restaurant meals
Fast food
Cable
Hotels, vacation homes
Rent
Electricity
"Owner's equivalent rent" (what homeowners would pay if they were renting their homes)

Sources: Bureau of Labor Statistics; Michael Balzer, University of Konstanz (Germany)

Matthew Bloch, Shan Carter and Amanda Cox/The New York Times

AUTHOR	Matthew Bloch, Shan Carter, and Amanda Cox (*New York Times*)
COUNTRY	U.S.
DATE	2008
MEDIUM	Online interactive application
URL	www.nytimes.com/interactive/2008/05/03/business/20080403_SPENDING_GRAPHIC.html
DOMAIN	Finance (consumer spending)
TASK	To provide an overview of the average American consumption in relation to price performance over a year
STRUCTURE	The visualization uses a Voronoi treemap algorithm to render consumption items.

DATA TYPE AND VISUAL ENCODING

Categorical:	Expenditure groupings
Encoding:	Spatial positioning (grouping) and line weight
Quantitative:	National spending shares as percentages
Encoding:	Area size
Quantitative:	Price performance within the one-year period (as percentages)
Encoding:	Color sequence: from blue (< 0%), to white (neutral), to yellow (> 7%) to brown (> 20%)

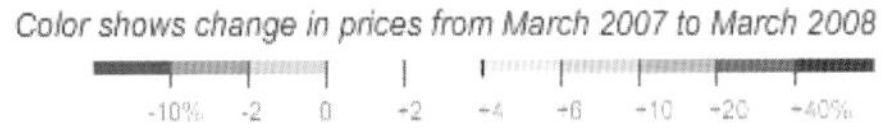

Color shows change in prices from March 2007 to March 2008

-10% -2 0 +2 +4 +6 +10 +20 +40%

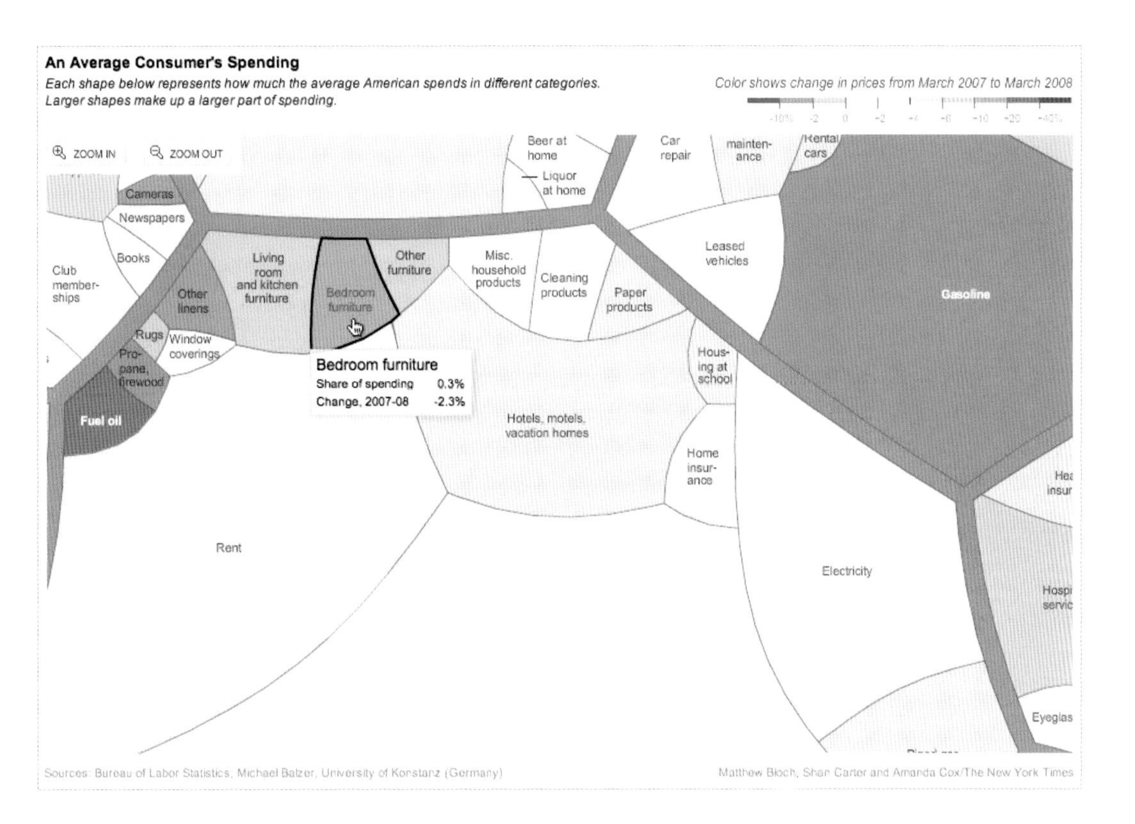

Michael Balzer and Oliver Deussen developed the algorithm for Voronoi treemaps in 2005 with the purpose of eliminating the aspect-ratio problems imposed by rectangle-based shapes in traditional treemaps.[44] Voronoi treemaps use arbitrary polygons instead of rectangular subdivisions. The layouts are computed by the iterative relaxation of Voronoi tessellations, which allows arbitrary shapes to be used as the outer container, such as circles and triangles. However, the comparison of area sizes, which was one of the problems raised earlier about rectangle-based treemaps, gets amplified in the Voronoi version, where partitions have very different shapes, with almost no base for comparisons.

On May 3, 2008, the *New York Times* published an interactive visualization titled "All of Inflation's Little Parts" that uses the Voronoi treemap algorithm to structure expenditure data. The visualization maps an average consumer's spending between March 2007 and March 2008. The data source is the Bureau of Labor Statistics, which collects prices on about 200 categories, in order to generate the Consumer Price Index. In the visualization, data are grouped into eight categories, each subdivided into common spending items. For example, within the category Transportation, the two largest spending items are Gasoline, with 5.2% of national shared spending, and New Cars and Trucks, with 4.6%.

Voronoi diagrams (such as Delaunay triangulations and convex hulls) are often used to record information about distances and regions of influence. The mathematical method has been used over time, and in various domains, such as anthropologic research examining cultural regions of influence, economic studies of market models, and computational problems looking for the nearest neighbor. An early use of a similar method that is particularly relevant to this book was made by the British physician Dr. John Snow, who is known in the visualization field for mapping the 1854 London cholera epidemic as a way to prove to the health authorities that the disease was spread by infected water and not an airborne disease, as was believed then (see page 135).

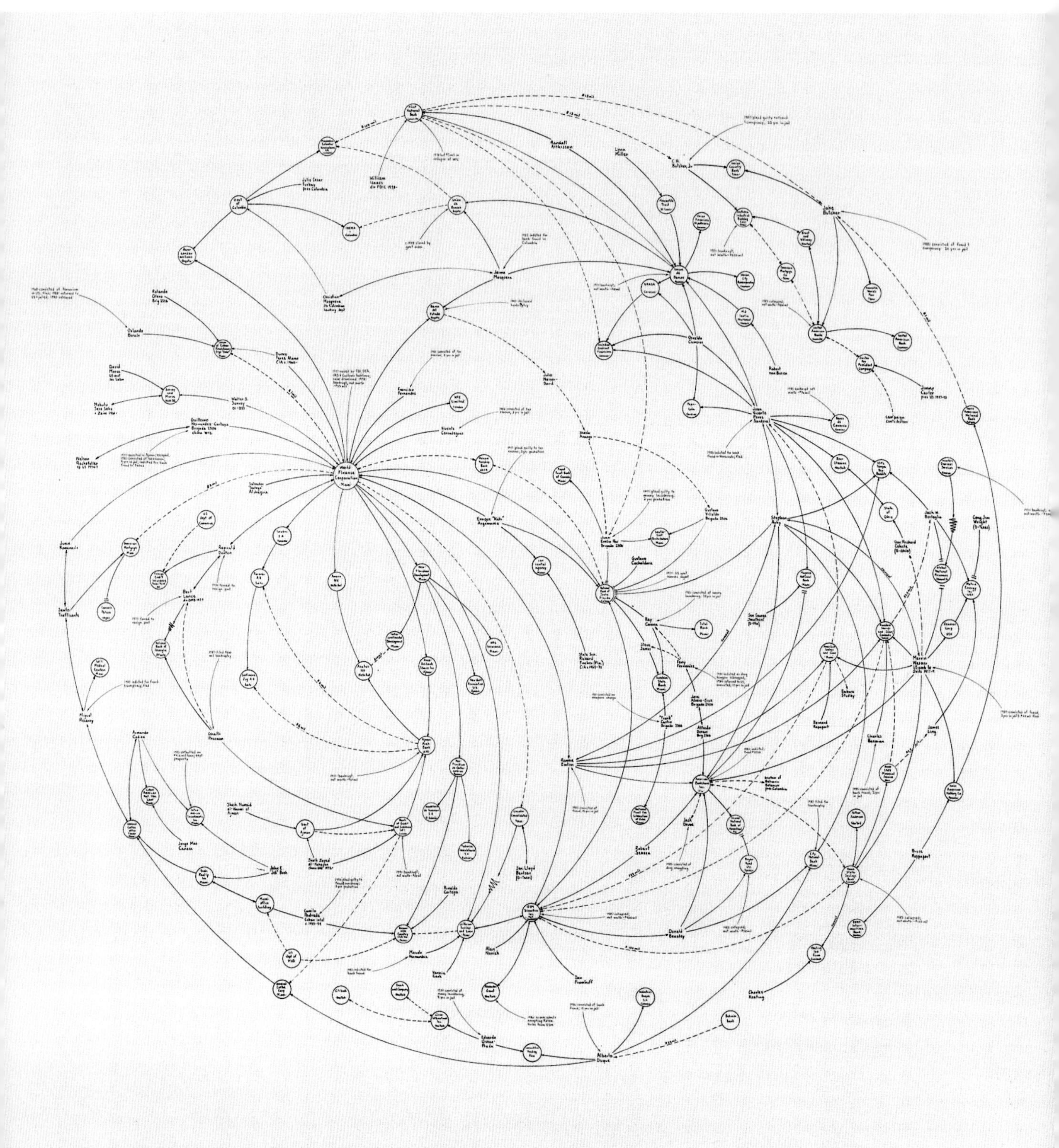

World Finance Corporation Miami
Jake Butcher
C.H. Butcher, Jr.
Jimmy Carter pres US 1977-81
Randall Atkisson
Lynn Miller
Jaime Mosquera
Julio Cesar Turbay pres Colombia
Orlando Bosch
Rolando Otero
Duney Perez Alamo
David Mora
Walter S. Surrey
Guillermo Hernandez-Cartaya
Nelson Rockefeller
Juan Romanacci
Santo Trafficante
Miguel Recarey
Armando Codina
Jorge Mas Canosa
Jeb Bush
Sheik Humaid
Camilo Padreda
Enrique "Kiki" Argomaniz
Emilio Nuñez
Gustavo Villoldo
Stephen Raby
Marvin Warner
Ronnie Ewton
Alfredo Duran
Jack Brown
Robert Sensen
Donald Beasley
Alan Novick
Dan Fountoff
Alberto Duque
Eduardo Orozco
Charles Keating
Bruce Rappaport
James Ling
Charles Bowman
Bernard Rapoport
Barbara Studley
Robert Vesco
Glenn Robinson
Francisco Fernandez
Ricardo Carbaga
Marcelo Hernandez

CHAPTER 2

RELATIONAL STRUCTURES: NETWORKS

Mark Lombardi, U.S.: *World Finance Corporation and Associates, c. 1970–84, Miami-Ajman-Bogota-Caracas* (7th version), 1999.

American artist Mark Lombardi began a series of drawings in 1994 that he called Narrative Structures, as he explains, "Each consists of a network of lines and notations which are meant to convey a story, typically about a recent event of interest to me, like the collapse of a large international bank, trading company or investment house. One of my goals is to map the interaction of political, social and economic forces in contemporary affairs."[13] The drawing reproduced here is one among several versions Lombardi created to depict the scandal involving the WFC and the central role it reputedly played in the trafficking of Colombian drugs. Robert Hobbs explains, "An important subtext of this work and other Lombardi pieces…is the wide-ranging collusion involved in global crimes."[14]

As the name indicates, relational structures organize data for which relationships are key to the system being visualized. Or to put it another way, there is much that can be learned by studying the patterns of connections between elements in the system—that is, the network of systems. Shneiderman and colleagues provide a good example in the context of social studies: "The focus of social network analysis is between, not within people. Whereas traditional social-science research methods such as surveys focus on individuals and their attributes (e.g., gender, age, income), network scientists focus on the connections that bind individuals together, not exclusively on their internal qualities or abilities. This change in focus from attribute data to relational data dramatically affects how data are collected, represented, and analyzed. Social network analysis complements methods that focus more narrowly on individuals, adding a critical dimension that captures the connective tissue of societies and other complex interdependencies."[1]

We are surrounded by networks, from metabolic to social networks, from transportation systems to power grids. Barabási explains that networks are at the heart of understanding complex systems, and "despite the apparent differences, the emergence and evolution of different networks is driven by a common set of fundamental laws and reproducible mechanism. Hence despite the amazing diversity in form, size, nature, age, and scope characterizing real networks, most networks observed in nature, society, and technology are driven by common organizing principles."[2]

The study of networks is not new, as shown by early research in fields as varied as biology, sociology, and mathematics, briefly described below. The scientific study of networks—network science—is, however, more recent and focuses on the study of patterns of connections in real-world systems. According to Barabási, four key characteristics distinguish network science as a discipline from early studies of networks: it is interdisciplinary; it examines empirical data; it is quantitative and mathematical in nature; and it relies on computational tools.[3]

Over the years, scientists from several fields have developed a set of tools for analyzing, modeling, and making predictions about complex systems using network science. Given the mathematical, computational, and statistical nature of these tools, this book offers only a glimpse into the fundamentals of this burgeoning field, with focus on visualizations. Visualizations have played a key role in network sciences by adding visual insight and intuition to the numerical analysis. By examining network representations from diverse disciplines, I present the core concepts of network analysis while discussing the challenges faced in visualizing them. For an in-depth examination and advanced study of the science behind networks, I recommend excellent books listed in the bibliography (see page 209). Important to remember is that new models and algorithms are constantly being devised by a growing number of researchers all over the world, and those can be found in scholarly papers and conference proceedings.

GRAPH THEORY

Network science originated in graph theory, and the mathematical foundations set by Leonhard Euler in the eighteenth century. The root is on the puzzle involving the city of Königsberg, the capital of eastern Prussia at the time, and its seven bridges: Can one walk across all seven bridges without crossing the same bridge twice?

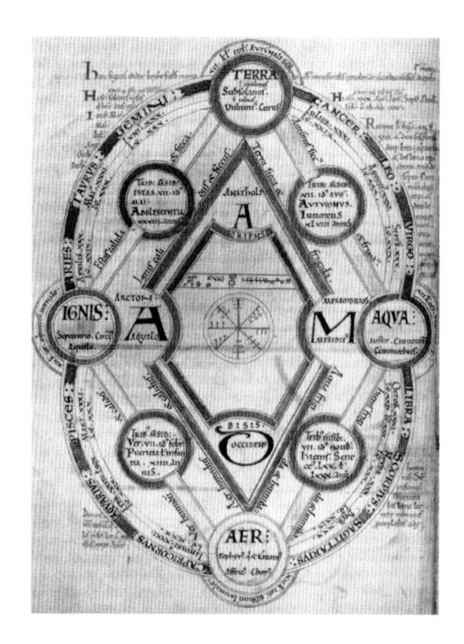

This diagram by Byrthferth de Ramsey, from a manuscript from around 1080, portrays the mysteries of the universe. It shows Adam in the center, surrounded by the four cardinal points (north to the left), the four elements, the four seasons, the four stages of life, and the twelve signs of the zodiac.

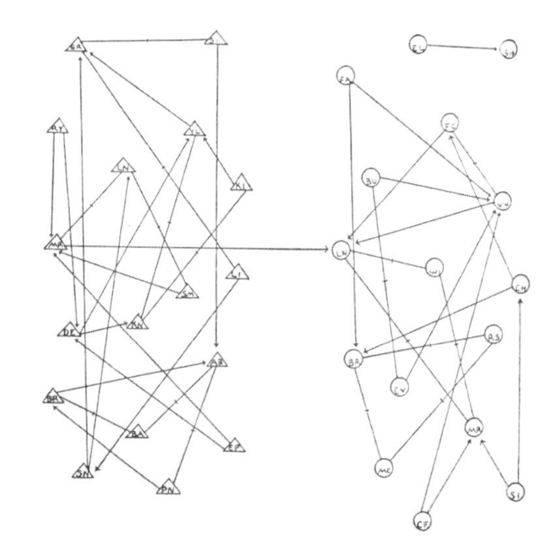

Considered one of the founders of social network analysis, the Romanian psychiatrist Jacob Moreno devised a method for evaluating relationships between individuals in groups or communities called *sociometry*. *Sociograms* are the visual counterpart he devised to represent information as graphs for studying the connecting roles of individuals in communities. His 1934 book *Who Shall Survive?* presents his theories and early network graphs.

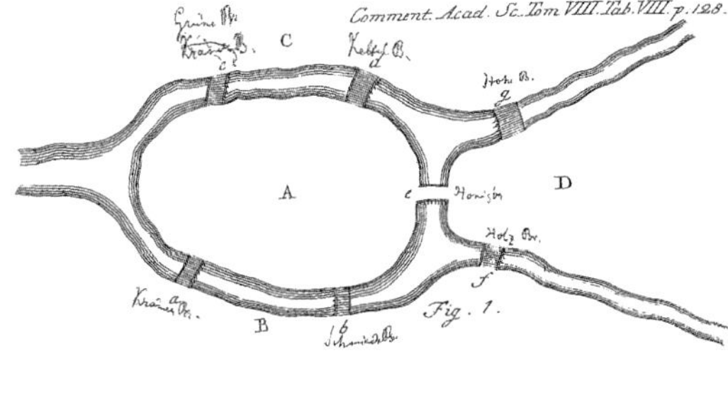

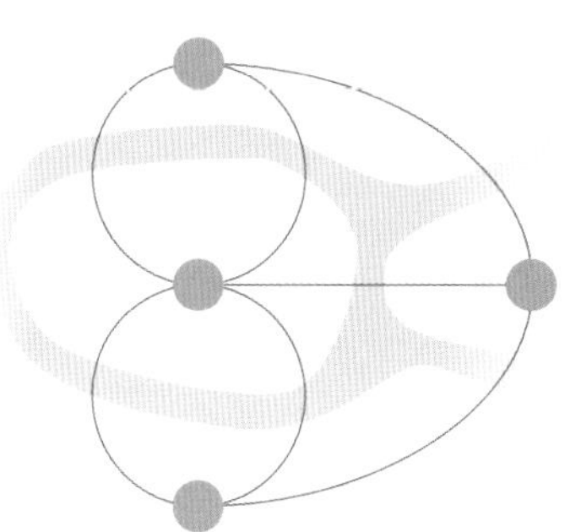

The image at the top appeared in the original paper by Euler in 1736, and it shows the seven bridges in the city of Königsberg. The diagram at the bottom depicts the same problem as a graph.

FIELD		
Computer Science	node	link
Mathematics	vertex	edge
Physics	site	bond
Sociology	actor	tie

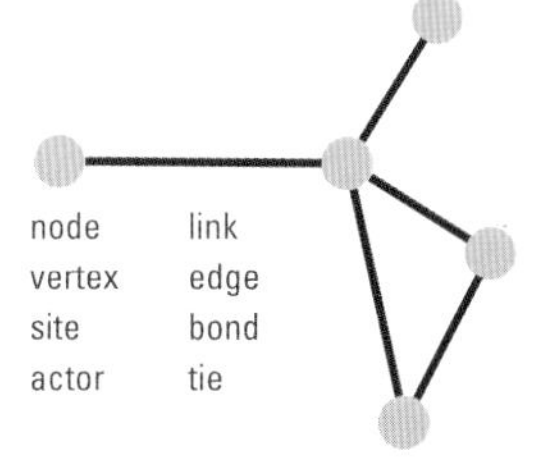

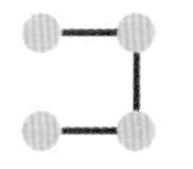

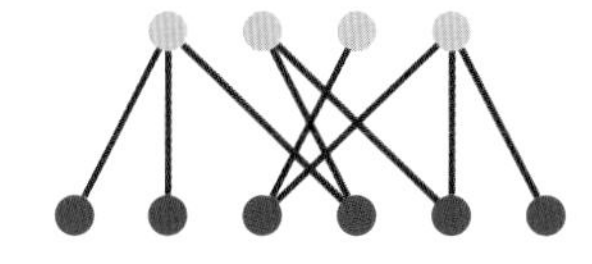

The center graph shows a bipartite network, and the top and bottom ones are the related one-mode projection.

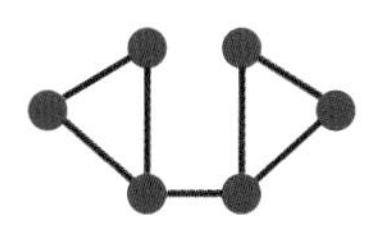

In 1736, Euler provided a mathematical proof showing that the path didn't exist. Euler's proof was the first time someone solved a mathematical problem by turning it into a graph, where land areas were represented as nodes and the bridges as links. Euler observed that except for the starting and ending nodes, all other nodes should have two links—in and out—or an even number of links, if an *Eulerian path*, as it came to be called, is to exist. Described in another way, "a network can have an Eulerian path only if there are exactly two or zero vertices of odd degree—zero in the case where the path starts and ends at the same vertex."[4]

BASIC ELEMENTS

Networks are collections of nodes and links with a particular structure, or topology. A network is also called a *graph* in mathematics. As Newman explains, "A network is a simplified representation that reduces a system to an abstract structure capturing only the basics of connection patterns and little else. Vertices and edges in a network can be labeled with additional information, such as names or strengths, to capture more details of the system, but even a lot of information is usually lost in the process of reducing a full system to a network representation."[5]

A node can be a machine, a person, a cell, and so on. A link represents the relations between two nodes. For example, in the Internet, nodes are computers or routers, and links are cables or wireless connections; in a neural network, nodes are neurons and links are the synapses. Different disciplines use different terminology to describe the elements of networks, but differences stop at the label conventions.

When all the nodes in the network are of the same type, say, in a friendship network, where all nodes are friends, the network is called *one mode*, *unimodal*, or *unipartite*. When there is more than one type of node, networks are called *multimodal* or *multipartite*. A common examined type is the bipartite network, also called a *two-mode* or an *affiliation network* (in sociology), which consists of two sets of nodes that only share links between sets, but not within them. For example, a network with two sets of nodes, persons and books, and the links showing who has read what is considered a bipartite network. Out of this network, we can construct two one-mode projections: person–person, where a node is a person and the nodes are connected if they have read the same books; and book–book, in which books are connected if they share the same readers. One-mode projections allow understanding of clusters based on common membership.

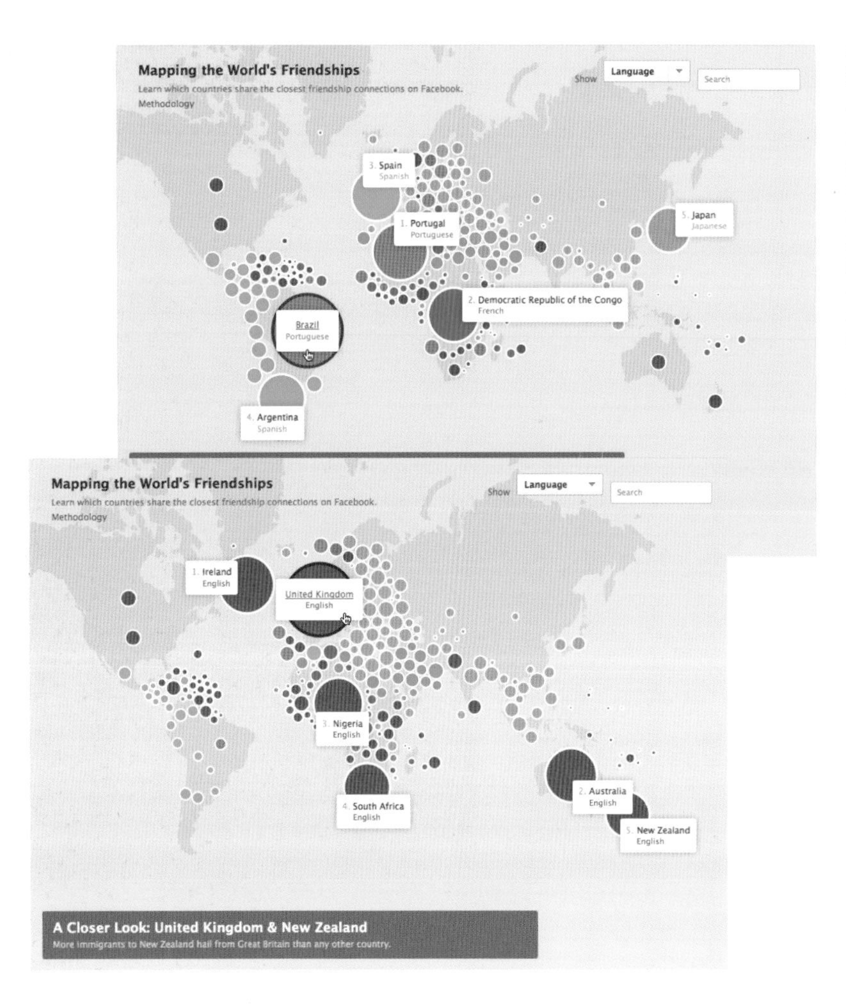

Stamen Design, U.S.: Interactive map of the world's friendship in Facebook, 2012.

The visualization shows trends in how friendship ties are dispersed around the globe, which were further contextualized by Stanford graduate in international relations, Mia Newman. The top image shows connections to Brazil, and it reveals, for example, a strong relationship with Japan. This is due to migration patterns, and more specifically, a large Japanese emigration to Brazil more than 100 years ago. The bottom image shows connections to the United Kingdom, this time with colors representing languages. This image shows strong ties with countries that once were Britain's colonies. A similar pattern is also found in connections of former empires, such as in Portugal and France.

www.facebookstories.com/stories/1574

Paul Butler (Facebook), U.S.: Map visualizing friendships in Facebook around the globe, 2010.

Perhaps what is most revealing about the image are the dark spots—in other words, the lack of connections in certain areas. It turns out, however, that those places are not uninhabited, nor isolated technologically; rather, these places are inhabited by populations with different choices of social media applications.

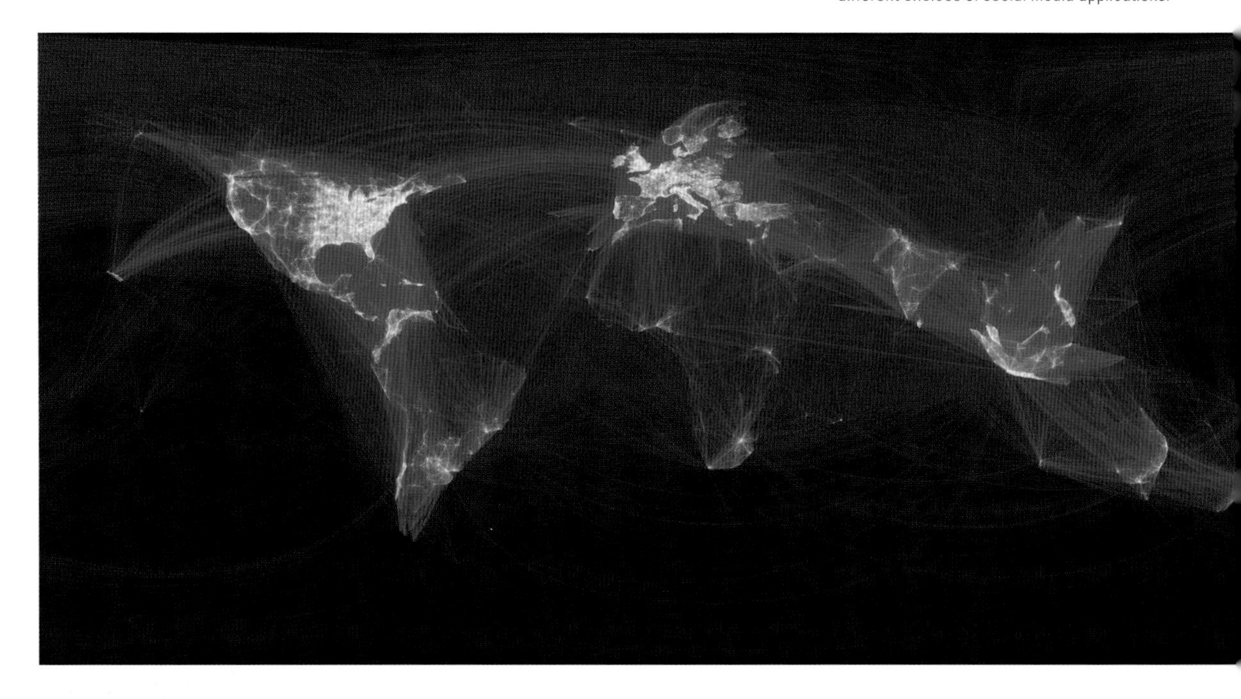

PROPERTIES
Links are described by any kind of interaction between nodes, from kinship to collaboration, from transactions to shared attributes. For example, in a social network, the links might stand for different kinds of interactions between people, such as family, friend, work-related, political affiliation, etc. In a trade network, with countries as the nodes, links might stand for types of transactions, such as import or export. Links might have properties describing the direction of the interaction (undirected or directed), and the weight of that connection (unweighted or weighted).

Undirected links, also known as symmetric edges, refer to mutual connections, such as those between couples. Undirected links have no origin destination attributes, and the lines are represented without indication of direction. Directed links, also known as asymmetric edges, are connections in which an origin destination between the nodes is known. It is an asymmetric relation because not all connections are reciprocated. For example, when someone makes a phone call or sends a message, we can identify who originated it (*from*), who it was designated for (*to*), and whether it was or was not reciprocated. In ecological networks, such as food webs, directed links show the prey-predator interactions. Directions are often represented with the addition of arrows to the link elements.

Unweighted links describe the existence of a connection without further indication of its nature. In other words, it is an on/off situation, where the presence of a link between two nodes denotes that there is an interaction between them without other qualifications. Weighted links, on the other hand, represent additional information about the interaction, such as its strength, weight, or value. For example, John calls Mary more frequently than he calls Joseph. The weight is often represented by the quality of the line, and most often quantities are represented by its width.

The number of immediate connections of a node provides the degree property of that node. In the case of directed networks, degrees are designated as "in degree"—the number of links destined *to* the node, and "out degree"—the number of connections originated at the node, or *from* it. Once we know the degree of a node, there are other metrics that can be analyzed, such as the notion of the degree centrality of a node in relation to the network, which attempts to answer questions about the "importance" of that node in the system. There are few ways that centrality can be measured, from the simple calculation of the node degree in

Similarity

Similarity is the tendency to group similar visual elements into a perceptual unit. It relates to nonlocational characteristics, such as color, shape, and texture, but it is not absolute and can occur in degrees. For example, we perceive the six lines below as forming different groups:

|||||| = 1 group
|||||_ = 2 groups

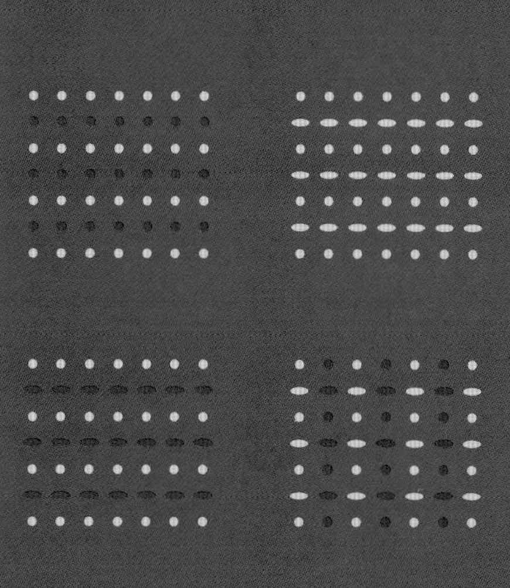

Similarity is essential to categorical association. For example, the use of color coding for categories can enhance the search and comparison between them. When associating more than one graphical variable, attention should be paid to whether they are integral or separable visual dimensions.

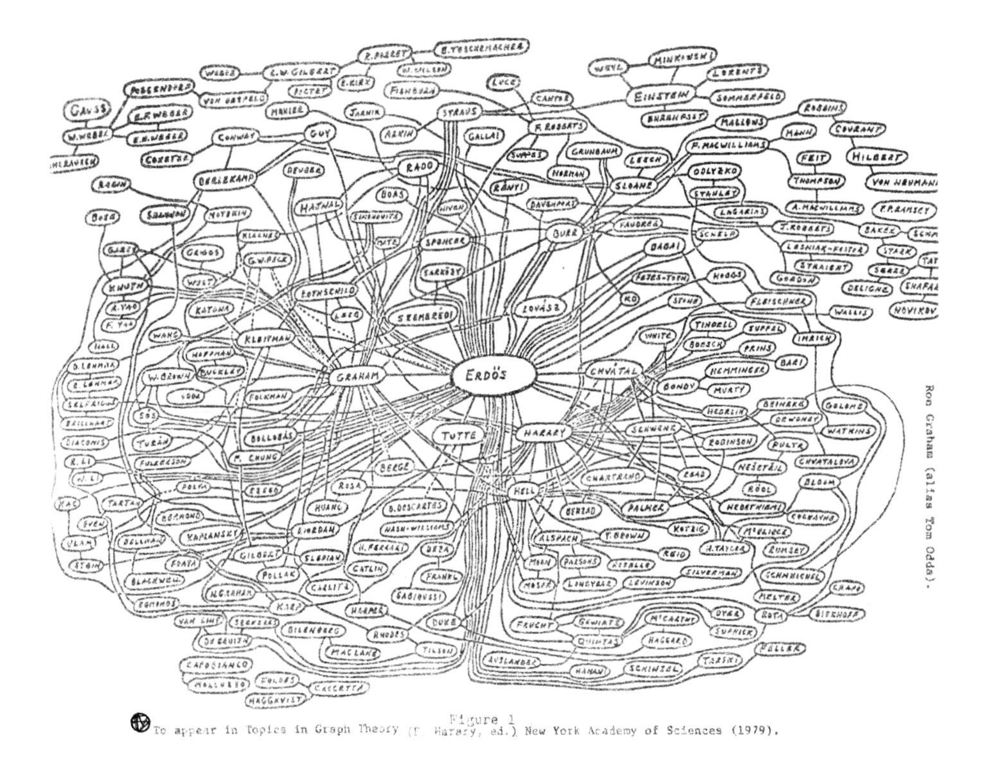

Paul Erdös published around 1,500 papers during his prolific career in mathematics, including important contributions to graph theory and random graphs. Ron Graham hand drew this diagram in the 1970s to portray the collaboration network of Erdös. The nodes are mathematicians, and links connect pairs who have jointly authored a paper with Erdös. As Easley and Kleinberg explain, "A mathematician's Erdös number is the distance from him or her to Erdös in this graph. The point is that most mathematicians have Erdös numbers of at most 4 or 5, and—extending the collaboration graph to include co-authorship across all the sciences—most scientists in other fields have Erdös numbers that are comparable or only slightly larger; Albert Einstein's is 2, Enrico Fermi's is 3, Noam Chomsky's and Linus Pauling's are each 4, Francis Crick's and James Watson's are 5 and 6, respectively. The world of science is truly a small one in this sense."[15]

relation to the total number of links in the network, to more complex methods involving paths, such as closeness and betweenness centrality. A common method is the eigenvector centrality, which considers the importance of nodes based not only on how many links the node has but also in relation to the degree centrality of its neighbors.

Another example is the study of degree distribution, which became a central measure after the discovery of the scale-free networks in 1999 by Albert and Barabási.[6] The model shows that the average number of connections follows a power law distribution: many nodes with few connections (small degree) and a few nodes with many connections (very high degree).

PATHS AND CONNECTIVITY

In order to understand distances in a network, scientists developed the concept of a path that is any sequence of nodes given that each consecutive pair of nodes is connected by a link. The path length provides the number of links in the route between a pair of nodes. When there are no paths between a pair of nodes, it means that a network is not connected and it is divided into subgroups, called "components" in network science. Other metrics were devised for questions related to distances; the shortest path between two nodes and the network diameter are two examples.

Ben Fry, U.S.: "*Isometricblocks*," 2003.

Ben Fry developed this interactive applet using the open source Processing environment, which he originally conceived and implemented with Casey Reas. His goal was to devise software that would combine scientific methods with visualization tools for haplotype and LD data. One can interactively switch between methods and look at the different visualization options. Animated transitions make comparisons easy to follow. One can also modify the parameters of the mathematics used to set boundaries on the blocks. Unfortunately, this caption is far from capturing the level of sophistication of this application, and further reading on how Fry developed it is strongly recommend by following the URL below. This screenshot shows the 3-D view option, an isometric projection, with blocks offset slightly in the *z*-axis to allow view of the lines depicting the transitions between blocks, while preserving the linear scaling of the nucleotide scale in the horizontal axis.

www.benfry.com/isometricblocks

There are qualitative aspects to these metrics, such as the small-world phenomenon, which describes the notion that the world feels small, given that the path length connecting two people is a short one. This notion originated in a series of experimental studies performed by Stanley Milgram and colleagues in the 1960s, which looked into the degrees of separation between chains of friends.[7] One such study asked 296 randomly chosen people to forward a letter in the fastest possible way to a destination person who lived in the suburbs of Boston and was a stockbroker. The instructions were to give the letter to someone they knew on a first-name basis and who would be more likely to know the target person. Among the 64 letters that arrived at the destination, the median path length was six. Later, this phenomenon came to be known by the popular notion of "six degrees of separation," a phrase not coined by Milgram but inspired by the 1990 play of this title by John Guare.[8]

Many network metrics have originated in the social sciences, and are now commonly utilized for quantifying network structures across many fields. The metrics and models have helped scientists examine networks in different domains while also looking for universal properties underlying these phenomena.

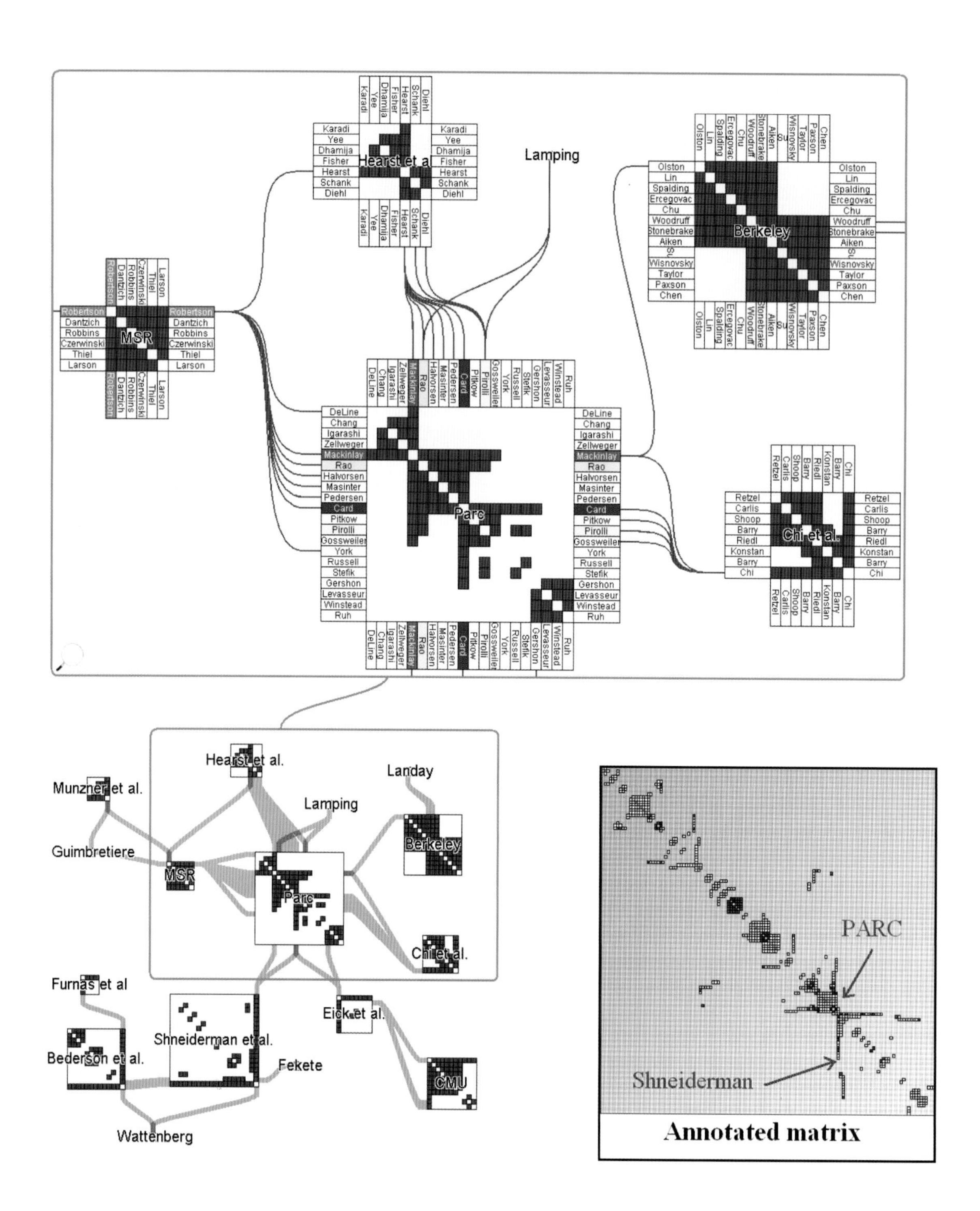

Hearst et al.
Karadi
Yee
Dhamija
Fisher
Hearst
Schank
Diehl
Lamping
Berkeley
Olston
Lin
Spalding
Ercegovac
Chu
Woodruff
Stonebrake
Aiken
Su
Wisnovsky
Taylor
Paxson
Chen
MSR
Robertson
Dantzich
Robbins
Czerwinski
Thiel
Larson
Parc
DeLine
Chang
Igarashi
Zellweger
Mackinlay
Rao
Halvorsen
Masinter
Pedersen
Card
Pitkow
Pirolli
Gossweiler
York
Russell
Stefik
Gershon
Levasseur
Winstead
Ruh
Chi et al.
Retzel
Carlis
Shoop
Barry
Riedl
Konstan
Chi
Munzner et al.
Guimbretiere
Landay
Furnas et al
Eick et al.
Shneiderman et al.
Bederson et al.
Fekete
CMU
Wattenberg
PARC
Shneiderman
Annotated matrix

Nathalie Henry Riche, Howard Goodell, Niklas Elmqvist, and Jean-Daniel Fekete, France: *NodeTrix*, 2007.

Following the pioneering work with reorderable matrices of Jacques Bertin, Riche and colleagues devised several tools to explore and understand networks in the digital environment. *NodeTrix* was directed at solving the problem of how to represent networks that are globally sparse with dense local communities. The interactive tool uses a hybrid representation that combines matrices, for depiction of dense areas, within a node–link diagram, which provides the global structure.[16]

The image is part of a larger examination of "20 Years of Four HCI Conferences." It shows the largest component of the coauthorship network of the IEEE Symposium on Information Visualization (InfoVis). Riche explains, "The lower right corner shows the overview of whole InfoVis matrix, labeling the main actors of this network: PARC and Ben Shneiderman. The largest cross identifiable is Ben, the most central actor in the InfoVis community. The *NodeTrix* representation in the lower left corner shows how Ben Shneiderman acts as a bridge to the other UMD researchers grouped in a community centered on Ben Bederson. Finally, the upper part of the figure is a zoomed-in *NodeTrix* view showing how the PARC community collaborates with other communities. It is interesting to note that Berkeley and Microsoft Research strongly collaborate with each other. Similarly Stuart Card, Jock Mackinlay and Ed Chi collaborators are strongly connected."[17]

TYPES OF REPRESENTATION

There are three main methods for representing networks: lists, matrices, and node–link diagrams. A complete list of links in a network provides an adjacency list, which can be used to store the structure of the network. Considering the large size of most networks, lists are unmanageable, and thus rarely used. A more effective mathematical tool is the adjacency matrix, a grid of nodes with the cells representing the presence or absence of a link between two nodes. A two-color scheme, or a 0/1 numeric system, usually suffices to indicate links in unweighted networks. Weighted networks require a more complex numerical or visual encoding to represent amounts in addition to the binary system of the existence of a link. One of the benefits of matrices is that by representing information about links in the cells, matrices avoid the problem of too many link crossings faced by most node–link diagrams.

The French cartographer Jacques Bertin worked extensively on matrices in the 1960s.[9] Bertin pioneered work on reordering rows and columns for revealing patterns in the representation, a strategy that has continued to this day with the development of several new algorithms.

Node–link representations use symbolic elements to stand for nodes, and lines to represent the connections between them. Physical network systems, such as power grids and transportation networks, provide the spatial attribute to locate both nodes and links into the spatial structure of the diagram. Most networks, however, are of abstract data, such as food webs and metabolic networks, and do not have *a priori* spatial properties for positioning elements in the visualization. The table on page 62 shows the most common types of layouts according to certain properties of the network. Each type points to real-world examples that are examined in this book.

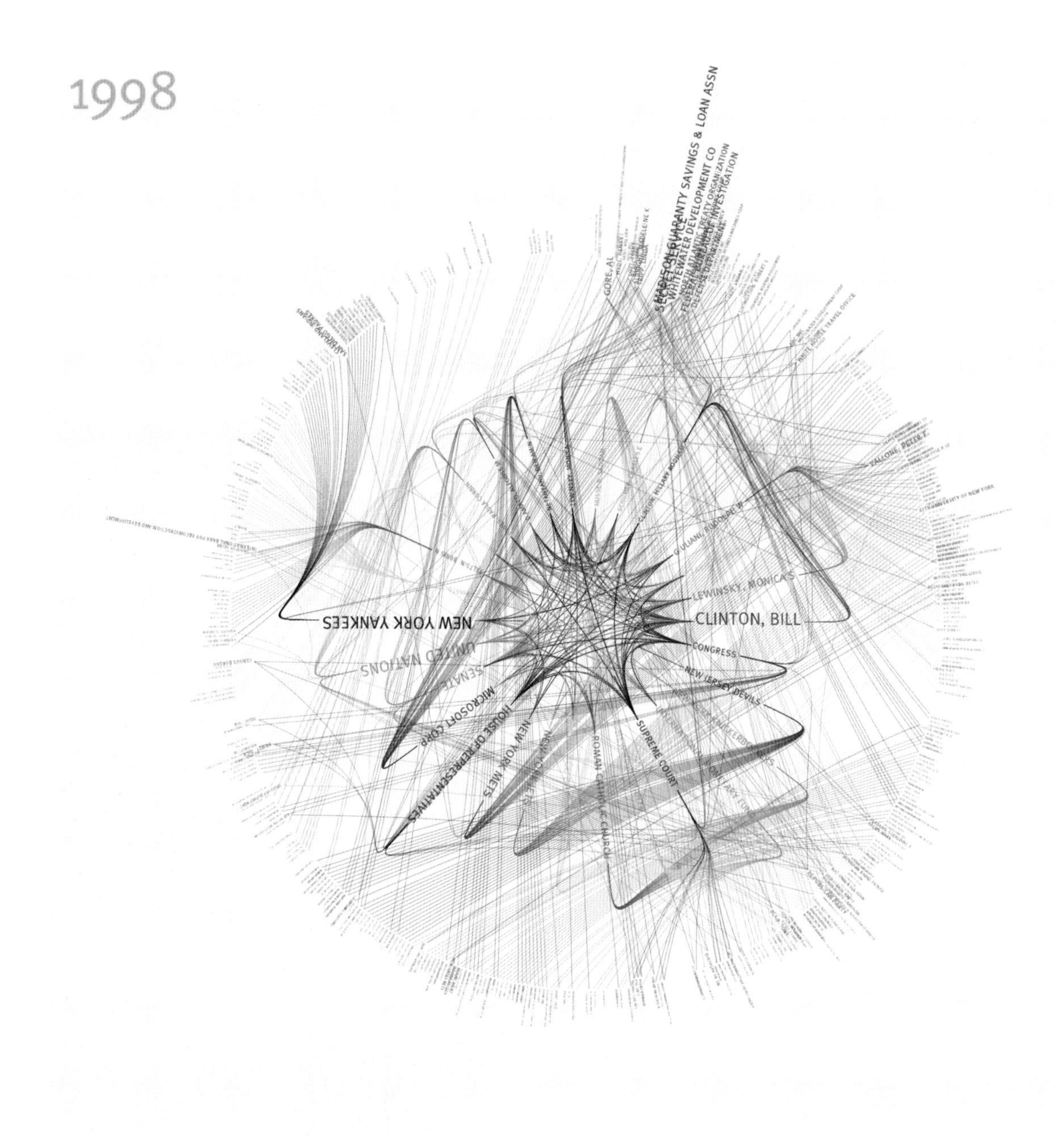

Jer Thorp, U.S.: "*New York Times 365/360,*" 2009.

The image is one of a series of visualizations that Canadian Jer Thorp created in Processing for portraying the top organizations and personalities for every year from 1985 to 2001, by occurrence in the *New York Times*. Lines indicate the connections between people and organizations.

CHALLENGES OF NODE–LINK DIAGRAMS

Most problems faced by node–link representations are caused by the occlusion of nodes and link crossings, which obliterates the structure it is supposed to reveal. This, however, is not a trivial problem, given the large datasets used in these graphs, and, perhaps, one of the reasons we so often see hairball network displays, which are hard to read and extract meaning from. New layout techniques and algorithms aim at minimizing the problem, and ultimately generating more legible graphs. This is an area receiving large attention by researchers in diverse fields, because the need for effective visual displays of networks grows with the accessibility to more and larger datasets. As Schneider contends, "It could be said that a graph is worth a thousand ties.... The ability to map attribute data and network metric scores to visual properties of the vertices and edges makes them particularly powerful. However, network visualizations are often as frustrating as they are appealing. Network graphs can rapidly get too dense and large to make out any meaningful patterns. Many obstacles like vertex occlusions and edge crossings make creating well-organized and readable network graphs challenging."[10]

One of the strategies pursued in interactive node–link visualizations is the ability to switch between different spatial layouts in order to discover meaningful properties of the network, while understanding relationships in new ways. Take, for example, the *SPaTo* application tool that allows examination of properties of a network by switching from a force directed node–link representation, to a circular graph, to a geographical map (see pages 76–77).[11] Similar to reordering rows and columns in matrices, the rearrangement of the spatial layout helps revealing hidden structures in the network.

Visual encoding of nodes and links is another area that affects the interpretation of network representations, in that complex systems are often described by more properties than we can perceive. Take, for example, the Human Disease Network, which is an amalgamation of more than seven subsystems—our limit to perceptually distinguish and cognitively remember stuff (see the box Magical Number Seven on page 97). However, eliminating categories from the eighteen disorder classes portrayed in the visualization would negatively affect the integrity of the information being communicated: "A platform to explore in a single graph theoretic framework all known phenotype and disease gene associations, indicating the common genetic origin of many diseases."[12]

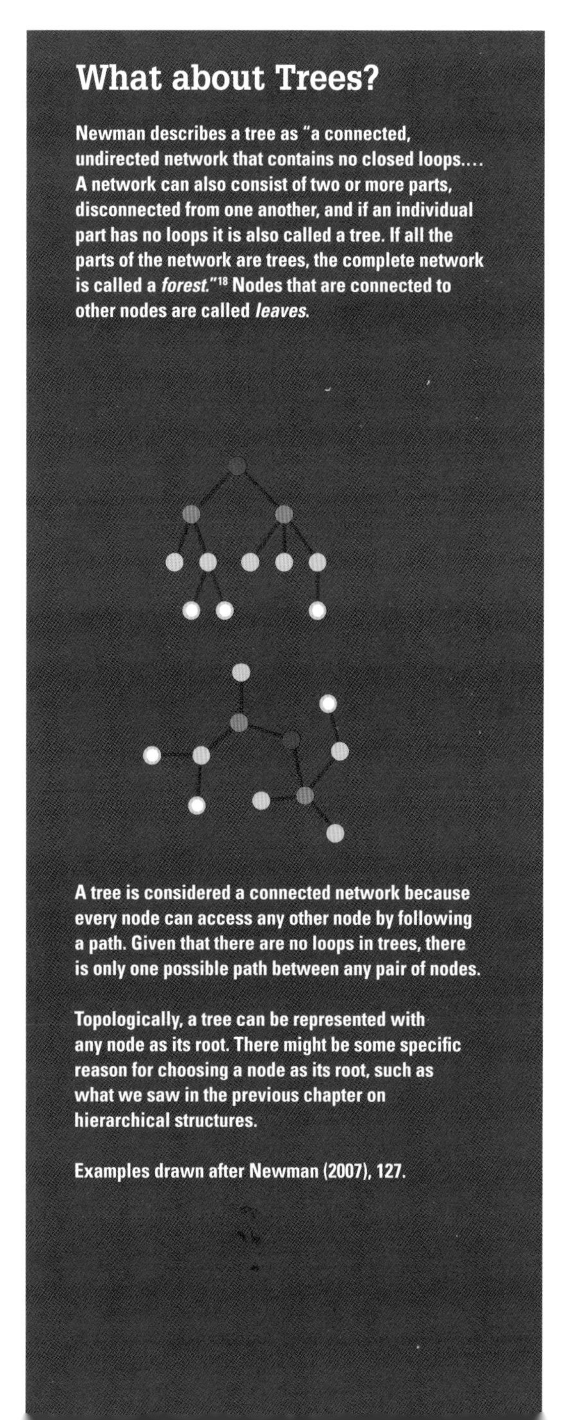

What about Trees?

Newman describes a tree as "a connected, undirected network that contains no closed loops.... A network can also consist of two or more parts, disconnected from one another, and if an individual part has no loops it is also called a tree. If all the parts of the network are trees, the complete network is called a *forest*."[18] Nodes that are connected to other nodes are called *leaves*.

A tree is considered a connected network because every node can access any other node by following a path. Given that there are no loops in trees, there is only one possible path between any pair of nodes.

Topologically, a tree can be represented with any node as its root. There might be some specific reason for choosing a node as its root, such as what we saw in the previous chapter on hierarchical structures.

Examples drawn after Newman (2007), 127.

Good Continuation

Good continuation is the tendency to construct visual entities out of visual elements that are smooth and continuous, or connected by straight or smoothly curving lines. For example, we perceive the six lines below as forming different groups:

— — — — — — = 1 group
— — — · · · = 2 groups

A common experience of the principle is found in most maps. Good continuation allows, for example, for state contours to be differentiated from roads or rivers. When representing data, we should pay attention to not creating nonintentional groupings due to good continuation.

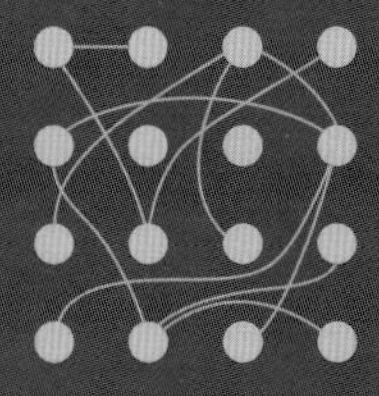

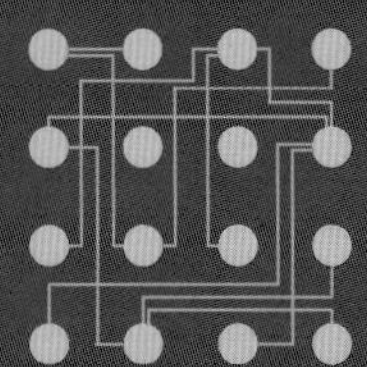

Good continuation plays an important role when designing networks with several connecting lines. It is easier to perceive smooth continuous lines than lines with abrupt changes in direction.

The same holds true for the placement of labels and the difficulties encountered in effectively positioning them, given the complexities of network representations. As with all other types of visualizations, labels carry important information, enabling one to understand what it is being revealed, from scales and measurements to categorical information. A common strategy in the case of node–link diagrams is placing labels inside the nodes. However, this is not always possible, such as in dense areas of the graph or in the case of small nodes with long labels. These limitations might be overcome in interactive visualizations, such as associating the cursor with actions that highlight nodes while revealing labels.

Other effective strategies involve enabling the user to change the camera view or zoom into the graph, for example. So-called *focus + context* techniques involve operations that keep the contextual view of the whole graph while enabling a selected area to be represented in detail. Presenting details as one gets closer is a strategy that has been used successfully in maps, in which the amount of details change in relation to the scale: the larger the scale, the greater the details, as in a neighborhood map, for example (see page 123).

There are several mechanisms for reducing the number of nodes and links, such as using thresholds in the process of generating the visualization, collapsing nodes into clusters, or enabling one to filter data, three commonly used operations. The interactive network visualization in the website theyrule.net uses collapsing nodes, which can be revealed on demand by the viewer by selecting the group symbol (a table). In the series of images created by Thorp depicting data from the *New York Times*, links were bundled to avoid too many edge crossings in the circular layout.

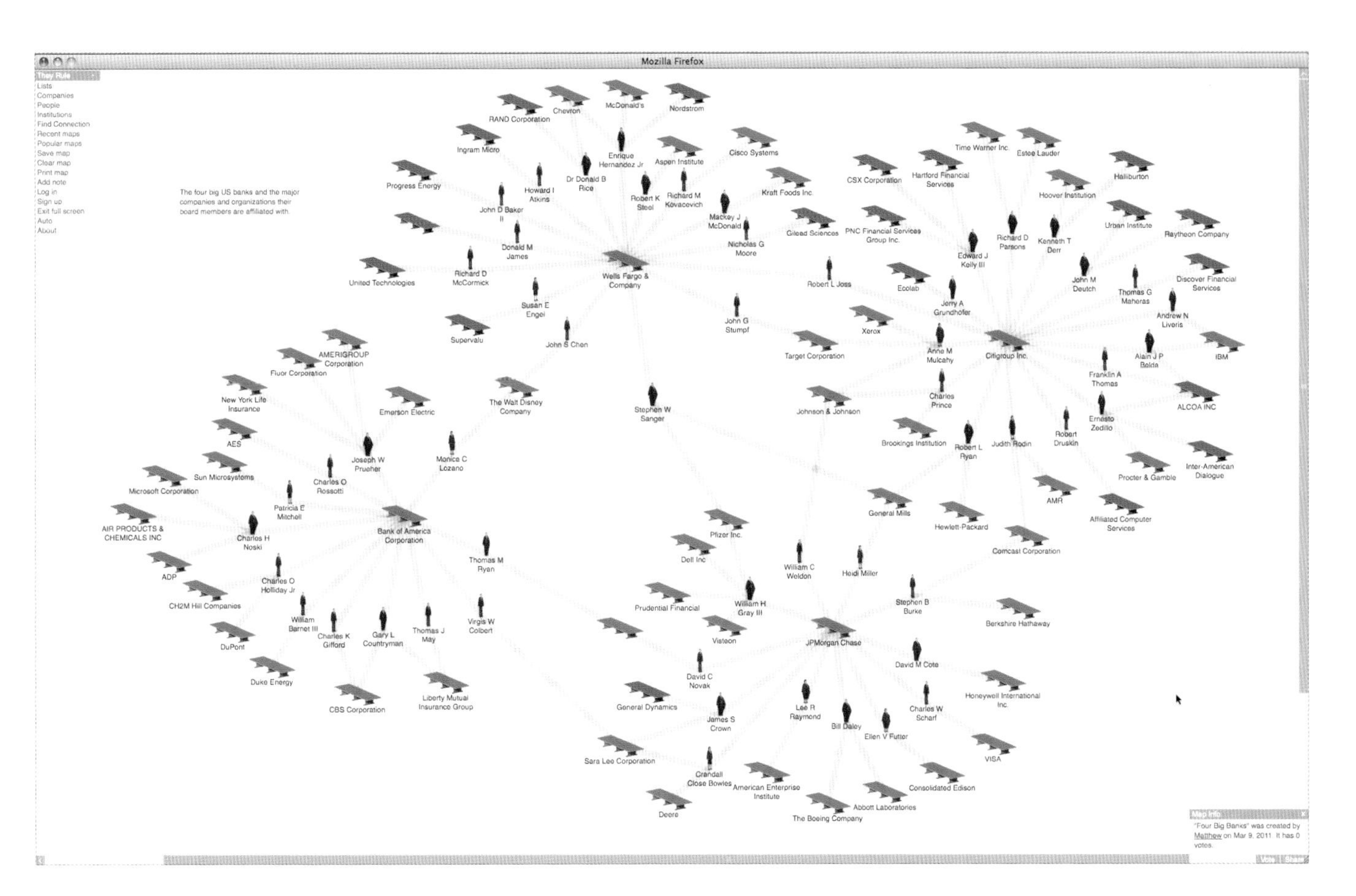

Josh On, U.S.: "They Rule," 2004.

The website theyrule.net allows visitors to examine the connections among board members of the top 1,000 U.S. companies. It presents information in a relational diagram. Originally created in 2001 by Josh On with a static set of 100 companies, the site was updated in 2004 to include the top 500 companies, and in 2011, with data made available through LittleSis.org, the site now offers access to 1,000 companies. There are two types of nodes: organizations (table) and board members (male and female figures). Board members get "fatter" according to the number of boards they participate in. Corporation symbols do not change size, but they can be collapsed so as to hide board members in two ways: hide unconnected members or hide all members. Links connect board members to the organizations they serve on as well as among members when they sit on the same boards. Visitors to the site can save and share resulting graphs together with their own annotations. On writes about the context for building the tool: "Hopefully They Rule will raise larger questions about the structure of our society and in whose benefit it is run."[19] The images reproduced here were listed in the Popular Maps section. The one above is titled "Four Big Banks," and it was created by user Matthew on March 9, 2011, and the one on the right is titled "Six Too Big to Fail Banks," also by Matthew on July 26, 2011.

www.theyrule.net

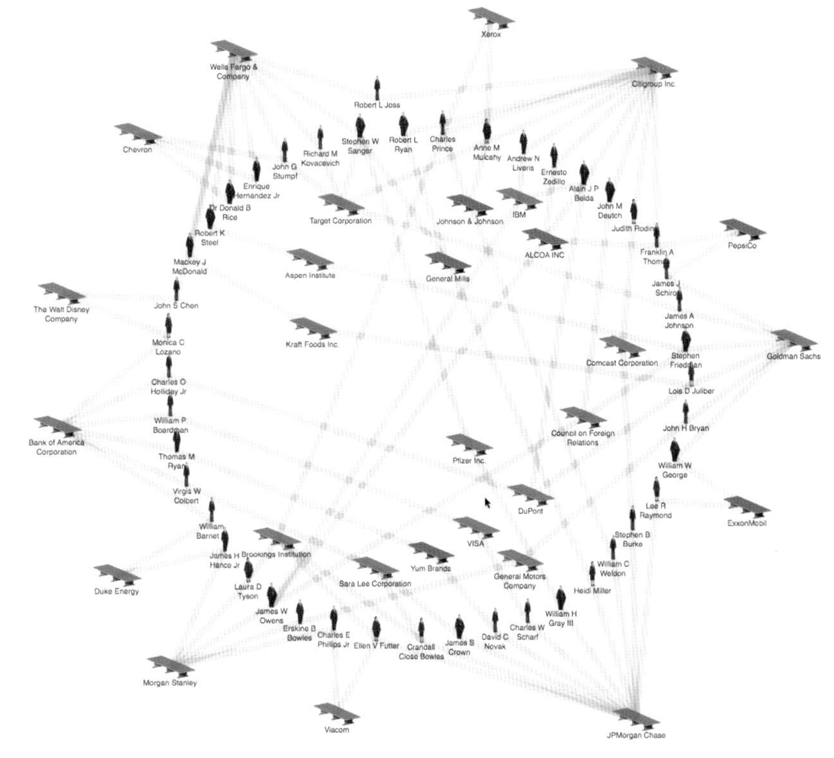

The human disease network

Goh K-I, Cusick ME, Valle D, Childs B, Vidal M, Barabási A-L (2007) *Proc Natl Acad Sci USA* 104:8685-8690

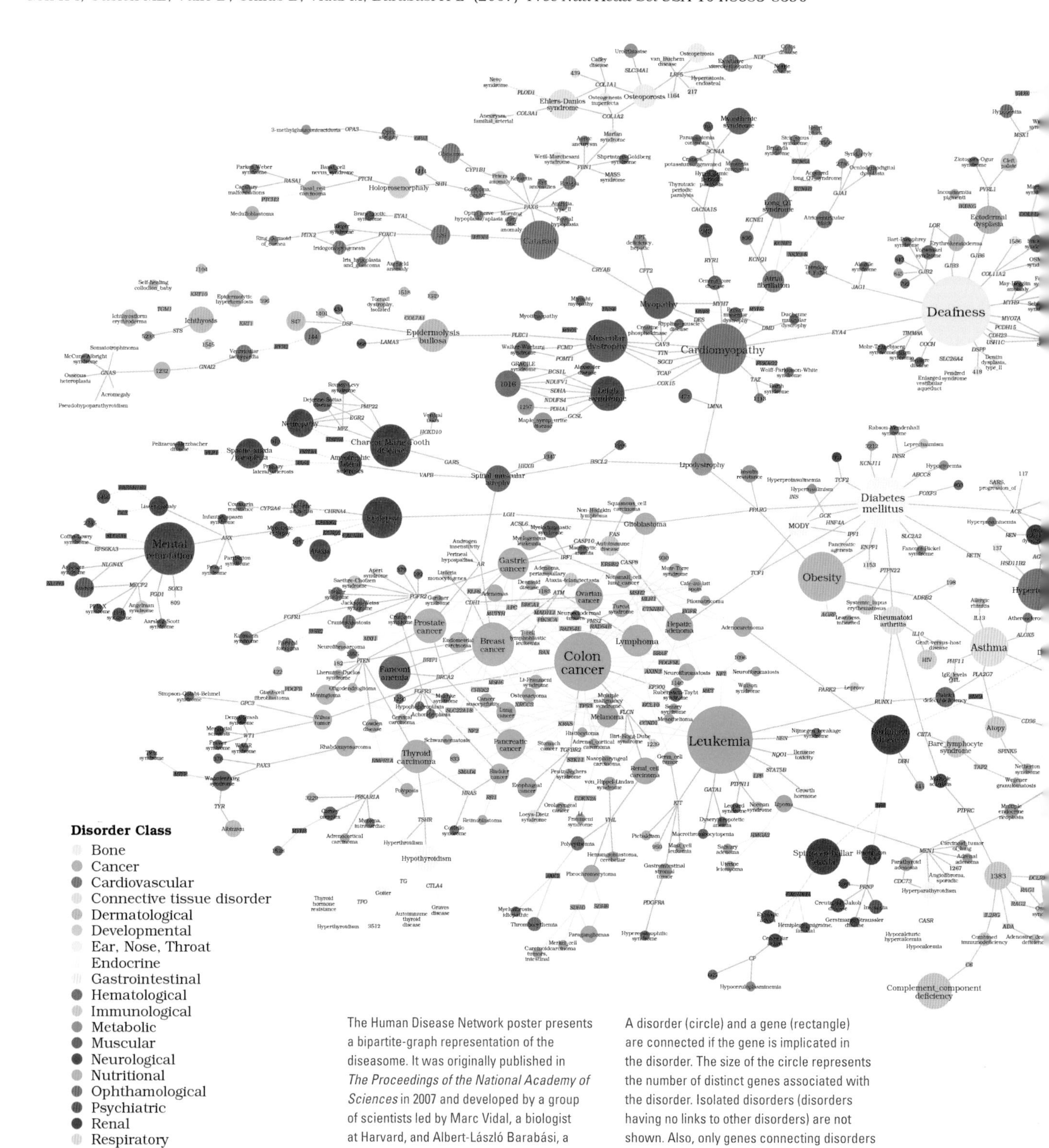

The Human Disease Network poster presents a bipartite-graph representation of the diseasome. It was originally published in *The Proceedings of the National Academy of Sciences* in 2007 and developed by a group of scientists led by Marc Vidal, a biologist at Harvard, and Albert-László Barabási, a physicist at Northeastern University.

A disorder (circle) and a gene (rectangle) are connected if the gene is implicated in the disorder. The size of the circle represents the number of distinct genes associated with the disorder. Isolated disorders (disorders having no links to other disorders) are not shown. Also, only genes connecting disorders are shown.[20]

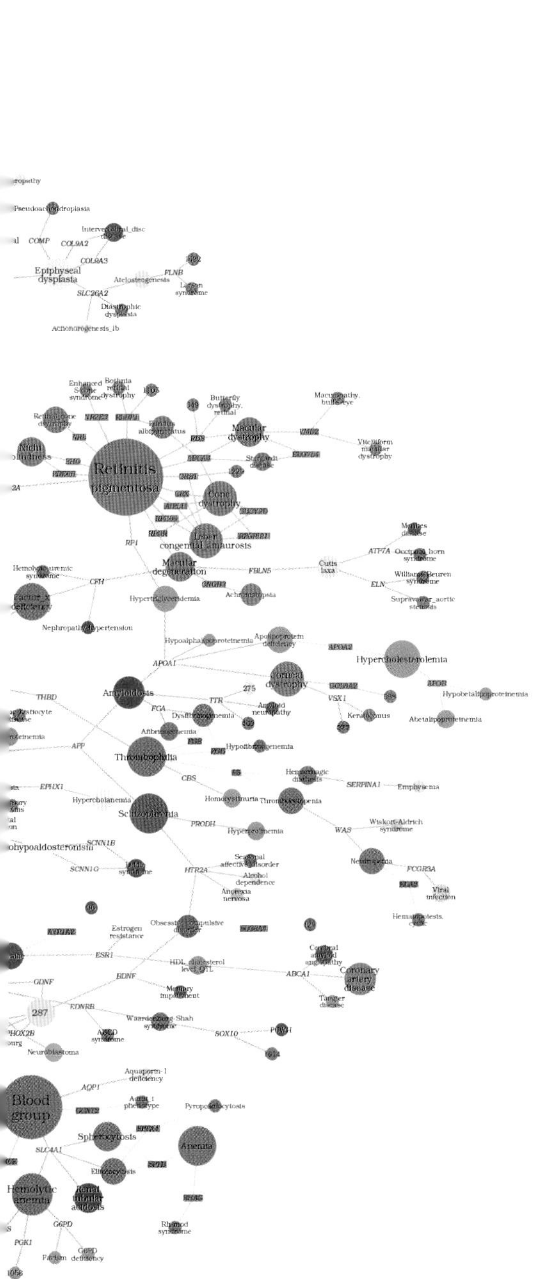

May 5, 2008

Mapping the Human ‘Diseasome’

Researchers created a map linking different diseases, represented by circles, to the genes they have in common, represented by squares.

Redefining Disease, Genes and All

Cataract
Myopathy
Epidermolysis bullosa
Muscular dystrophy
Cardiomyopathy
Leigh syndrome
Deafness
Retinitis pigmentosa
Charcot-Marie-Tooth disease
Epilepsy
Mental retardation
Gastric cancer
Diabetes mellitus
Myocardial infarction (heart attack)
Alzheimer's disease
Obesity
Hypertension
Prostate cancer
Breast cancer
Fanconi anemia
Colon cancer
Lymphoma
Asthma
Thyroid carcinoma
Leukemia
Parkinson's disease
Blood type
Hemolytic anemia

TYPE OF DISEASE
Cancer
Bone
Skeletal
Connective tissue
Muscular
Dermatological
Cardiovascular
Hematological
Renal
Endocrine
Immunological
Gastrointestinal
Nutritional
Metabolic
Ear, nose, throat
Ophthalmological
Respiratory
Developmental
Neurological
Psychiatric
Multiple types
Unclassified

SCALE
Each circle represents a disease or disorder and is scaled in proportion to the number of genes associated with that disease
30 genes
15
5
1

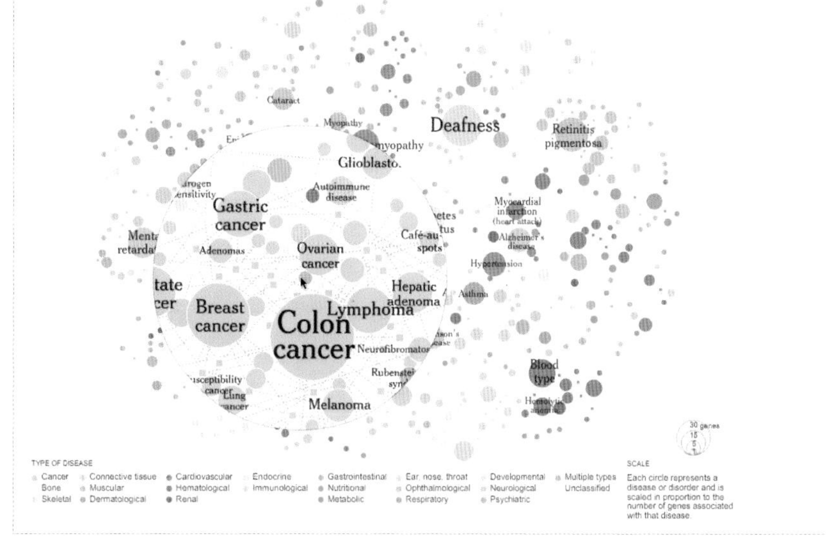

In 2008, the *New York Times* published the scientific discovery and created an interactive disease map to accompany the article "Redefining Disease, Genes and All."

www.nytimes.com/interactive/2008/05/05/science/20080506_DISEASE.html.

most common types of network layouts

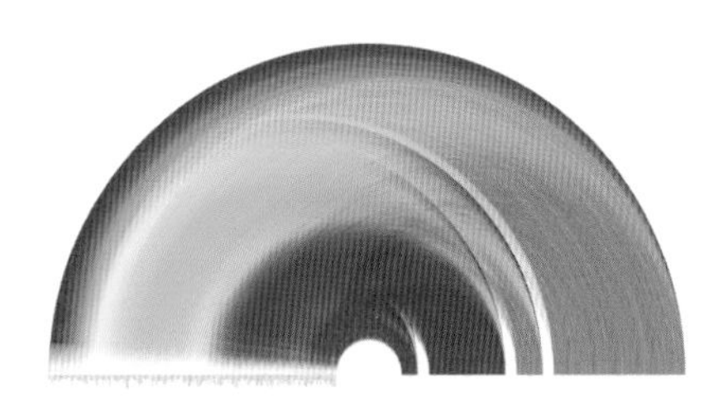

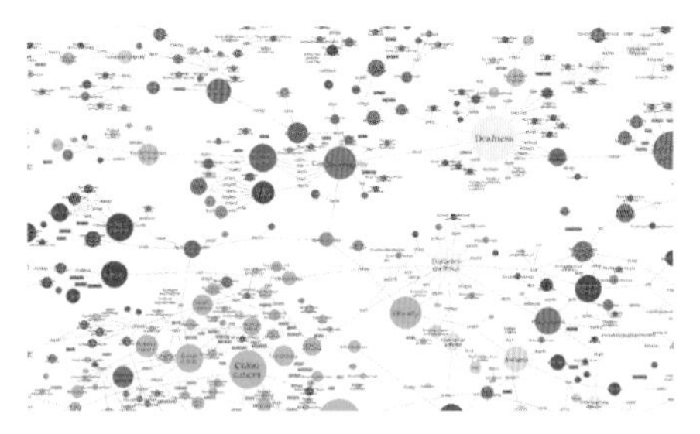

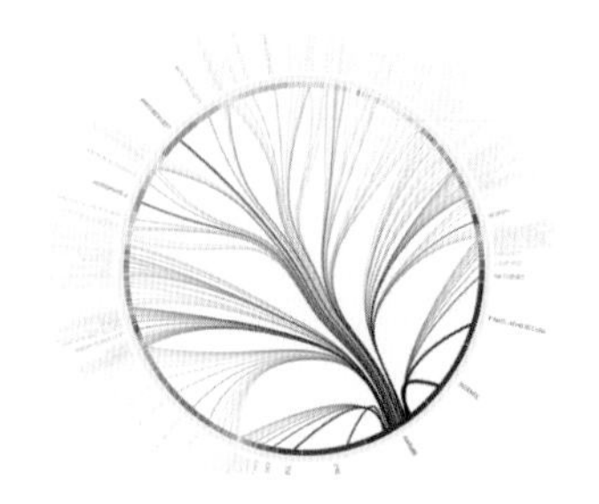

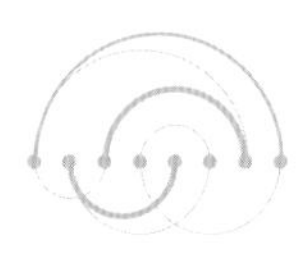

LINEAR:

Nodes are organized linearly and the links are usually arcs connecting nodes.
Con: It's hard to identify clusters and is only feasible for small datasets.

FORCE DIRECTED:

There are many algorithms that use an iterative process to locate nodes according to physical forces.
Con: There are too many node occlusions and link crossings in dense areas.

CIRCULAR:

Nodes are organized around the circumference and usually groupe by categories. Links cross the circ and are usually bundled so as to simplify the crossings.
Con: It's hard to identify clusters.

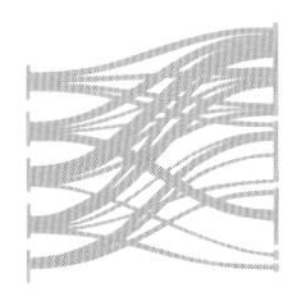

SANKEY TYPE DIAGRAMS:

Nodes are organized vertically and the links horizontally.

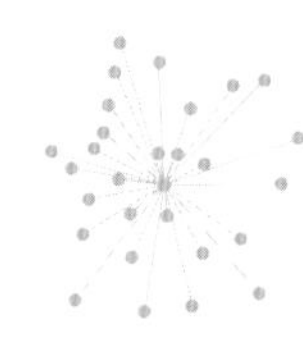

FORCE DIRECTED:

Force directed graphs centered on a node.

POLAR OR RADIAL:

Nodes are organized around a central node, with their position related to the number of hops it takes to reach it.

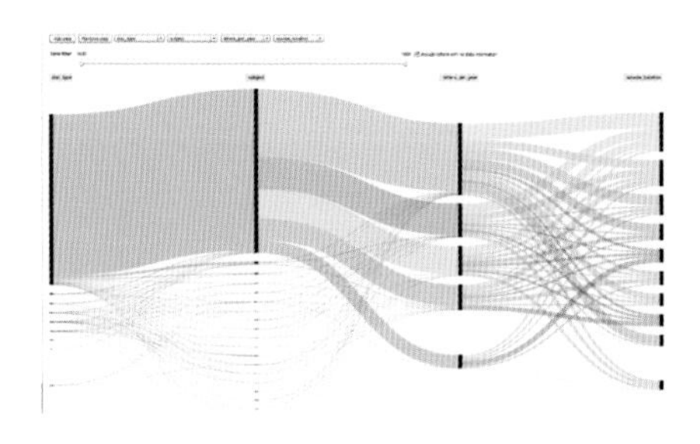

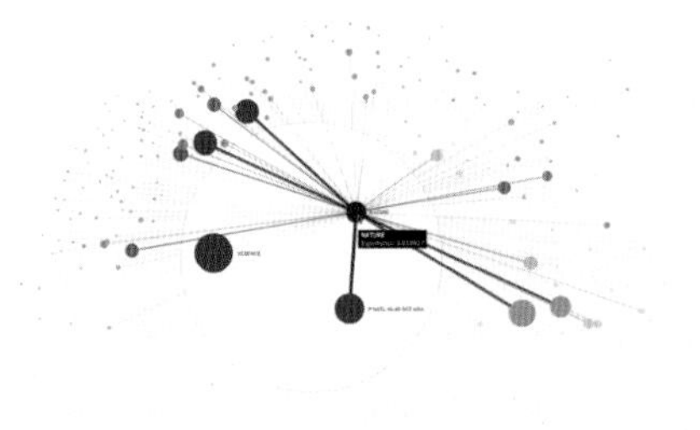

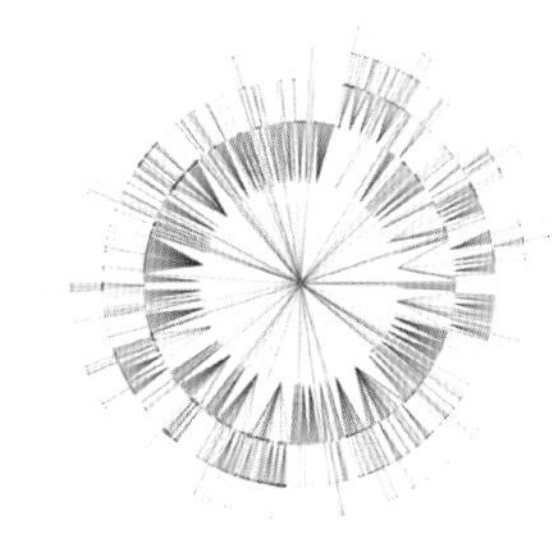

most common layouts centered on nodes

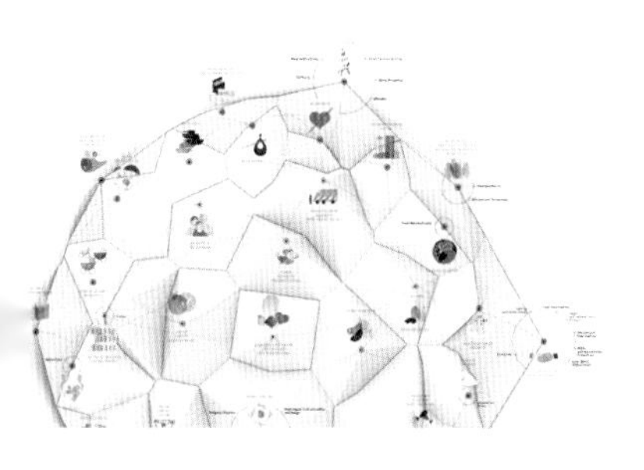

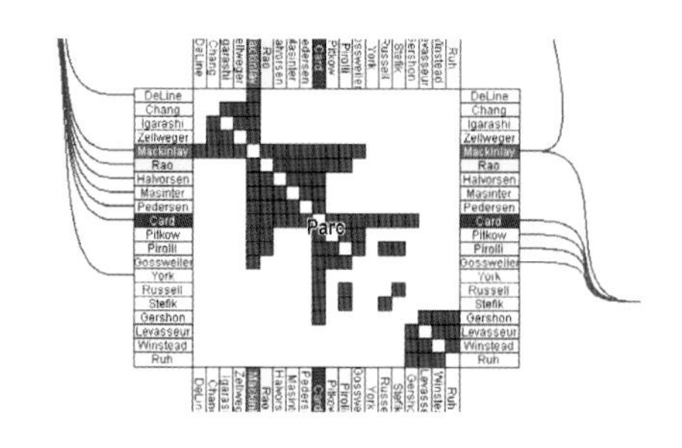

COMMUNITY STRUCTURE:

The focus is on community structures.

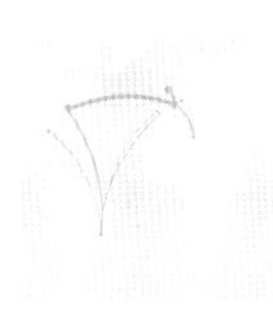

GEOGRAPHY BASED:

Spatial location of a node is provided by its geo position.

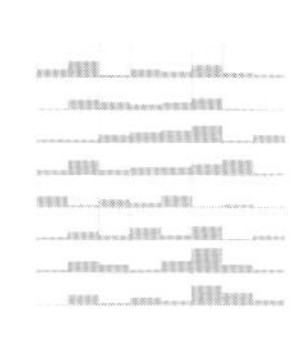

MATRIX:

Grid of nodes with link information positioned within the cell.

RADIAL COMMUNITY STRUCTURE:

Nodes are organized around a central community

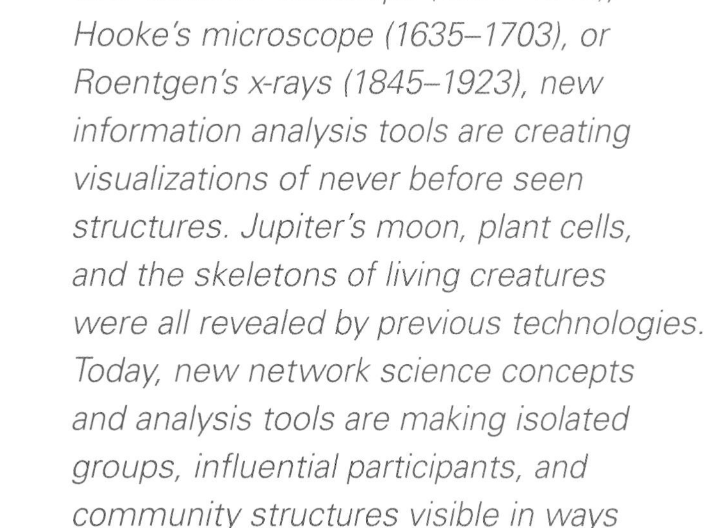

Like Galileo's telescope (1564–1642), Hooke's microscope (1635–1703), or Roentgen's x-rays (1845–1923), new information analysis tools are creating visualizations of never before seen structures. Jupiter's moon, plant cells, and the skeletons of living creatures were all revealed by previous technologies. Today, new network science concepts and analysis tools are making isolated groups, influential participants, and community structures visible in ways never before possible.

Ben Shneiderman

CASE STUDY

CIRCULAR + LINEAR + TREEMAP + FORCE DIRECTED

Visualizing Information Flow in Science

http://well-formed.eigenfactor.org

The visualization "well-formed.eigenfactor: Visualizing information flow in science" was devised by Moritz Stefaner in collaboration with Martin Rosvall, Jevin West, and Carl Bergstrom at the Bergstrom Lab, University of Washington.

The project examines a subset of the citation data from Thomson Reuters' *Journal Citation Reports* from 1997–2005. It depicts 400 journals and around 13,000 citation edges, which ensures coverage of the top journals in each field.

The Eigenfactor® project calculates a measure of importance for individual journals—the Eigenfactor score—while also measuring the citation flow and a hierarchical clustering based thereon. The authors explain how they approached the problem of visualizing the citation network, saying, "Our project extends the visual vocabulary in this area: on the one hand, by repurposing existing techniques, such as radial edge bundling and treemaps; on the other hand, by inventing novel approaches like magnetic pins as flow indicators and an alluvial diagram to represent change over time in cluster structure."[21]

Stefaner created a set of four interactive visualizations, and each allows one to explore emerging patterns in the scientific citation network: citation patterns, changes over time, clustering, and map. All visualizations were created in 2009 using Flare, the ActionScript library for creating visualizations that runs in the Adobe Flash Player.

AUTHORS Moritz Stefaner (visualization), Martin Rosvall, Jevin West, and Carl Bergstrom (Eigenfactor score)
COUNTRY Germany and U.S.
DATE 2009
MEDIUM Online interactive application
URL http://well-formed.eigenfactor.org
DOMAIN Scientific citation network
TASK To provide an overview of information flow in science
STRUCTURE Set of four visualizations, each with a different structure

DATA TYPE AND VISUAL ENCODING
Categorical: Four scientific fields: medical sciences, natural sciences, formal sciences, social sciences
Encoding: Color: Purple, green, blue, orange
Quantitative: Eigenfactor score
Encoding: Radial diagram: Length of arc segment
Flow diagram: Thickness of line
Treemap: Area size of squared shape
Map: Area size of circle
Quantitative: In and out citation flows for each journal
Encoding: Radial diagram: Line width and opacity
Flow diagram: Not encoded
Treemap: "Magnetic pins" size
Map: Area size of circle
Temporal: Five years in the dataset
Encoding: Flow diagram: Horizontal axis

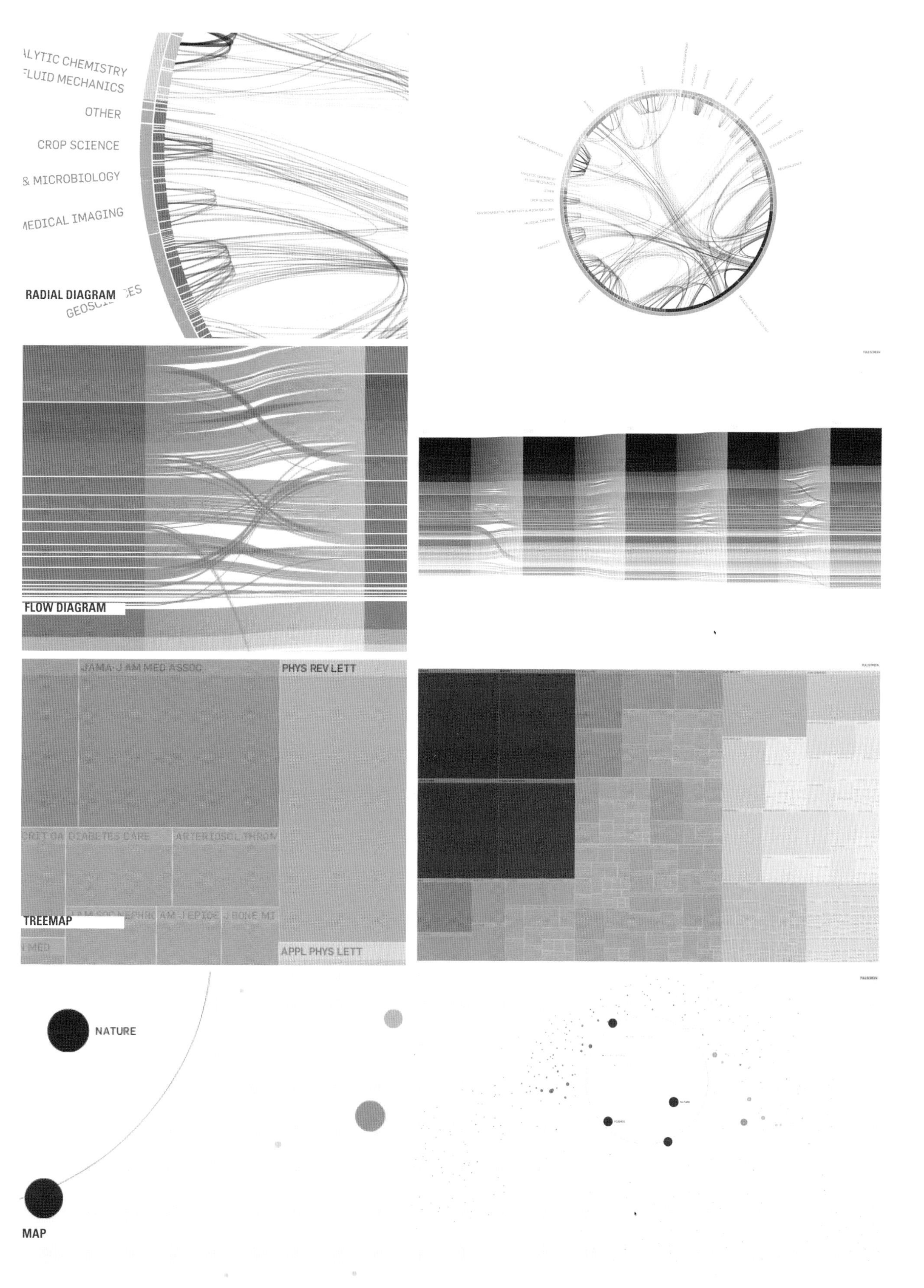

ALYTIC CHEMISTRY
FLUID MECHANICS
OTHER
CROP SCIENCE
& MICROBIOLOGY
MEDICAL IMAGING
RADIAL DIAGRAM
FLOW DIAGRAM
JAMA-J AM MED ASSOC
PHYS REV LETT
CRIT CA
DIABETES CARE
ARTERIOSCL THROM
TREEMAP
APPL PHYS LETT
NATURE
MAP

CITATION PATTERNS

The radial diagram gives an overview of the citation network. The color scheme depicts the four main groups of journals, which is carried out through the whole set of visualizations. The outer ring portrays major fields within each of the four groups, which is further subdivided into individual journals as represented in the innermost ring. Each journal's segment is scaled by the Eigenfactor score. The citation links follow the cluster structure, using the hierarchical edge bundling technique, originally devised by Danny Holten.[22] Line width and opacity represent connection strength.

Selecting a single journal (inner ring) or a whole field (outer ring) displays all citation flow coming in or out of the selected segment. The color is based on the cluster color of the origin node.

NATURE

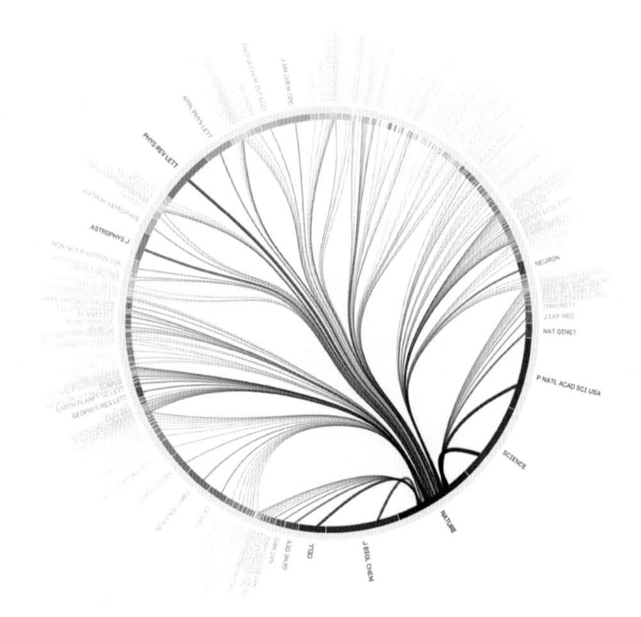

CHANGE OVER TIME

The authors call it an *alluvial* diagram, and it displays changes in the Eigenfactor score and clustering over time. It was inspired by stacked bar charts and Sankey diagrams. The latter technique is discussed in the Fineo case study later in the chapter (see page 70).

The journals are grouped vertically by their cluster structure and horizontally by year. Bars belonging to the same journal are connected. The visualization portrays five years in the dataset, each corresponding to a column: 1997, 1999, 2001, 2003, and 2005.

Clicking on a line highlights a journal over the years, allowing one to examine clusters the journal has been part of, track changes of influence, and determine its cluster structure.

NATURE (1997)

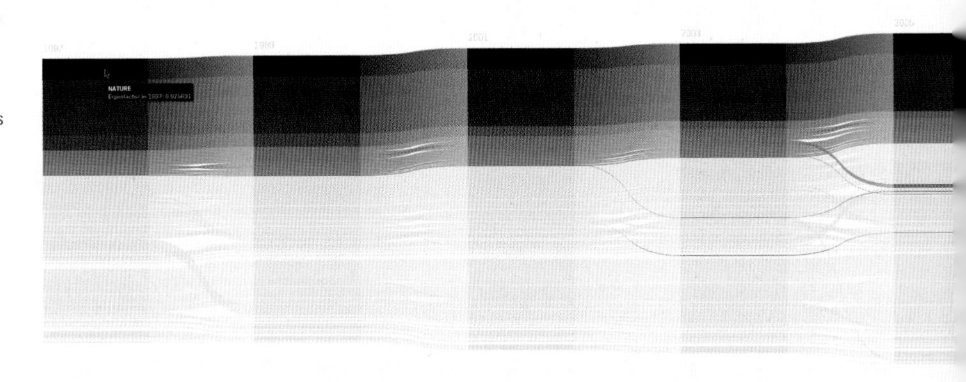

CLUSTERING

The structure of this visualization is the squarified treemap layout algorithm, discussed in detail in the case study of chapter 1, *SmartMoney Map of the Market* (see page 30). The size of each square corresponds to that journal's Eigenfactor score.

Clicking on a journal (square) displays the amount of citation flow from other journals. The flow is indicated by "magnetic pins" depicting both incoming (white arrow) and outgoing (black arrow) citation flow for any selected journal. The arrow size indicates the amount of citation flow.

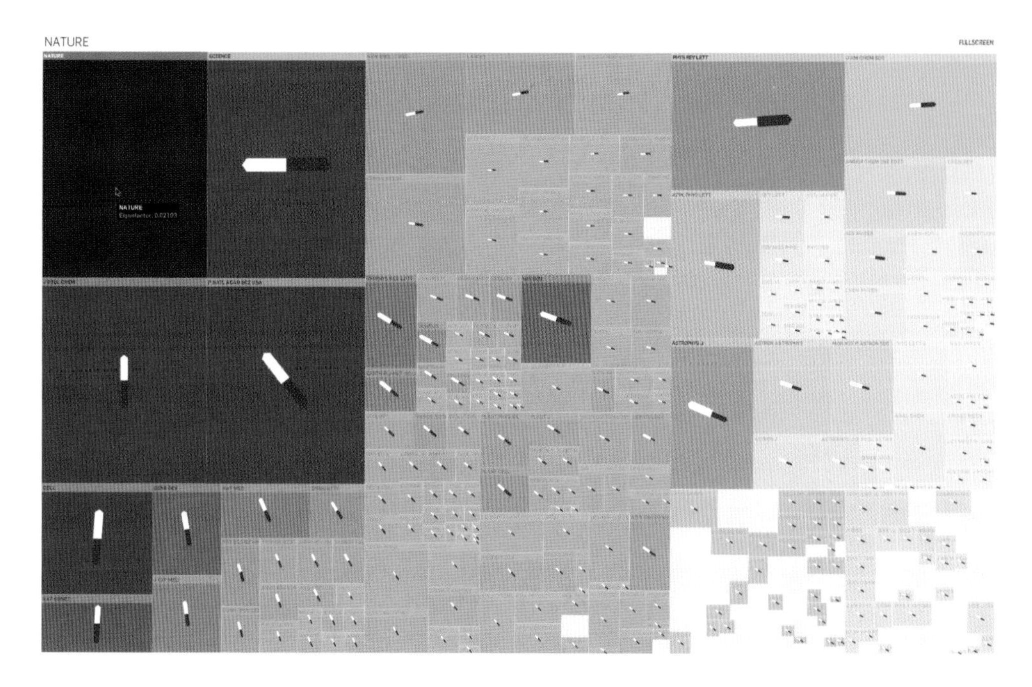

MAP

Called a map by the authors, this visualization locates journals that frequently cite each other closer together. To enlarge a part of the map for closer inspection, one can drag the white magnification lens around.

Clicking on a journal redraws the map into a force directed graph centered on that node, that is, the journal's citation network (nodes and links). The journal's area size resizes to represent the relative amount of citation flow (incoming and outgoing) with respect to the selection. When nodes are not selected, the areas are scaled by the Eigenfactor score.

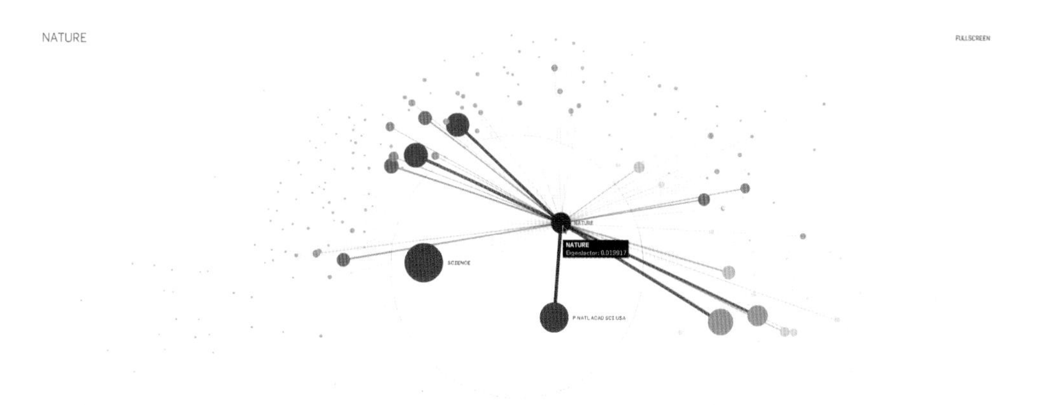

CITEOLOGY

3,502 CHI/UIST PAPERS AND THE **11,699** CITATIONS BETWEEN THEM

1982 1983 1985 1986 1988 1989 1990 1991 1992 1993 1994 1995 1996 1997 1998 1999 2000 **2001** 2002 2003 2004 2005 2006 2007 2008 2009 2010

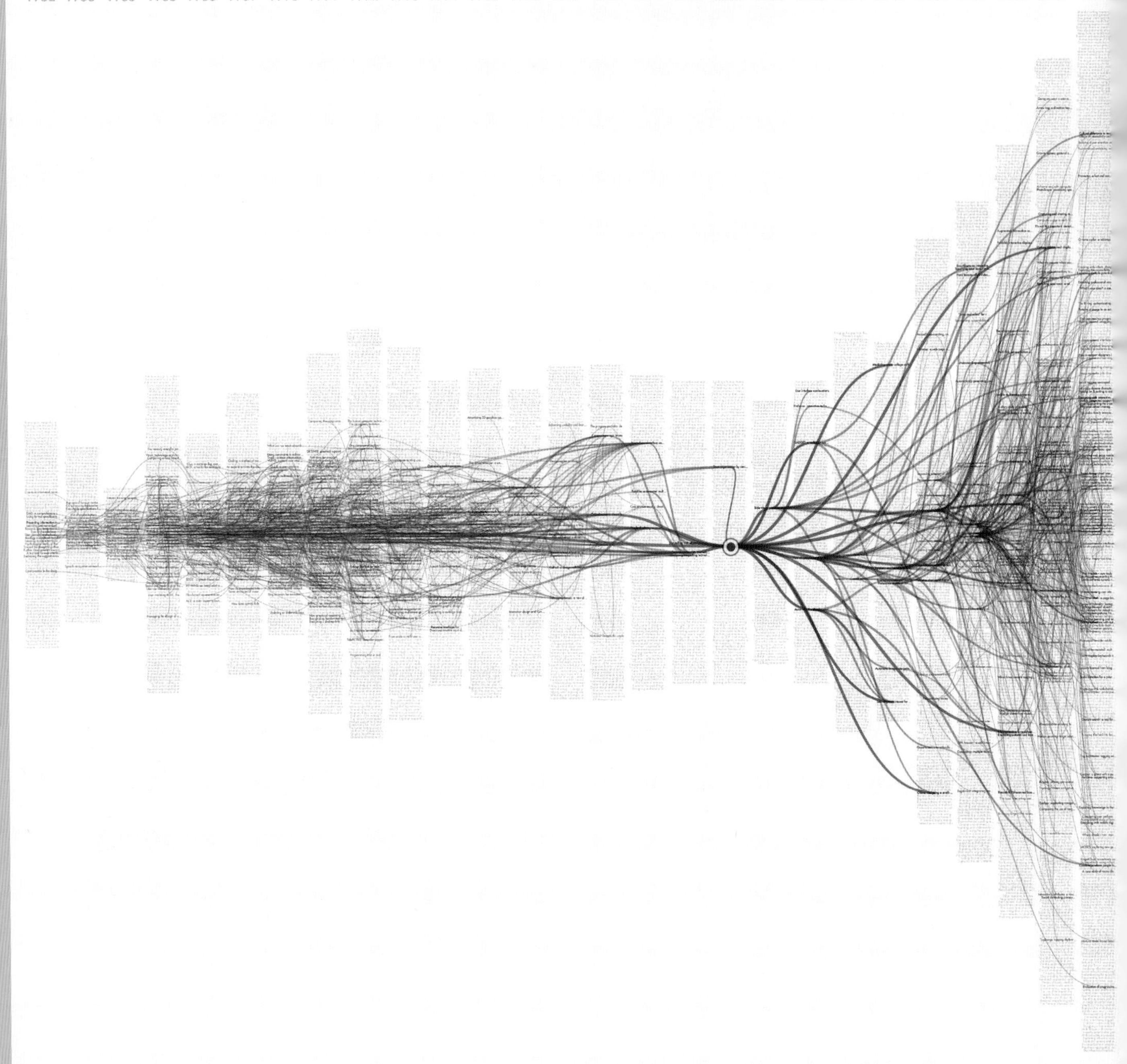

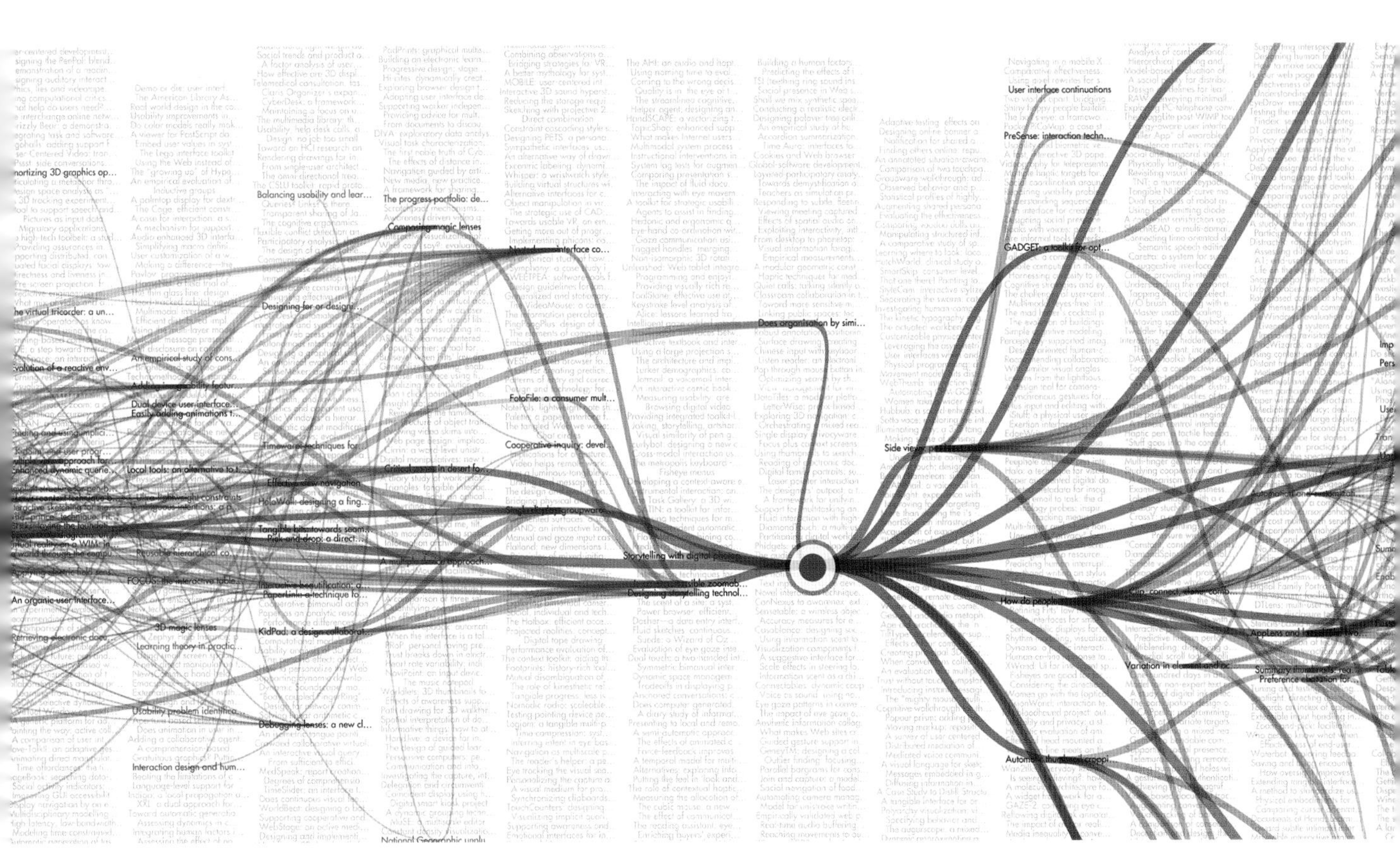

Justin Matejka, Tovi Grossman, and George Fitzmaurice (Autodesk Research), Canada: "*Citeology*," 2011.

Citeology is an interactive visualization application that looks at the relationships between research publications through their use of citations. In total, 11,699 citations were made from one article to another within the collection of 3,502 papers published at two series of conferences by the Association for Computing Machinery (ACM) between the years 1982 and 2010: the Conference on Human Factors in Computing Systems (CHI) and the Symposium on User Interface Software and Technology (UIST) on Computer-Human Interaction.

Time runs horizontally and is measured in years, with the omission of 1984 and 1987, when conferences didn't occur. Papers are organized vertically by year and positioned starting at the center of each column and sorted by the frequency of citations. In other words, the papers with the largest number of citations are found at the horizontal center of the visualization. The initial twenty-five characters of papers form the lines that represent each accordingly. Because the type is too small to read on the screen, hovering over one of the lines provides the paper title. When a paper is selected, the program draws its citation network, rendering in blue connections to papers cited in the paper (descendants) and in red papers that cited it (ancestors). Thickness and opacity of the connecting lines encode age, such that lines connecting close generations are thicker and opaque in contrast to thinner and more transparent lines for further generations. The shortest path between two papers can be found by means of interactions once a paper has been selected and its *citeology* rendered.

www.autodeskresearch.com/projects/citeology

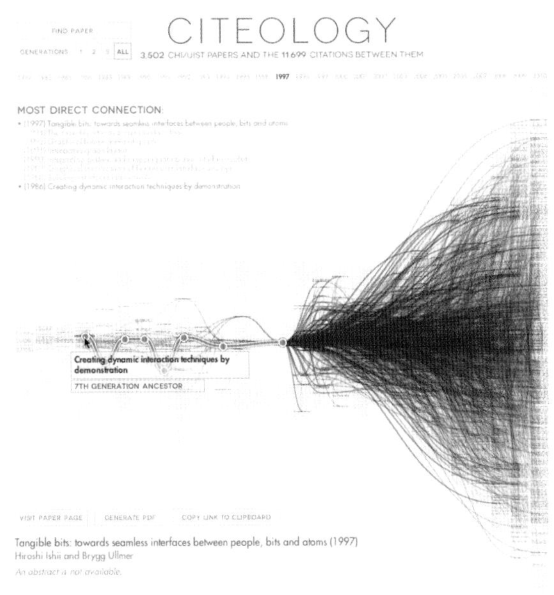

CASE STUDY

LINEAR STRUCTURE

Fineo

http://fineo.densitydesign.org

First published in 1898 to depict energy flows and energy losses in a steam engine, the Sankey diagram was named after its creator, the Irish engineer Matthew H. P. R. Sankey.[23] Sankey diagrams are flow diagrams in which the widths of bands are scaled to the corresponding quantities of flow. Common examples are found in energy and financial systems, because they require understanding of the flow distribution of a phenomena.

Fineo is an interactive application created by DensityDesign Research Lab in 2010. The exploratory visualization uses the structure of a Sankey diagram with the purpose of representing relations between multidimensional categorical data. Sankey diagrams have a networklike structure, with nodes and weighted links. By using the continuous flows of connections, the tool allows easy comparison between dimensions at both local (pairs) and global (all dimensions) levels of the phenomena. The team explains, "Flows in Sankey diagrams act much more like 'rivers' (as opposed to threads) in which you lose memory of the previous steps. This can be useful in those cases in which the user is more interested in relating different data dimensions next to each other more than centering the visualization partition around a leading dimension."[24]

Bendix and Kosara devised in 2006 the Parallel Sets interactive visualization for exploring categorical data.[25] The method extends the parallel coordinates methodology by representing the set of categories along each axis, while scaling the categories according to their corresponding frequencies. Although it is similar at first glance with Parallel Sets, *Fineo* depicts data in a nonhierarchical way. In *Fineo*, axes are independent of each other, and they can be reordered to facilitate comparison between pairs of dimensions, such that one can read the visualization from all directions (left or right).

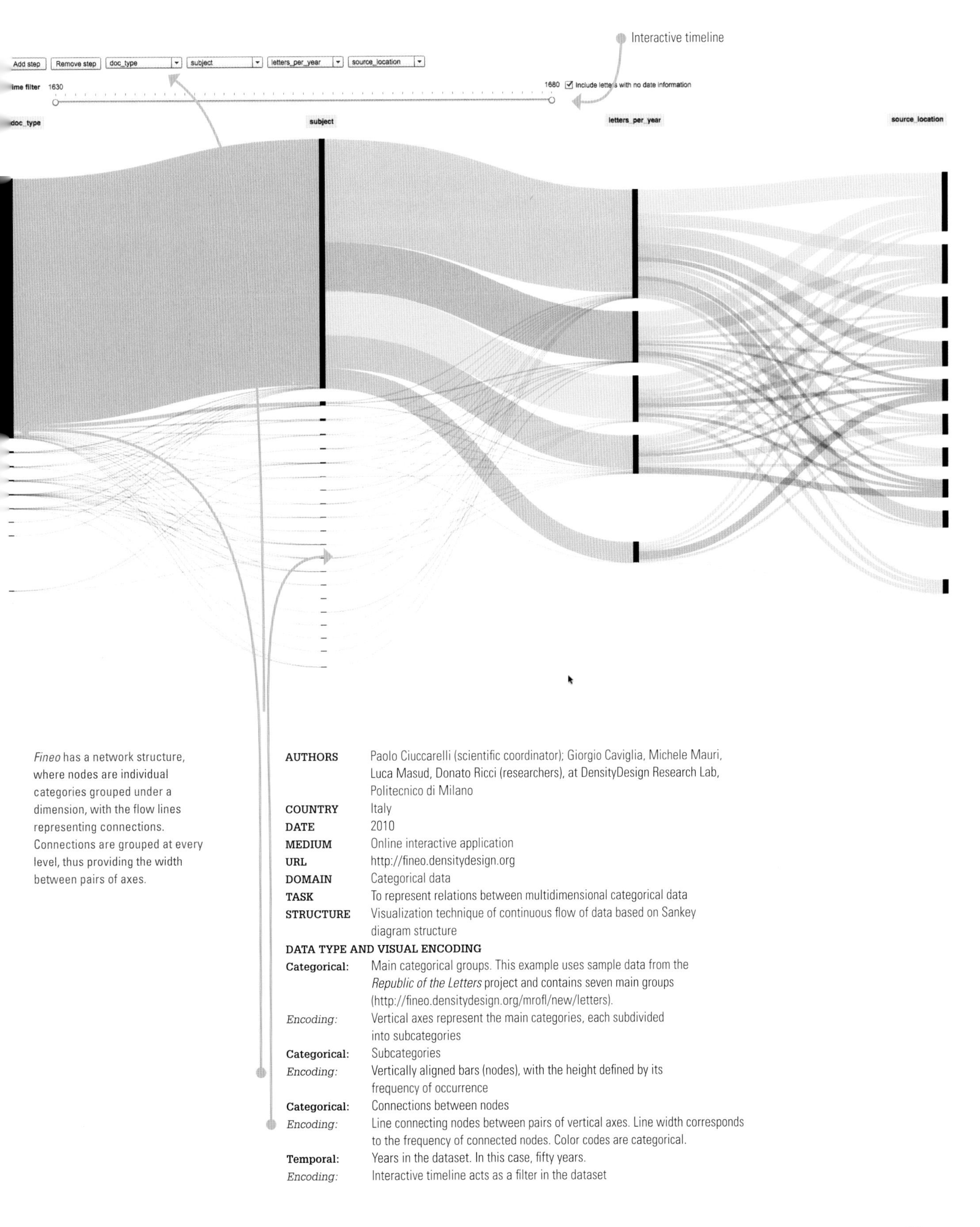

Fineo has a network structure, where nodes are individual categories grouped under a dimension, with the flow lines representing connections. Connections are grouped at every level, thus providing the width between pairs of axes.

AUTHORS Paolo Ciuccarelli (scientific coordinator); Giorgio Caviglia, Michele Mauri, Luca Masud, Donato Ricci (researchers), at DensityDesign Research Lab, Politecnico di Milano

COUNTRY Italy

DATE 2010

MEDIUM Online interactive application

URL http://fineo.densitydesign.org

DOMAIN Categorical data

TASK To represent relations between multidimensional categorical data

STRUCTURE Visualization technique of continuous flow of data based on Sankey diagram structure

DATA TYPE AND VISUAL ENCODING

Categorical: Main categorical groups. This example uses sample data from the *Republic of the Letters* project and contains seven main groups (http://fineo.densitydesign.org/mrofl/new/letters).

Encoding: Vertical axes represent the main categories, each subdivided into subcategories

Categorical: Subcategories

Encoding: Vertically aligned bars (nodes), with the height defined by its frequency of occurrence

Categorical: Connections between nodes

Encoding: Line connecting nodes between pairs of vertical axes. Line width corresponds to the frequency of connected nodes. Color codes are categorical.

Temporal: Years in the dataset. In this case, fifty years.

Encoding: Interactive timeline acts as a filter in the dataset

Wesley Grubbs (creative director), Nicholas Yahnke (programmer), Mladen Balog (concept artist) at Pitch Interactive, U.S.: "2008 Presidential Candidate Donations: Job Titles of Donors," 2008.

The arcs in this diagram connect the job titles (left) to the amounts donated to Obama in the 2008 presidential campaign (right). Job titles are organized by most common to least common among the top 250 job titles of donors to Obama. Donations are organized by dollar amounts, with the first group standing for less than $100, followed by $100 to $500, $500 to $1000, and ending with amounts over $1000. The dollar group segments are sized according to the total percentage of donation amount from the donors listed.

Wesley Grubbs (creative director), Nicholas Yahnke (programmer), Mladen Balog (concept artist) at Pitch Interactive, U.S.: "US Federal Contract Spending in 2009 vs. Agency Related Media Coverage," 2010.

The graphic plots U.S. federal agency spending in 2009 against media coverage of those agencies in the same year. Each agency is represented by a stripe proportional to its budget presence. The graphic reveals that there is a dramatic mismatch between what American taxes fund and which issues occupy national discourse. It is clear for example, that defense spending accounts for the majority of the federal budget, almost 70%.

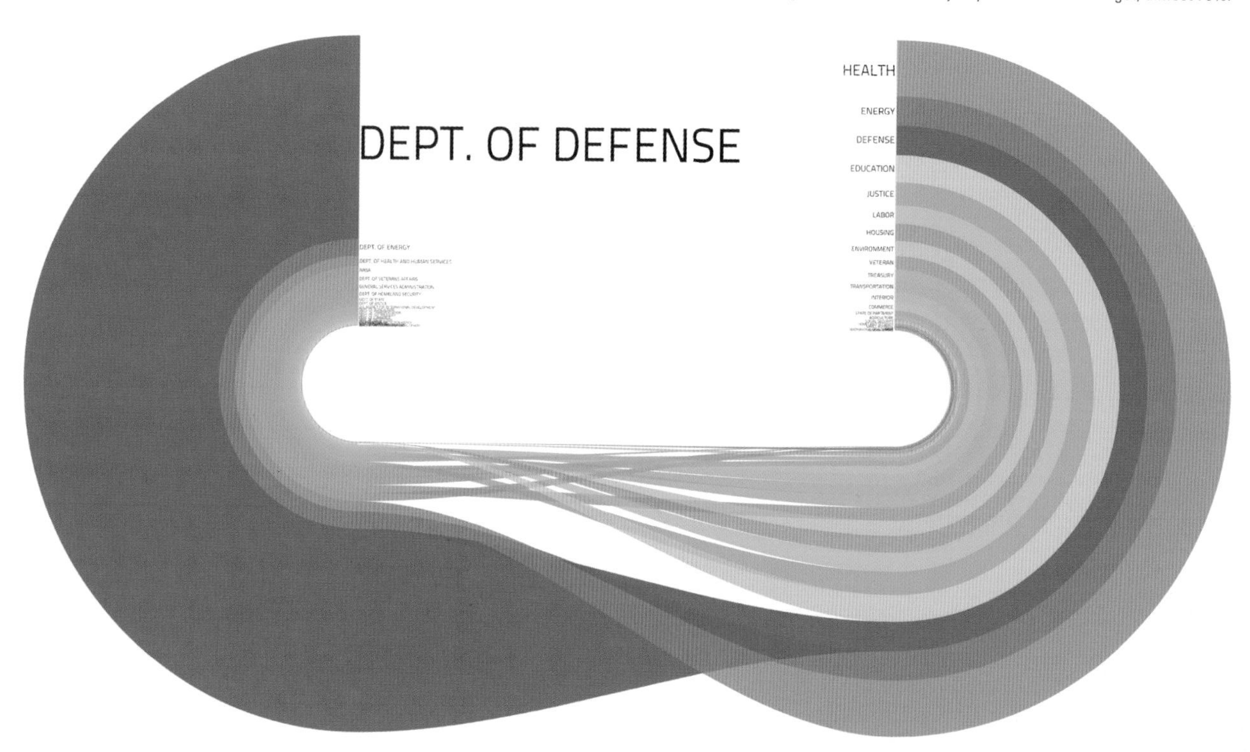

Mike Bostock, Shan Carter, and additional reporting by Amanda Cox (*New York Times*), U.S.: "Over the Decades, How States Have Shifted," 2012.

The flow diagram visualizes how American states have shifted parties over the years, from 1952 to 2012. Time is organized vertically with each row representing an election year. The horizontal axis depicts the size of the parties. Each line represents a state. For example, one can select a line and see the path taken by a state across elections, and whether it has changed, and how much. Note the information on the left-hand side, that provides contextual information and helps the viewer further interpret the diagram.

www.nytimes.com/interactive/2012/10/15/us/politics/swing-history.html

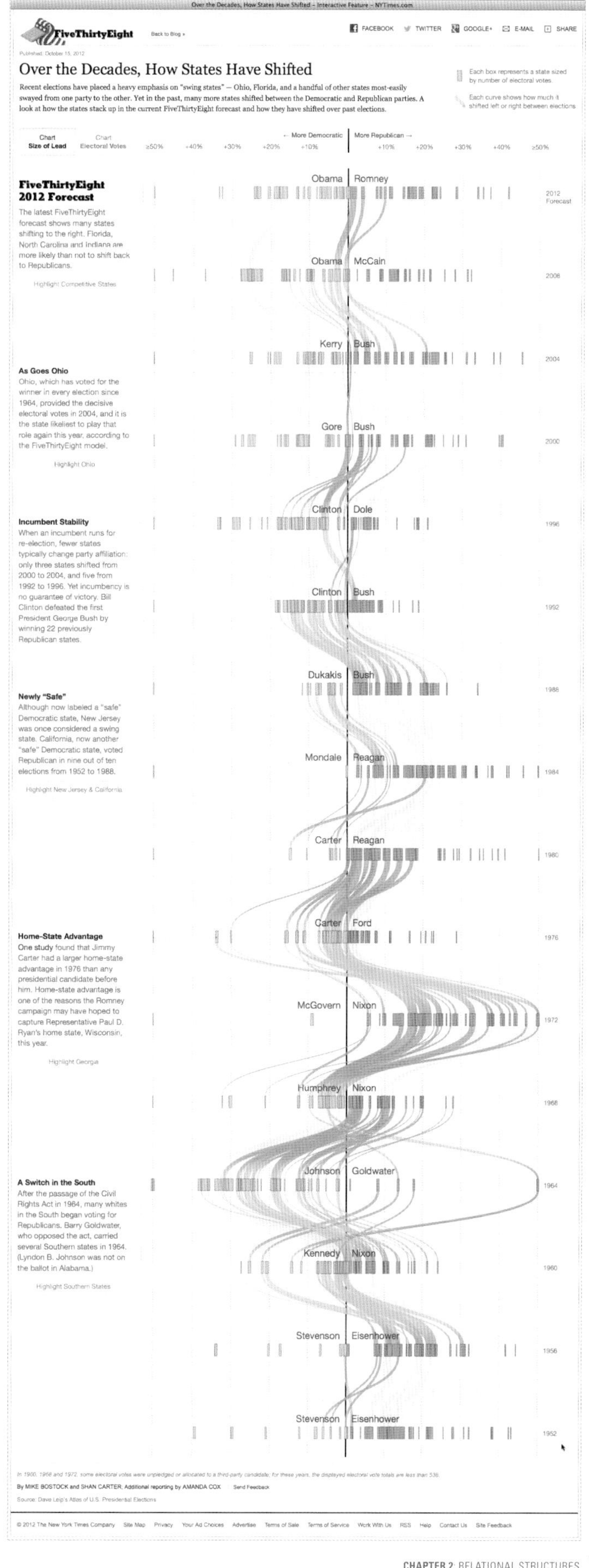

Common Fate

The common fate principle is the tendency to group elements that are moving in the same direction. For example, we tend to perceive the six lines below as forming different groups:

\\\\\\ = 1 group
\\\/// = 2 groups

Parallel lines are easier to perceive and will be grouped into a unit, whereas nonparallel lines are perceived individually.

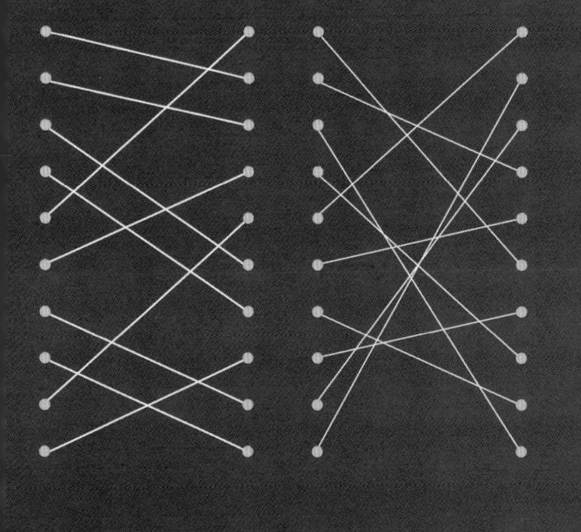

CASE STUDY

GEOGRAPHY BASED

GLEAMviz

www.GLEAMviz.org

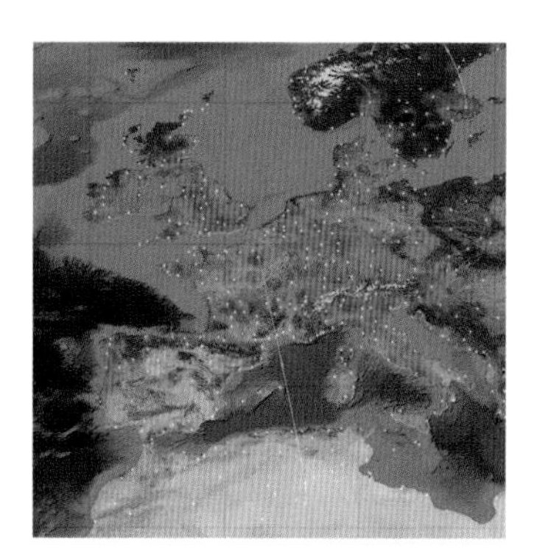

GLEAMviz is a client-server software system that can model the worldwide spread of epidemics for human transmissible diseases such as influenza-like illnesses. GLEAMviz makes use of a stochastic and discrete computational scheme to model epidemic spread called GLEAM—Global Epidemic and Mobility model. The model is based on a geo-referenced metapopulation approach that considers 3,362 subpopulations in 220 countries of the world, as well as human mobility taking into account air travel flow connections and short-range commuting data.[26]

Epidemic forecasts are complex and need to consider a series of parameters within the social context. Vespignani and colleagues explain, "GLEAM uses real-world data covering the distribution of the worldwide population, their interactions and journeys, and the spatial structure and volumes of national and international air traffic. By combining these datasets with realistic models of infection dynamics, GLEAM can deliver forecasts for the spreading pattern of infectious diseases epidemics. We have thoroughly tested and validated GLEAM against historical epidemic outbreaks including the 2002/03 SARS epidemic. In 2009, GLEAM has been used to produce real-time forecasts of the unfolding of the H1N1 pandemic."[27]

GLEAMviz offers three types of visualization:

- A 2-D map depicting the spread of the infection with charts showing the number of new cases at various levels of detail.
- A 3-D globe with a concise overview of the spread.
- Geographic and concentric views by SPaTO visual explorer depicting how the structure of the airport network influences the notion of distance. The outputs remap all the transportation hubs according to the time it takes for the infection to reach them from the moment of outbreak.

GLEAMviz, which is publicly available for download, allows setting up and executing simulations, and retrieving and visualizing the results. It was developed by an international team lead by Alessandro Vespignani (team coordinator) and Vittoria Colizza. It is hosted at three institutions: College of Computer and Information Sciences and Department of Health Sciences, Northeastern University, Boston, MA, USA; Complex Networks & Systems Group, ISI Foundation, Turin, Italy; and INSERM, Unite Mixte de Recherche 707, Paris, France.

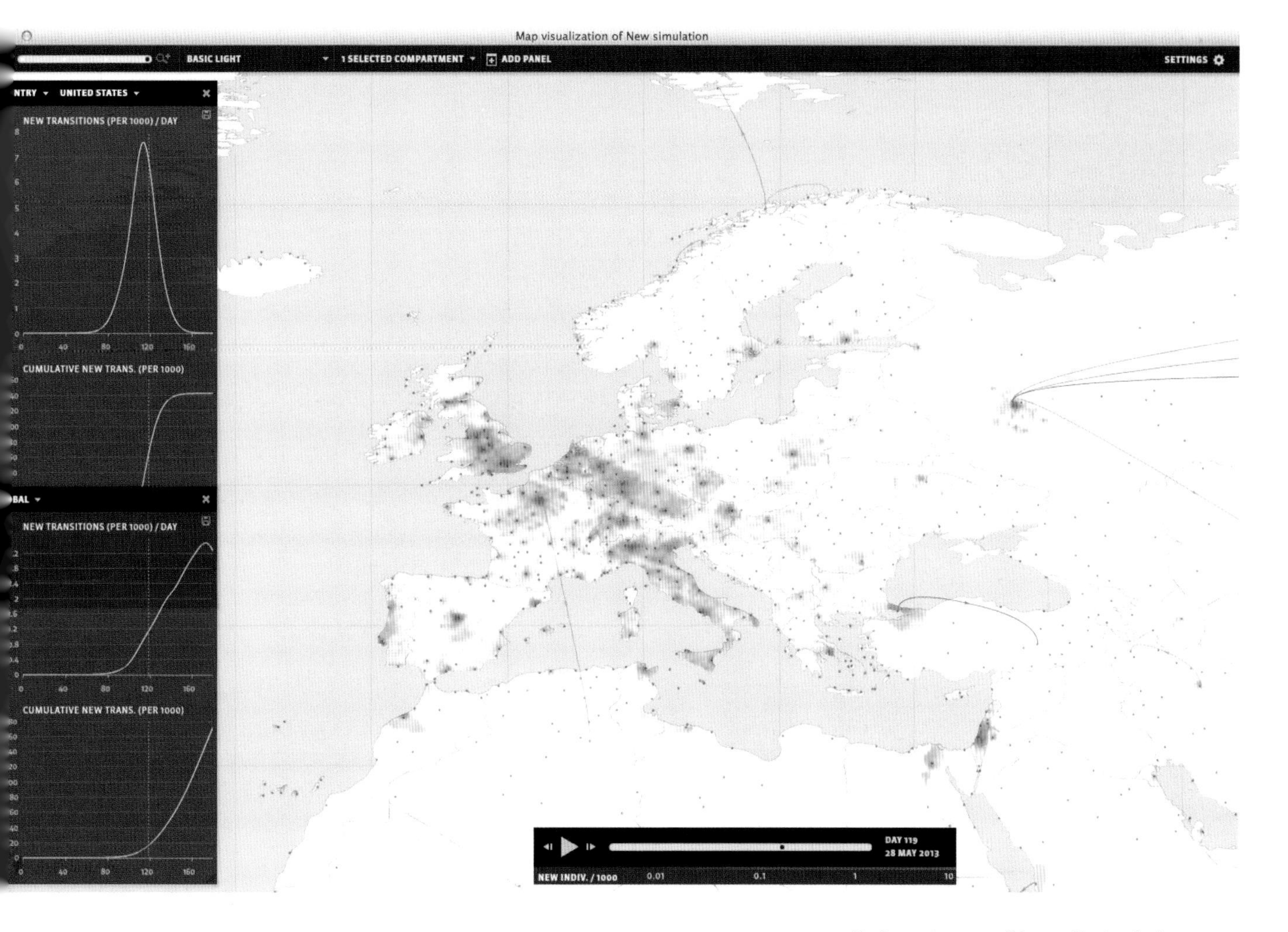

The image shows one of the possible visualization outputs in GLEAMviz: a 2-D geo-temporal evolution of the epidemic. The map shows the state of the epidemic on a particular day. Infected population cells are color coded according to the number of new cases of the quantity that is being displayed. Detailed information is provided on demand by clicking on a city. The evolution of the epidemic can be viewed as an animation by using the play button at the bottom of the interface. The two sets of charts (on the left) depict the incidence curve and the cumulative size of the epidemics for selectable areas of interest. There are three options for map backgrounds: Blue Marble map by NASA's Earth Observatory, a dark or white solid color.

Among the types of visualization available at GLEAMviz is this 3-D globe showing an overview of the disease spread.

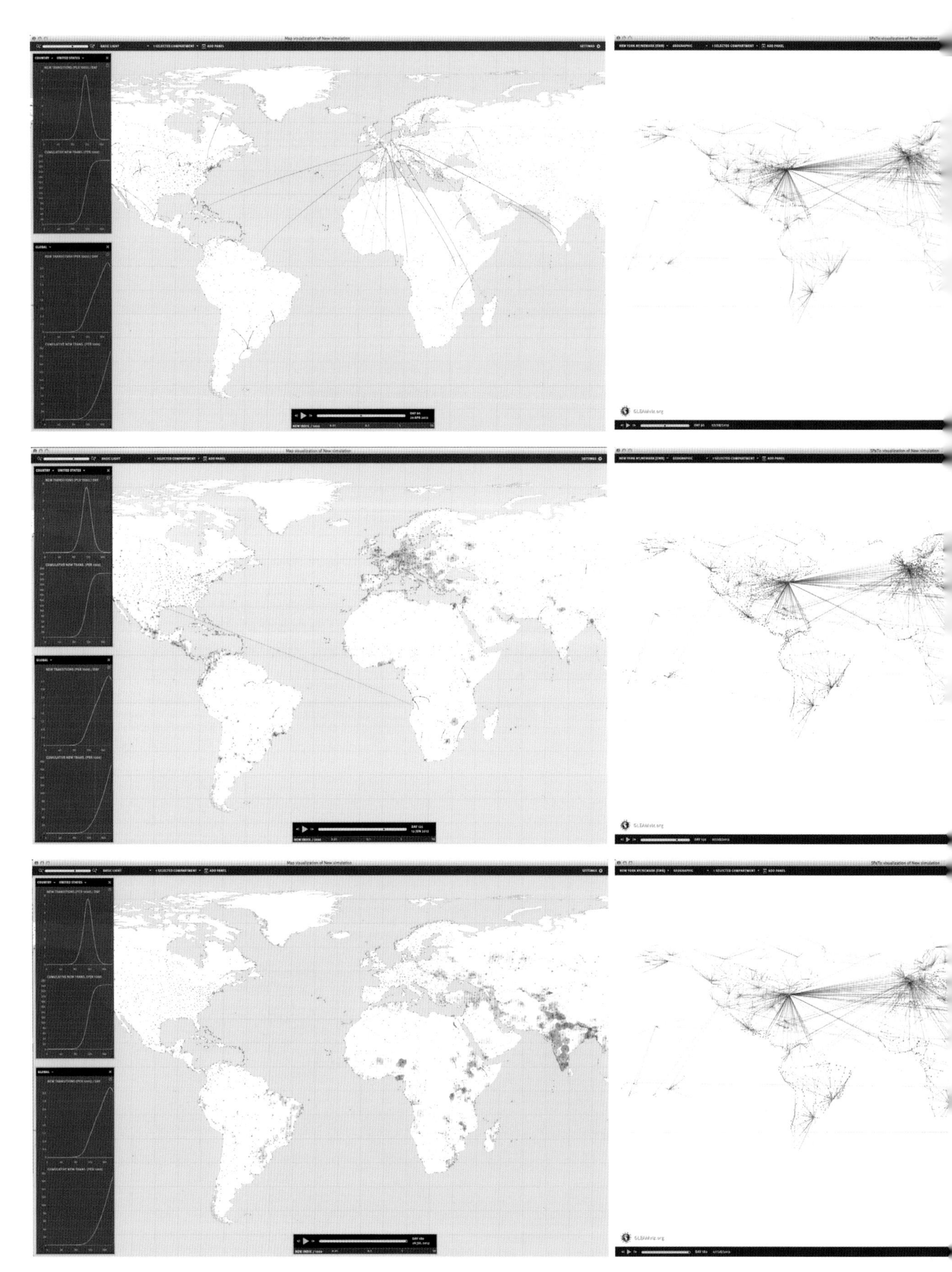

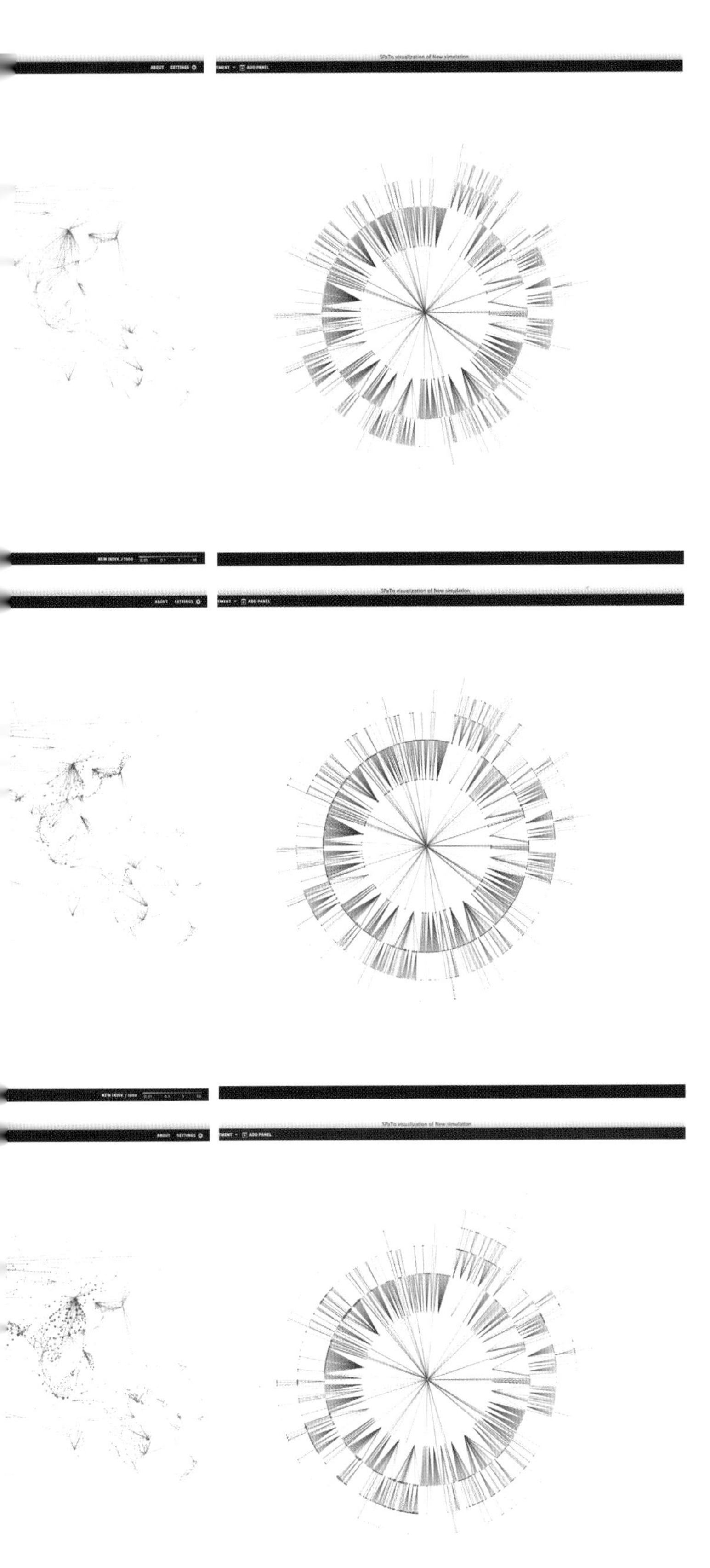

The three sets of images show the temporal evolution of an Influenza Like Illness (ILI) started in New York City simulated and visualized using the GLEAMviz simulator. The model uses real-world data on population and mobility networks to predict when and where people will interact and potentially transmit the infection. The sets show the result of disease spread for days 90 (top), 130 (center), and 180 (bottom). The left image in each set shows the geo-temporal evolution of the epidemic for each particular day. The arrows show the spread of infection. The color of each census area shows the local number of transitions into the infected compartment (incidence). The two black chart panels on the left show the incidence and total number of cases in the United States (top) and in the globe (bottom) as a function of time.
The remaining images are renditions from *SPaTo Visual Explorer*, a visualization tool integrated into GLEAMviz. *SPaTo Visual Explorer* is an interactive tool for the visualization and exploration of complex networks developed by Christian Thiemann in the research group of Dirk Brockmann at Northwestern University. The system provides two views: geographic and concentric. It uses a radial distance corresponding to "effective" network distance, that is, the shortest-path distance to the central node. As Thiemann explains, "By reducing a network to the shortest-path tree of a selected root node, we obtain a local but simpler view of the network that can be easily visualized. With the ability to quickly change the root node, the program allows us to explore the network from different perspectives."[28]

COMMUNITY STRUCTURE

Universal Exposition, Milan, 2015

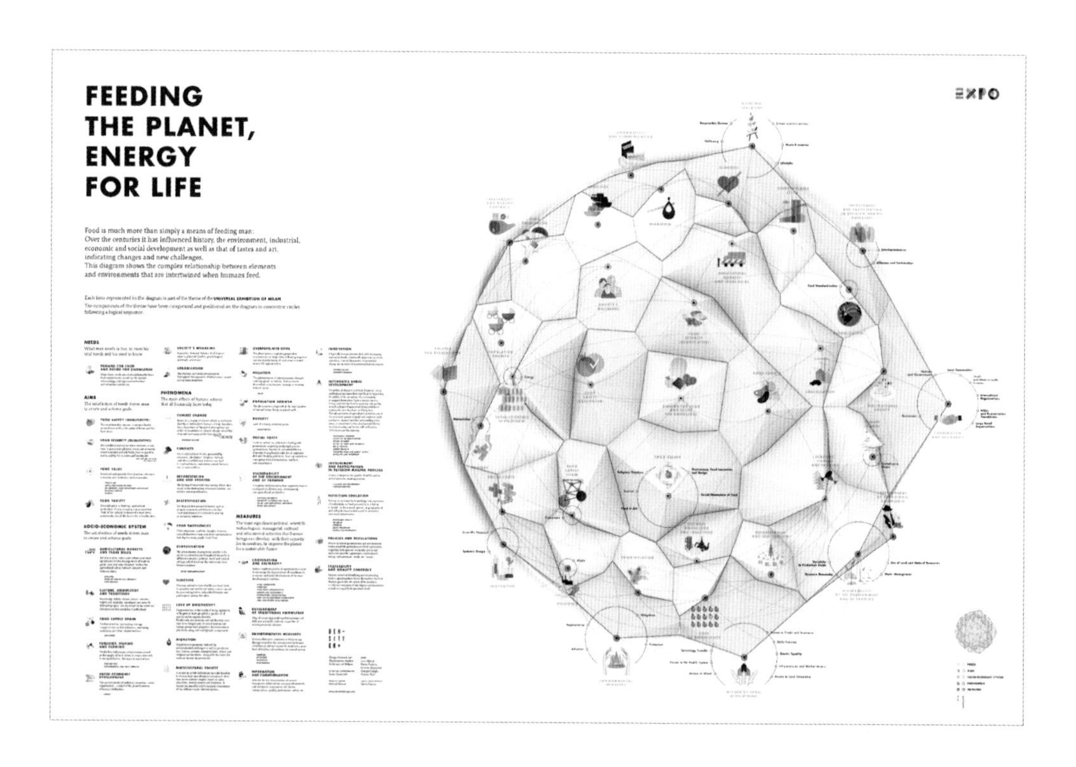

The city of Milan, Italy, will host the 2015 Universal Exposition around the topic of food with the theme "Feeding the Planet, Energy for Life." The organizers of Expo 2015 invited the Italian research laboratory DensityDesign at the Politecnico di Milano to devise a visualization that would communicate the topic to a general audience. The final poster depicts relationships between food production and consumption, social and environmental concerns, and technological and sustainability issues. The following spread provides an explanation of the design process, from the technical graph to the design of symbols.

The design team at DensityDesign Research Lab, Politecnico di Milano consisted of Paolo Ciuccarelli (Scientific Coordinator), Michele Mauri (Project Leader), Giorgio Caviglia, Lorenzo Fernandez, Luca Masud, Mario Porpora, and Donato Ricci (Team). Gloria Zavatta took part in the theme development.

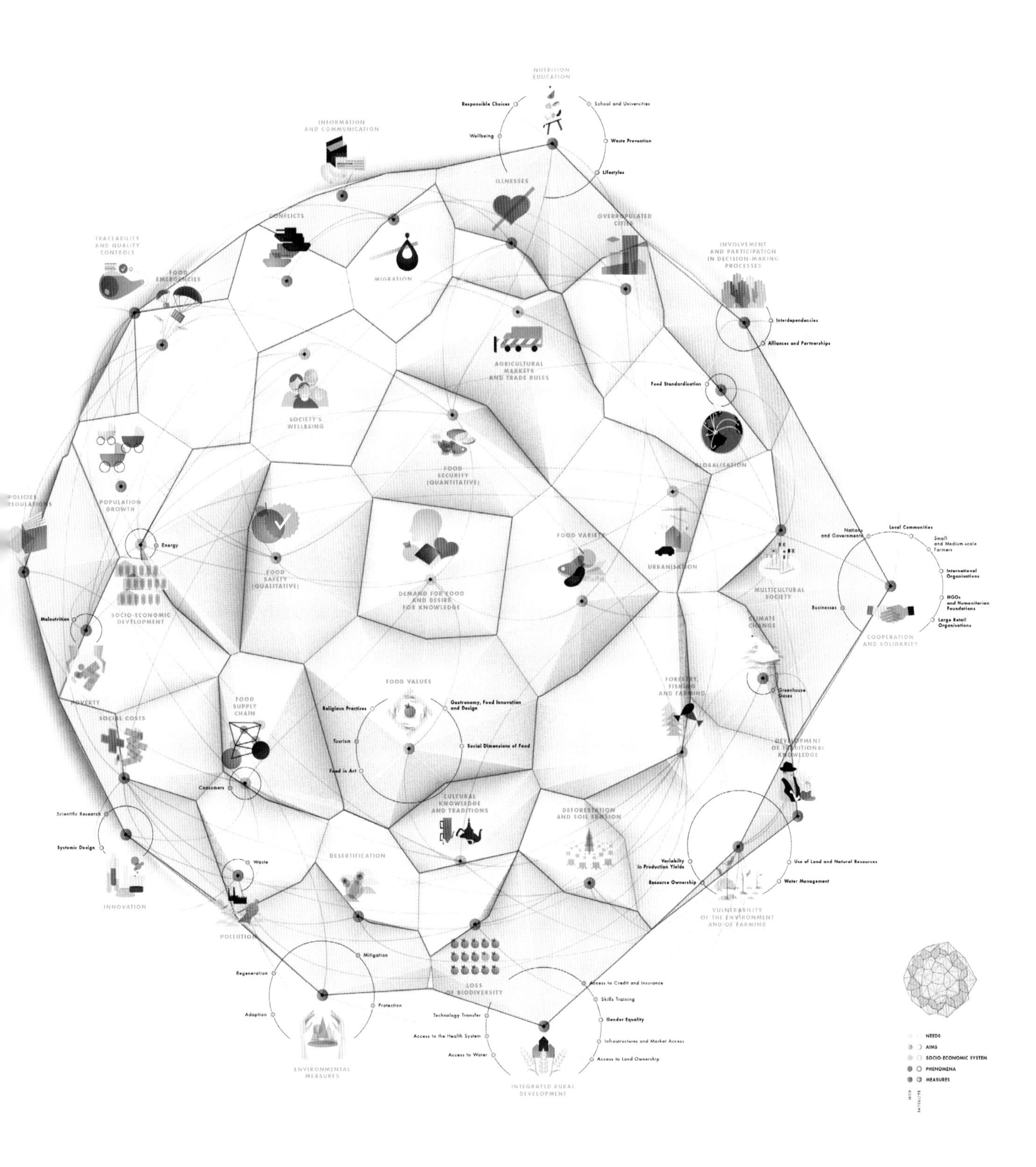
NUTRITION EDUCATION
Responsible Choices
School and Universities
Wellbeing
Waste Prevention
Lifestyles
INFORMATION AND COMMUNICATION
ILLNESSES
CONFLICTS
MIGRATION
OVERPOPULATED CITIES
TRACEABILITY AND QUALITY CONTROLS
FOOD EMERGENCIES
INVOLVEMENT AND PARTICIPATION IN DECISION-MAKING PROCESSES
Interdependencies
Alliances and Partnerships
AGRICULTURAL MARKETS AND TRADE RULES
Food Standardisation
SOCIETY'S WELLBEING
GLOBALISATION
FOOD SECURITY (QUANTITATIVE)
POPULATION GROWTH
Energy
FOOD SAFETY (QUALITATIVE)
DEMAND FOR FOOD AND DESIRE FOR KNOWLEDGE
FOOD VARIETY
URBANISATION
MULTICULTURAL SOCIETY
Nations and Governments
Local Communities
Small- and Medium-scale Farmers
International Organisations
NGOs and Humanitarian Foundations
Businesses
Large Retail Organisations
COOPERATION AND SOLIDARITY
SOCIO-ECONOMIC DEVELOPMENT
Malnutrition
POVERTY
CLIMATE CHANGE
Greenhouse Gases
FOOD VALUES
Religious Practices
Gastronomy, Food Innovation and Design
Tourism
Social Dimensions of Food
Food in Art
FOOD SUPPLY CHAIN
SOCIAL COSTS
FORESTRY, FISHING AND FARMING
DEVELOPMENT OF TRADITIONAL KNOWLEDGE
Consumers
CULTURAL KNOWLEDGE AND TRADITIONS
DEFORESTATION AND SOIL EROSION
Scientific Research
Systemic Design
INNOVATION
Waste
DESERTIFICATION
Variability in Production Yields
Resource Ownership
Use of Land and Natural Resources
Water Management
VULNERABILITY OF THE ENVIRONMENT AND OF FARMING
POLLUTION
Mitigation
Regeneration
Adaption
Protection
ENVIRONMENTAL MEASURES
LOSS OF BIODIVERSITY
Access to Credit and Insurance
Skills Training
Technology Transfer
Gender Equality
Access to the Health System
Infrastructures and Market Access
Access to Water
Access to Land Ownership
INTEGRATED RURAL DEVELOPMENT
NEEDS
AIMS
SOCIO-ECONOMIC SYSTEM
PHENOMENA
MEASURES

THE NETWORK

The first step involved the identification of subthemes and the examination of interactions among them. For that, DensityDesign created a series of network diagrams that started with hand sketches and ended with the digital version reproduced here.

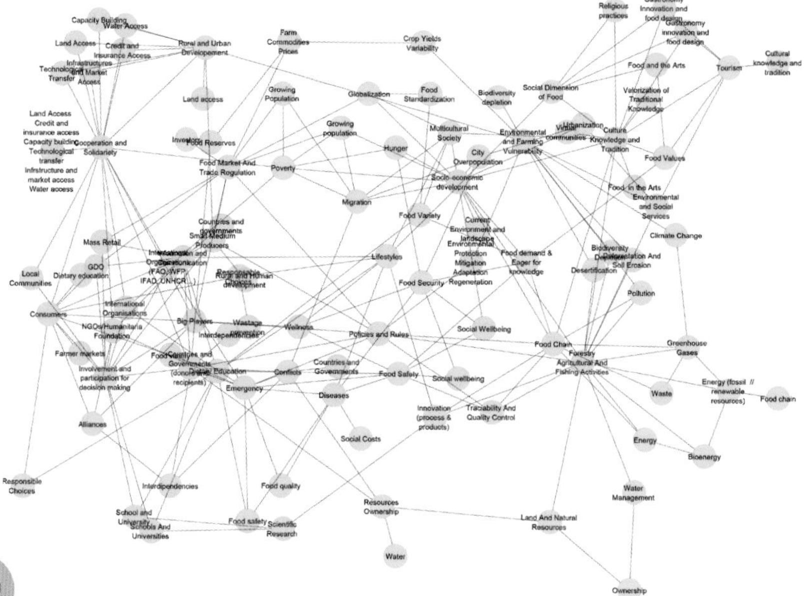

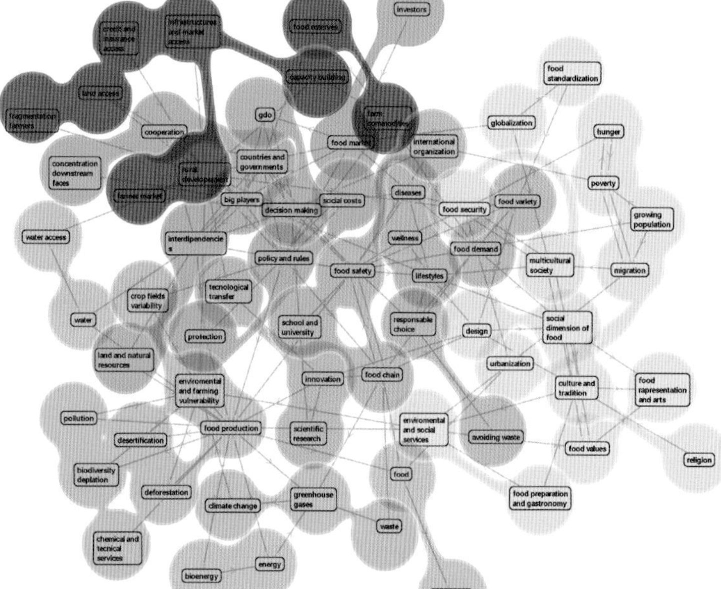

CLUSTERING

After creating the relational structure, they grouped the subthemes into five categories:

- Needs: The needs of humans to live and to meet vital needs, and our needs to know;
- Aims: The satisfaction of our needs drives humans to create products and to achieve goals;
- Socioeconomic system: The productive, social, economic environment;
- Phenomena: The main effects of human actions that all humanity faces today;
- Measures: The most significant political, scientific, technological, managerial, cultural, and educational activities that human beings can develop, with their capacity for innovation, to improve the planet for a sustainable future.

Each color stands for one of five categories structuring the subnetworks within the main theme.

THE GRAPHICAL LAYOUT

With the subnetworks organized into five categorical groups, they started studying the best visual representation with which to communicate the story to the general audience. In the series of representations, we see the iterations of the design process toward a layout that would maintain the complexities of the theme without the technicality of the initial network diagram. In this process, each subtheme became a hub in the network with their connected nodes. More important, the subnetwork within the Needs category was centralized in relation to the whole network and surrounded by the other four groups. The last step in the graphical structure was the introduction of the landscape metaphor. Using Delaunay triangulation, they assigned areas to the groups so as to depict the network as a Voronoi diagram. Each node is represented as a mountain peak, with its height provided by the number of connections (the node degree).

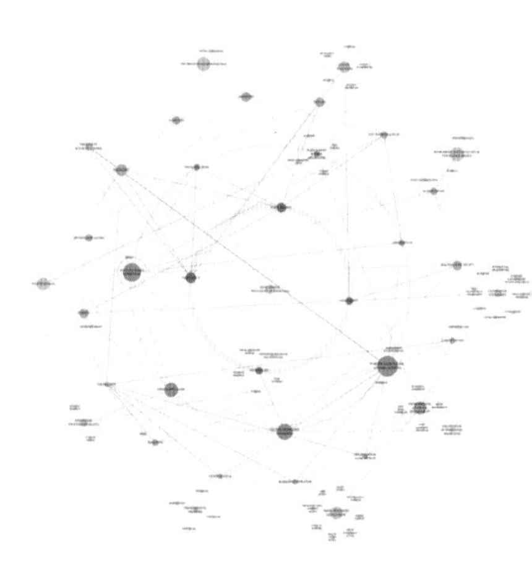

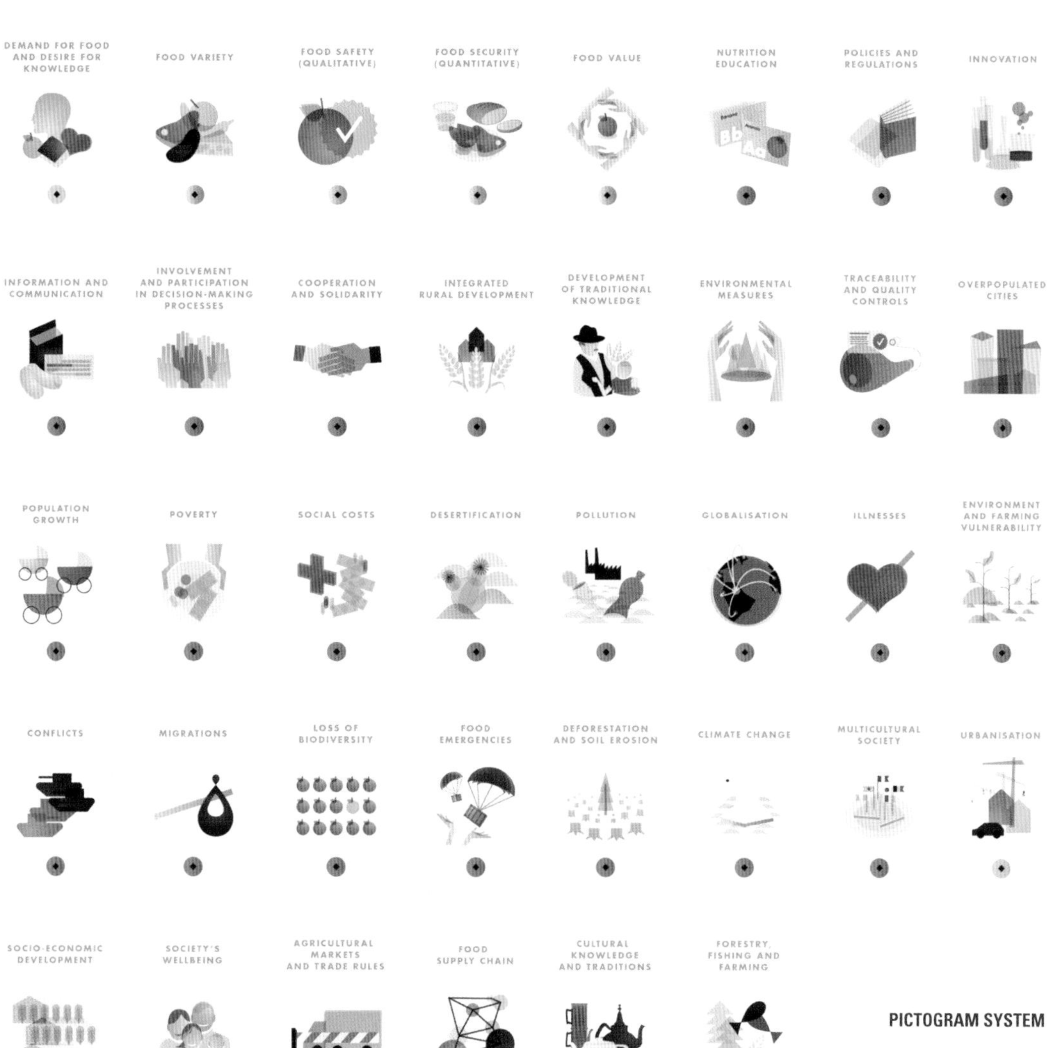

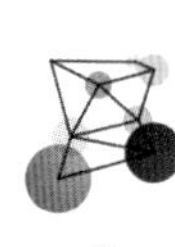

PICTOGRAM SYSTEM

The last stage involved the creation of a series of pictograms to convey each theme. The color code stands for the five main themes. Each hub is represented by a diamond shape inside a circle of its theme color, and other nodes are represented by outlined circles, again color coded for themes.

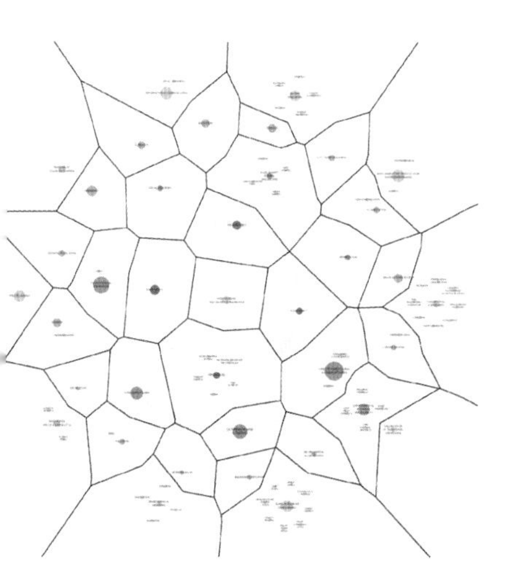

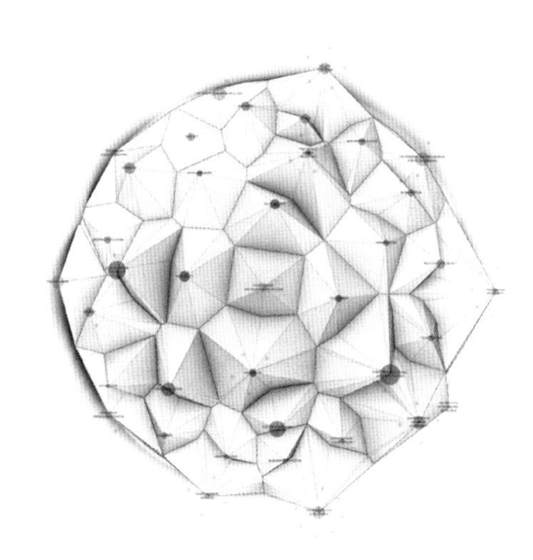

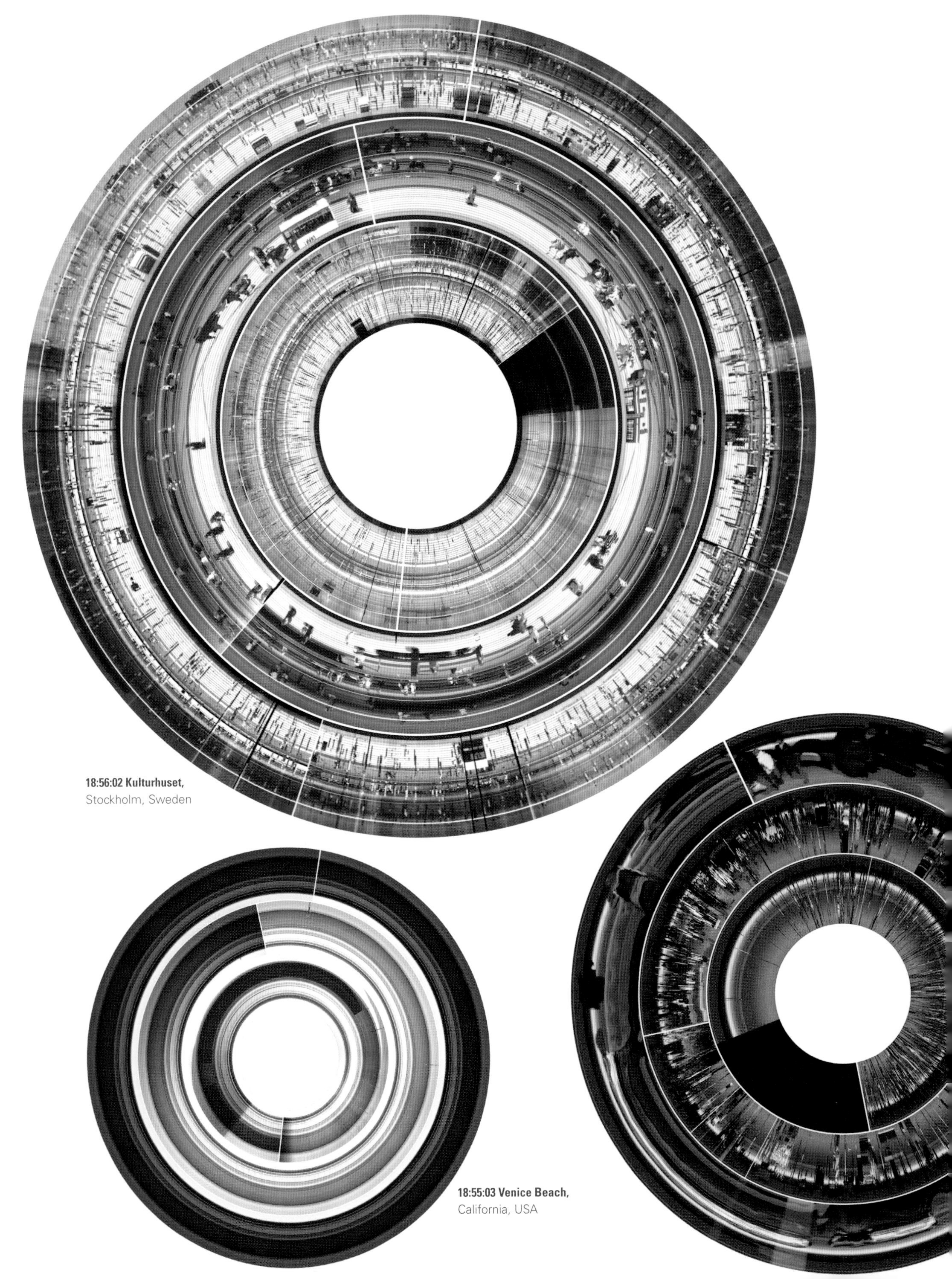

18:56:02 Kulturhuset,
Stockholm, Sweden

18:55:03 Venice Beach,
California, USA

CHAPTER 3

TEMPORAL STRUCTURES: TIMELINES AND FLOWS

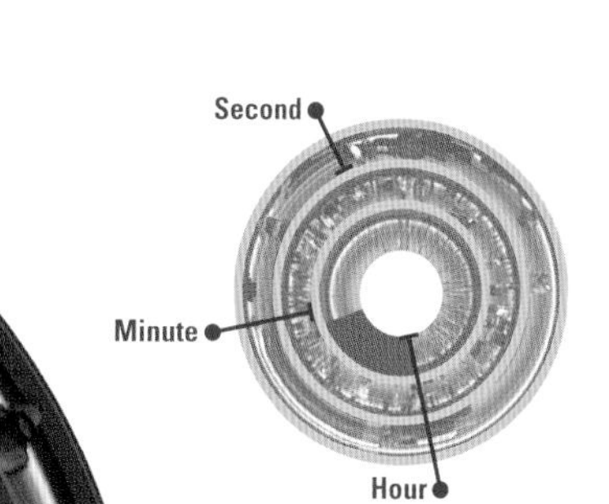

Jussi Ängeslevä and Ross Cooper, U.K.: "Last Clock," 2002.

Similar to an analog clock, the interface has three concentric circles, each representing a measure of time, with the outermost ring standing for seconds. The interface is connected to a video source that feeds the clock at each level, so that at every second a new image is added, coinciding with the clock "hand." The video can be any source devised by the authors, including a recent application for the iPad, which allows anyone to create their clocks with personal footage (https://itunes.apple.com/us/app/last-clock/id460584423?mt=8).

17:42:54 Ebisu,
Tokyo, Japan

Time is an abstract concept and, thus, not inherently visual. Much of the terminology we use for time is based on our concrete experience of space and of the physical environment. In the seminal book *Metaphors We Live By*, Lakoff and Johnson explain that the expressions we use to describe temporal experiences in most idioms emerge from our concepts of "containers" and "moving objects." "The 'time is a moving object' metaphor is based on the correlation between an object moving towards us and the time it takes to get to us. The same correlation is a basis for the 'time is a container' metaphor (as in 'he did it *in* ten minutes'), with the bounded space traversed by the object correlated with the time the object takes to traverse it. Events and actions are correlated with bounded time spans, and this makes them 'container objects.'"[1]

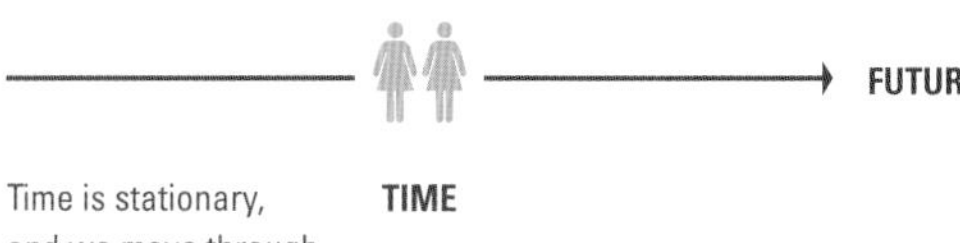

Time is stationary, and we move through it in the direction of the future.

TIME

Time is a moving object that moves toward us.

The diagram depicts two subcases of the same metaphor "time goes past us, from front to back." In both cases, the relative motion happens in relation to us, with the future in front and the past behind.

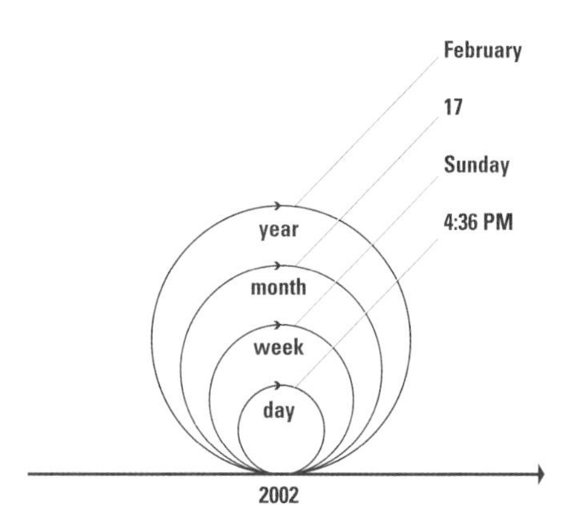

This diagram, after Zerubavel, shows the linear and circular visions of time. He explains, "Locating a particular historical instant in 2002, for example, does not preclude it from also being designated as 4:36 PM on Sunday, 17 February, thereby placing it on four different wheels that are nevertheless rolling along an unmistakably straight road."[22] Another way to depict linear and cyclical time is portrayed in the diagram below, in which recurrence is understood if we read it vertically.

LINEAR

Winter 2002	Spring 2002	Summer 2002	Fall 2002
Winter 2003	Spring 2003	Summer 2003	Fall 2003
Winter 2004	Spring 2004	Summer 2004	Fall 2004
Winter 2005	Spring 2005	Summer 2005	Fall 2005

CYCLICAL

There are two ways in which we conceive of time moving:

- The subject is moving (ego-motion) and time is stationary, as in the expressions "the weeks *ahead*" (expressing the future); "all is *behind* us" (past);
- Time is moving and we are stationary, as in the expressions "the *following* weeks" (future); "the *preceding* weeks" (past).

These two orientations are used without contradiction, such as when we say, "We are looking *ahead* to the *following* weeks." As Lakoff and Johnson explain, we tend to assign a front/back orientation to moving objects, with the front facing the direction of motion.[2] For example, we designate a "front" to a satellite, which is spherical, based on the direction of its orbit. The same holds true when using the moving object metaphor to reason about time, such that if we are the moving targets, we move in the direction of time, as in "time is ahead" or "I look forward." If we consider time moving toward us, then time faces us, as in expressions like "the time has arrived" and "I face the future." In other words, how the motion is viewed, whether the subject or time is moving, will determine the front/back relationship: "What we have here are two subclasses of 'time passes us': in one case, we are moving and time is standing still; in the other, time is moving and we are standing still. What is in common is relative motion with respect to us, with the future in front and the past behind."[3]

MEASURING TIME

It's interesting to note that most of our systems for measuring time are cyclical, such as clocks and calendars. Furthermore, these systems are also anchored in our physical experiences, as Umberto Eco recalls: "All the 'clocks' used by man, at least until the invention of mechanical time-pieces, were in their way linked to our bodily location. Time was measured against the visible motion of the stars and the 'rising' and 'setting' of the Sun, that is, movements that only exist in relation to our point of view (indeed, objectively speaking, it was the Earth that was moving, of course, but we did not know it and we did not really care)."[4]

The history of measuring time is a rich one, and unfortunately outside the scope of this book. But, it is worth recalling that these are conventions established and agreed upon. For example, according to the U.S. Naval Observatory, there are six principal calendars in current use around the world: Gregorian, Hebrew, Islamic, Indian, Chinese, and Julian calendars. However, most countries in the world have adopted the Gregorian calendar for their daily civic activities and international interactions. Pope Gregory XIII introduced the calendar in 1582, which is based on a solar set of rules, with days as the elemental cycle provided by the rotation

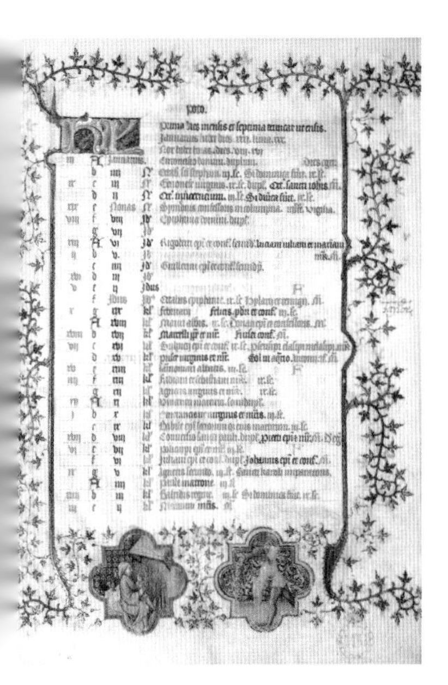

Fourteenth-century *Calendarium Parisiense* indicating holidays according to the Roman tradition.

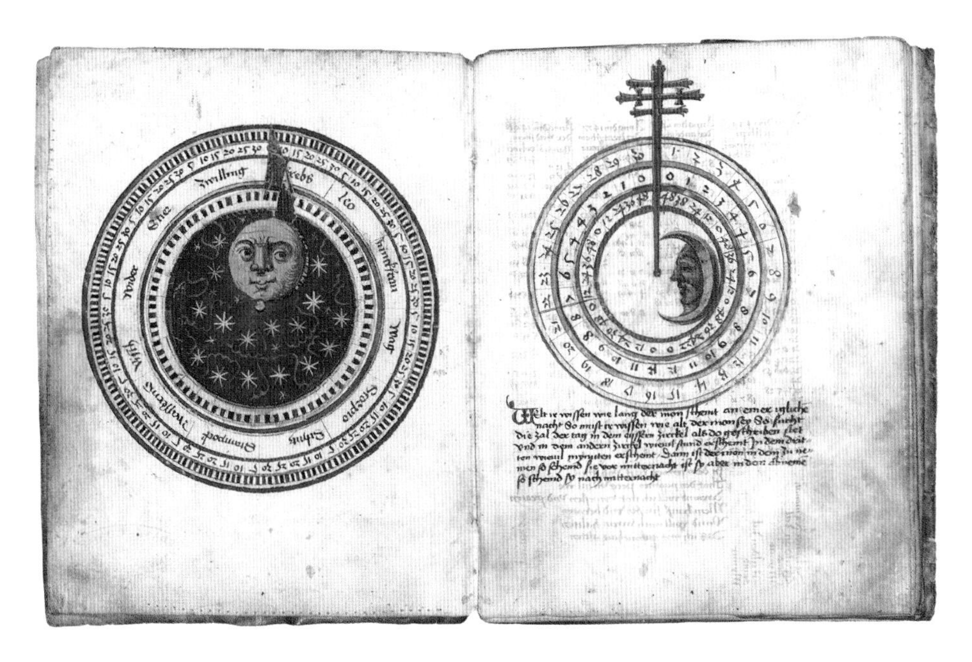

This 1496 manuscript shows medieval calendars with depictions of the positions of the Sun and the Moon.

of the Earth on its axis. Because of its roots in Christianity, many countries have kept their original calendars for religious purposes, such as the Islamic lunar calendar, and the Hebrew, Indian, and Chinese lunisolar calendars.[5]

Another aspect of our temporal experiences is the time perceived, as when we express that "the day was too long." Discussions around the nature of time can be traced back to the fourth century, as Eco describes: "Augustine tells us, we can measure neither the past, nor the present, nor the future (since these never exist), and yet we do measure time, whenever we say that a certain time is long, that it never seems to pass or that it has passed by very quickly. In other words, there is a nonmetric measure, the sort we use when we think of the day as boring and long or when a pleasurable hour has gone by too swirly. And here, Augustine pulls off an audacious coup de théâtre: He locates his nonmetric measure in our memory. The true measure of time is an inner measure. Centuries later, Henri Bergson would also contrast metric time with the time of our consciousness or 'inner durée.'"[6]

Beginning again and again
is a natural thing
even when there is a series.
Beginning again and again and again
explaining composition and time
is a natural thing.

Gertrude Stein

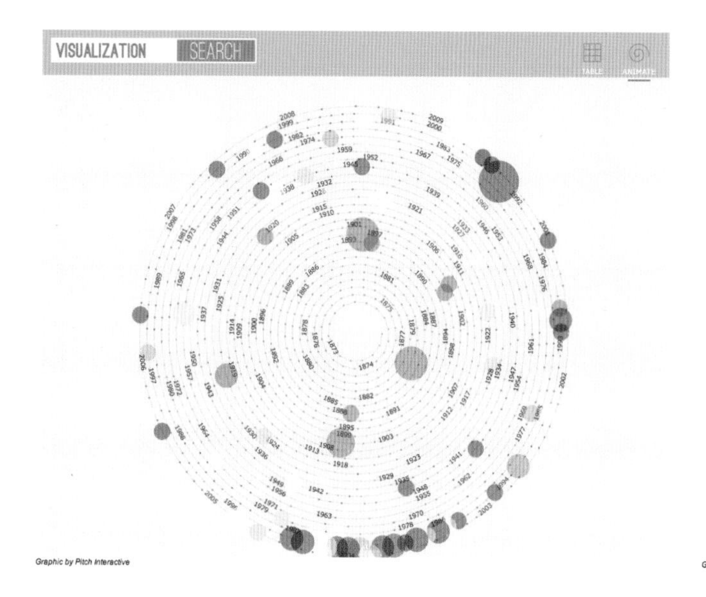

Graphic by Pitch Interactive

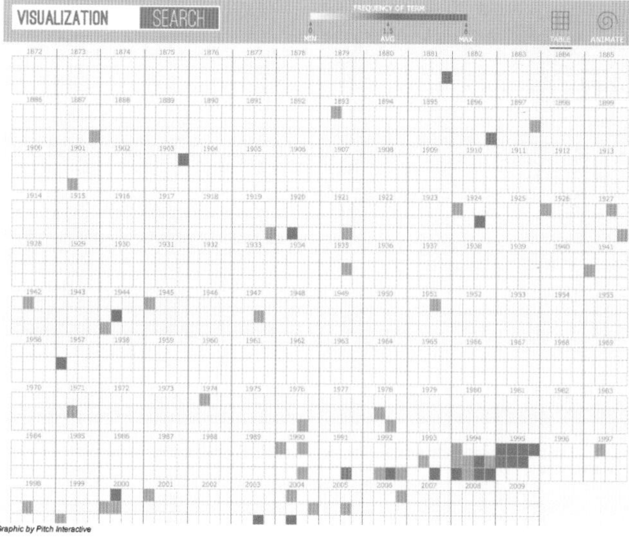

Graphic by Pitch Interactive

Wesley Grubbs (creative director), Nicholas Yahnke (programmer), Mladen Balog (concept artist) at Pitch Interactive, U.S.: "*Popular Science* Archive," 2009.

In 2009, *Popular Science* magazine worked with Google to digitize the magazine's archives back to its inception in 1872, transforming 1,563 issues into searchable data. The *Popular Science Archive* Explorer is an interactive online tool created by Pitch Interactive, where one can access the data, including reading the issues. It is possible to search for any single word (the example reproduced here is for "visualization") and to check the frequency of its appearance over the years. The frequency of words is color coded from gray to orange, and, in the case of the circular diagram, the area size of circles also stand for frequency. It is interesting to compare how trends are revealed in the two temporal structures available—calendar-based grid and the cyclical concentric circles—even though the latter does not present the years aligned.

www.popsci.com/content/wordfrequency#war

STRUCTURING MODELS

Our philosophical notions of time also affect how we spatially structure time. Our conceptual models and corresponding visual structures are organized around the dichotomy between linear and cyclical times, as Stephen Jay Gould explains, "At one end of the dichotomy—I shall call it time's arrow—history is an irreversible sequence of unrepeatable events. Each moment occupies its own distinct position in a temporal series, and all moments, considered in proper sequence, tell a story of linked events moving in a direction. At the other end—I shall call it time's cycle—events have no meaning as distinct episodes with causal impact upon a contingent history. Fundamental states are immanent in time, always present and never changing. Apparent motions are parts of repeating cycles, and differences of the past will be realities of the future. Time has no direction."[7]

Gould's discussion attests to the ongoing philosophical debate over the topologies of time. But, as we shall see in this chapter, in the modern world there has been a predominance of the linear model when depicting historical time. This is mainly due to the influence of Isaac Newton's *Principia* (1687), and his definition of an absolute, true and mathematical time (in opposition to time as measured in cycles). On the other hand, we find the cyclical model used in visualizations mostly portraying periodic patterns in the data. A recent example is the *New York Times*' interactive graph depicting "How Different Groups Spend Their Day," and examined in the case

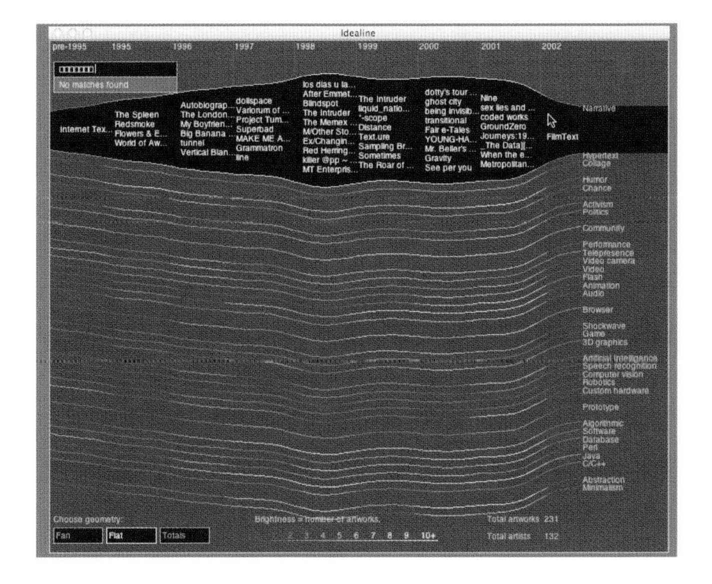

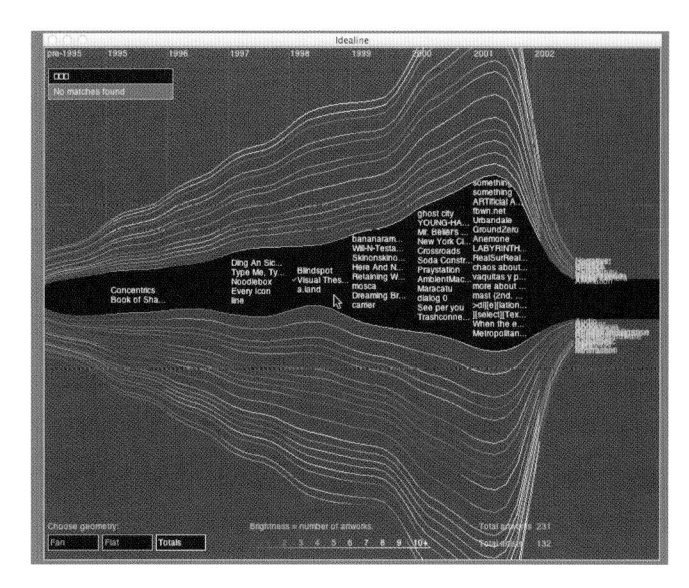

Martin Wattenberg, U.S.: "Idea Line," 2001.

"Idea Line" was the first web commission by the Whitney Museum of American Art. Martin Wattenberg created it in 2001 as a visualization of the history of software and Internet art during the early years of net artworks. Works are arranged in a fanned timeline, in which the dividing luminous lines stand for the amount of works in that yearly period. Connections between works are also highlighted, as invitations for further explorations. Wattenberg explains, "The Idea Line was designed to let you follow these threads of thought yourself, and discover how each work is part of a larger tapestry."[23]

http://whitney.org/Exhibitions/Artport/Commissions/IdeaLine

study section. It is within this functional framework, rather than the philosophical one, that the models will be discussed in the book: when to structure data so as to reveal periodicity, sequence, or a combination of both.

REPRESENTATIONS OF HISTORICAL TIME

Historical time is typically represented with the graphical form of timelines, which are chronological and sequential narratives of relevant historical events. Although ubiquitous nowadays, timelines were not invented until the eighteenth century. Initially, chronologies were represented as lists and tables, and we still see large use of these graphical structures, as one can attest by incursions on the web, or by looking at our own résumés, for example.

Different from lists, where each line stands for an event independent of the temporal interval between them, in timelines, space communicates temporal distances, and negative space becomes a relevant graphical element pregnant with meaning. Units of space may represent uniform or nonuniform temporal intervals. In the first case, all spatial units stand for the same temporal interval, whereas in the latter, spatial and temporal intervals vary.

Timelines tend to facilitate comparison between the temporal and other attributes of events. For example, timelines might reveal meaningful patterns by enhancing the perceptual grasp of events clustered in time, but at different locations, in the world.

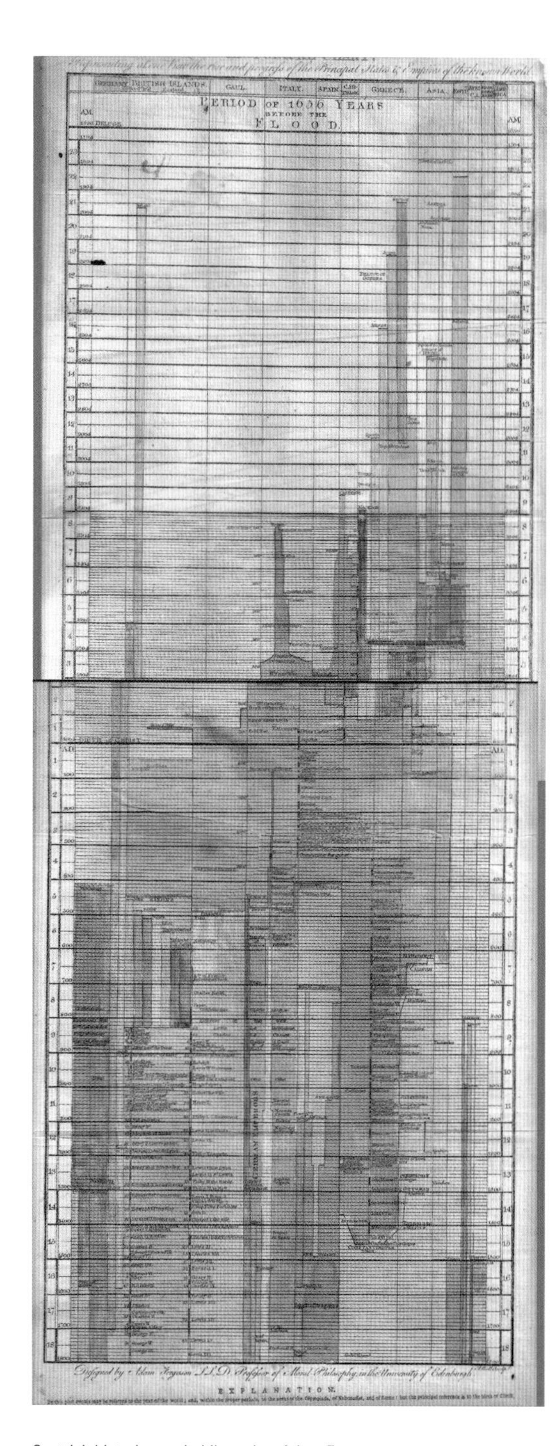

Scottish historian and philosopher Adam Ferguson (1723–1816) created this timeline of historical events to accompany his article titled "History," published in the second edition of the *Britannica Encyclopedia* in 1780. Time is depicted vertically, with the earliest time at the top, 2344 BCE. The timeline focuses on the birth and death of civilizations, that are organized horizontally and color coded to help differentiate between nations.

VERTICAL VERSUS HORIZONTAL AXES

We tend to order items using either a vertical or a horizontal orientation. Tversky explains that our preferences are grounded in perception: "The perceptual world has two dominant axes: a vertical axis defined by gravity and by all the things on earth correlated with gravity; and a horizontal axis defined by the horizon and by all things on earth parallel to it. Vision is especially acute along the vertical and horizontal axes. Memory is poorer for the orientation of oblique lines, and slightly oblique lines are perceived and remembered as more vertical or horizontal than they were."[8]

The vertical orientation has precedence over the horizontal, as we see in the dominance of language expressions associated with up/down orientation. Lakoff and Johnson have shown that we tend to naturally correspond "up" with positive feelings such as good, happy, strong, whereas "down" is identified with bad, sad, weak, and so on.[9] In representations of time, however, the horizontal orientation is prevalent.

In chronological lists, time is ordered vertically, and in all cultures we start at the top of the page. In tables and timelines, we find time ordered either vertically or horizontally. The first graphical timelines that appeared in the mid-eighteenth century depicted time horizontally, with time moving from left to right, as we shall see below. The orientation corresponds to the horizontal preference for depicting time, and the directionality of the authors' European writing systems. Literature in perception and cognition has shown that we tend to use the direction of our writing systems to order events over time. Studies conducted by Tversky and colleagues have shown that "people who wrote from left to right tended to map temporal concepts from left to right and people who wrote from right to left tended to map temporal concepts from right to left. This pattern of findings fits with the claim that neutral concepts such as time tend to be mapped onto the horizontal axis. The fact that the direction of mapping time corresponded to the direction of writing but the direction of mapping preference and quantitative variables did not may be because temporal sequences seem to be incorporated into writing more than quantitative concepts, for example, in schedules, calendars, invitations, and announcements of meetings."[10]

THE BEGINNING OF UNIFORM TIMELINES

In uniform timelines, time is represented following Newton's mathematical notion of an absolute and uniform container of events. The innovation brought first by Jacques Barbeu-Dubourg and then by Joseph Priestley, who added lines to show duration, emphasizes the visual perception of time in a unifying structure provided by the simultaneity of events. Priestley acknowledged the influence of "chronological tables" done by the seventeenth-century scholars Francis Tallents and Christoph Helvig (Helvicus), who depicted

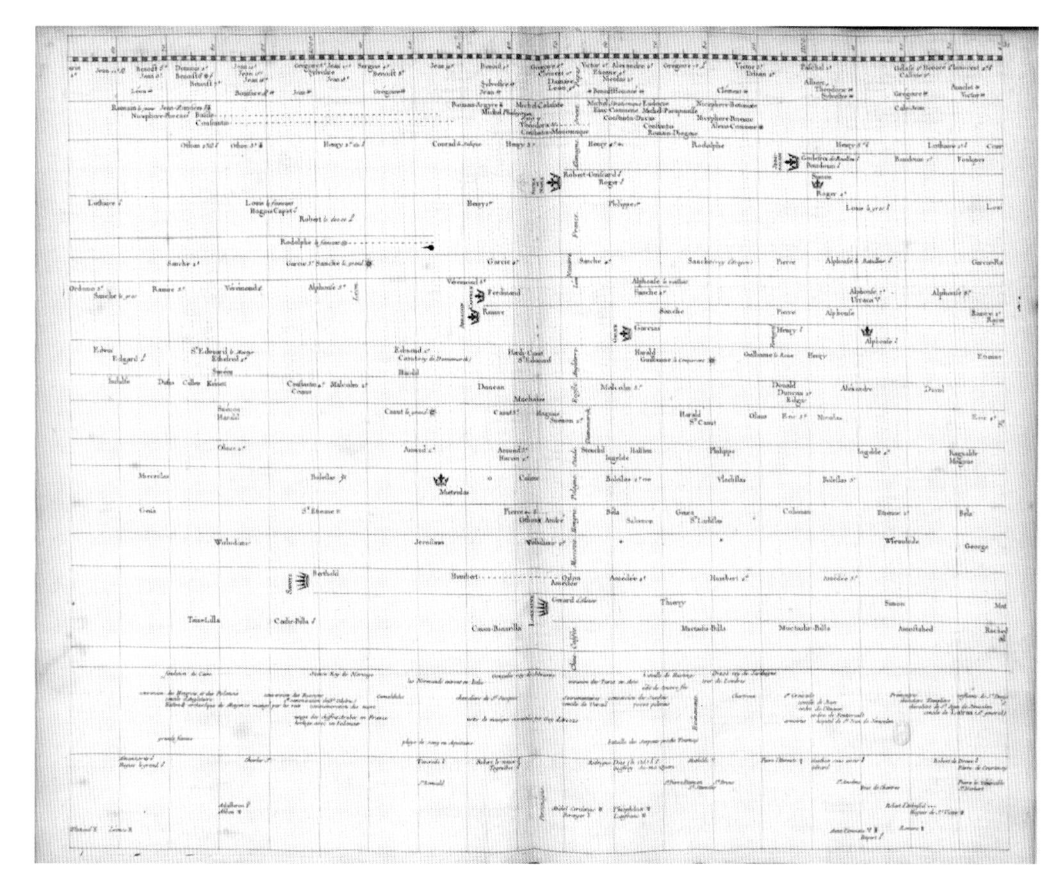

not only dates and events but also information on kingdoms and geography.[11] The tables used a grid with uniform spatial structure, but space did not stand for uniform temporal intervals. Intervals were defined according to meaningful events, such as shifting dates in historical periods.

The use of space to denote the historical temporal dimension, and more specifically temporal intervals, appears in the mid-eighteenth century. In 1753, Jacques Barbeu-Dubourg (1709–1779), French doctor, botanist, and philologist, created a 5.4-foot chart (1.6 m) depicting history from the Creation to his time. The chart is considered the first to have depicted a uniform timescale by dividing space arithmetically. To view sections of this long paper diagram, Barbeu-Dubourg constructed a device with a manual scrolling mechanism. His objective, as described in the accompanying explanatory document, was to use vision to amplify cognition, in that by looking at his chart, one would not need to use one's memory; rather, it would suffice to scroll the chart to the desired point in time. By mapping time uniformly, the chronography (graph of chronological time) enabled easy comparison of temporal intervals.[12]

The "*Chronographie Universelle*" by Frenchman Jacques Barbeu-Dubourg (1709–1779) was published in 1753. In this 5.4-foot (1.6 m) paper roll, Barbeu-Dubourg depicts the main events for each century starting at the time of Creation, a total of 6,480 years. This timeline is considered the first to have used a uniform timescale to represent historical events, with each year represented by 0.1 inch (2.5 mm). Barbeu-Dubourg constructed a device to facilitate viewing the long diagram, as depicted in the diagram above. Names and events are positioned horizontally according to when they occurred in time and grouped vertically either by country or under the general category of "*évènments mémorables.*" Barbeu-Dubourg understood history as having two ancillary fields, geography and chronology, as Wainer explains: "By wedding the methods of geography to the data of chronology he could make the latter as accessible as the former. Barbeu-Dubourg's name for his invention, chronographie, tells a great deal about what he intended, derived as it is from *chronos* (time) and *graphein* (to write). Barbeu-Dubourg intended to provide the means for chronology to be a science that, like geography, speaks to the eyes and the imagination."[24]

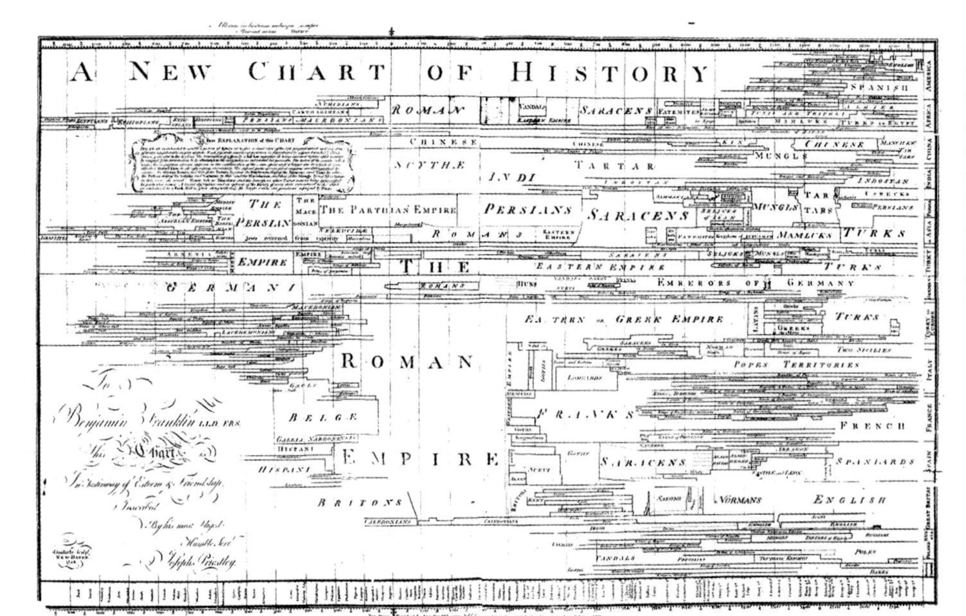

"A New Chart of History" by Joseph Priestley was published in 1769. Designed for a general public and with a pedagogical purpose, some versions of the graph add color codes to the previous conventions devised by Priestley to depict historical events over time. The colors visually enhance the perception of empires that crossed different geographical boundaries—in this graph, depicted horizontally.

PRIESTLEY'S TIMELINES OF HISTORICAL DATA

Joseph Priestley (1733–1804), British theologian, scientist, and philosopher, published in 1765 the first of a series of timelines, the "Chart of Biography." Similar to Barbeu-Dubourg, Priestley represented time linearly using equal intervals throughout the chart. Among Priestley's innovations is the use of lines to represent duration: line lengths stand for the duration of depicted lives, thus resulting in a chart of lifelines. In the accompanying essay, "A Description of a Chart of Biography," Priestley asserts that we make use of spatial expressions such as "short" and "long" to describe periods of time, expressions that naturally fit into the visual representation of lines and intuitively describe quantities as measurable distances. He points to the cognitive advantages of his linear representation of time: "It follows from these considerations that to express intervals of time by lines facilitates an operation which the minds of all men have recourse to, in order to get a just and clear idea of them; and that the view of a number of lines, drawn exactly in proportion to a number of intervals of time to which they correspond, will present to the mind of any person a more just and distinct idea of the relative lengths of the times they represent than he could have formed to himself without that assistance."[13]

The "Chart of Biography" is 3 X 2 feet (90 X 60 cm) and depicts a period between 1200 BCE and Priestley's own time in the eighteenth century, covering around 3,000 years and the lives of 2,000 famed persons. The names are organized into six themes, divided by lines and ordered from top to bottom as follows:

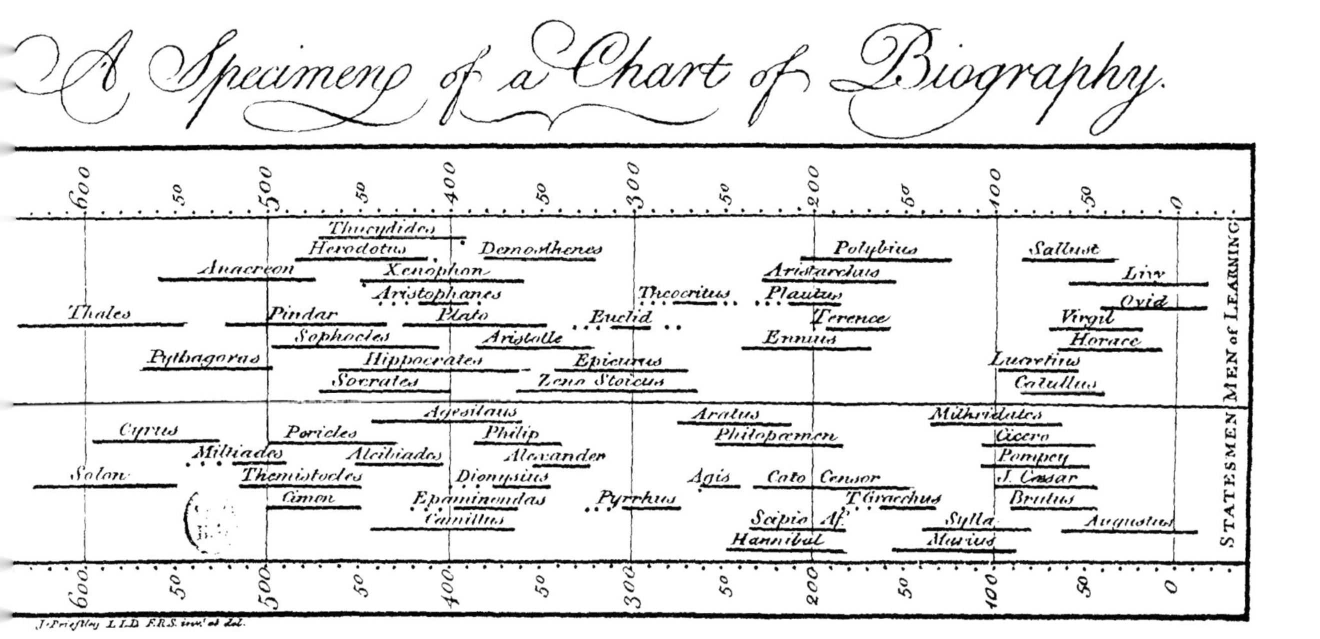

This diagram is a sample of the "Chart of Biography" created by Joseph Priestley and published in 1765. Note the conventions devised by Priestley to depict uncertainty in the lives of famed persons, with dots placed at the beginning or the end of lifelines.

Historians, Antiquaries, and Lawyers; Orators and Critics; Artists and Poets; Mathematicians and Physicians; Divines and Metaphysicians; Statesmen and Warriors. The criterion for the order was that of relevance, with the Statesmen as the most important group placed at the bottom for easy access. To facilitate comparisons, Priestley located the lifelines of persons with connections near each other, the same for people for whom he considered closeness to be advantageous: "Almost any number of lives may be compared with the same ease, to the same perfection, and in the same short space of time."[14]

Priestley acknowledged that not all dates had the same level of accuracy, for which he devised a graphical system to differentiate uncertainties: lives with known dates for birth and death were depicted with solid lines, and uncertain dates were represented with dots. Dates known to be "about" a certain time were depicted by a dot below the line. Lines starting or ending with dots represented uncertainty of dates for birth or death, respectively. Finally, for the case when nothing was known, Priestley drew a dashed line where he believed to be the most probable date.[15] The only verbal notations were the written names placed above the lines.

Another graphical element used by Priestley was a solid line under a lifeline to depict the period when an author was considered to have flourished: "When it is said that a writer flourished at or about a particular time, a short full line is drawn about two thirds before and one third after that particular time, with three dots before and two after it; because, in general, men are said to flourish much nearer the time of their death than the time of their birth."[16]

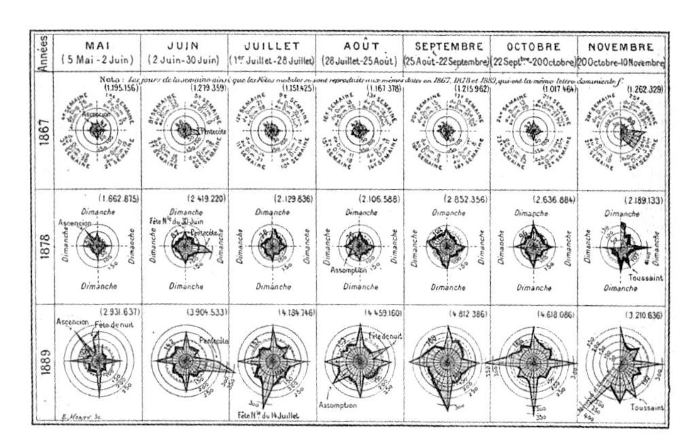

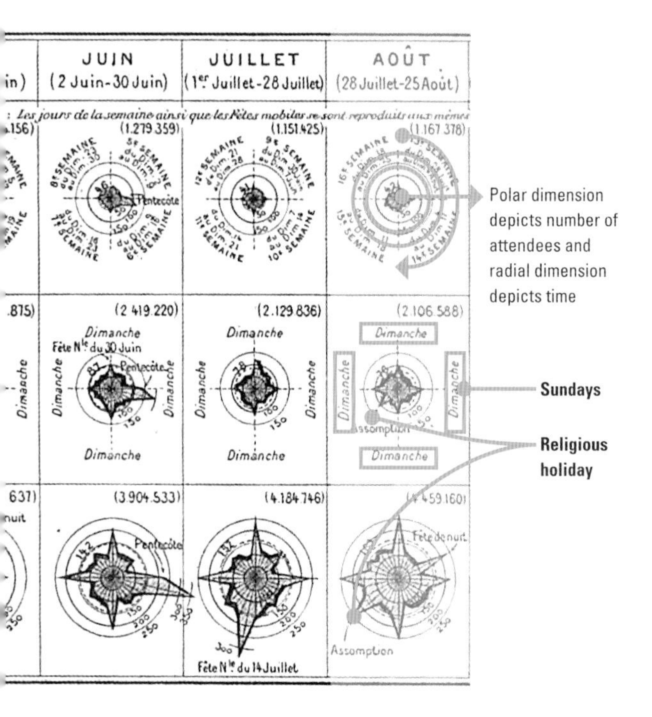

The diagram "Statistics of the Universal Exhibitions in Paris" by Émile Cheysson was compiled soon after the 1889 exhibition and compares its attendance to the previous two events in Paris in 1867 and 1878 (vertical axis) by depicting statistics month by month (horizontal axis). To facilitate comparison across the years, the position of Sundays and other holidays are kept in the same location in all graphs, also highlighted with additional notes.

Priestley originally drew the "Chart of Biography" as a visual device to facilitate understanding of his "Lecture upon the Study of History," during which he presented it for the first time. Later, Priestley decided to print the chart to provide his students with the pedagogical material.[17] Both the "Chart of Biography" (1765) and "A New Chart of History" (1769) were devised for the general public as reference aids of historical context and were used with this purpose by teachers for several decades (both went through more than twenty editions). Priestly used the same timescale and graphical encoding in the two charts to enable the reader to move between them: they cover the same historic period, beginning and ending at the same dates, and they depict the same statesmen.[18]

The charts, however, are too big in dimensions and, consequently, they are hard to reproduce, or even to look at the whole at once. But, sectioning the charts obliterates their significance, because the purpose is to provide historic context to the topics depicted. The charts make sense only when viewed as a whole: It is the broad view that communicates the historic content and context. This is a paradox that anyone attempting to create timelines faces, especially when using uniform timescales.

Rosenberg writes about Priestley's influence during and after his time: "As aids to the study of history, Priestley's charts were recommended by numerous pedagogical manuals of the day. As models for the graphic presentation of data, they exerted a deep influence: They were, in fact, the only precedent recognized by William Playfair, the central figure in the early development of statistical graphics. Perhaps the most important interpretation of Priestley's timelines occurs in Playfair's *Commercial and Political Atlas* of 1786 and his *Inquiry into the Permanent Causes of the Decline and Fall of Powerful and Wealthy Nations* of 1805. In these works, Playfair explicitly juxtaposes historical timelines of the sort pioneered by Priestley with the line graphs that had, by then, become Playfair's own stock and trade."[19]

EARLY TEMPORAL STRUCTURES IN OTHER DISCIPLINES

William Playfair (1759–1823) created several line graphs to represent economic data as a function of time, which were first published in his *Commercial and Political Atlas* in 1786. It is interesting to note that out of the forty-four charts published in this volume, only one chart was not a line graph. Due to a lack of temporal data for the exports and imports of Scotland, Playfair saw the need to devise a graphical representation in which time was not one of the dimensions, and the innovation resulted in the first known bar chart. Initially, Playfair considered it a less effective representation,

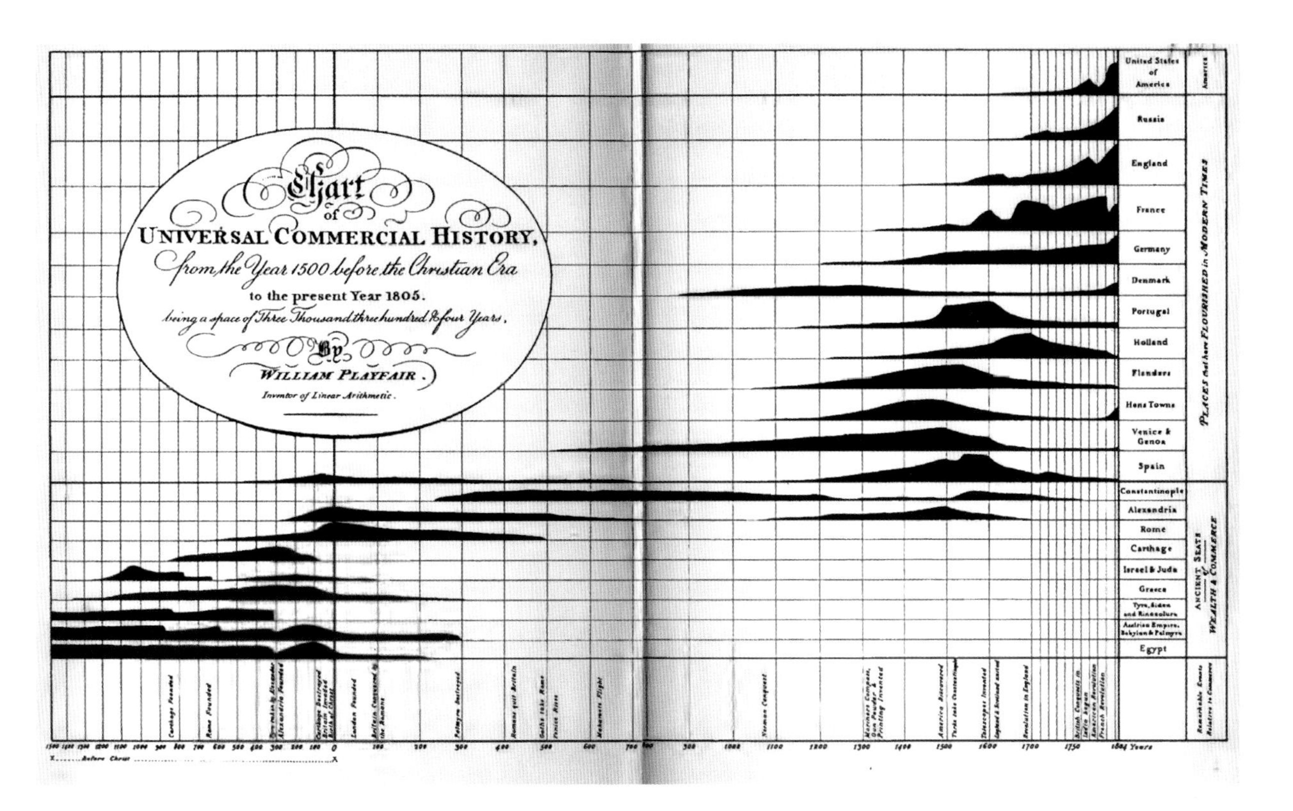

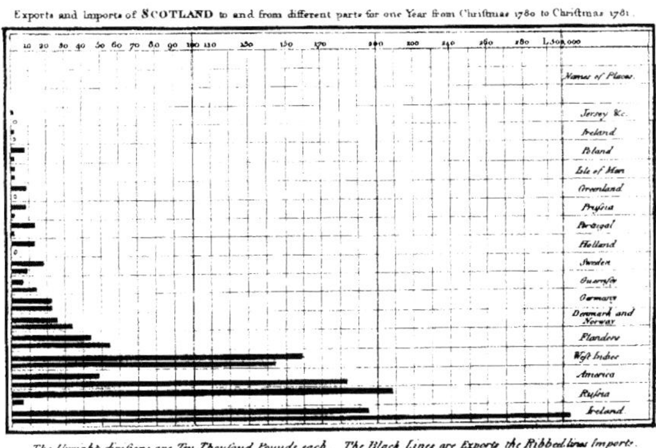

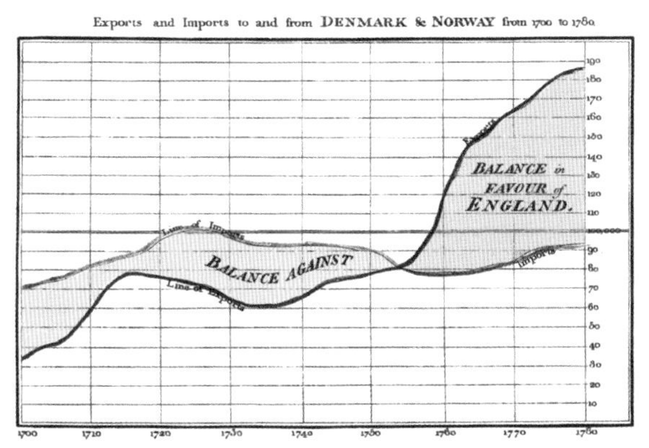

The first known bar graph was designed by William Playfair and published in his *The Commercial and Political Atlas*. It depicts the Exports and Imports of Scotland to and from different parts for one year, from Christmas 1780 to Christmas 1781. Different from all other graphical representations in the book, this was the only bar graph, because Playfair had to be inventive in the face of the lack of temporal data. At first, he thought the bar graph was "much inferior in utility" than the timelines, a position he changed in later editions of the atlas.[25] The other two graphs show data depicted over time: Exports and Imports to and from Denmark and Norway from 1700 to 1780 (bottom), and Universal Commercial History from 1500 BCE to 1805 (top). The latter was influenced by Priestley's timelines, and it depicts the rise and fall of nations over 3,000 years. It is interesting to note the change in the temporal scale. Wainer and Spence explain that Playfair's graphs "were remarkably similar to those in use today; hachure, shading, color coding, and grids with major and minor divisions were all introduced in the various editions of the Atlas. Actual, missing, and hypothetical data were portrayed, and the kind of line used, solid or broken, differentiated the various forms. Playfair filled the areas between curves in most of the charts to indicate accumulated or total amounts. All included a descriptive title either outside the frame or in an oval in the body of the chart. The axes were labeled and numbered where the major gridlines intersected the frame."[26]

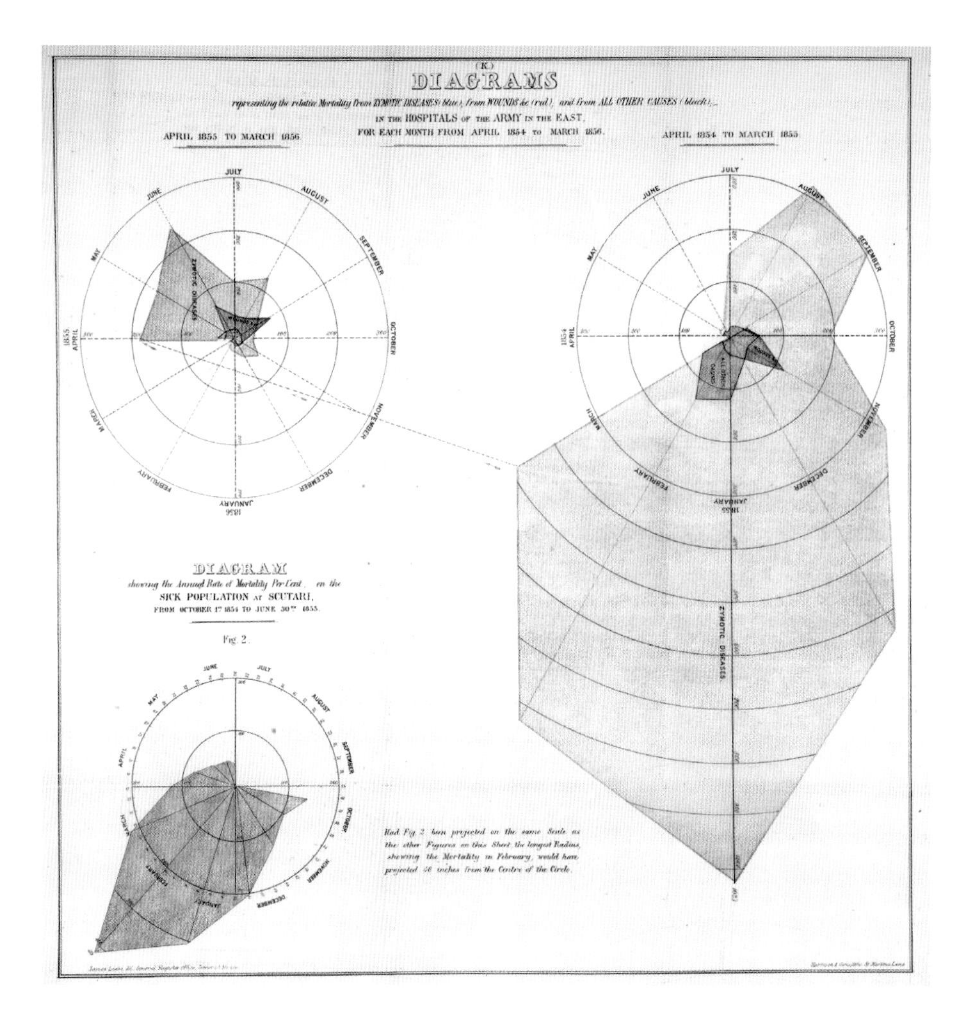

The British nurse, Florence Nightingale, published in 1858 the "Diagrams Representing the Relative Mortality from Zymotic Diseases (blue), from Wounds &c. (red), and from All Other Causes (black), in the Hospitals of the Army in the East, for Each Month from April 1854 to March 1856" with the intent to promote better sanitation and administration in civilian and military hospitals. Later, Nightingale changed the technique to "coxcomb" graphs reproduced on the right.

as he writes in the first edition of the atlas: "The chart ... does not comprehend any portion of time, and it is much inferior in utility to those that do."[20] The pie chart, another graphical invention by Playfair, was described in chapter 1 (page 36).

The British nurse Florence Nightingale used a cyclic model of time to represent medical data. Published in 1858, the "Diagram of the Causes of Mortality in the Army in the East" depicts the causes of death by plotting mortality data using a polar graph, also known as "rose charts." Unlike pie charts, in rose charts all wedges have the same angle, and each stands for a time period. The circumference is divided into twelve wedges, each standing for a month of the year. The quantitative data are represented in the polar axis, and depicted by the length of each radius, not the area, as expected. Despite that the graph presents two-dimensional elements (the wedges), the amounts are depicted linearly, which is disguising at first, especially considering that the graph does not provide a measuring scale.

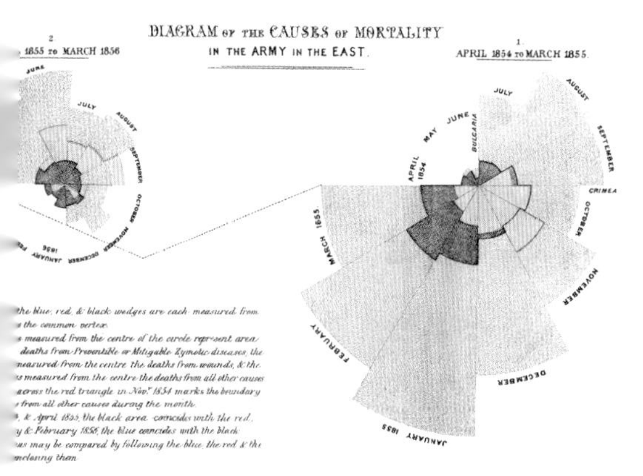

This "Diagram of the Causes of Mortality in the Army in the East" was devised by the British nurse Florence Nightingale and published in 1858. It is a polar graph, not a pie chart, such that the radius of each wedge depicts the number of deaths for each month. Color stands for the types of death causes: preventable diseases are in blue, war wounds in red, and fatalities in black.

Although Nightingale didn't invent rose charts, her graph became a landmark in medicine because it was instrumental in persuading the British government of the need for better health care systems. The graph efficiently demonstrates that the majority of deaths were not the result of accidents of war; rather, they were caused by preventable factors, such as lack of hygiene and infectious diseases. According to Friendly, the method was devised by Guerry, who published in 1829 the first known rose diagram "to show seasonal and daily variation in wind direction over the year and births and deaths by hour of the day."[21]

Other early examples of graphical representations portraying temporal data are medical reports, such as fever curves in the nineteenth century. Time schedules and productivity diagrams became common graphical devices in the second half of the nineteenth century with advances in industrialization. Page 8 shows an early example of the Paris–Lyon train schedule designed by Etienne-Jules Marey in 1885.

GRAPHICAL CONVENTIONS

Most of the graphical inventions discussed previously, such as timelines and line graphs, are remarkably similar to their contemporary counterparts, as we see in the visualizations in this chapter. It is worth noting the graphical conventions devised by Priestley, which continue unchanged to this day when we create timelines. Priestley's graphical system comprises the following main graphical elements:

- **Timescale:** Timescale is uniform and represented arithmetically, following Newton's notion of absolute time.
- **Time indicators:** Dates are inscribed at the top and at the bottom, and connected by lines to facilitate perception of the temporal divisions. In Priestley's timelines, the grid is that of a century, with decades marked with dots.
- **Thematic sections:** Horizontal thematic sections are separated by lines. In the "Chart of Biography," the divisions are thematic (Statesmen, Artists, etc.), and in "A New Chart of History," the divisions are geographic.
- **Line indicators:** Line lengths are used to depict duration. In Priestley's timelines, they stand for lifelines.
- **Line differentiators:** Levels of uncertainty in the data are graphically depicted by the quality of lines (solid or broken lines), and with the addition of dots.
- **Color code:** Color was added to "A New Chart of History" to encode the empires that are noncontiguous spatially.

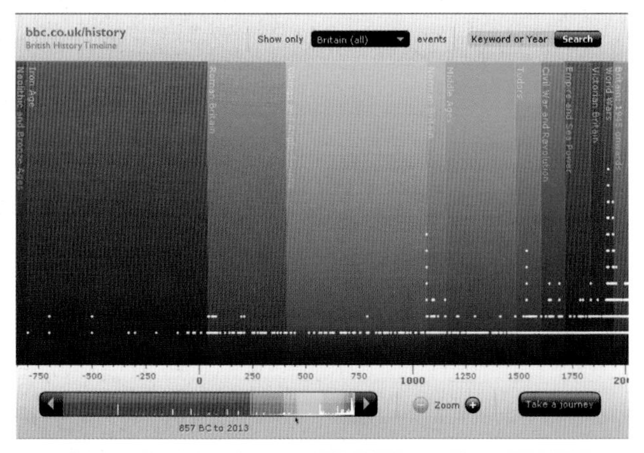

The online *British History Timeline* by the BBC provides a great pedagogical tool to learn about events taking place in the United Kingdom from the Neolithic era to the present day. It allows visitors to explore historical events that can be filtered by regions of the United Kingdom as well as by date. Detailed information on events appears connected when they have developed over time. It was designed and built by AllofUs and conceived by the BBC History website team.

www.bbc.co.uk/history/interactive/timelines/british/index_embed.shtml

Most of the graphical conventions devised by Playfair for his several graphical inventions, including the pie chart, the bar graph, and the line and area graphs, are also preserved in current visualizations without many changes.

NONUNIFORM TIMESCALES

Timescales facilitate comparison over time, including our understanding of events diachronically. However, not all data are suited for depictions using a uniform timescale. The early timelines examined are good examples of how uneven the densities across the diagrams are, especially when depicting large spans of time. It is not uncommon that the most recent periods in history tend to have more information, whereas older times are almost devoid of events. As such, some representations benefit from the use of nonlinear timescales. For example, when using a logarithmic scale, the wider regions in the timeline can be used for depicting the periods with denser data.

Among the most innovative possibilities opened up by computerized interactivity is the ability to scale time, in other words, the ability to zoom in and out in time in similar ways to how we zoom in space. Take for example, the online tool BBC *British History Timeline*, which uses a uniform timescale but enables the viewer to delve into the data and learn about events synchronically.

TIMELINES IN THE DIGITAL ENVIRONMENT

Similar to their printed ancestors, digital timelines enable navigation through time by means of sliding back and forth along the linear structure, not much different from how one moved the timeline in Barbeu-Dubourg's mechanical device.

The inclusion of other contexts, which Priestley initiated by adding historical context to his charts, has been expanded in the digital realm with associating diverse datasets toward new insights. Nontemporal categories (e.g., geographical, philosophical, etc) are often mapped in the opposite axis and layered to allow easy comparison within the ordered temporal dimension.

There are other enhancements to timelines brought forward by computerized interactivity, such as the ability to filter data according to specified thresholds, to delve into content, and to zoom in and out of time, as mentioned earlier.

Magical Number Seven

George A. Miller published in 1956 the seminal article "The Magical Number Seven, Plus or Minus Two," where he examines our limited capacity for receiving, processing, and remembering information. The article introduces three areas that, despite showing similar span capacities, should not be considered uniformly, because each involves different cognitive processes:

1. Our span of absolute judgment can distinguish about seven categories.
2. Our span of attention encompasses six objects at a glance.
3. Our span of working memory is about seven items in length.

Miller distinguishes between absolute judgment and immediate memory, in that the first is limited by the amount of information, while the latter is limited by the number of items, independent of the amount of bits. He continues, "In order to capture this distinction in somewhat picturesque terms, I have fallen into the custom of distinguishing between bits of information and chunks of information. Then I can say that the number of bits of information is constant for absolute judgment and the number of chunks of information is constant for immediate memory. The span of immediate memory seems to be almost independent of the number of bits per chunk, at least over the range that has been examined to date."[27]

Miller stresses the importance of grouping the input into meaningful units as a mechanism to increase our capacities for memory. Some strategies of grouping are discussed throughout the book in the boxes dedicated to the Gestalt principles. Another powerful strategy discussed by Miller, and borrowed from communication theory, is recoding, or devising a code to the input to contain fewer chunks with more bits per chunk. To illustrate the point, he shows how we could increase the amount of information by recoding a sequence of eighteen binary digits:

Binary Digits (Bits)		1 0 1 0 0 0 1 0 0 1 1 1 0 0 1 1 1 0
2:1	Chunks	10 10 00 10 01 11 00 11 10
	Recoding	2 2 0 2 1 3 0 3 2
3:1	Chunks	101 000 100 111 001 110
	Recoding	5 0 4 7 1 6
4:1	Chunks	1010 0010 0111 0011 10
	Recoding	10 2 7 1
5:1	Chunks	10100 01001 11001 110
	Recoding	20 9 25

When encoding data, we should consider our small capacity for making unidimensional judgments, despite that our capacity increases with the number of dimensions, but not by a large amount. For example, Miller shows that our capacity for judging the position of a dot in a square is 4.6 bits, which is larger than the 3.25 bits for the position of a point in an interval.[28] Although our total capacity increases with the combination of dimensions, our accuracy for a particular variable decreases. He concludes, "People are less accurate if they must judge more than one attribute simultaneously."[29]

Furthermore, Miller suggests three basic devices we can use to increase the accuracy of our judgments and the limits of our span:[30]

1. To make relative rather than absolute judgments;
2. Or, if that is not possible, to increase the number of dimensions along which the stimuli can differ;
3. Or to arrange the task in such a way that we make a sequence of several absolute judgments in a row (which introduces mnemonic processes).

Considering that we have limited capacity to perceive information accurately, his results are crucial to the process of visualizing data. First, visualizations should rely mostly on relative judgment rather than on absolute ones. The latter can be provided as additional information, especially in interactive applications. A number of experiments have been conducted to examine our relative judgments of visual variables, and a summary is presented on page 129 discussing two fundamental laws: Weber's and Steven's. Second, we should be careful not to exceed our own perceptual and cognitive limits by presenting more than seven levels of data at once.

When more than seven levels are needed, we should strive to group information into familiar units to expand our limited working memory capacity. For example, the design and use of glyphs depicting integrated variables can extend our visual working memory capacity. However, we need to pay attention not to incur mismatches, as illustrated by the Stroop effect image below.[31]

RED GREEN YELLOW BLUE BLACK GREEN PURPLE BLUE BLACK
ORANGE GREEN RED GREEN YELLOW BLUE BLACK GREEN PURPLE

GREEN RED BLUE YELLOW PURPLE RED BLACK GREEN BLUE
BLACK ORANGE GREEN RED GREEN YELLOW BLUE BLACK GREEN

CASE STUDY

REPRESENTING EVENTS OVER TIME

As we saw in the introduction to this chapter, the most common use of temporal structures is found in representations of historical events. Timelines might have a uniform and a nonuniform scale, as well as be organized horizontally or vertically. Another common metaphor used throughout history is the branching tree, presented extensively in the first chapter on Hierarchies. Similar to the linear vectorized structure of timelines, tree-structures organize time in one direction, mostly spacing elements nonuniformly, while emphasizing notions of progress and causality. The examples in this section focus on visualizations imparting a sense of narrative to the diagrammatic representation of events over time. Although the selected visualizations are static, the sense of immersion is emphasized by the expressive visual vocabulary contextualizing the events depicted.

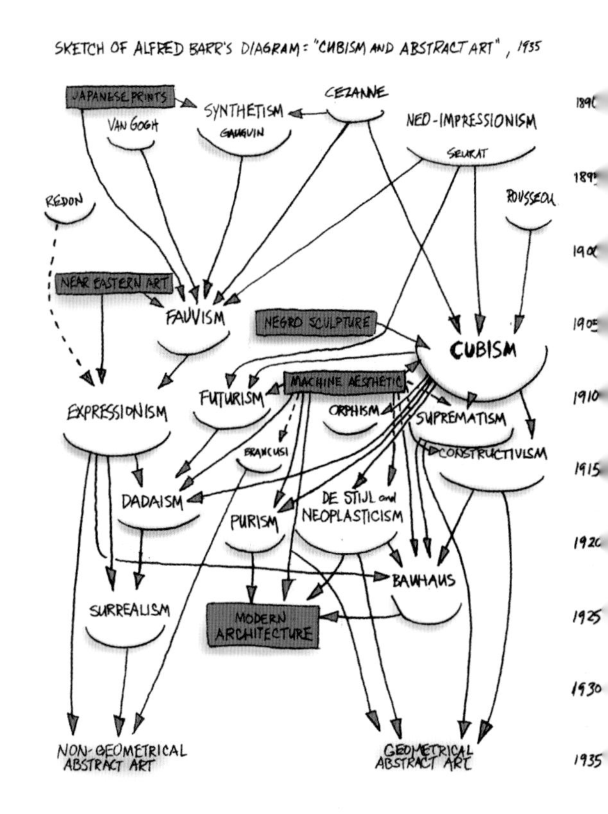

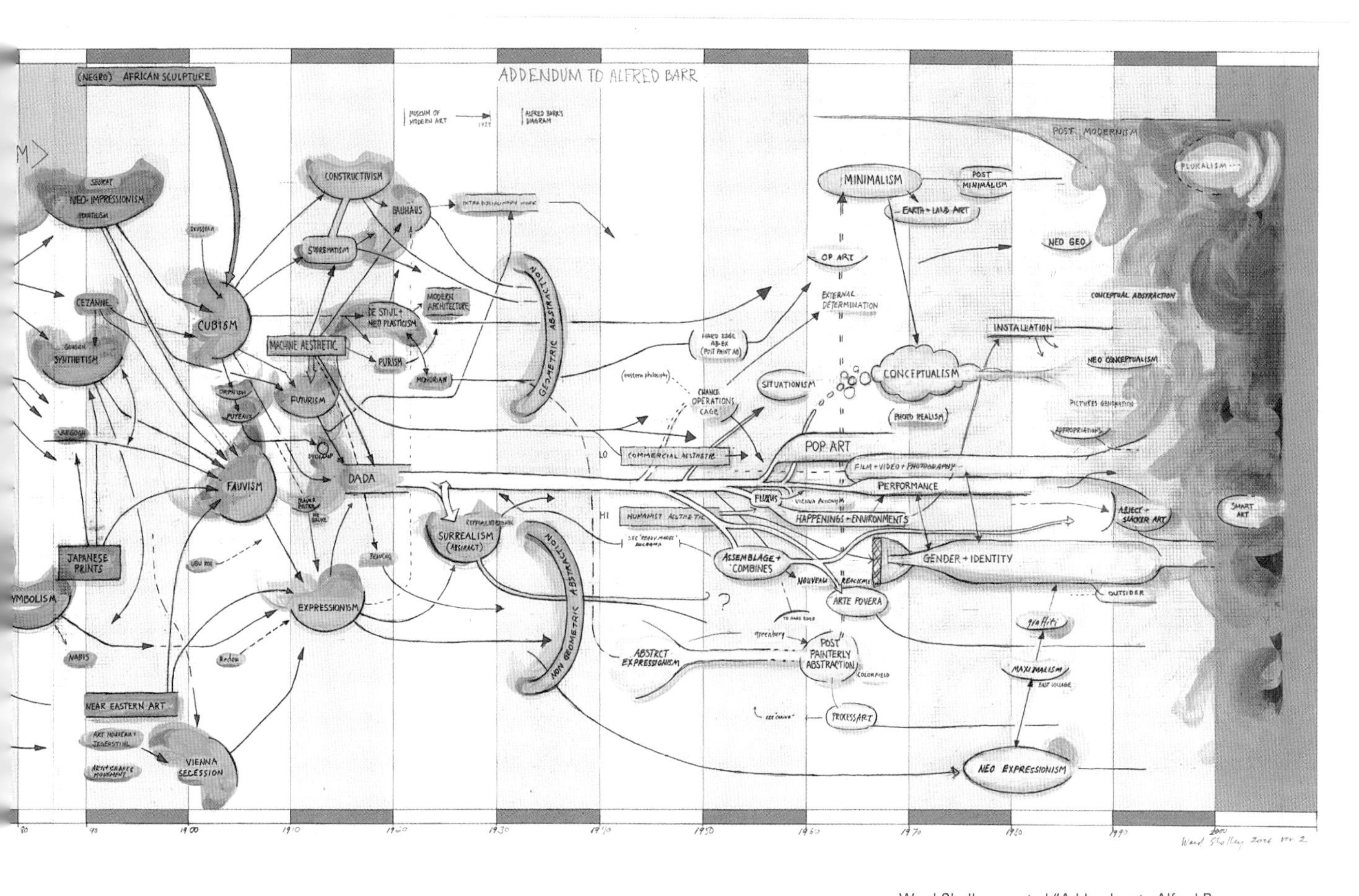

Alfred Barr, the first director of the Museum of Modern Art in New York City, drew this "Diagram of Stylistic Evolution from 1890 until 1935" to explain the origins of abstract art. We see it here in a sketch by artist Ward Shelley, who was largely influenced by how Barr sets forth his diagrammatic narrative.

Ward Shelley created "Addendum to Alfred Barr, ver. 2" in 2007, which extends Barr's original diagram, positioning it at the center and depicting both past and future events around it. The chart starts with the Enlightenment and the rivalry between painters Peter Paul Rubens and Nicolas Poussin, and ends in 2000. The diagram keeps the original diagrammatic vocabulary of using arrows to show direction of influence. The three colors stand for separating the three components of the graph and separating before and after the original Barr diagram. Time is well demarcated on the top and bottom of the work, which is reinforced by the gray bands.

In describing this work, Shelley writes, "I like to present narratives with sprawling information-rich panoramas. Yet these diagrams are radical reductions of written sources I've researched. I have had to choose who and what to include, who and what not. Because the variables that I have to work with are extremely limited, the people and events I use are reduced to symbols that are plotted in relationship to each other in diagrams. Even within such limitations, it is possible to tell a compelling story."[32]

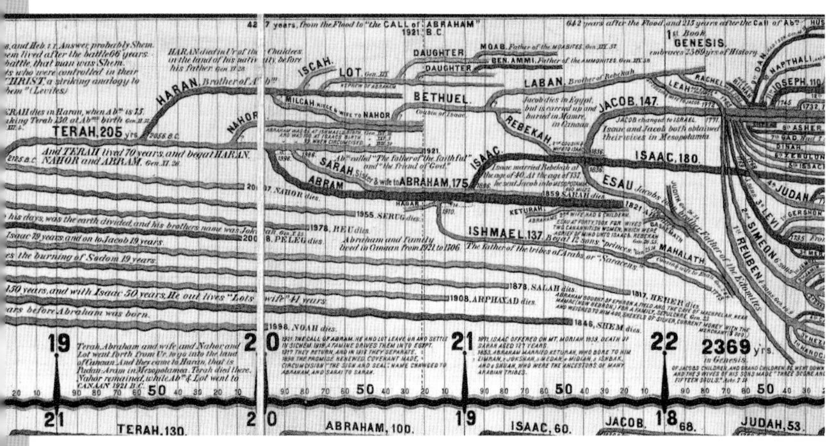

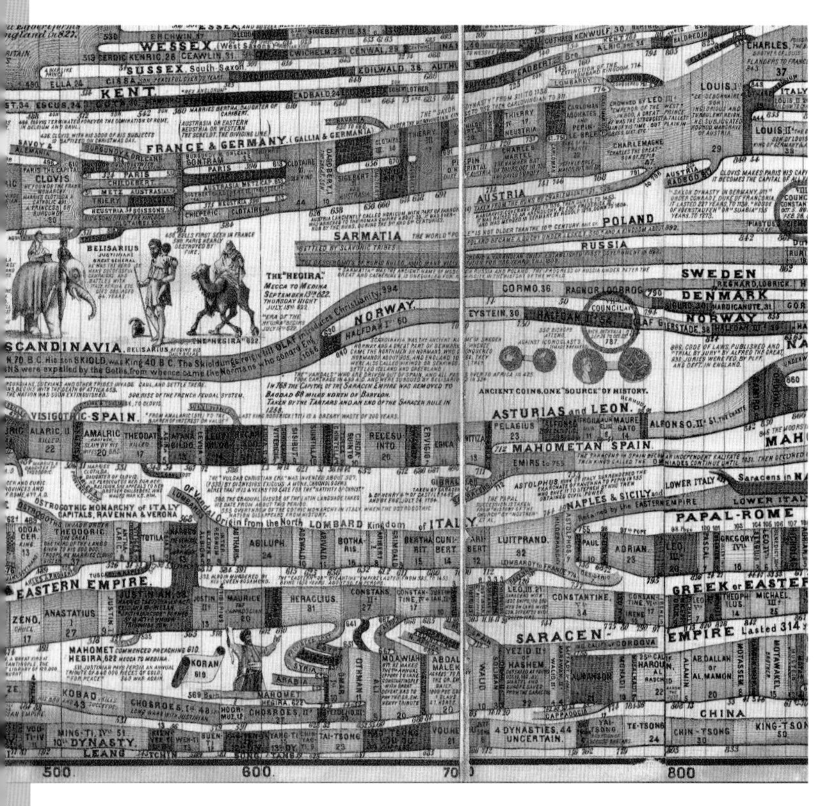

Sebastian C. Adams was an educator and a senator for Oregon who designed and first published the "Synchronological Chart of Universal History" in 1871. The timeline is monumental in scope, covering almost six millennia, as well as in size, measuring 27 inches in height by 260 inches in length (68.6 X 660.4 cm), and folded into twenty-one full-color panels. Adams based his research on *The Annals of the World* by James Ussher. Adams saw the chart as an educational tool for studying the places and times of religious and historical events. At the very beginning of the timeline it reads: "The object of this CHART is to assist the mind in clearly fixing, along down the stream of time, the time when the events of the world took place. The *time when* (i.e., Chronology) and the *place where* (i.e., Geography) 'are the two great eyes of history'"[35] (emphases in the original). It's interesting to note that Adams names the key to the chart an "Explanation of the Map," which provides detailed description of how the chart was constructed, including notes on the content. Time runs horizontally, with the earliest time at the far left. Time is uniformly depicted, starting at 4004 BCE, and ending at 1878 CE. Every century is clearly demarcated by century pillars and further subdivided into decades. Nations and kingdoms run parallel to time, with all sorts of annotations and illustrations. The images reproduced here are from the third edition of 1878, printed in the United States by Strobridge & Co., lithographers of Cincinnati, Ohio.

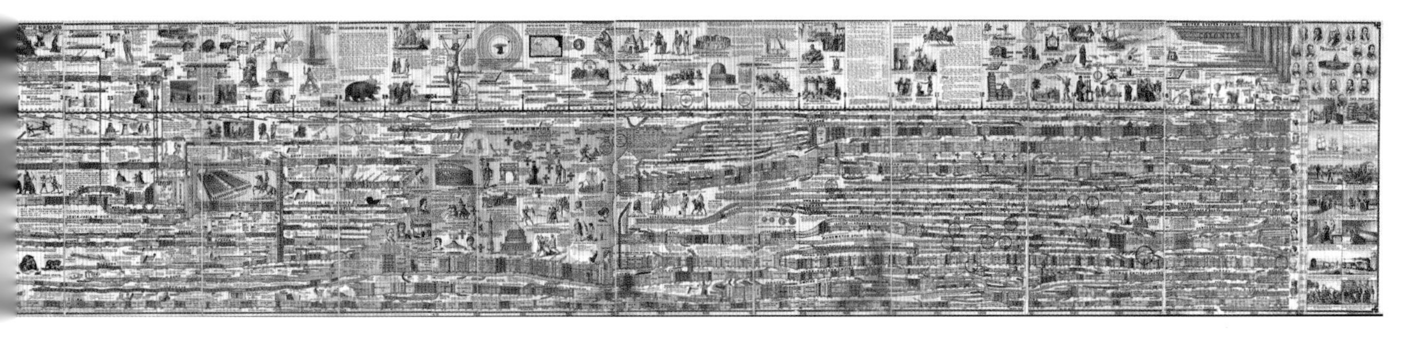

In the fascinating book *Maciunas' Learning Machines*, Schmidt-Burkhardt imparts the traditions of diagramming events over time, with a focus on the large work on charts and diagrams by Fluxus initiator George Maciunas. She goes on to write, "This work by Shelley presents data in such a way as to render explicit the continuity, coherence, and contingency of the history of Fluxus for a contemporary audience."[33] *The Extra Large Fluxus Diagram* illustrates the people and work involved with the experimental art movement Fluxus and pays homage to Maciunas. Shelley's diagram traces the Fluxus movement from its beginnings, with John Cage's 1956–58 composition classes at the New School and Karlheinz Stockhausen's seminars in Darmstadt, up to the death of Maciunas in 1978. Shelley writes about his practice, "My paintings/drawings are attempts to use real information to depict our understandings of how things evolve and relate to one another, and how this develops over time. More to the point, they are about how we form these understandings in our minds and if they can have, in our culture, some kind of shape."[34]

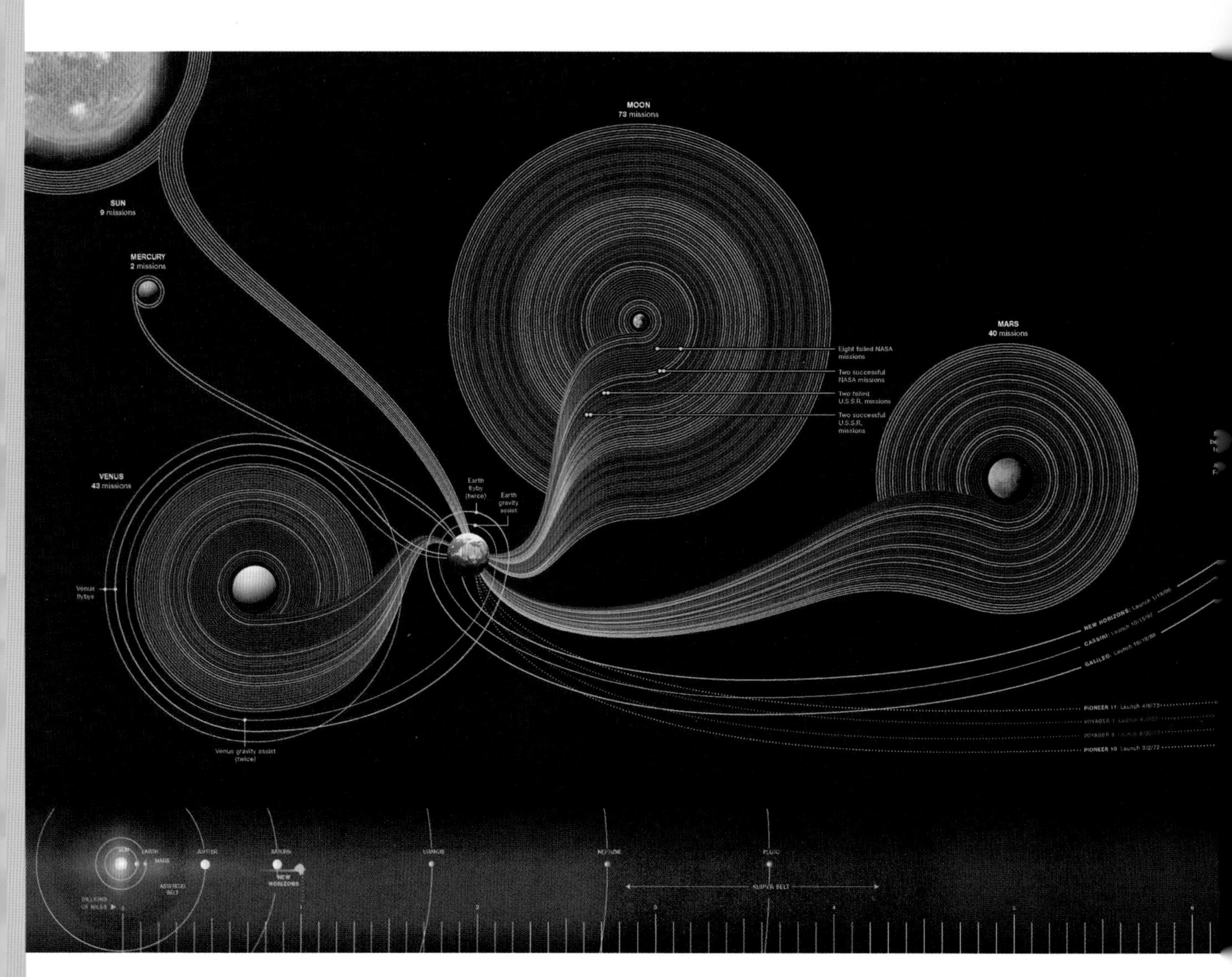

Sean McNaughton (*National Geographic* magazine) and Samuel Velasco (5W Infographics), U.S.: "Fifty Years of Space Exploration," 2010.

This magnificent infographic depicts exactly what the name indicates, "Fifty Years of Space Exploration." It shows nearly 200 solar, lunar, and interplanetary missions, starting with the first attempts to reach Mars in 1960 and Venus in 1961, up to our time. It includes ongoing missions, such as the *New Horizon* scheduled to enter in Pluto's orbit in 2015. Structured as a map, we learn about temporal events based on their spatial trajectories, and the paths that accumulate around their objects of interest. Take, for example, the large number of missions to the Moon, in total seventy-three. We learn about past and future interest in different planets, such as the new *MESSENGER* mission to Mercury. At the bottom of the graph, there is a line depicting the relative distances between the planets.

http://books.nationalgeographic.com/map/map-day/index

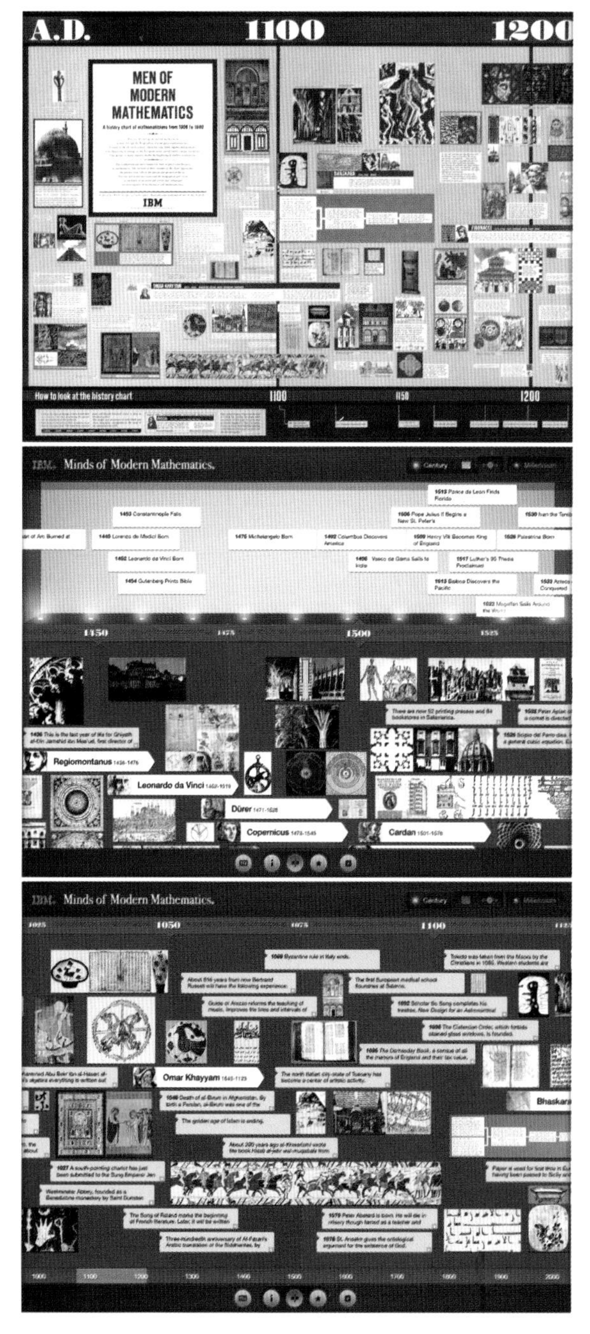

Original design by Charles and Ray Eames, U.S.:
iPad app "Minds of Modern Mathematics," 2012.

IBM has recently released an iPad version of the celebrated 50-foot (15 m) infographic on the history of math created by the husband-and-wife design team of Charles and Ray Eames. The timeline covers the period between 1000 and 1960, and it was part of the exhibition "Mathematica: A World of Numbers ... and Beyond" displayed at the IBM pavilion at the 1964 World's Fair in New York City. The app *Minds of Modern Mathematics* offers access to "more than 500 biographies, milestones and images of artifacts culled from the Mathematica exhibit, as well as a high-resolution image of the original timeline poster."[36] It is interesting to note the differences of affordances between the static long poster and the interactive timeline. The latter follows the original design, with additional functionality that facilitates reading the extensive material printed in the initial design.

https://itunes.apple.com/us/app/minds-of-modern-mathematics/id432359402?mt=8

CASE STUDY

REPRESENTING AMOUNT OVER TIME

It took several decades before the graphic methods devised by William Playfair at the end of the eighteenth century became widely known. Wainer and Spence explain the oppositions his inventions encountered in his own time both in the U.K. and in continental Europe: "Adoption of the new methods had to wait until the second half of the nineteenth century when Minard and Bertillon used some of Playfair's inventions in their cartographical work. In the United Kingdom, Playfair was almost completely forgotten until 1861, when William Stanley Jevons enthusiastically adopted Playfair's methods in his own economic atlas."[37] Nowadays, bar graphs, line graphs, pie charts, and area graphs are ubiquitous. We find them everywhere, from newspaper articles to textbooks, and depicting all sorts of content, from economic to entertainment data. More important, most people are familiar with these statistical schemes and know how to read them. As in other areas covered in this book, new methods have been devised for plotting quantitative data over time. The case study examines recent examples that have reached the general public beyond the confines of visualization research.

Fernanda Viégas and Martin Wattenberg, U.S.:"History Flow," 2003.

History Flow is a visualization made by Martin Wattenberg and Fernanda Viégas in 2003 with the objective of examining the human dynamics behind group editing. It depicts how articles were written and edited by several authors in the collaborative environment of Wikipedia, just two years after its deployment online. When we read articles on Wikipedia, we are mostly unaware of the history behind the article's complex "manufacturing" process. This can be accessed through the link "history" at the bottom of each page, which provides a list of links to the full edit text of all previous versions, including the authors, as well as timestamps of their interventions, the data used in this project. For the text analysis, Viégas and Wattenberg used an algorithm by Paul Heckel that enabled them to track the movement of large passages of text, while also offering the possibility of keeping track of word-size tokens. Then came the encoding process aimed at visually documenting positions and correspondences between passages that had changed. After several iterations that are explained in detail in *Beautiful History: Visualizing Wikipedia* they arrived at the visualization reproduced here.[38]

Time runs horizontally, with earlier time at the far left. It is measured by editions rather than by normal temporal units, even though it can be spaced by date, which deemphasizes revisions happening in rapid succession of each other. In other words, each vertical line corresponds to a version of the article. Horizontal lines represent chunks of text that have been edited. Color encodes the authors. In this way, it is possible, for example, to see which parts were edited by a particular author in a singular version as well as across time. A list and key to the authors is positioned at the far left of the interface, and one can select a name to view that particular author's participation in the article. Given that they wanted to assign each author with a unique color identifier across the entire encyclopedia, they decided to assign colors randomly. They explain, "We settled on an unusual choice of encoding in which our software chose random bright, saturated colors for each user. These weren't genuinely random, but were based on the Java 'hashcode' of an author's name. This technique ensured that the colors were consistent across diagrams, and that there was the widest possible range of variation. For anonymous editors, we chose a light shade of gray."[39]

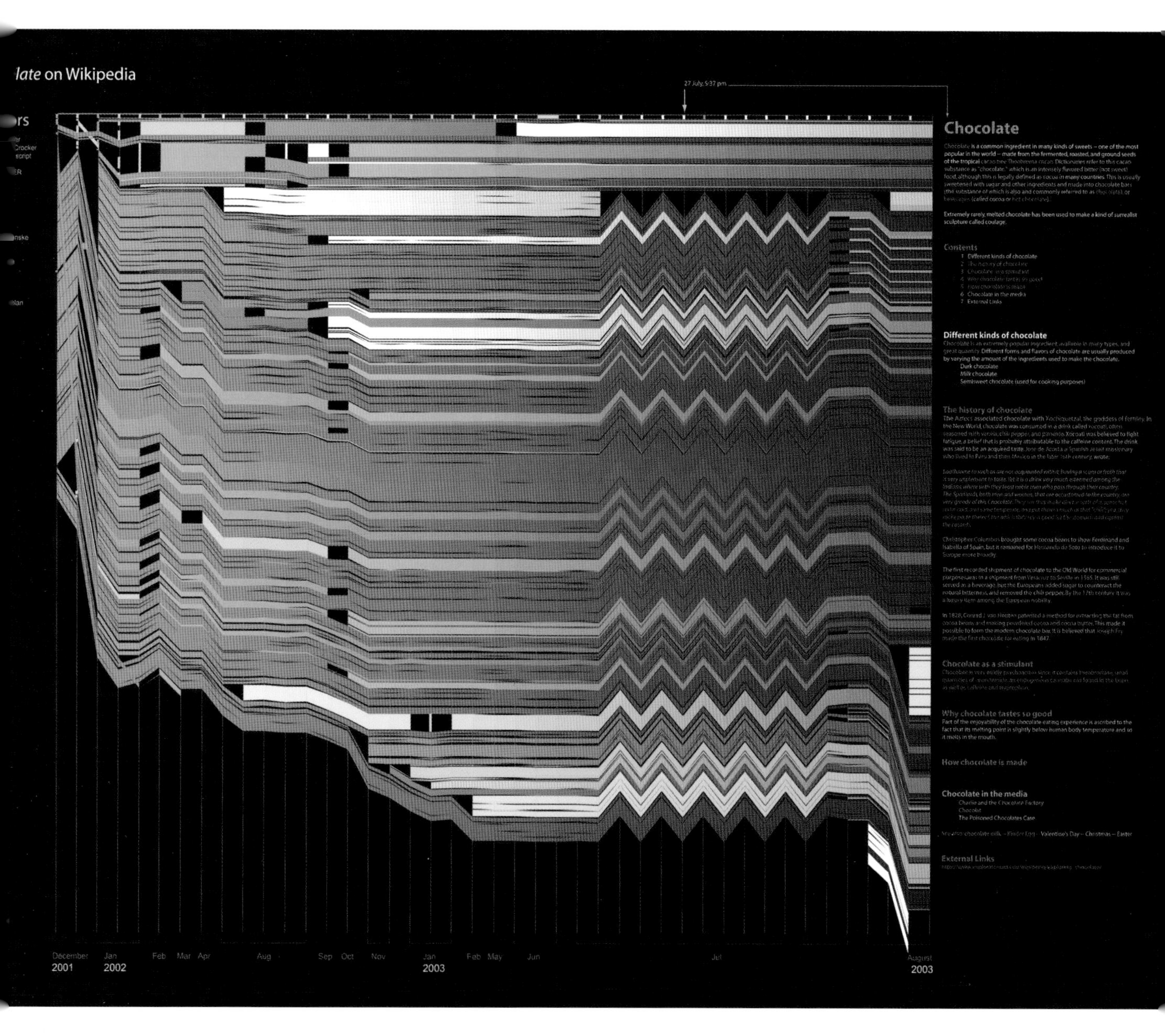

Looking at this image, it is possible to examine patterns of behaviors. For example, the zigzag lines reveal "edit wars," in which authors repeatedly reverted one another's changes. The image shows the history of the Wikipedia article on chocolate and, according to Viégas and Wattenberg, the zigzag depicts an argument on whether a certain type of surrealist sculpture exists or not. Another feature that we see implemented in this image is the possibility of accessing the text itself, which can be read at the right-hand side of the interface.

Bestiario, Spain: "Research Flow," 2009.

The online exploratory tool designed by the Spanish studio Bestiario is a good example of the possibilities opened up by computerized interaction, such as the ability to filter data and to zoom in time.

www.bestiario.org/research/flow

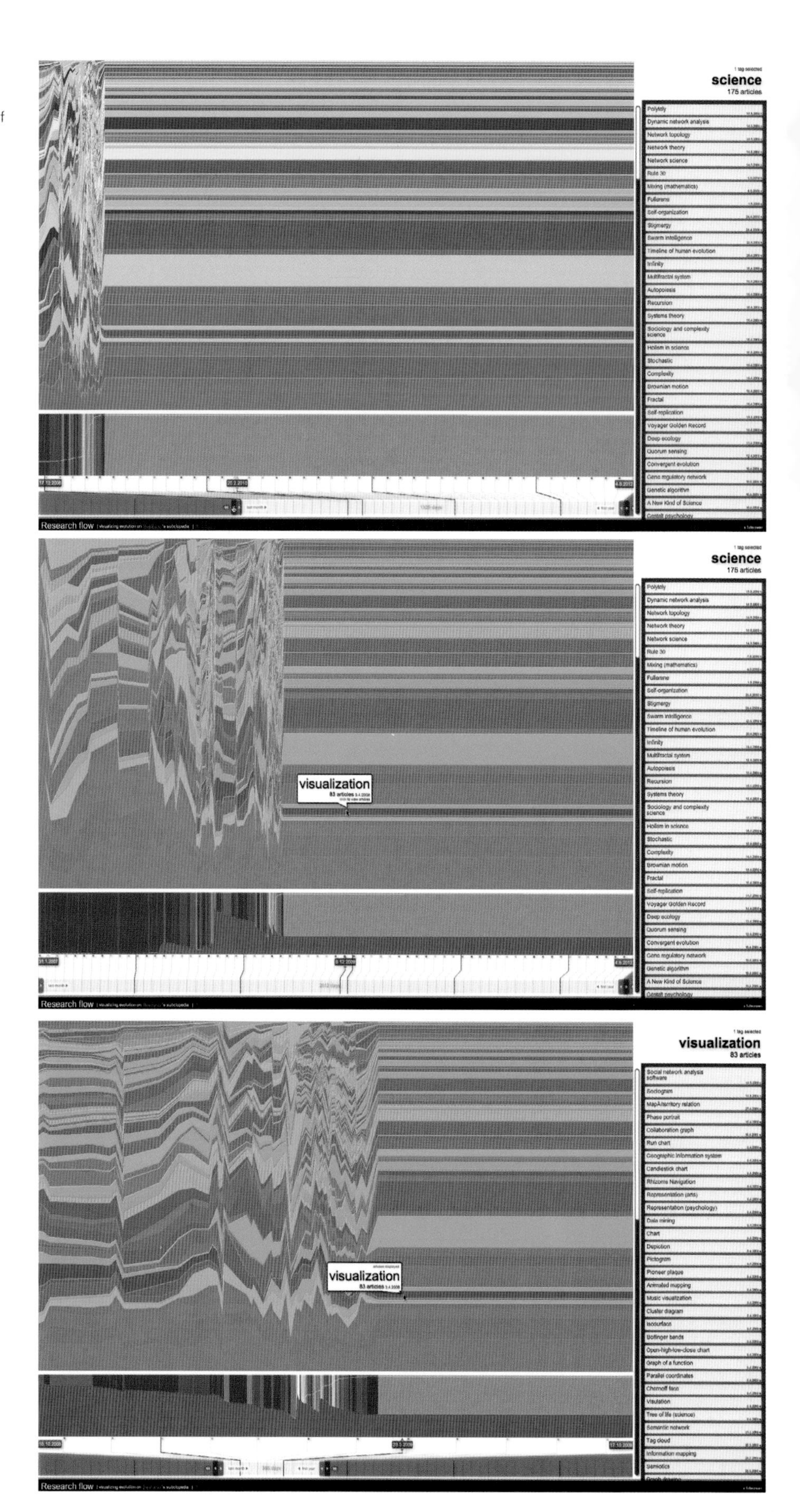

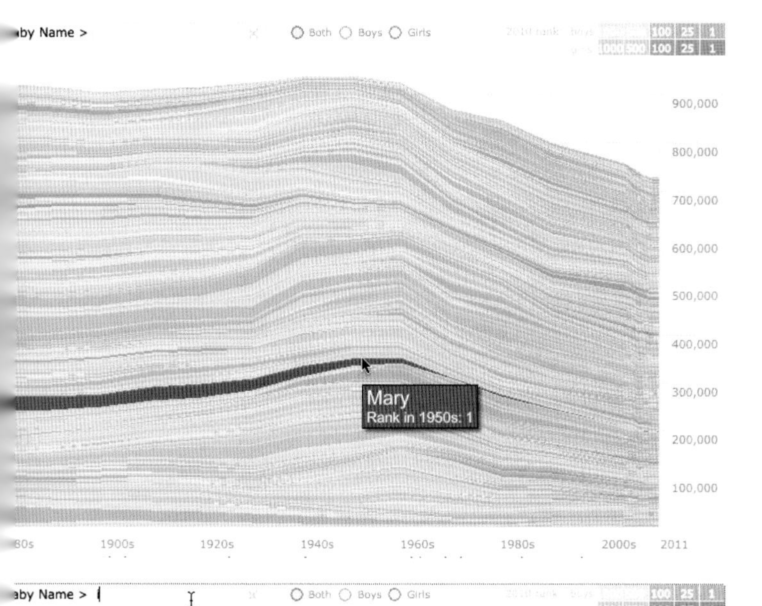

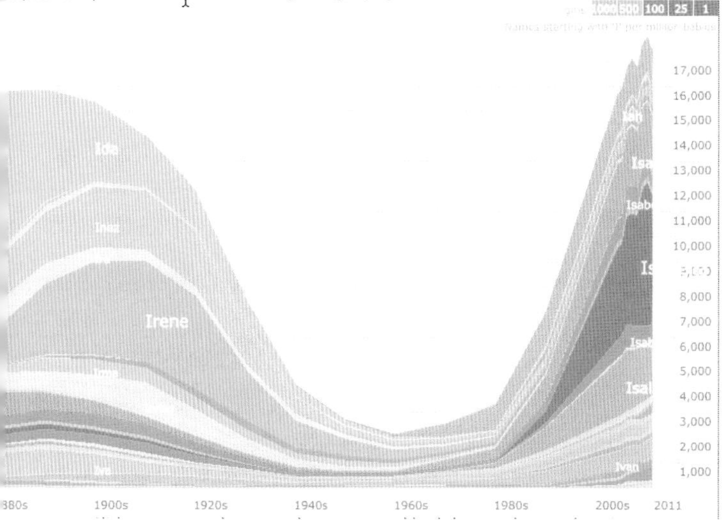

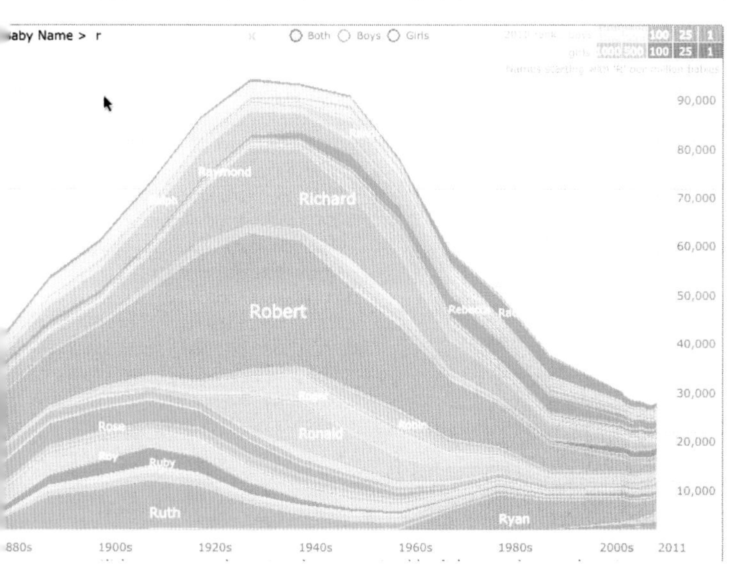

Martin Wattenberg, U.S.: "NameVoyager," 2005.

The *NameVoyager* is a web-based visualization of historical trends in baby naming designed by Martin Wattenberg in 2005. The visualization became very popular, and Wattenberg credits it to the public nature of the web-based application, because it enables social data analysis. The structure is familiar to most viewers, and for the quantitative time series it uses the stacked graph method. Time is represented horizontally from left to right. The vertical axis represents the frequency of occurrence for all names in view in terms of occurrences per million babies. Each stripe represents a name, and the thickness of a stripe is proportional to its frequency of use at the given time step. Girl names are color coded in pink and boys in blue. There is an additional attribute of brightness encoding the stripes for popularity; currently popular names are darkest and stand out the most. Wattenberg explains, "The idea behind this color scheme is twofold. First, names that are currently popular are more likely to be of interest to viewers—many people will probably want to know statistics on Jennifer, but few are looking for Cloyd. Second, the fact that the brightness varies provides a way to distinguish neighboring name stripes without relying on visually heavy borders."[40] Similar to search engines, *NameVoyager* lets you type in a name and see a graph of its popularity over the past century. Because it renders data as one types each letter, it is possible to see trends provided by name fashion, given by their similar sounds.

www.babynamewizard.com/voyager

Herbert Bayer, U.S.: "Diagram of the Chronology of Life and Geology," 1953.

The "Diagram of the Chronology of Life and Geology" appeared in the spectacular *World Geo-Graphic Atlas* designed by well-known designer Herbert Bayer and published by the Container Corporation of America in 1953. It tells the story of geology and life on Earth as a function of time. On the right-hand side, the spiral represents time. Time is portrayed backward, with the starting point (or the end of data in the diagram) at the top right, when human life starts, closer to the label "future." It regresses to the beginning of our planet, millions of years back. The choice of the spiral is not arbitrary; rather, it enables, on one hand, the representation of such a huge span of time and, on the other, focus on the period when life occurs. The scale of time is in millions of years, with numbers positioned along the timeline. Horizontal lines connect specific times in the spiral with the whole diagram. The lines mark the different phases of the Earth's history. Each phase is labeled and presents numerical information about its duration (also in millions of years). Phases are grouped into Eras, labeled in red. From right to left, the diagram displays the chronology of geological formations (mountains in black), plant life (green vertical lines), and animal life (red vertical lines). Each categorical group is represented graphically (pictograms) and verbally. Line variations represent quantitative information about each species, including those that went extinct.

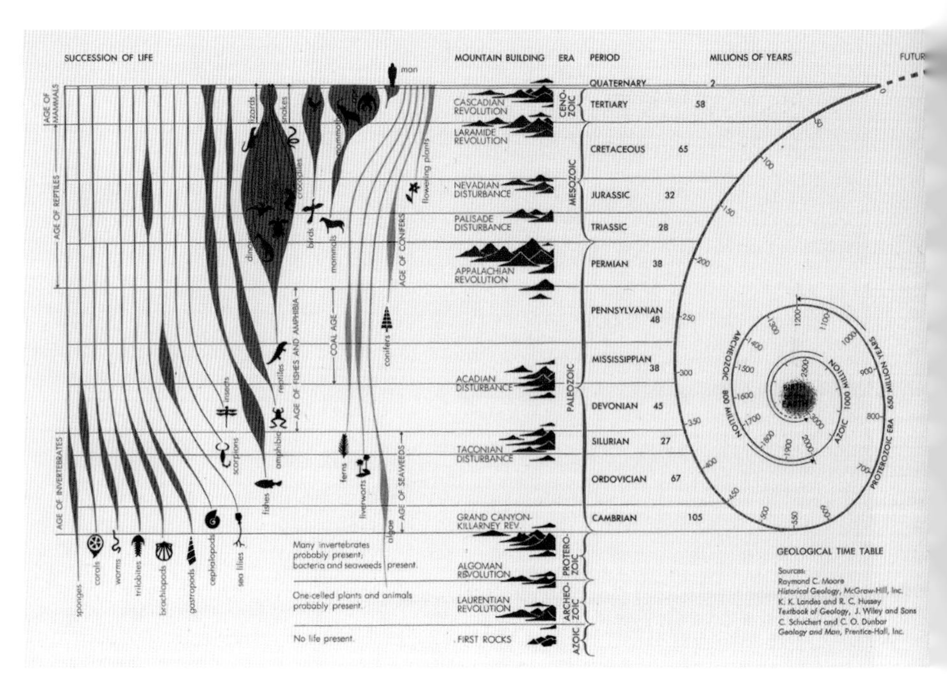

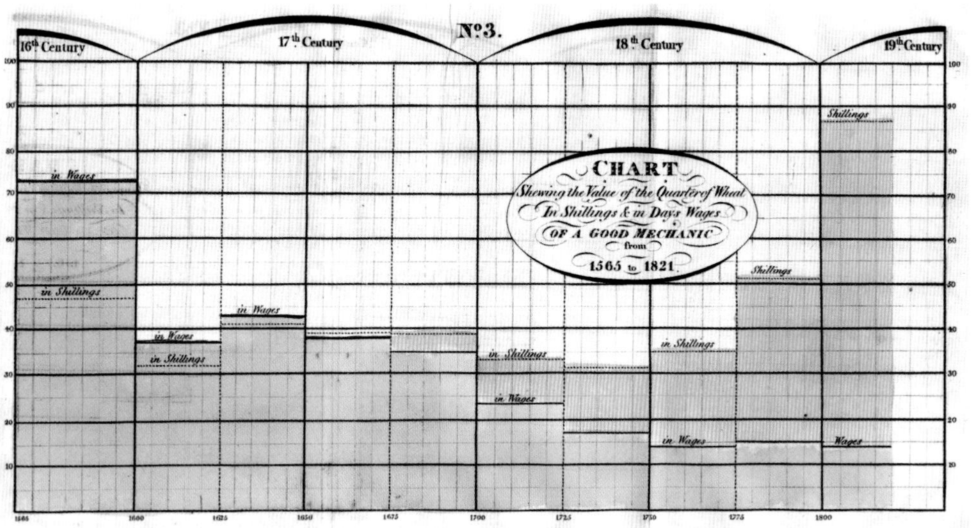

William Playfair created the "Chart Shewing the Value of the Quarter of Wheat in Shillings & in Days Wages of a Good Mechanic from 1565 to 1821" with the purpose to compare wages against the cost of wheat. It was published in *A Letter on Our Agricultural Distresses, Th Causes and Remedies: Accompanied wi Tables and Copper-plate Charts, Shewin and Comparing the Prices of Wheat, Bre and Labour, from 1565 to 1821.*

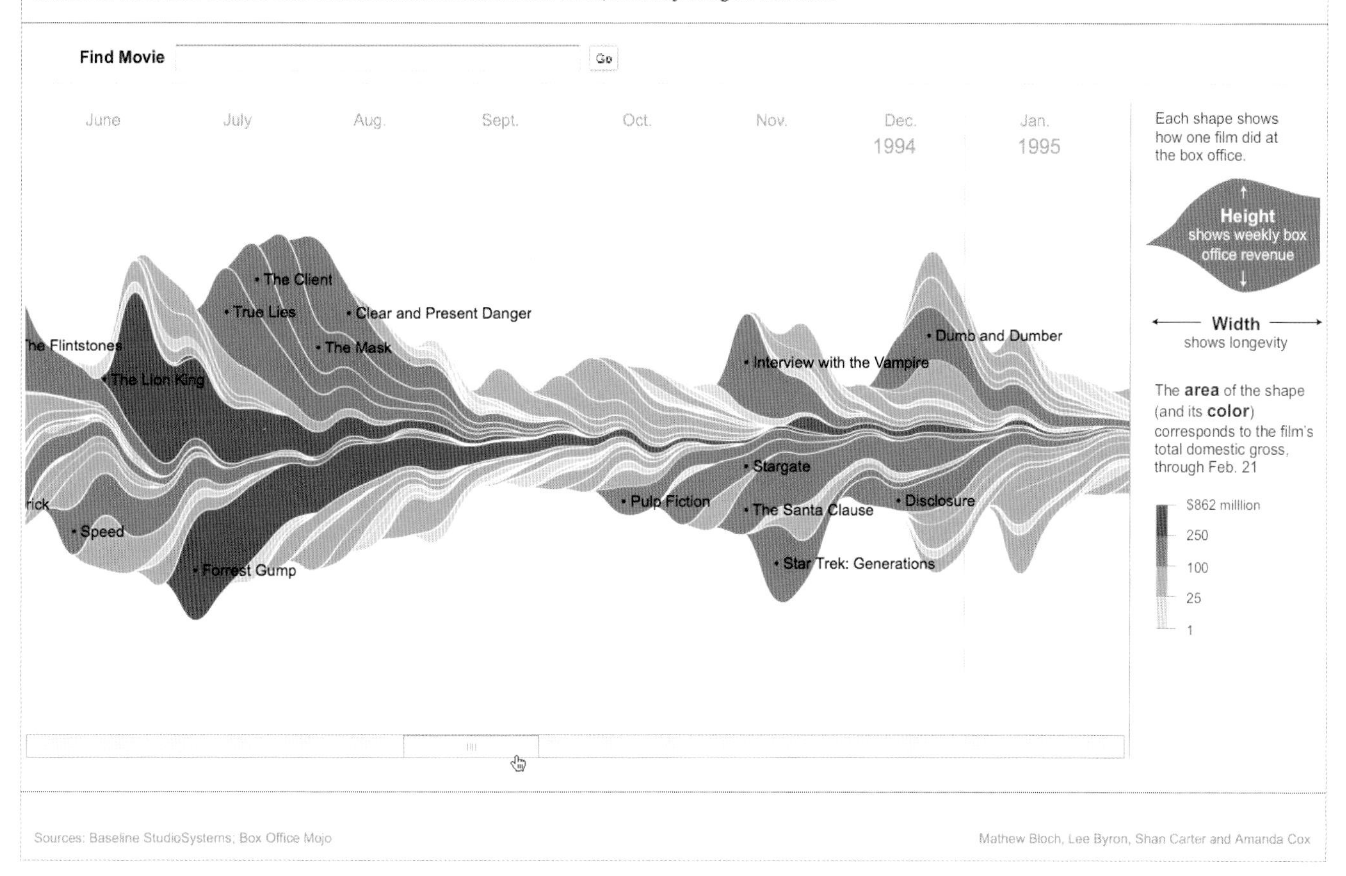

Matthew Bloch, Lee Byron, Shan Carter, and Amanda Cox (*New York Times*), U.S.: "The Ebb and Flow of Movies: Box Office Receipts 1986–2008," 2008.

The visualization depicts box office revenues for 7,500 movies over twenty-one years. The "Ebb and Flow of Movies: Box Office Receipts 1986–2008" was published in February 2008 by the *New York Times* both on the printed version and online. It was designed by Mathew Bloch, Lee Byron, Shan Carter, and Amanda Cox. The visualization uses the *Streamgraph* method devised by Lee Byron, which arranges the layers in an organic stacked form. The method was inspired by *ThemeRiver*, a method devised by Havre and colleagues in 2000, a technique that creates a smooth interpolation from discrete data and generates a symmetrical layout of the layers centered around the horizontal axis, rather then stacked in one direction.[41] *Streamgraph* also borrowed techniques from *NameVoyager* by Wattenberg, described on the previous page.

The graph reproduced here depicts the dichotomy between box office hits and Oscar nominations that was discussed in the original article. Time is represented horizontally from left to right. The height of each band of film represents the box office revenue per week, and the width its longevity. The area of the shape corresponds to the film's total domestic gross through February 21, 2008. The same is true of color, which has a four-color palette that ranges from pale yellow (low gross) to saturated orange (high gross).

Stacked graphs in general involve trade-offs, because the heights of individual layers add up to the overall height of the graph. With the purpose to spotlight stacked graphs as an interesting object of study, Byron and Wattenberg discuss several issues with the legibility of stacked area graphs with a fixed and varying baseline in the informative paper "Stacked Graphs—Geometry & Aesthetics."[42]

www.nytimes.com/interactive/2008/02/23/movies/20080223_REVENUE_GRAPHIC.html

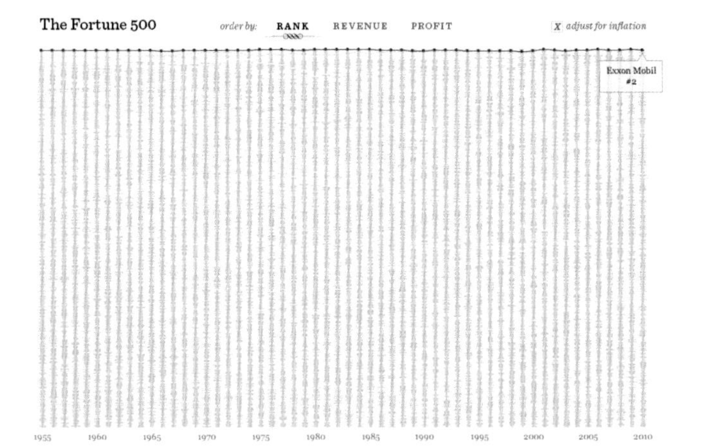

Ben Fry, U.S.: "*The Fortune 500,*" 2011.

Ben Fry created the online tool *The Fortune 500* in 2011. The series of interactive line graphs shows how the tool depicts the 500 companies on *Fortune* magazine's annual list of America's largest corporations. There are three ways in which one can compare the companies from 1955 to 2010: by Ranking, Revenue, and Profit, with the possibility to adjust for inflation. A log scale is used for plotting data in revenue and profit. Fry explains that the application was built with publicly available data found on Wikipedia. His intent was "to show how 84,000 data points could be easily viewed and navigated in an interactive piece."[43]

http://fathom.info/fortune500

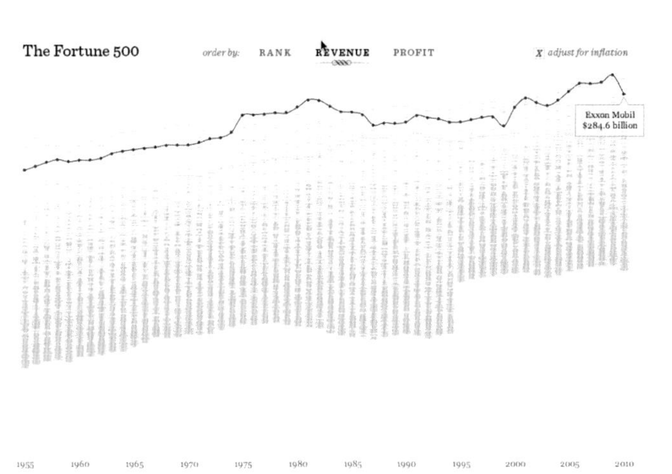

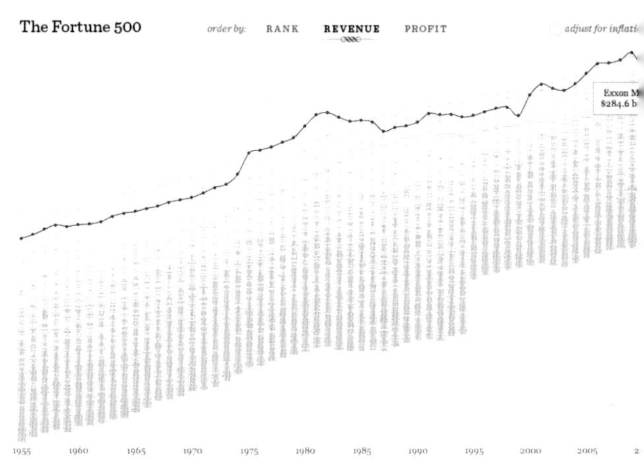

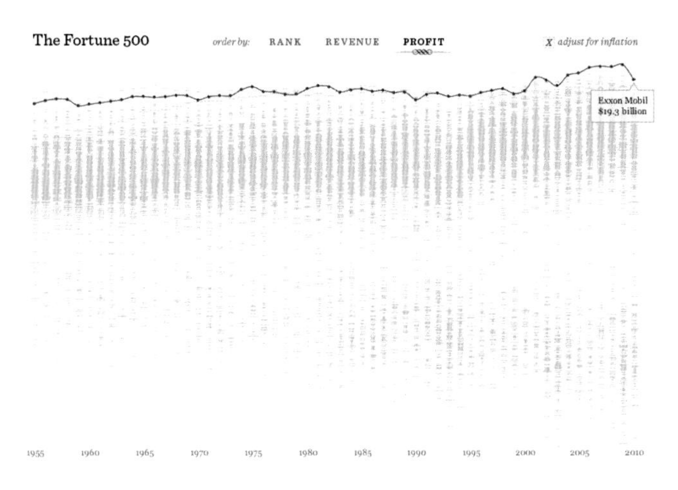

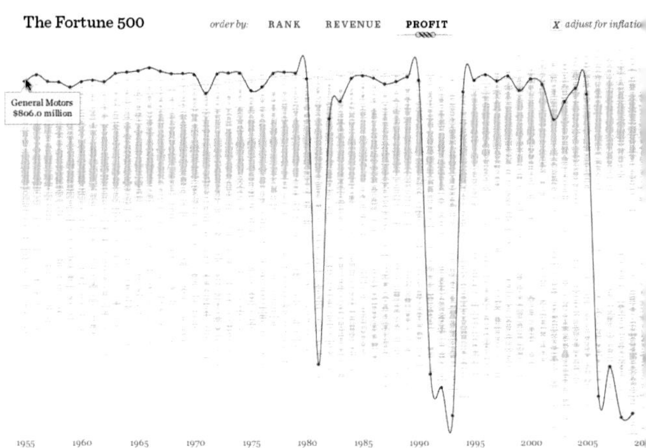

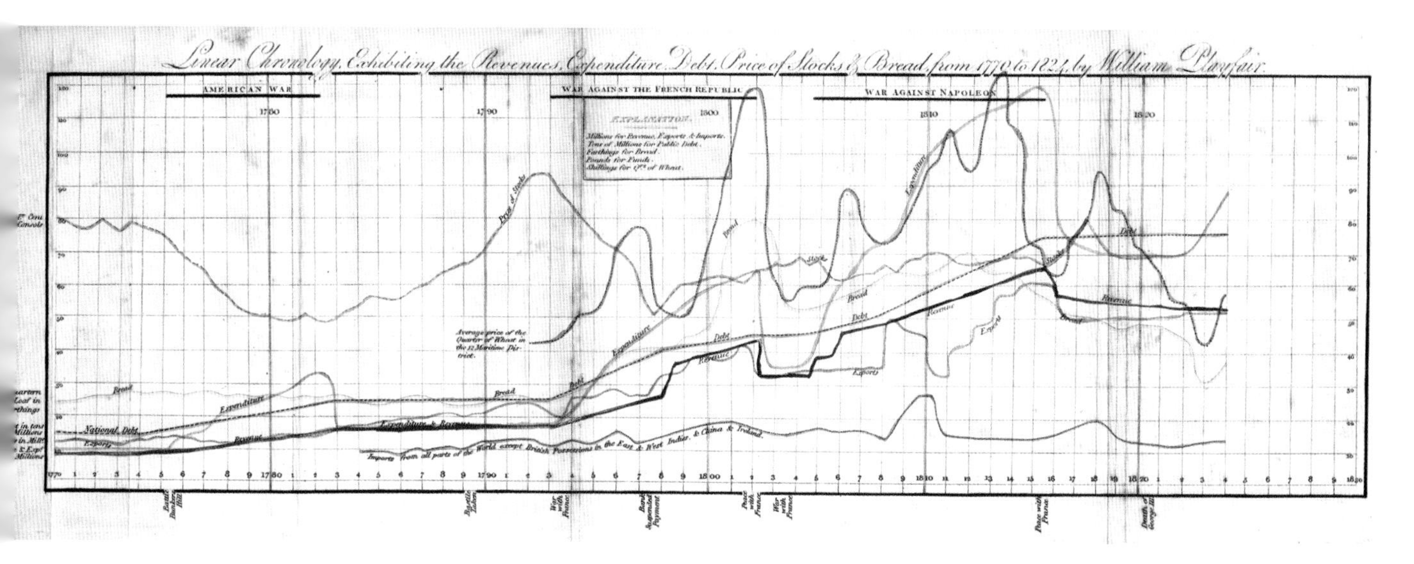

William Playfair devised "Linear Chronology, Exhibiting the Revenues, Expenditure, Debt, Price of Stocks & Bread, from 1770 to 1824" for reproduction in the *Chronology of Public Events and Remarkable Occurrences within the Last Fifty Years; or from 1774 to 1824*. Delaney explains, "This volume was intended to be a perpetual publication, adding a year on at the end while removing one from the beginning, so that it would continually present a record of the last fifty years. Here, Playfair's popular time line has been extrapolated beyond his death (1823) for another year."[44] Color encodes categorical data, for example, red for revenue, green for expenditure, yellow for bread, and so on. Note the addition of main historical events to the year marks on the horizontal axis at the bottom.

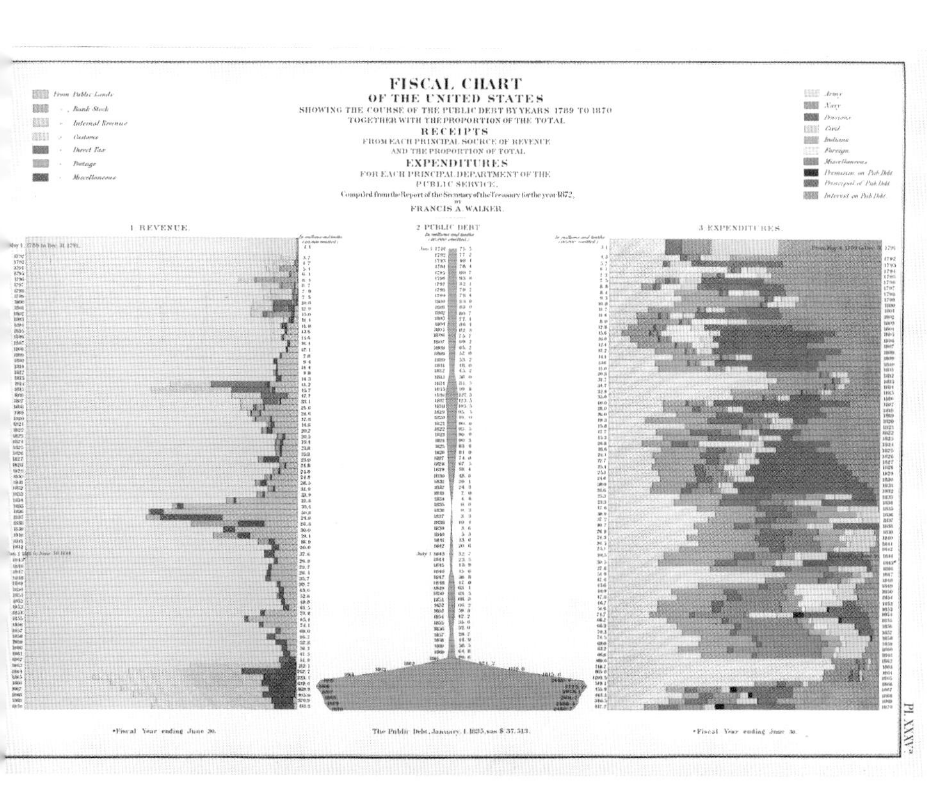

Francis A. Walker (1840–1897) compiled this fiscal chart of the United States showing the course of the public debt over years. It covers a period from 1789 to 1870 and is represented in a vertical scale, with earliest dates at the top. It includes the proportion of the total receipts from each principal source of revenue and the proportion of total expenditures for each principal department of the public service. It was published in 1874 in the *Statistical Atlas of the United States,* based on the results of the ninth census (1870).

Shan Carter, Amanda Cox, Kevin Quealy, and Amy Schoenfeld (*New York Times*), U.S.: "How Different Groups Spend Their Day," 2008.

When data are portrayed linearly, hourly trends are not easily perceived, because it is impossible to compare events occurring at the same periods. For that we need to aggregate values, as in this example from the *New York Times*' "How Different Groups Spend Their Day." The interactive visualization depicts data as a stack area graph of activities performed (as percentages) by different demographic groups over the course of a day. Color encodes the different activities, such as sleeping, eating, socializing, etc.

When the goal is to visualize trends in people's routines, the period we deal with is the twenty-four-hour cycle of the day. We know a day starts at 00:00 and ends at 23:59. But structuring data around this temporal convention usually interrupts certain patterns. To avoid this issue, for example, this visualization starts at 4:00 AM instead of at 00:00, because it focuses on daily activities. The result is an effective use of space, in which the most relevant data fall into the center of the visualization, with sleeping times divided into the sides. To avoid this problem, it is often recommended to closely examine the data because they provide good indications of the most appropriate time stamps to start and end the time series.

www.nytimes.com/interactive/2009/07/31/business/20080801-metrics-graphic.html

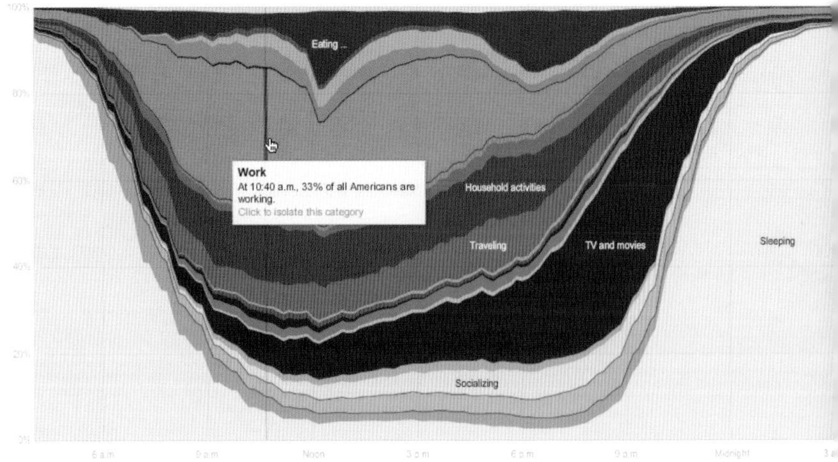

People ages 65 and over

At 2 p.m., about 1 in 15 people over age 65 is asleep. Older people also spend more time eating (particularly breakfast).

Everyone Employed White Age 15-24 H.S. grads
Men Unemployed Black Age 25-64 Bachelor's
Women Not in lab... Hispanic Age 65+ Advanced

Eating ... Shopping Work Household activities TV and movies Sleeping Relaxing and thinking Socializing

6 a.m. 9 a.m. Noon 3 p.m. 6 p.m. 9 p.m. Midnight

The unemployed

On average, the unemployed spend about a half-hour looking for work. They tidy the house, do laundry and yard work for more than two hours, about an hour more than the employed.

Everyone Employed White Age 15-24 H.S. grads
Men Unemployed Black Age 25-64 Bachelor's
Women Not in lab... Hispanic Age 65+ Advanced

Eating and drinking Shopping Education Job search Household activities TV and movies Sleeping Traveling Socializing

6 a.m. 9 a.m. Noon 3 p.m. 6 p.m. 9 p.m. Midnight

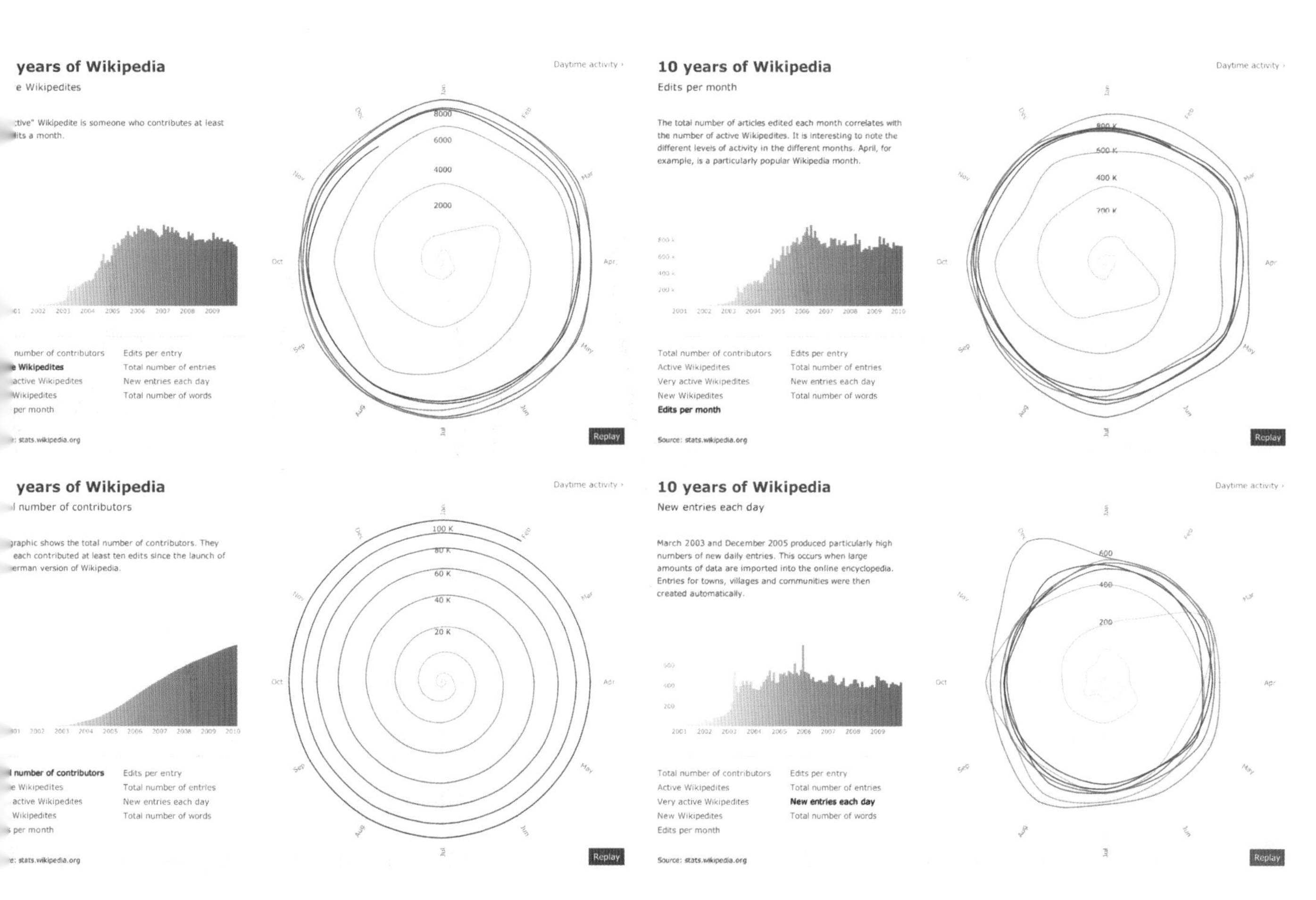

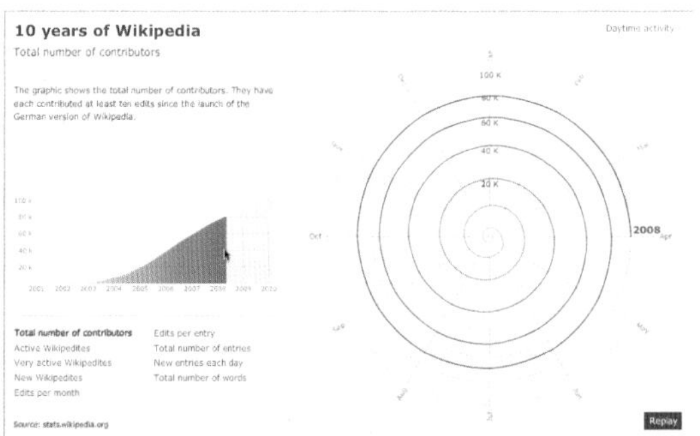

Gregor Aisch, Germany: "10 Years of Wikipedia," 2011.

Circular or spiral structures are often used when the goal is to show a continuous timescale, as well as to reveal periodic data. Spirals are best at depicting continuous data over many cycles, similar to several concentric circles. Different from linear time series, which depict data by aggregating values, in spirals we can represent individual amounts per temporal unit. In this visualization depicting "10 Years of Wikipedia," Gregor Aisch used a polar line chart to reveal the periodical growth patterns of a few selected metrics in relation to the daily activity curves of the top 100 editors. The interactive visualization was developed by Gregor Aisch with Marcus Bösch and Stellen Leidel (editors) for the *Deutsche Welle* at the occasion of the encyclopedia's anniversary in 2011.

There are few antecedents to the circular schema, such as Nightingale's rose chart and the star and polar diagrams (see page 92, 94, 95).

http://visualdata.dw.de/en/wikipedia

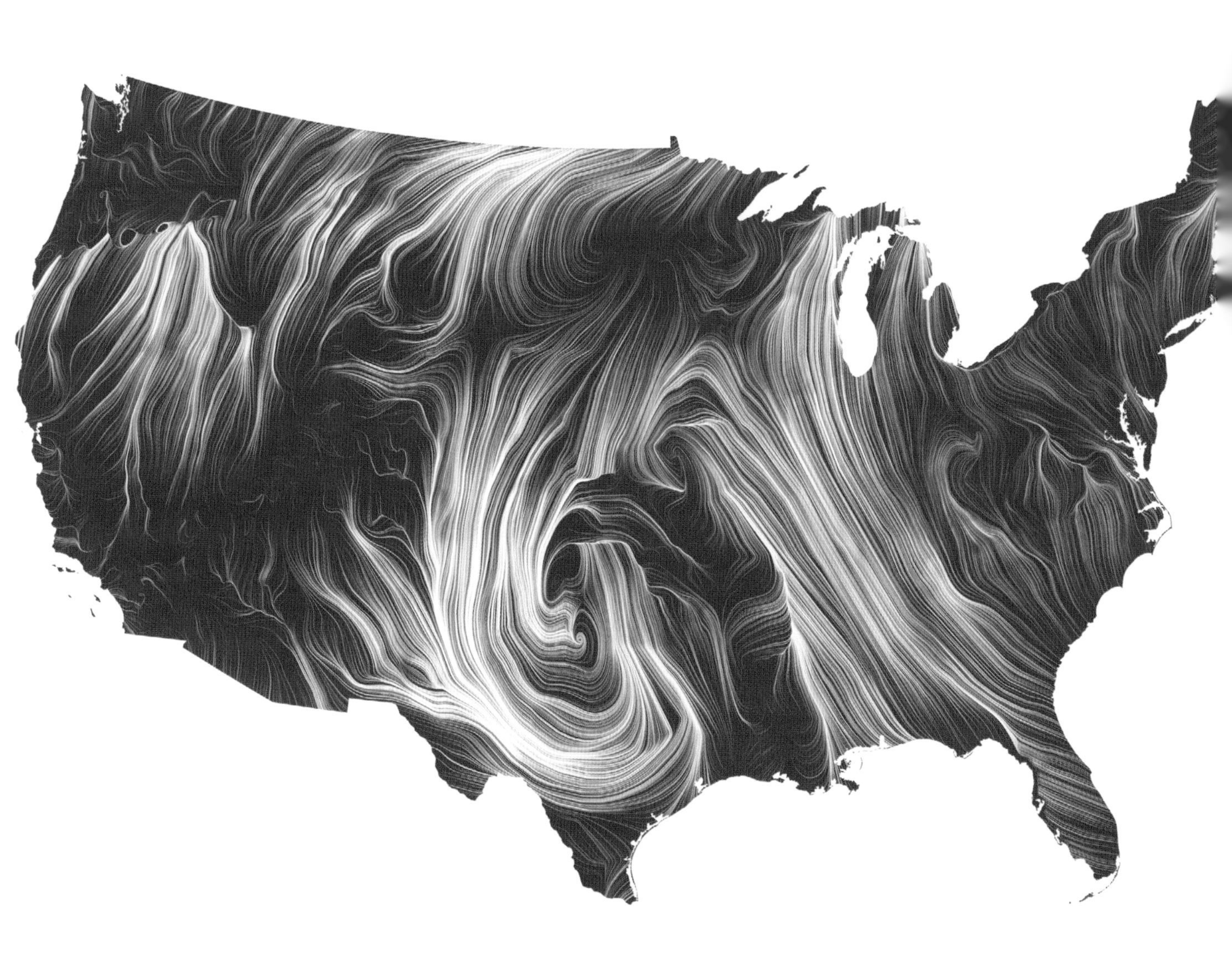

CHAPTER 4

SPATIAL STRUCTURES: **MAPS**

Fernanda Viégas and Martin Wattenberg, U.S.: "Wind Map," 2012.

The 2012 "Wind Map" is a personal art project by Fernanda Viégas and Martin Wattenberg devised to visualize the wind as a source of energy. The project shows wind forces over the United States using data from the National Digital Forecast Database and is revised hourly. The varying weights of lines represent the velocity of the wind flows. The screenshot depicts a "living portrait" at a given date. Patterns are easily distinguished given the orientation and thickness of lines, which ultimately reveal the hidden geography.

http://hint.fm/wind

We encounter the term **map,** as well as the act of **mapping** in diverse fields of knowledge, all, however, with the shared characteristic of being "a diagram or collection of data showing the **spatial distribution** of something or the **relative positions** of its components."[1] The oldest (c. 1527), and perhaps the most frequent, use of the term *map* refers to representations of geographical data, ranging from the Earth's surface to parts of it.[2] Maps are used in other disciplines, such as genetics, in diagrammatic representations of the order and distance of the genes (see page 53), and in mathematics, as correspondences between two or more sets of elements. These are just two fields in which maps are frequently used.

This chapter focuses on **thematic maps**, which are representations of attribute data (quantitative and qualitative) on a base map. The latter is provided by the fixed positional data defined by geometry, such that spatial (geographic) relations are represented using locational reference systems (e.g., latitude/longitude, projections). In other words, and as the name suggests, thematic maps display a theme that can be a number of phenomena, such as social, political, economic, or cultural issues, with the purpose of revealing patterns and frequencies in the geography where they occur. As Robinson explains, "One of the major reasons for making a thematic map is to discover the geographical structure of the subject, impossible without mapping it, so as to relate the 'geography' of one distribution to that of others."[3]

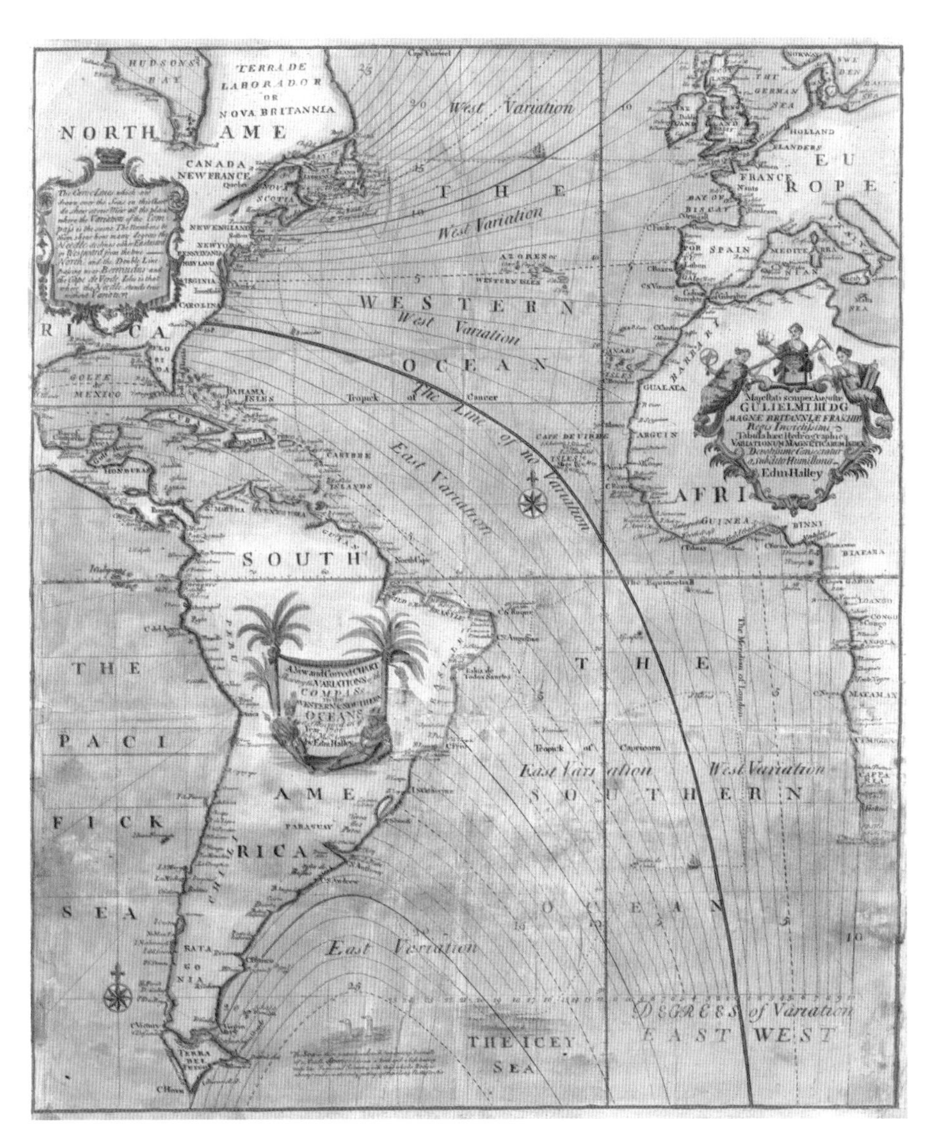

"A New and Correct Chart Showing the Variations of the Compass in the Western & Southern Oceans as Observed in the Year 1700," was created by Englishman Edmond Halley and published in 1701. It is the first known use of isolines.

BRIEF HISTORY

Thematic maps can be traced back to the second half of the seventeenth century, with large advances in the nineteenth century, when most graphical methods were devised between 1820 and 1860.[4] Initially, thematic maps represented data in the natural sciences. The 1701 isoline map of the magnetic fields by the Englishman Edmond Halley (1656–1742) is considered the first of these. The portrayal of social phenomena appeared a century later, and the first modern statistical map is credited to Frenchman Charles Dupin (1784–1873), and his 1826 choropleth map of France displaying levels of education by means of shaded gray administrative areas.[5] "As data built up from environmental observations and measurements during the Enlightenment," Robinson expounds, "attention shifted from place to space. Focus shifted from analytical concern with the position of features to holistic concern with the spatial extent and variation of features. Thus, the idea of distribution was born. The conceptual leap from place to space led to distributional representations called thematic maps."[6]

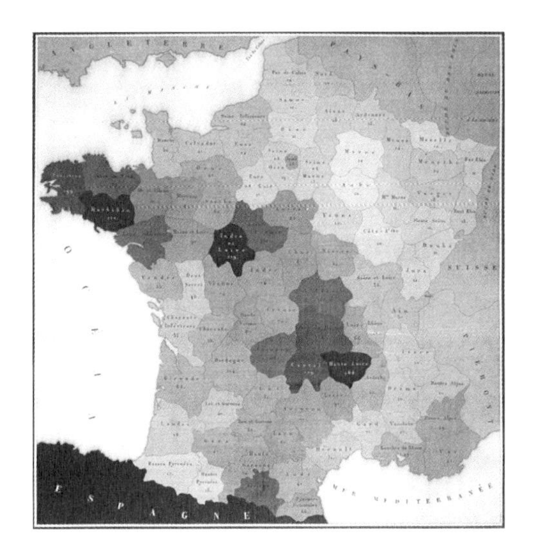

Baron Pierre Charles Dupin is credited with having created the first modern statistical map in 1826. The map, also the first known choropleth map, depicts with shades from black to white the distribution and intensity of illiteracy in France. It is an unclassed choropleth map, in which each unique value is represented by a unique gray value. Classes in choropleth maps started being used in the early 1930s.

The enumeration of population was recorded during Egyptian, Greek, and Roman times, all of which used data primarily for administrative purposes, such as taxation. It is from the Romans, in fact, that the word *census* is derived from the Latin *censere,* "to estimate." The systematic collection of social data started only in the late eighteenth century, with the first population census carried out by Sweden in 1749, followed by other countries, such as the United States in 1790, and France and England in 1801.

By 1870, most European countries, as well as the United States, were systematically collecting, analyzing, and disseminating official government statistics on population, trade, and social and political issues in publications such as statistical atlases, international expositions, and conferences.[7] The International Statistical Congress, which met eight times between 1835 and 1876, served as an important international forum for the discussion and promotion of the use of graphical methods, as well as attempts to set forth international standards.[8]

A thematic map is concerned with portraying the overall form of a given geographical distribution. It is the structural relationship of each part to the whole that is important. Such a map is a kind of graphic essay dealing with the spatial variations and interrelationships of some geographical distribution.

Arthur H. Robinson

ADVANCES IN THE MID-1800S

Overall, the use of graphs for illustration and analysis outside the domains of mathematics and the physical sciences was rare prior to the mid-nineteenth century, despite the graphical inventions of William Playfair in the late 1700s (see page 93). The unprecedented development in the mid-1800s of graphic methods to analyze data in many ways was fueled by most countries' recognition of the importance of numerical information in planning for the general welfare of the population (social, economic, etc).

This period also marks the birth of new disciplines, such as statistics, geology, biology, and economics, to mention a few. New techniques developed by the emerging disciplines influenced each other as well as traditional fields like cartography, and led to advances in thematic maps that are examined in this chapter. For example, most innovations in graphical methods for statistical maps were devised by engineers and not by cartographers.[9] As Friendly stresses, "What started as the 'Age of Enthusiasm' in graphics and thematic cartography, may also be called the 'Golden Age,' with unparalleled beauty and many innovations."[10]

As a side note, it is relevant to consider that we are currently experiencing a similar phenomenon powered by the collection of all sorts of digital data and the need to visually analyze them. Furthermore, we see the effect on several disciplines, from physics to biology, from political sciences to literature, all permeated by the growing field of data visualization.

MAP DESIGN

Visualizing data with maps involves making decisions in three basic areas: projection, scale, and symbolization. This chapter focuses on the latter, and a brief explanation follows with regard to the first two items. There is vast literature on map making, and further readings are strongly recommended. A list of the books used here as resources, together with other suggestions, can be found at the end of this book.

Map projections are mathematical transformations of the curved three-dimensional surface of the globe onto a flat, two-dimensional plane. All map projections involve transformations that result in distortions of one or more of the geometric properties of angles, areas, shapes, distances, and directions. Throughout the years, different projections have been devised for transposing the globe into the plane.[11]

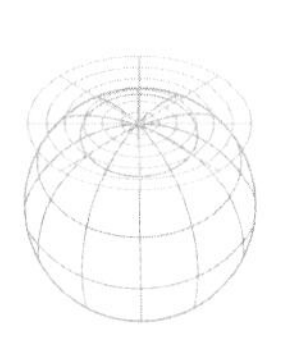
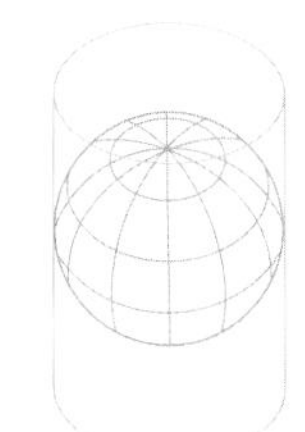
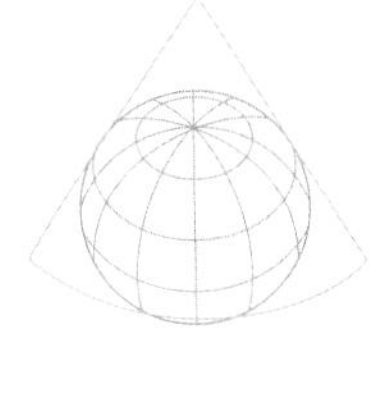
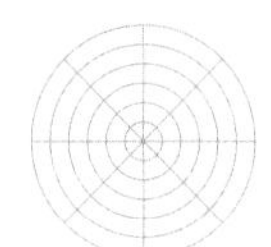
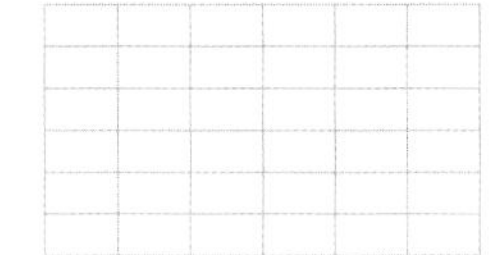
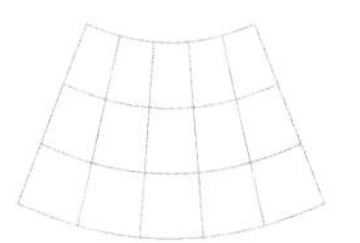

There are three basic surfaces upon which the sphere is projected: plane, cylinder, and cone. Each results in three kinds of map grids: azimuthal, cylindrical, and conic.

There are three basic *developable surfaces*—plane, cylinder, and cone—which result in three kinds of map grids—azimuthal, cylindrical, and conic. Distortion increases with the distances from the point or line of contact—tangent or secant—between the developable surface and the globe. For this reason, cartographers recommend cylindrical projections for continents around the equator (e.g., Africa, South America), conic projections for middle-latitude continents (e.g., Asia, North America), and azimuthal projections for polar regions.[12]

There are a variety of projections for each developable surface. Choosing a map projection involves understanding the geometric properties that one needs preserved with minimized distortion.

PROJECTIONS

Robinson and colleagues warn, "There is no such thing as a bad projection—there are only good and poor choices."[29] All map projections result in distortions of one or more of the geometric properties of angles, areas, shapes, distances, and directions. As illustrated on the right, some projections preserve areas but not local angles; all projections distort large shapes, some more than others; all projections distort some distances; and so on. Distortions should be taken into consideration when selecting the projection that best fits the purpose of the map.

The maps on this page use Tissot's *indicatrix*, a graphic device that illustrates distortion when circles change into ellipses. Changes in geometry indicate the amount of angular and/or areal distortion at any particular location in the map. The device was devised by French mathematician Nicolas Auguste Tissot in 1859.

The **Mercator projection** is conformal. Areas and shapes vary with latitude, especially away from the Equator, reaching extreme distortions in the polar regions. All indicatrices are circles as there are no angular distortion.

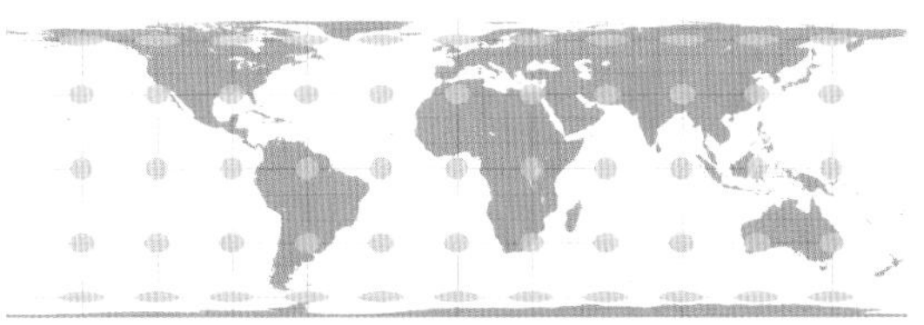

The **equal-area cylindrical projection** preserves area. Shapes are distorted from north to south in middle latitudes and from east to west in extreme latitudes.

In the **Mollweide projection,** shapes decrease in the north–south scale in the high latitudes and increase in the low latitudes, with the opposite happening in the east–west direction.

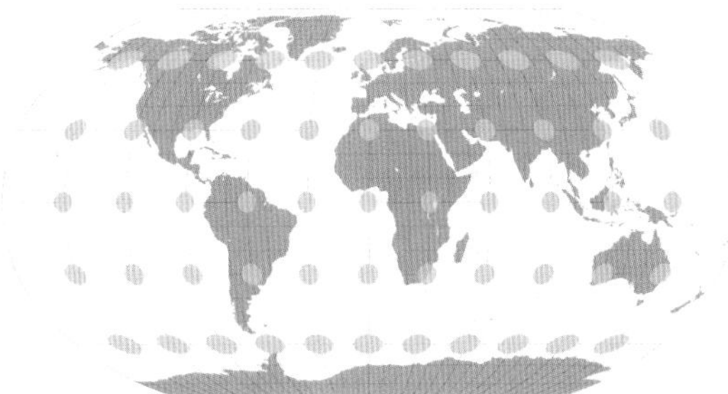

In the **Robinson projection,** all points have some level of shape and area distortion. Both properties are nearly right in middle latitudes.

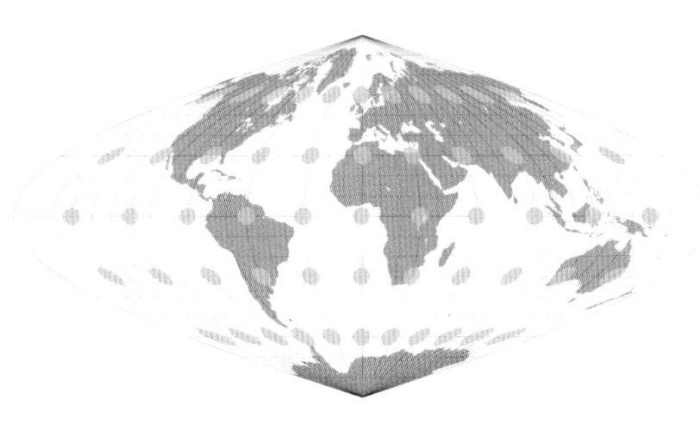

The **sinusoidal projection** preserves area, such that areas on the map are proportional to same areas on the Earth. Shapes are obliquely distorted away from the central meridian and near the poles.

In this Mercator projection map, Alaska and Brazil seem to be of similar size, when in reality Brazil is five times as large as Alaska. If used to compare land areas, a projection that preserves area should be selected, such as equivalent or equal-area projections. The illustration is based on the example in *Elements of Cartography*.[30]

For example, in 1569, the Flemish cartographer and mathematician Gerardus Mercator (1512–1594) introduced the Mercator projection, which helped solve a major problem of early navigators by providing a plane so that a straight line on the map would result in a line of constant bearing. On the other hand, if it is used to compare land areas, the Mercator projection is largely ineffective, because the regions, especially those at higher latitudes, are enlarged to a great extent.

Equivalent or *equal-area* projections preserve all relative areas, and are useful for visualizations in which the comparison of areas on the map is crucial, especially in the case of world maps. For example, dot-distribution maps rely on accurate area representation for the effective comparison of dot densities between regions on the map.[13] Maps used for instruction and small-scale general maps also require equivalent projections. Most common equal area projections are Alber's equal area, Lambert's equal area (especially recommended for middle-latitude areas, such as the United States), Mollweide (good for world distributions), and the Goode's homolosine.[14]

Conformal or *orthomorphic* projections conserve angular relationships, such that the angle between any two intersecting lines will be the same on the flat map as on the globe. Even though conformal projections also distort shapes, the result is less pronounced than in other projections, with preservation of the shape of small circles. They are often used for large-scale maps and include most modern topographic maps.[15] Conformal projections are also common in navigational charts. The conformal projections frequently used are Mercator, transverse Mercator, Lambert's conformal conic, and the conformal stereographical.[16]

Projections cannot preserve both angle and area—in other words, projections cannot be both conformal and equivalent. Monmonier explains, "Not only are these properties mutually exclusive, but in parts of the map well removed from the standard line(s), conformal maps severely exaggerate area and equal-area severely distort shape."[17] There are, however, projections that offer acceptable compromises between conserving area and conserving angles. A good example is provided by the Robinson projection, devised by geographer Arthur Robinson for the National Geographic Society, and used for its general-purpose world reference map between the years 1988 and 1998. Monmonier recommends a low-distortion projection, such as the Robinson projection, for world maps in which the representation of both land and ocean areas are important, and the Goode's homolosine equal-area projection when only the land areas are relevant.[18]

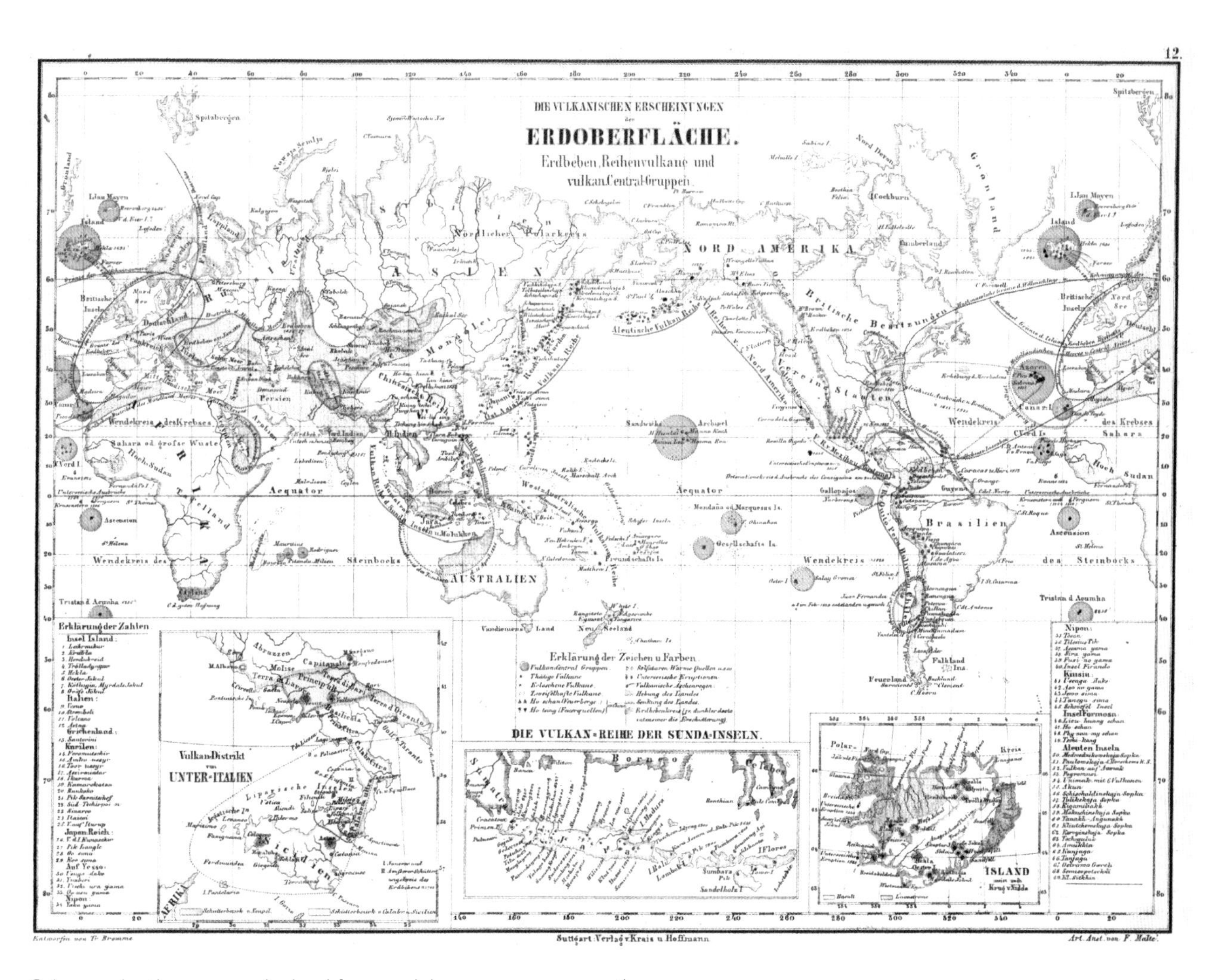

Considering that all projections will cause distortions, when using whole world maps, "recentering" the projection to favor parts of the globe is usual. Rather than using the usual European-centered projection, this 1851 map depicting volcanic activity around the world by Traugott Bromme is centered on Asia. Delaney expounds, "The large yellow circle around Indonesia and part of Australia shows the destructive reach of Mount Tambora's explosive eruption on April 11, 1815. Its magnitude has been given a 7 on today's Volcanic Explosivity Index, the highest rating of any volcanic eruption since the Lake Taupo (New Zealand) eruption circa AD 180." The map was part of a companion volume to Humboldt's *Kosmos*. Color encodes categorical data, with red dots standing for eruptions, green circles for volcanic regions, and colored lines for ranges.[31]

Other projections were devised for special purposes; among the most common are the *azimuthal*, the *plane chart*, and the *Robinson* projection—the latter a compromise between the conformal and the equal-area projections, as explained previously.

The **map scale** refers to the degree of reduction of the map. It is the ratio between a distance on the map and the corresponding distance on the Earth. The ratio is often presented in the map by a verbal statement in addition to a graphic bar. The distance on the map is always expressed as one, such that in a map scale of 1:10,000, 1 unit on the map represents 10,000 units on the Earth. Because the units are the same in either side of the scale, units do not need to be stated. The ratio scale is a dimensionless number.

Two factors should be considered when selecting the map scale: the objective of the map and the intended output. The goal of the visualization will suggest the geographical scope of the map.

For example, if the goal is to portray political inclinations within a country, a world map is too small a scale, causing important details to be missed; if the goal is to study the distribution of languages around the globe, a world map is needed.

Similar to other types of visual displays, maps involve simplifications and generalizations. As Monmonier explains, "Generalization results because the map cannot portray reality at a reduced scale without a loss of detail."[19] As a result, it is often the case that symbols take more space than what they represent. For example, in order to make symbols legible and meaningful, lines demarcating the border of countries in a world map could be proportionately as wide as several miles, depending on the line thickness and the map scale. Symbol exaggeration is not uncommon in maps, but exaggeration should not hinder comprehension of that which the symbol represents.

Cartographers recommend that most thematic maps include features such as coastlines, major rivers and lakes, political boundaries, and latitude–longitude lines.[20] Deciding on which features to include will depend on the purpose of the map, with the caveat that the map scale imposes the level of details depicted in it. For example, a map portraying the transportation of goods in a country should include its major road system, which might not be needed for a map showing temperature, for example. The amount of features to include in a thematic map should suffice for the effective matching of the mental model of the spatial relations portrayed in the map in front of us. A locator inset map can always be added to maps to provide farther geographic context, effective in both static and dynamic maps.

The base map should provide enough contextual information about the general geographic space without eclipsing the visual representation of the thematic data. In other words, the base map elements should be depicted with similar degrees of generalization while being deemphasized and less detailed than the thematic distributions layered onto them. The same is true for how the geographic information is visualized, in that most world maps don't need to carry the level of detail for coastlines, for example, as a large-scale map of an island would. The smaller the map's scale, the less physical space available for visual marks and details. Robinson and colleagues alert, "This does not mean that symbols should merely shrink in size as map scale increases. Rather, the smaller the scale, the less feature detail there should be."[21]

SPECTRUM OF CARTOGRAPHIC SCALES

Monmonier explains, "Maps are scale models of reality. That is, the map almost always is smaller than the space it represents."[32]

Sometimes, map scales are presented as fractions rather than ratios, but both carry the same information regarding the relationship between the map and Earth. Thinking about fractions can help viewers more easily grasp map scales, because the larger the fraction, the larger the map scale will be. For example, ½ is larger than ¼, the same way that 1:10,000 is larger than 1:50,000. The larger the scale, the greater the map's capacity for details.

The graph to the right is based on Monmonier's figure "Spectrum of cartographic scales, with selected examples and ranges for common applications."[33] Two series of maps illustrate the different scales depicted in the diagram. The maps were created by Stamen Design, which has experimented with different renditions for open source maps.

Prettymaps

Initially designed in 2010, Prettymaps is an interactive map composed of multiple freely available, community-generated data sources: Flickr, Natural Earth, and the OpenStreetMap (OSM) project. Stamen explains that the map has "four different raster layers and six data layers (that means all the map data is sent in its raw form and rendered as visual elements by the browser) that may be visible depending on the bounding box and zoom level of the map."[34]

Dotspotting

Dotspotting (2011) is the first project Stamen released as part of CityTracking, a project funded by the Knight News Challenge.

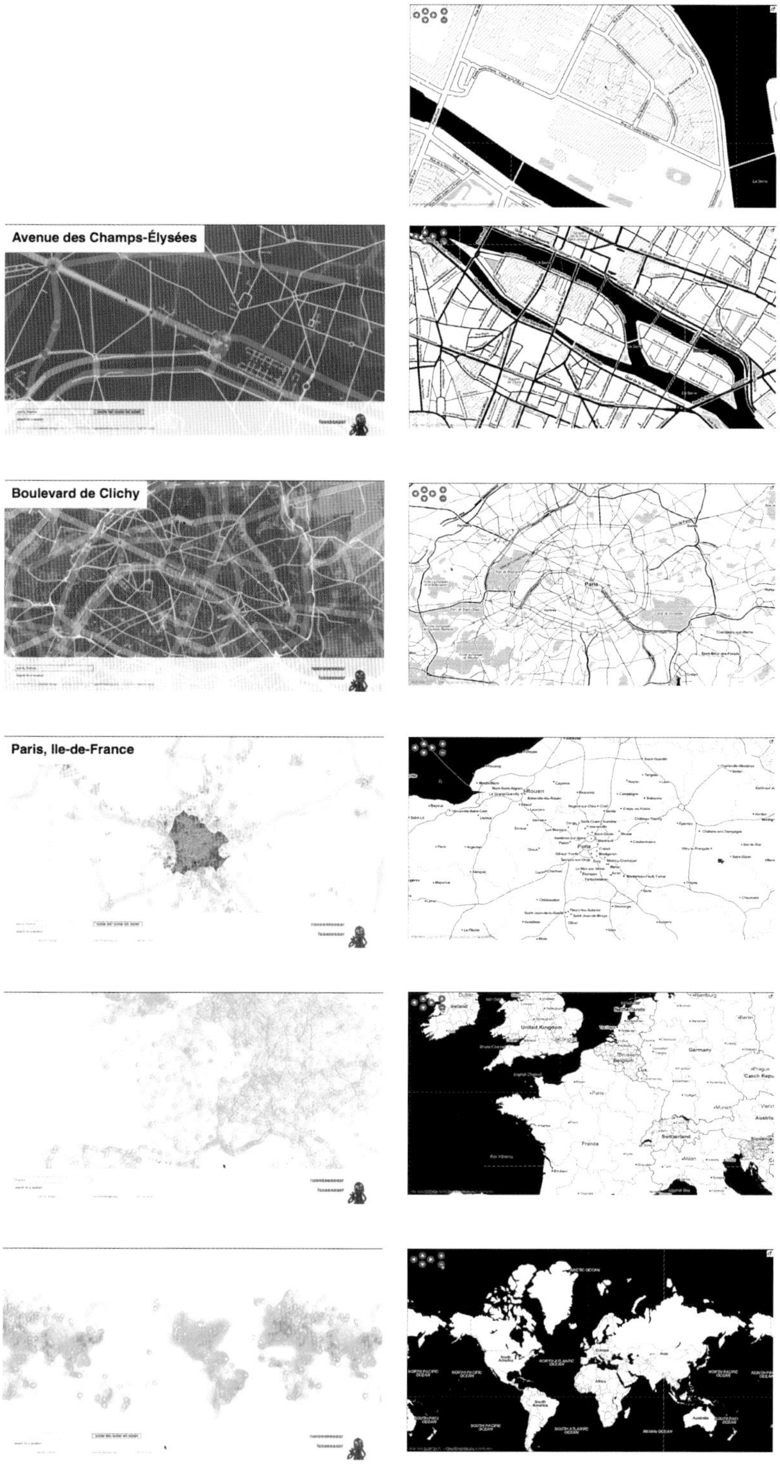

Avenue des Champs-Élysées

Boulevard de Clichy

Paris, Ile-de-France

PRETTYMAPS

http://prettymaps.stamen.com

DOTSPOTTING

www.dotspotting.org

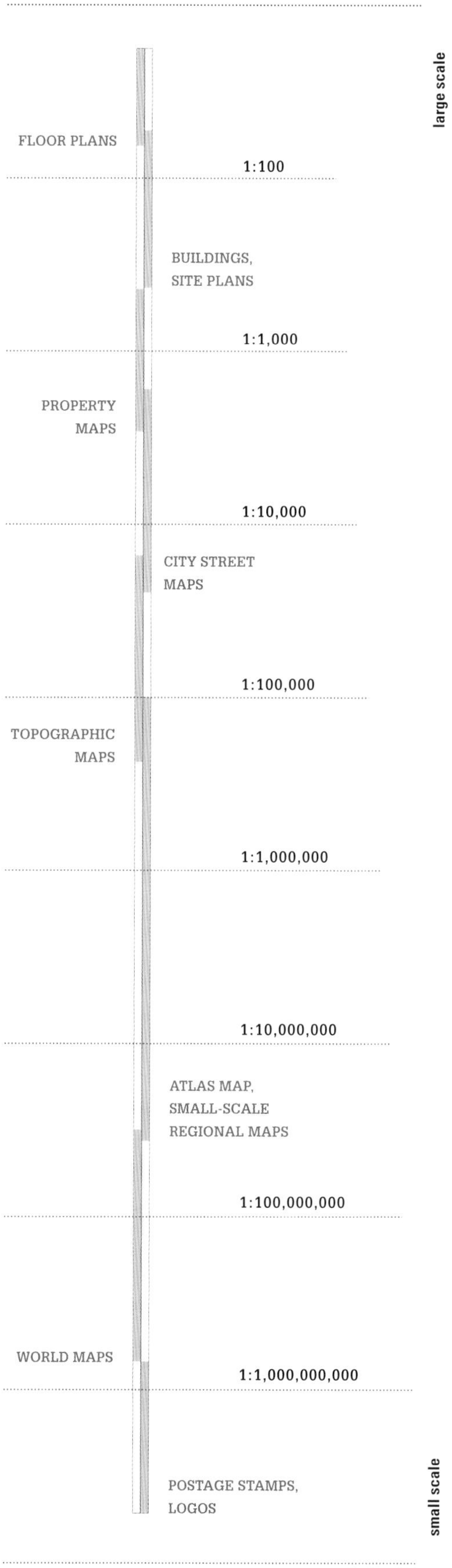

large scale

FLOOR PLANS

1:100

BUILDINGS,
SITE PLANS

1:1,000

PROPERTY
MAPS

1:10,000

CITY STREET
MAPS

1:100,000

TOPOGRAPHIC
MAPS

1:1,000,000

1:10,000,000

ATLAS MAP,
SMALL-SCALE
REGIONAL MAPS

1:100,000,000

WORLD MAPS

1:1,000,000,000

POSTAGE STAMPS,
LOGOS

small scale

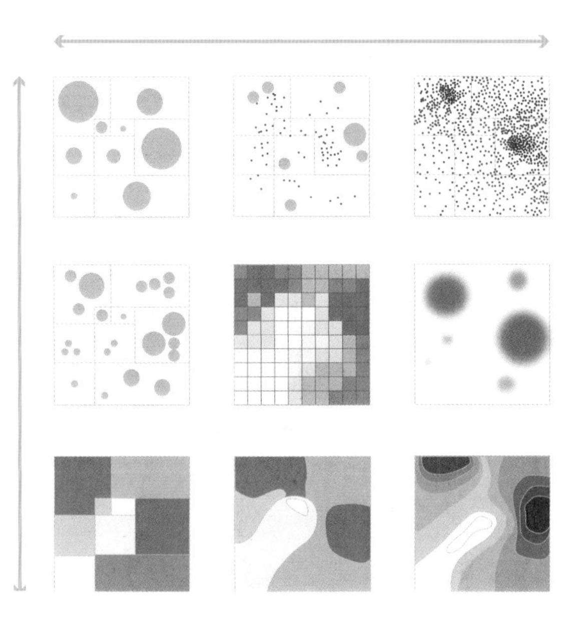

The diagram presents the syntactics of map forms. It suggests the appropriate schema for interpretation of map forms based on the typology of data models. The diagram below provides examples of phenomena. The two diagrams were drawn after MacEachren.[35]

Visual encoding is the process of matching the phenomena to be visualized, which is provided by the dataset (data scale and attributes), to the most suitable type of representation (graphical elements and visual properties). Visual encoding in cartography is often called **symbolization**.

DATA

In cartography and geo-informatics, **data** are divided into spatial phenomena (geography) and nonspatial phenomena, called thematic data. **Thematic** or **nonspatial phenomena** involve three levels of measurement (data scales) that increase in descriptive richness: nominal, ordinal, and quantitative.[22] Nominal scales, often called categorical or qualitative, allow differentiation between features (e.g., "A is different from B"), as well as sorting features into meaningful groups. Names of counties and political parties are examples of qualitative data. In addition to differentiation by class, ordinal data enable ranking, although without indication of magnitudes. For example, we can order the largest to the smallest counties in terms of population, without knowing the extent of differences among them. Quantitative data can be measured and are often numerically manipulated using statistical methods. For example, we can say, "County A has twice as many residents as county B." Or, given the area and population of counties, we can calculate the population densities (see appendix Data Types on page 204).

The **data attribute** of dimension is one of the most important characteristics when considering how to conceptualize visual marks in cartography, as well as in most other fields. For example, a point data such as a building (nominal) or an aggregated value of population (quantitative) in a city (nominal) can be symbolized by point marks. Area phenomena, such as the population density (quantitative) of a county (nominal), can be represented by area marks. In summary, data can have zero, one, two, or three **dimensions**, and be represented by the geometric elements of point, line, plane, and volume, respectively.

Another attribute relevant to thematic maps is whether data are **discrete** or **continuous**. Discrete data are composed of individual items, such as the cities on a map, which is different from continuous data, like temperature. Sometimes, discrete data, such as population, is transformed into continuous data by mathematical computations, as in the population density of an administrative unit. In some cases, this might not be ideal, if we consider that the population density will be visually represented as uniformly covering the entire area of the unit, and not depicting the "real" location of where people reside. On the other hand, this might not be easily avoided, in view that most social data are collected by administrative units.

Thematic maps can depict several sets of nonspatial data simultaneously. When a thematic map portrays exclusively one set of data, it is called **univariate**. If it shows two distinct sets of data, it is called **bivariate**, and for more than two sets, maps are called **multivariate**. For example, a map depicting population density would be a univariate map, and if in addition to the population density it portrays political affiliation, it would be considered a bivariate map. There is a limit on how many layers of visual information can be represented in a map without loss of legibility. Multiples are often used to represent such cases, as Bertin warns, "In any problem involving more than two components, a choice must be made between the construction of several maps, each one forming an image, and the superimposition of several components on the same map."[23]

The data sources and any data manipulation should be indicated on the map, and they are most often reported in the legend. It is valuable information that enables verification of the sources, the accuracy of the representation, and the reliability of the map.

TITLES AND LEGENDS

In general, titles provide the context for interpreting the visualization at hand. Titles should be as direct as possible and introduce the subject being represented on the map: the geographic, topical, and temporal context.

Legends or keys are essential to the effectiveness of any visualization and should be positioned in close proximity to the marks for which they stand for, to avoid forcing the viewer to search for meaning (grouping principle). Whenever possible it is recommended to include the verbal description, or label, for marks in the visualization itself, either in place of or in addition to the legend.

For ease of detection, marks should have the exact same appearance as on the map itself, including the size and orientation of symbols. Our perception of visual marks is sensitive to orientation, in that a symbol rotated 90 degrees or 180 degrees will be perceived differently, and might even be unrecognized with the additional burden of having to relearn it. For example, a square rotated 45 degrees becomes a diamond, which in this case also has a different verbal description.

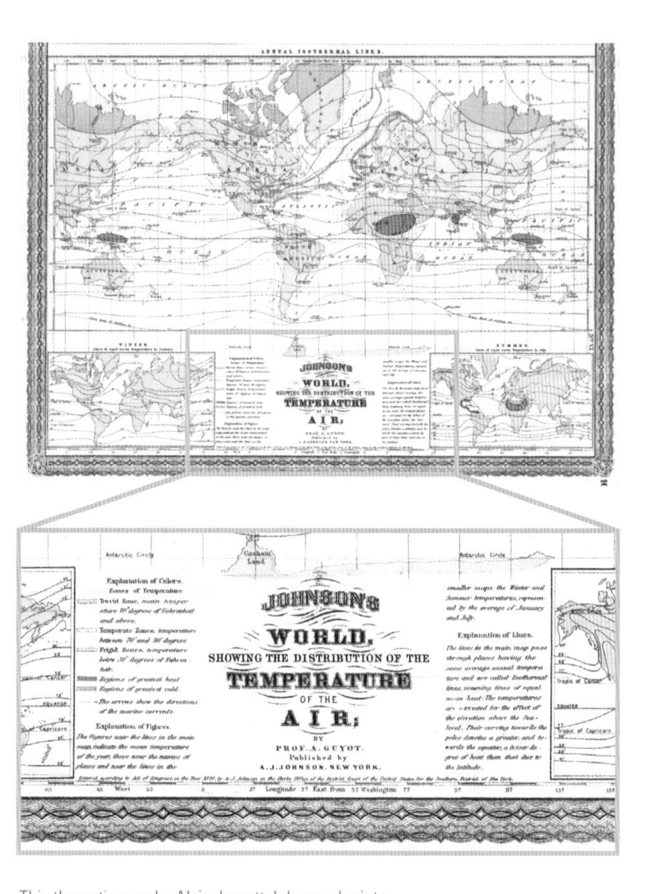

This thematic map by Alvin Jewett Johnson depicts the average air temperatures for different parts of the world. It was published in the 1870 edition of his *New Illustrated Atlas*. Similar to other early thematic maps reproduced in the chapter, Johnson explains in length how to read the encoding.

Segregation between Figure and Ground

The segregation between figure and ground principle describes the tendency to organize visual elements into units and to construct relationships. In this process some elements are selected as figure and the remaining as ground.

A central factor in perceiving objects is the detection of boundaries. Figure and ground should be easily distinguished. Otherwise, ambiguity is produced and they can be perceived as reversible.

Segregation between figure and ground is a dynamic process: perception shifts from one to the other possible image without stability. In the image above, we either perceive two white faces on a yellow background or a yellow vase on a white background—but not the two simultaneously.

Studies have shown that certain graphical variables enhance segregation of figure and ground. For example, the graphical variable of scale can influence how we perceive objects: a small shape in a larger shape will be viewed as the figure.

Another cue that has been reported is the tendency to perceive lower regions in the display as more figurelike than regions in the upper portion. The two images above are identically constructed. Despite the shift in color, people tend to perceive the bottom region as the figure.

VISUAL VARIABLES

Bertin is considered to be the first to have proposed a theory of graphical representation of data for use in maps, diagrams, and networks, published in his seminal book *Semiology of Graphics* in 1967 in France, with the first English edition in 1983. His theory is based on semiology and associates the basic graphic elements with visual variables and types of phenomena. Although Bertin's system has been widely adopted by cartographers and designers when selecting the appropriate type of marks for encoding data, it also has been expanded to include other variables not considered initially. One finds in the literature various proposals for expansions that are geared toward different purposes and the needs of specific fields.[24] For example, most proposals have added the variable of color saturation to the other color variables of hue and value. Other proposals include tactual elements in maps for visually impaired users and dynamic variables for maps changing over time.

The system presented here builds on Bertin's initial framework with the addition of variables from other systems that are relevant to the visualizations analyzed throughout this book. The system is not prescriptive; rather, the goal is to provide guidelines for appropriately matching types of phenomena (described previously) with graphic elements and visual variables. For example, in cases involving ordered data, visual order should be perceived in the corresponding visual encoding. If that is not the case, then the visual encoding is unsuitable and could be misleading. As Ware explains, "Good design optimizes the visual thinking process. The choice of patterns and symbols is important so that visual queries can be efficiently processed by the intended viewer. This means choosing words and patterns each to their best advantage."[25]

The basic **graphic elements**, the primitives of visual representation, and their semantics are[26]

- **Point** has no dimension and provides a sense of place.
- **Line** has one dimension and provides a sense of length and direction.
- **Plane** has two dimensions and provides a sense of space and scale.

The **visual variables** correspond to visual channels and the way features are extracted in our brains. As Ware explains, "Visual information is first processed by large arrays of neurons in the eye and in the primary visual cortex at the back of the brain. Individual neurons are selectively tuned to certain kinds of information, such as the orientation of edges or the color of a patch of light."[27] Going back to chapter 1, in the section on the model of human visual information processing, you will notice that the variables listed below are among the preattentive features illustrated on page 23.

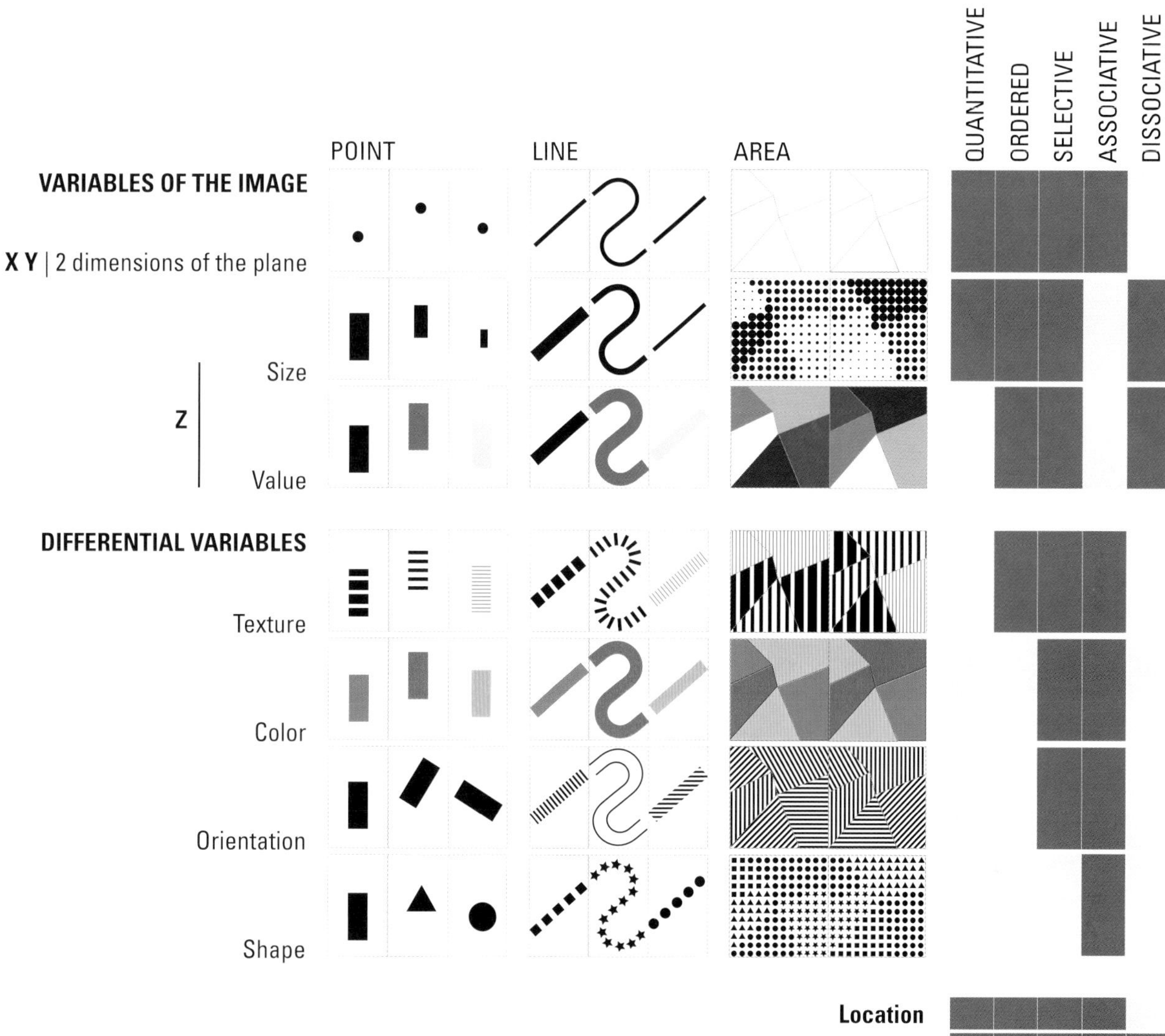

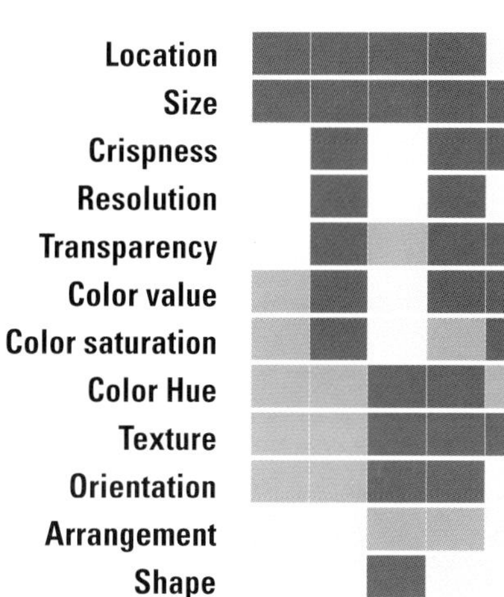

BERTIN'S SYSTEM OF PERCEPTUAL VARIABLES

Jacques Bertin introduced the term *visual variables* in his seminal book *Semiologie Graphique*. The diagram above presents his system of perceptual variables with the corresponding signifying properties. Dark gray stands for appropriateness.[36]

Bertin's system has been extended over time to include other variables, such as color saturation. Also included in the bottom table is a new visual variable introduced by MacEachren, *clarity,* that consists of the three subvariables listed in the table: crispness, resolution, and transparency. Other variables considered by map makers, but not included here, refer to motion, like velocity, direction, and frequency for example. The table was compiled after MacEachren, with middle gray standing for "marginally effective."[37]

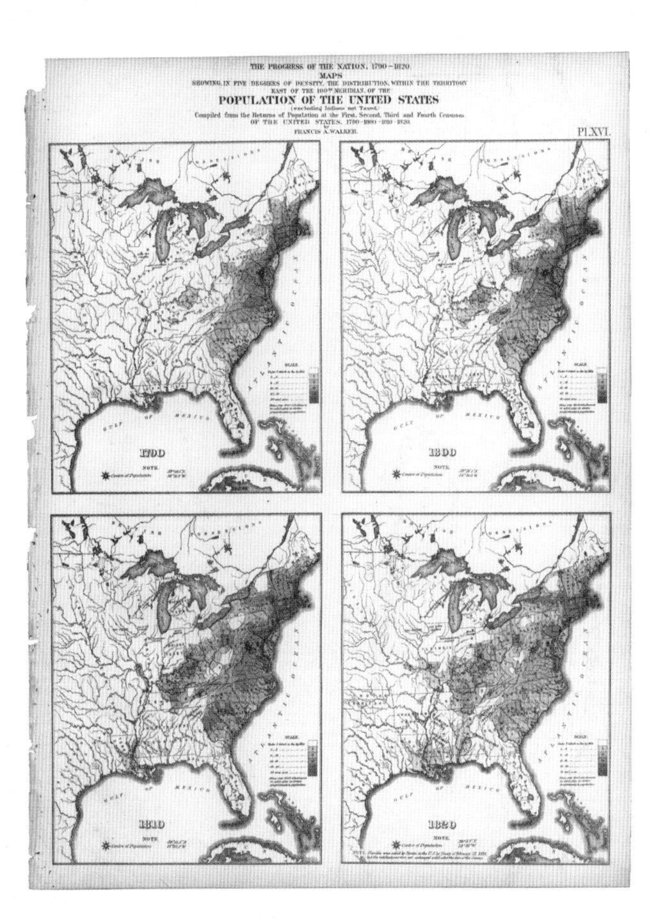

The multiple maps by Francis A. Walker depict the population of the United States for the years 1790, 1800, 1810, and 1820 compiled with data from the first through fourth censuses accordingly. "The Progress of the Nation, 1720–1820 Maps" are classed into five groups of population density, from white (under 2 inhabitants to the sq. mile) to dark gray (90 and over). The maps were published in the *Statistical Atlas of the United States* in 1874, for occasion of the results of the ninth census.

These features can increase the performance of tasks requested by visualizations, such as target detection, boundary detection, region tracking, and counting and estimation.

The visual variables are organized into two functional groups: positional (in space, or where; and in time, or when) and visual properties of the entity (what). Positional variables are processed separately in the brain and have a dominant role in perceptual organization and memory; they are described by the two dimensions of the plane (*x* and *y*), the time dimension (display time), and spatial arrangement.[28] Nine visual properties are considered: shape (and texture shape), size, color hue, color value, color saturation, orientation (and texture orientation), texture arrangement, texture density, and texture size.

Different from other visualizations, thematic maps are not concerned with conceptualizing the topological structure, which is provided by the geographic information in the form of the base map. All other visualizations in this book require the crucial step of deciding on the most appropriate topological structure, especially with regard to visual representation of abstract data.

GRAPHICAL METHODS

There are six graphical methods used primarily in thematic maps for representing all sorts of qualitative and quantitative data:

1. **Dot distribution maps**
2. **Graduated symbol maps**
4. **Isometric and isopleth maps**
5. **Flow and network maps**
3. **Choropleth maps**
6. **Area and distance cartograms**

What follows is a brief historical account of these techniques with a brief examination of recent best practices.

WELL-KNOWN VISUAL ILLUSIONS TO WATCH FOR

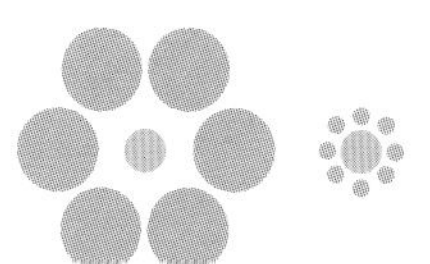

The *Ebbinghaus illusion* or *Titchener circles* is an optical illusion of relative **size** perception. The two yellow circles are of identical size. The one surrounded by large circles (left) appears smaller in size than the one surrounded by small circles (right).

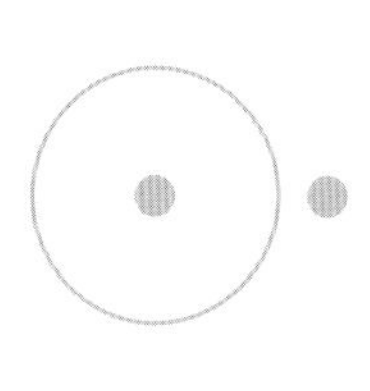

The *Delboeuf illusion:* Two identically sized circles that are near each other appear to have different **sizes** when one is surrounded by a ring. If the surrounding ring is closer to its inner circle, it will appear larger than the nonsurrounded circle, whereas it will look smaller if the surrounding ring is larger. The *Delboeuf illusion* is similar to the *Ebbinghaus illusion.*

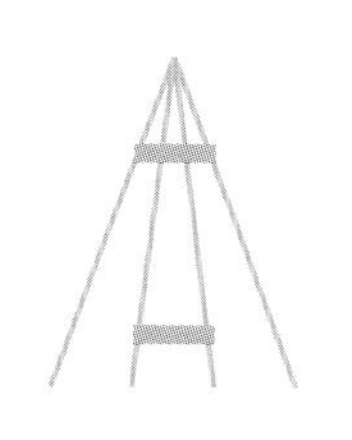

The *Ponzo Illusion:* two identically sized lines appear to have different **sizes** when placed over lines that seem to converge as they recede into the distance.

The *Muller-Lyer illusion* is an optical illusion of relative **length** perception: The three horizontal lines are identical, but they appear to have different lengths depending on the direction of the arrow, if pointing inward or outward the line segment.

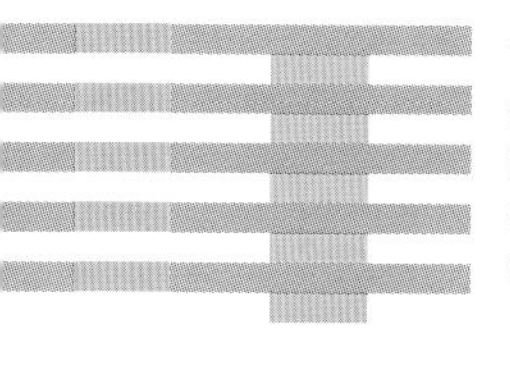

The *White's illusion:* the yellow rectangles on the left are perceived as lighter than the rectangles on the right, despite having the exact same color hue and **color brightness**.

The *Zöllner illusion* is an optical illusion of the misperception of **orientation**: The horizontal lines are parallel, but they do not appear parallel due to the different angles of the shorter lines.

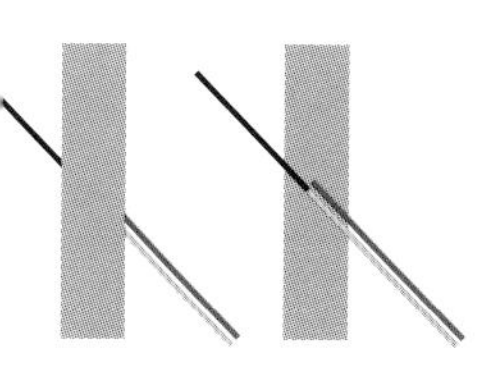

The *Poggendorff illusion* is an optical illusion of misperception of **position.** We perceive the red line to be a continuation of the black line when there is an obstacle between them. The apparent position shifting disappears when we remove the rectangle.

Relative Judgments in Perception: Weber's Law + Stevens' Law

The nineteenth-century experimental psychologist Dr. Ernst H. Weber (1795–1878) noticed that the minimum amount by which stimulus intensity must be changed in order to produce a noticeable variation in sensory experience between two stimuli is proportional to the magnitude of the original stimulus. The minimum amount is also called the Difference Threshold or Just Noticeable Difference (JND). Imagine that we are holding one kilogram in each hand and that we add weight to one of the hands, up to when we start perceiving differences, for example at around 1.1 kilograms. The difference threshold (or the JND) in this case would be 100 grams, and the Weber fraction would equal 0.1. The fraction can be used to predict JND for other magnitudes, such that we know we would need at least 500 grams to notice changes in sensory experience when we start with a 5-kilogram weight, because we wouldn't perceive differences by only adding 100 grams to this initial amount.

Gustav T. Fechner (1801–1887) built a theory around Weber's discovery, which he called Weber's law (also known as the Weber-Fechner law), stating that the subjective sensation is proportional to the logarithm of the stimulus intensity. In other words, the stimulus varies in geometric progression to a corresponding arithmetic progression of the sensation.

In 1975 Stanley Smith Stevens showed that the relationship between the magnitude of a physical stimulus and its perceived intensity follows a power law. His results show, for example, that the power for visual length is 1.0 (totally accurate), for visual area it is 0.7, and for redness (saturation) it is 1.7. In other words, when the dimension of the area attribute increases, so does our tendency to underestimate it. The opposite happens in relation to saturation: our tendency increases to overestimating it. The graph above uses data from Stevens' seminal paper.[38]

STEVENS' PSYCHOPHYSICAL POWER LAW

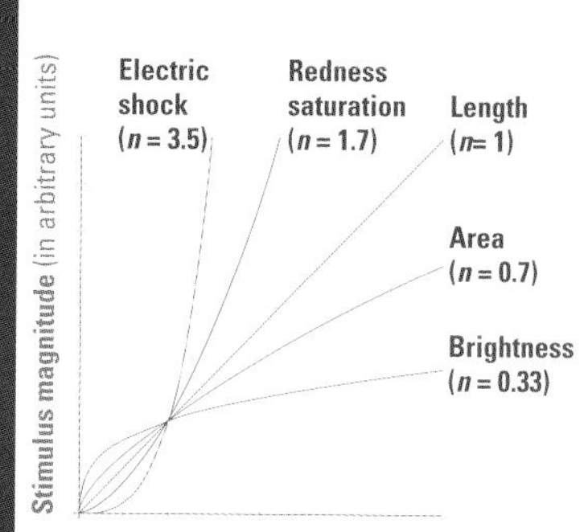

Wilkinson cautions, "The presence of bias in human information processing does not imply that we should normalize the physical world to an inferred perceptual world."[39] On the other hand, if the goal is to represent differences in scale of the elements being represented, then we should pay closer attention to the bias, so as to afford discrimination between visual marks.

One implication to visual encoding is that the larger the number of visual attributes shared by marks, the harder it will be to note differences among them. Take, for example, the difficulties in reading text formatted using only uppercase letters, in contrast to uppercase and lowercase renditions.

Kosslyn advises, "Except for very large or very small starting levels, a constant proportion of the smaller value must be added in order for a larger value to be distinguishable...The law applies to size, lightness, thickness, density of dots, cross-hatching, and type of dashes."[40]

CASE STUDY

DOT DISTRIBUTION MAPS

Dot distribution maps aim at revealing the spatial distribution of phenomena using the basic element of a point as the visual mark. The maps can depict two sets of discrete data: discrete phenomenon with known geo-location information, such as medical mappings, or discrete phenomena with smooth variation, like most maps depicting census data, in which symbols are distributed within the corresponding geographic area in order to portray densities (not the specific locations of the phenomena). Whole numbers, rather than derived numbers, should be used in either case to equate to the value of symbols. In the first case, a dot equates to one phenomenon, and in the latter, it corresponds to an aggregated value (e.g., one dot representing 1,000 people).

Given the current access to geo-tagged digital data, we now see a proliferation of maps with a one-to-one correspondence between datum and symbol. In these maps, dots are positioned according to a precise location (*x*-, *y*-coordinates) given by the phenomenon. The maps by Eric Fischer using Flickr data are good examples.

This 1830 map by Frère de Montizon depicts population in France by administrative departments. It is the earliest known use of irregularly spaced dots as an encoding. Each dot stands for 10,000 people. The innovation of dot distribution maps went unnoticed for a while, as Robinson explains, "except for a few rather crude, large-scale applications, without clear unit values... in medical mapping, we sill see that this basically simple, logical idea had to wait some thirty years to be reinvented and much longer than that to become generally known."[43]

But, not all datasets contain geo-locational information for individual occurrences. Rather, most data are provided by enumeration tracts, as exemplified in the demographic map published by the *New York Times*. In these cases, three parameters should be taken into account when creating the map: the unit value, the dot size, and the dot location.

Assigning the unit value and the unit size largely affect how the map is perceived. For example, if the dot size is too small, and each unit equates to large numbers, the map might be perceived as representing phenomena that are sparser than in actuality. Similarly, if a dot size is too large, and each unit equates to small numbers, the map might give a wrong impression of high density. Problems get even harder in datasets with large density variations, for which some cartographers have used a combination of graduated and distributed dot methods. Decisions on dot placement are also not trivial and will affect perception. For manually positioning dots, it is recommended to group features according to a center of gravity within the statistical unit, as well as cross relating with other meaningful geographic information, such as topography and the location of cities. For example, in maps portraying agricultural data, it would be meaningful not to cluster symbols in urban areas. The smaller the statistical area, the easier and more meaningful the distribution of symbols will be. There are, however, a number of available programs for producing dot distribution maps, because most maps are now produced digitally.[41] Also recommended is the *nomograph* developed by J. Ross Mackay as a tool to help determine the relationship between dot size and unit value.[42]

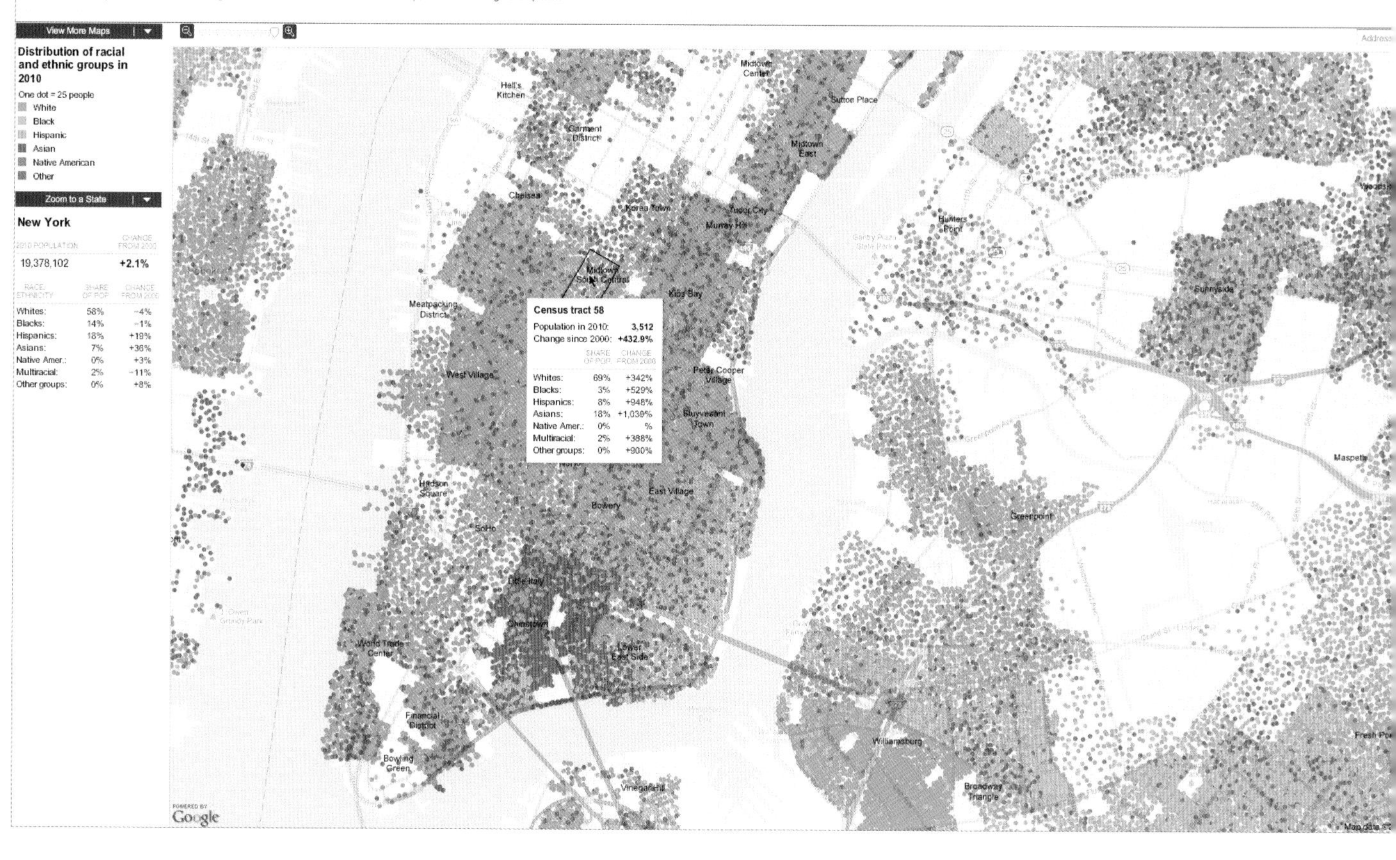

Matthew Bloch, Shan Carter, and Alan McLean (*New York Times*), U.S.: "Mapping the 2010 U.S. Census," 2010.

The *New York Times* published an online series of interactive maps showing data from the 2010 census (Census Bureau; socialexplorer.com). The maps depict population growth and decline, changes in racial and ethnic concentrations, and patterns of housing development.

This map and the maps on the next page portray the distribution of racial and ethnic groups in the United States. The technique is dot distribution, where one dot in the map stands for twenty-five people. Dots are evenly distributed across each census tract or county. Because the map is interactive, one can look at different parts of the country and learn about their specific ethnical configurations, including trends provided by changes from the previous census in 2000.

http://projects.nytimes.com/census/2010/map

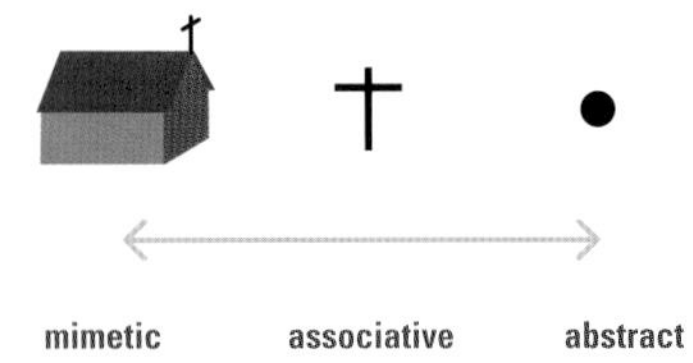

The diagram exemplifies different types of point marks that can be used in maps as well as other visualizations: pictorial, associative, and geometric.

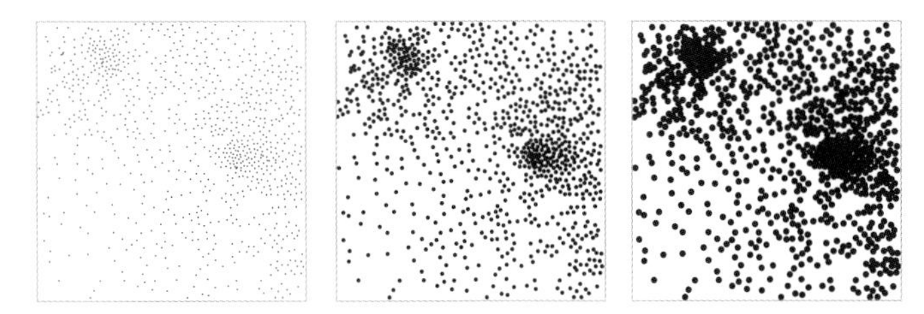

Changes in the size and value of the marks cause different impressions of the data in dot distribution maps. When the dots are too small, as in the first image, the patterns are hardly perceived. The converse situation happens in the far right image, where the dots are too large, giving an erroneous impression of densities. [44]

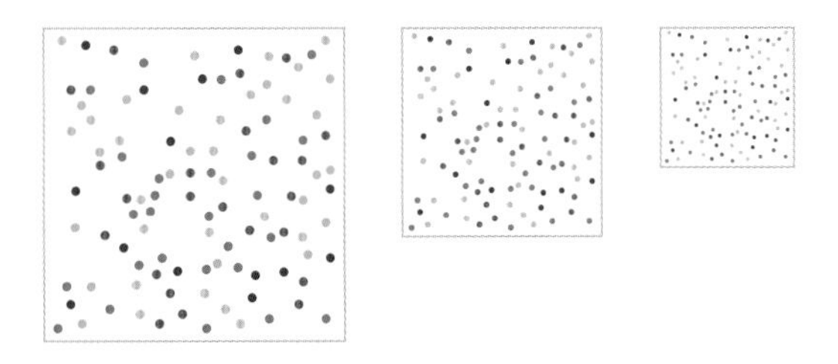

The smaller the marks, the harder it is to distinguish between the color hues of the marks.

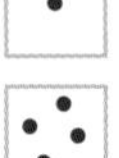

Legends are required in the case of maps where one dot equates to an aggregated value. This will help provide the viewer with some sense of estimation, especially because there is a tendency to perceive a dot with one instance. It is recommended to represent three examples of low, middle, and high densities in the map. Marks in the legend should have the same size as those in the map. Another important detail is to choose a round number for the unit value.

The circle is the most common shape, though some maps use the visual variable of shape to differentiate between categories (nominal scale). Color hue is also often used for this purpose, especially in the case of multivariate dot maps, though color hue should be used with care because it is difficult to perceive color differences in marks that are too small.

Dot maps provide an intuitive way for understanding data distribution, because variations in pattern are readily available, as clustering, for example. Dot maps are effective in portraying relative densities and, conversely, bad at displaying absolute quantities. There is, however, a tendency to underestimate the number of dots and the differences of densities between areas. As such, it is important that the unit value be a round number and clearly stated. It also helps to provide legend samples that illustrate different densities in the map, such as representations of low, middle, and high densities. As mentioned in the section on map projections, dot distribution maps require equal-area map projection, because the areas are not distorted, which is required for comparison of densities.

Because points are nondimensional elements, once the variable size is added to represent scale, the two dimensions of the plane are also added. What was a point is now a plane used to represent ordinal and quantitative data in a proportional symbol map, the focus of the next case study: graduated symbol maps.

These maps are from the same online series by the *New York Times* depicting data from the 2010 census reproduced on page 131. It is worth noting how changes in scale provide different views of the data and varying perceptions of patterns, an artifact of the dot distribution technique as discussed on this spread.

Ben Fry, U.S.: "Dencity," 2011.

In 2011, Ben Fry designed "Dencity" to show the global population density as the world reached the 7 billion milestone. Circles with varying size and hue encode population density, with larger and darker circles covering areas with fewer people. The visual encoding is effective, because the map highlights the populous areas. Fry writes, "Representing denser areas with smaller circles results in additional geographic detail where there are more people, while sparsely populated areas are more vaguely defined."[45]

Ben Fry, U.S.: "Zip code map," 2004.

In 2004, Ben Fry created this map out of curiosity about the system behind ZIP codes. The map is constructed out of all the ZIP codes in the United States. For each ZIP code number, the software positions a dot in space according to the latitude–longitude coordinates provided by the U.S. Census Bureau. The result is the rendition of the U.S. map with a clear understanding of population density in the country, because there are more ZIP code numbers in denser areas. Considering that it is an interactive online tool, it is possible to search for ZIP codes as well as highlight areas that share the same partial numbers, such as all codes starting with 0, or with 33, and so on. A detailed description of this project, together with the source code, can be found in his book *Visualizing Data*.[46]

http://benfry.com/zipdecode

This map depicts the cholera epidemic of 1854 in the south of London, considered one of the worst ever, killing around 500 people in ten days within a perimeter of 250 yards (228 m).[47] The British anesthesiologist Dr. John Snow mapped the outbreak in an effort to argue for his theory that cholera was a waterborne illness, not an airborne disease, as was believed at the time. Dr. Snow used the General Register Office's weekly mortality report of London as the source for laying out the individual deaths (represented as bars) in relation to the water sources (represented as circles) in the urban area of St. James, Westminster. To the official data, he added local knowledge, such as information provided by Reverend Whitehead, who also had mapped the outbreak.[48]

The map did not pioneer the use of point marks to depict disease occurrences. As Robinson explains, "An Inquiry into the Cause of the Prevalence of the Yellow Fever in New York" from 1797 by Seaman is considered to be the first of its kind.[49] Several medical practitioners in the beginning of the nineteenth century in Europe used maps as a means to understand environmental aspects of disease outbreaks. In medicine as well as in other fields, maps served as visual arguments of spatially grounded theories.

In the book *Disease Maps*, Tom Koch describes how "Snow developed a spatial theory that was tested in the map. This was not propaganda but an attempt at science. The map was the embodiment of Snow's proposition that if cholera was waterborne then its source had to be water, in this case, the Broad Street pump at the epicenter of the outbreak."[50] His spatial theory is more evident in the second version of the map, to which Dr. Snow added a dotted line to represent the walking distances of the neighbor population to the infected water pump. In other words, the line provided a temporal measure of how long it took to get to water sources.

Dr. Snow's map did not bring an end to the cholera epidemic, nor did it convince the health authorities of the waterborne theory. Discussions around the nature of cholera only settled in 1883, when bacteriologist Robert Koch identified Vibrio cholera as the waterborne agent.[51] The map, however, helped advance understanding of a public health issue (cholera epidemic) by revealing the disease pattern (inherently numerical) in the spatial context (walking distances to water pumps).

Steve Johnson, in his book *The Ghost Map*, writes about its legacy: "Snow's map deserves its iconic status. The case for the map's importance rests on two primary branches: its originality and its influence. The originality of the map did not revolve around the decision to map an epidemic, or even the decision to encode deaths in bars etched across the street diagram. If there was a formal innovation, it was that wobbly circumference that framed the outbreak in the second version, the Voronoi diagram. But the real innovation lay in the data that generated that diagram, and in the investigation that compiled the data in the first place. Snow's Broad Street map was a bird's eye view, but it was drawn from true street-level knowledge."[52]

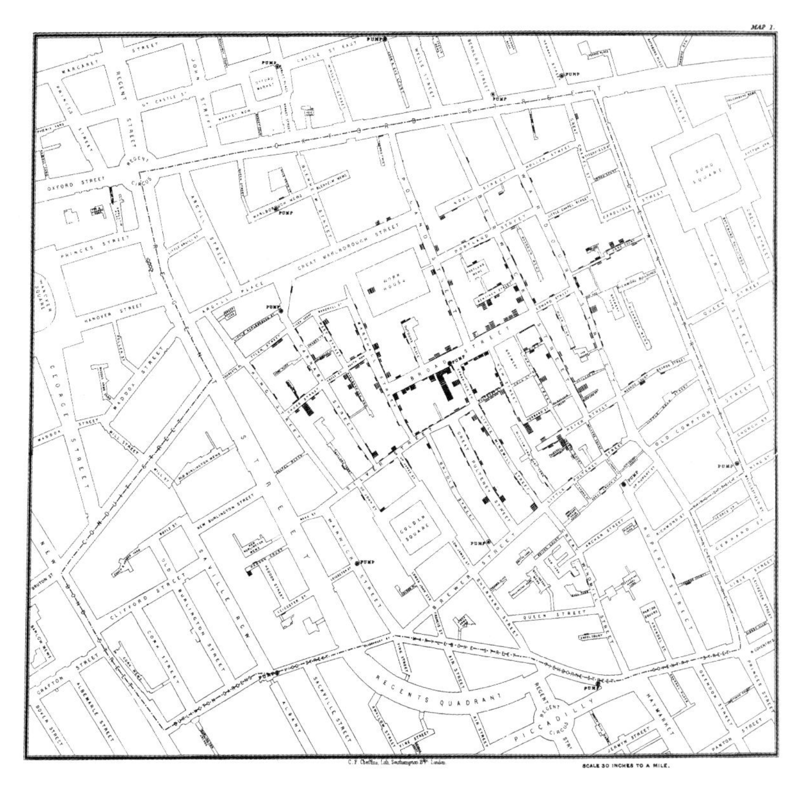

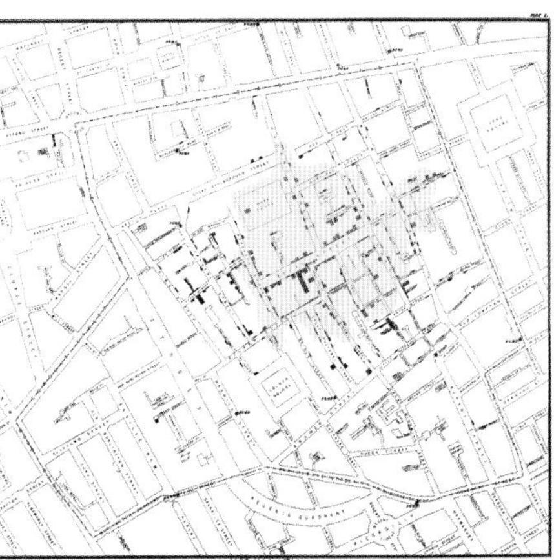

The yellow area corresponds to the line Dr. Snow drew on the map to depict the equal walking distances between the Broad Street water pump and other pumps.

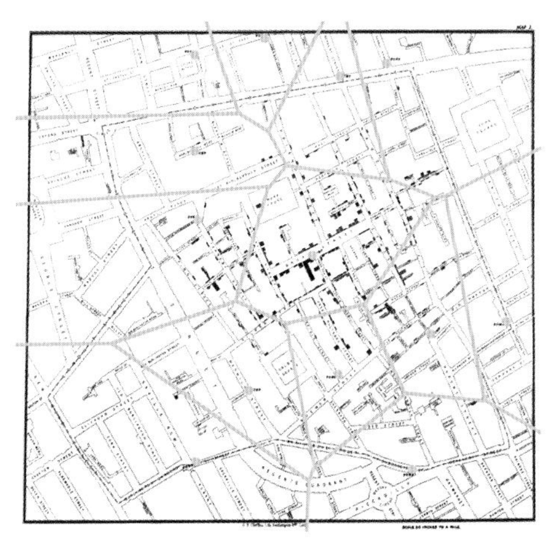

Dr. Snow did not use a Voronoi diagram in his efforts to understand the cholera outbreak. However, when we draw a Voronoi diagram onto the original map, it shows that the cell containing the largest number of deaths coincides with the one where the Broad Street water pump is located.

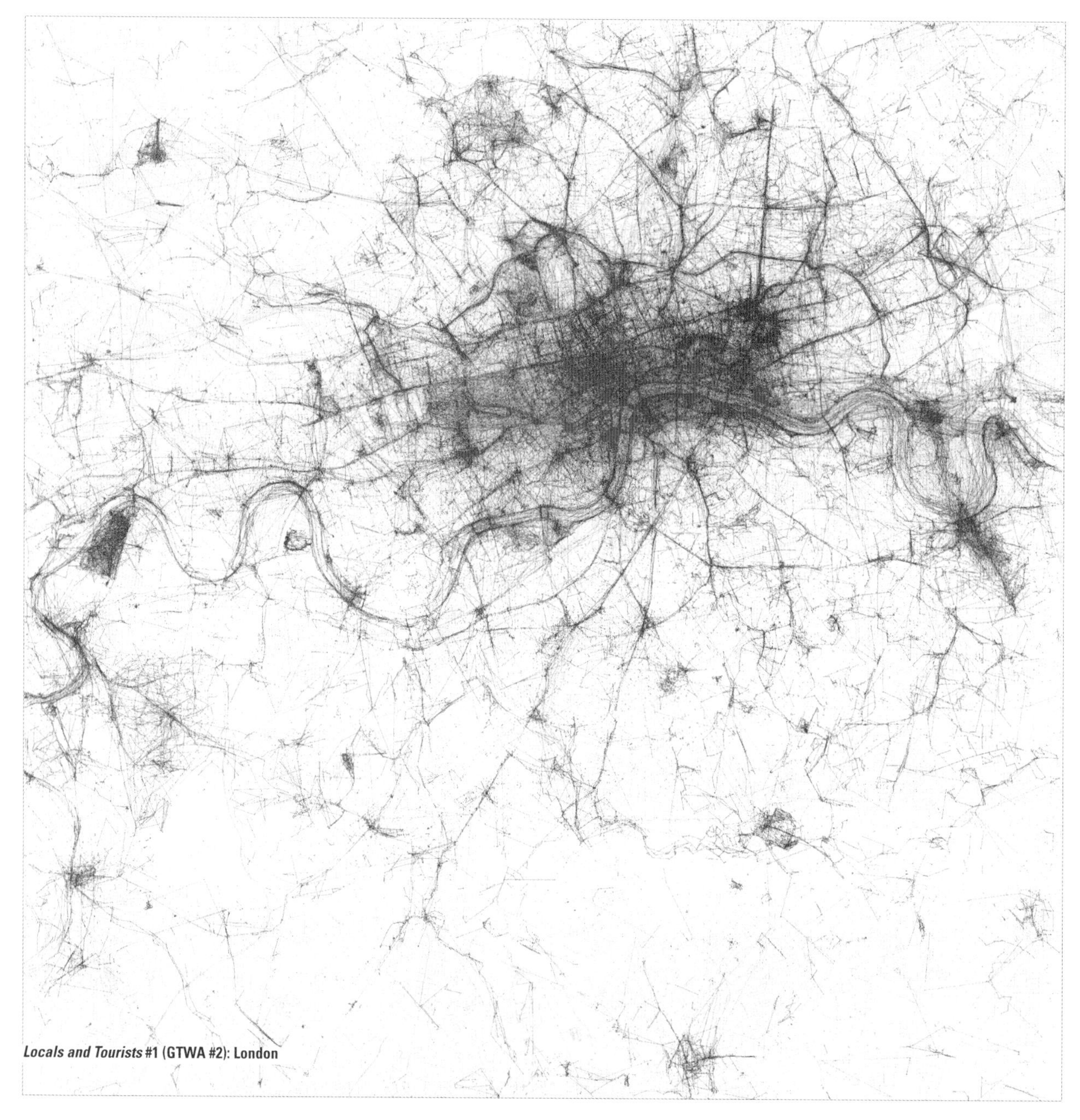

Locals and Tourists **#1 (GTWA #2): London**

Eric Fischer, U.S.: "Locals and Tourists," 2010.

Eric Fischer created this set of thematic maps "Locals and Tourists" in 2010. The dots depict the location of photos that were geo-tagged and uploaded to the photo server Flickr. By analyzing the frequency of photos taken in the locations, Fischer was able to categorize photographers into three groups according to the criteria and color code as follows:

- Local photographers (blue dots): Locals are those who have taken pictures in this city over a range of a month or more.
- Tourists (red dots): Tourists are defined by two criteria: those who took pictures in this city for less than a month but also seem to be a local of a different city, provided by the number of photos there.
- Undefined (yellow dots): Undefined stands for images for which it was not possible to determine whether or not the photographer was a tourist, because pictures were not taken anywhere else for over a month.

www.flickr.com/photos/walkingsf/sets/72157624209158632

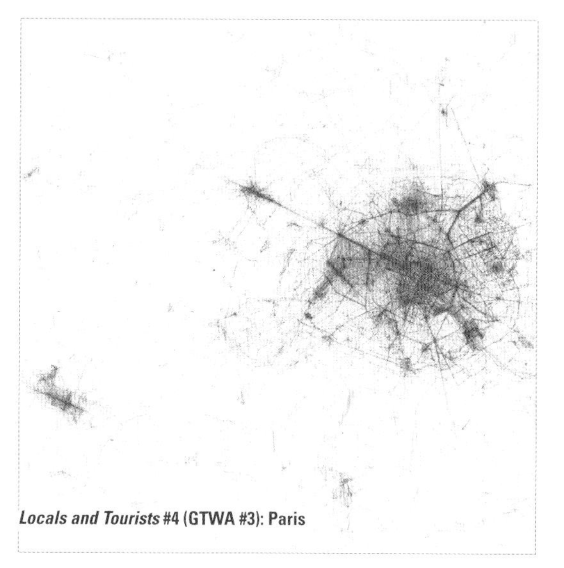
Locals and Tourists #4 (GTWA #3): Paris

Locals and Tourists #36 (GTWA #40): Moscow

Locals and Tourists #2 (GTWA #1): New York

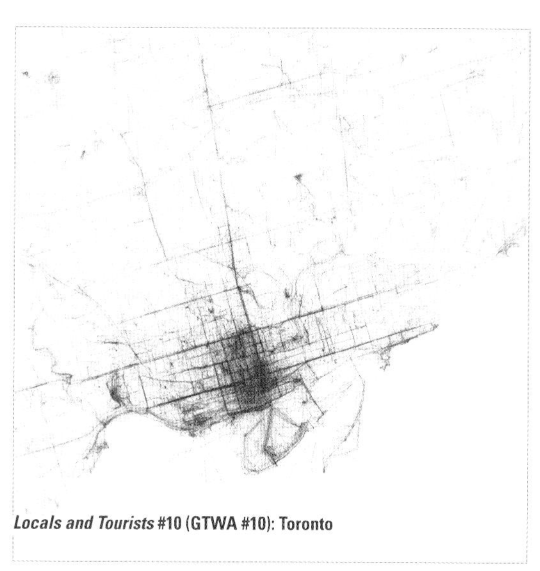
Locals and Tourists #10 (GTWA #10): Toronto

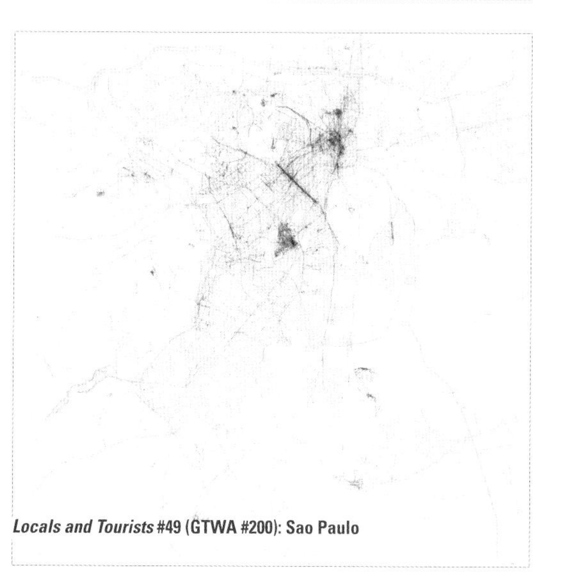
Locals and Tourists #49 (GTWA #200): Sao Paulo

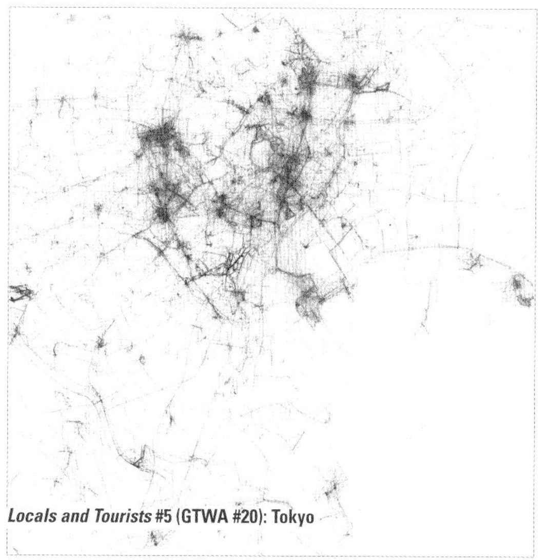
Locals and Tourists #5 (GTWA #20): Tokyo

CASE STUDY

GRADUATED SYMBOL MAPS

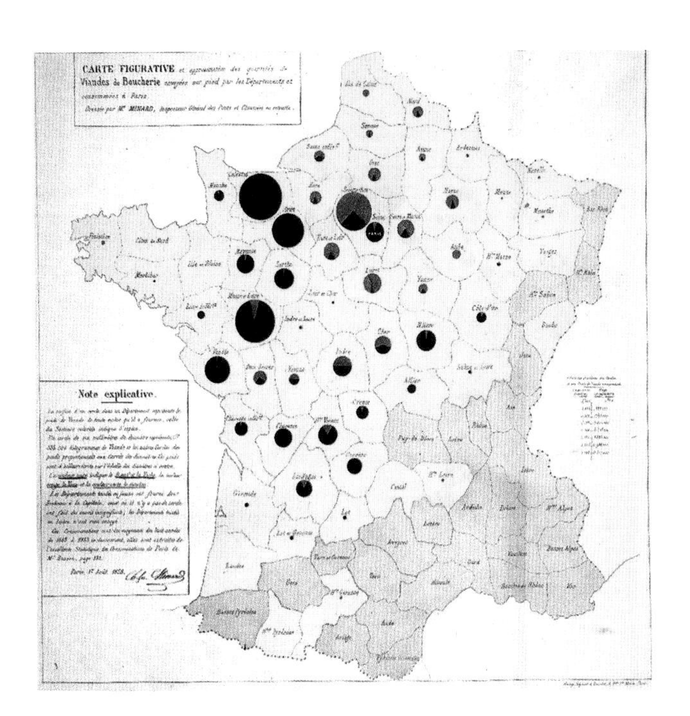

This 1858 map by Charles Minard is considered the first to have used graduated pie charts in maps.[53] It portrays the amount of butcher's meat supplied by each French department to the Paris market between the years 1845 and 1853 ("Carte figurative et approximative des quantités de viandes de boucherie envoyés sur pied par les départements et consommés à Paris"). Each circle is scaled to represent the proportional quantities of meat supplied by the administrative departments. The wedges of the pie charts refer to relative amounts of beef (in black), veal (in red), and mutton (in green). The color encoding the base map stand for departments supplying meat (in yellow) and not supplying meat (in bister). The departments lacking circles supplied meat, but in too small amounts to be noted.

Graduated symbol maps use the visual variable of size to proportionally represent magnitudes of thematic discrete data. The size is proportional to the quantities represented, but not dependent on the geographical area over which it stands. This characteristic helps avoid problems of confounding geographic area with data values, as in the case of choropleth maps (see page 142).

There are two main variables to consider when designing a graduated symbol map: the shape of the symbol and the scaling. The shape of the marks can vary, and the most common shape is the circle, although we see rectangular bars as well as triangles being used. There have been attempts at three-dimensional symbols, where the scaling is done to the cube rather than to the square root. But, if area perception is already hard in two dimensions, and often underestimated, then it gets even more problematic judging relative sizes of quantities provided by volumes. Glyphs have also been used for depicting more than one variable. The 1858 map by Minard is the first known example, where pie charts are used to portray different kinds of meat.

Selecting the scaling method is perhaps the biggest challenge in proportional symbol maps, as well as in choropleth maps. There are two ways to scale the size of symbols: classed, when size is range graduated, and unclassed, when sizes follow a proportional system.

In unclassed systems, the number of categories is equal to the number of data values. If there are five values, then there will be five encodings. For representing a large number of values, the most common strategy is the use of percentages. This strategy is more commonly employed in choropleth maps using color value graduation, rather than for scaling symbols, because differentiation would be almost impossible.

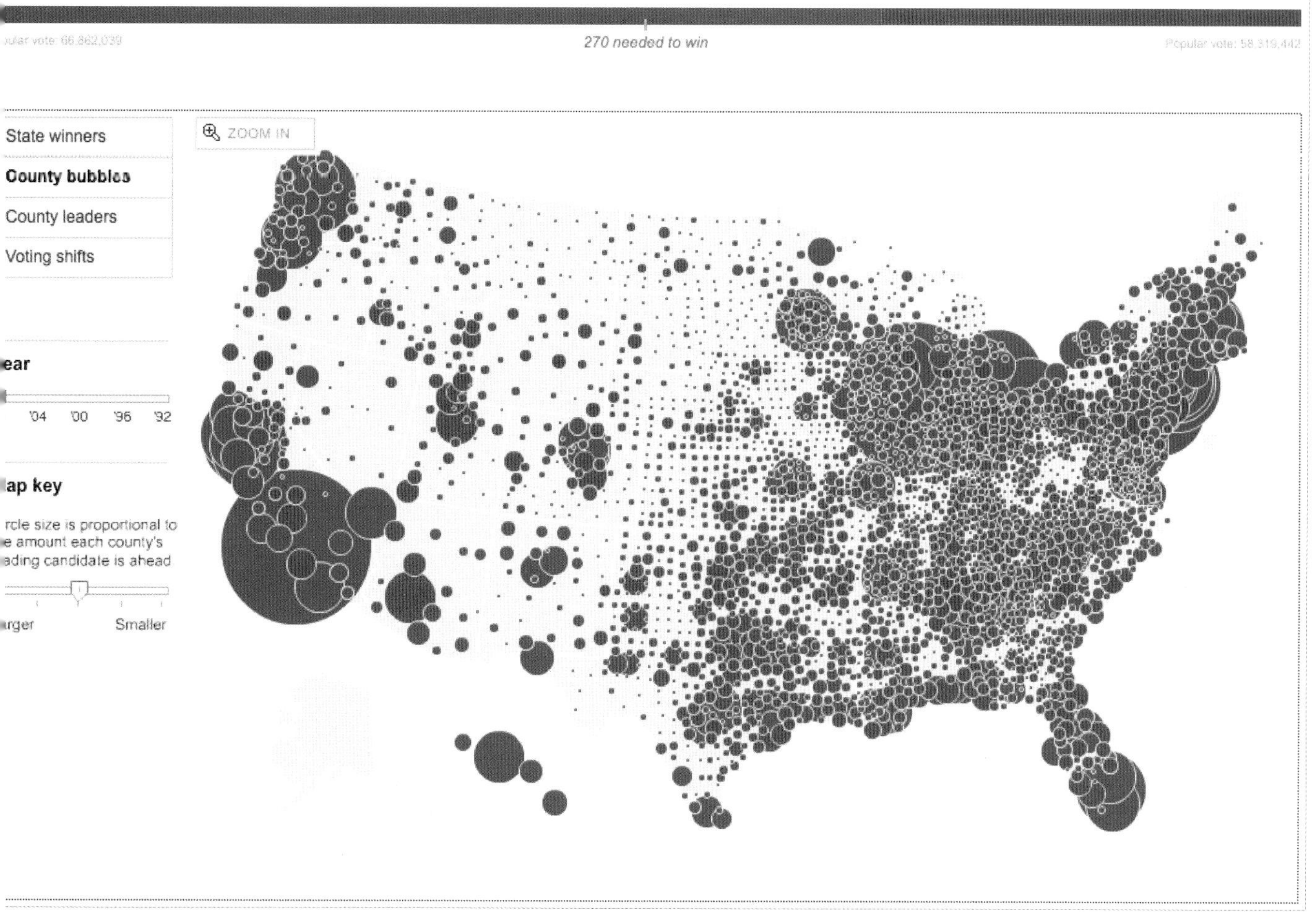

Two issues should be considered in classed systems because they influence how data are represented and thus perceived: the number of classes and the method for dividing the data. A differing number of classes influences the patterns revealed in the visualization, and it is recommended to experiment with the number of groups before making a final decision. The same holds true for the methods used for breaking down quantities (see the box Making Meaningful Groups on page 141). It is highly recommended to first analyze the data to understand certain characteristics, such as distribution. For example, using quantile methods—dividing quantities into groups of equal numbers—for representing skewed data is a poor choice, in that identical values will be divided into different groups, and different values will be grouped together. Color values and color saturation might be used to map other data attributes; however, perception is hindered in small marks.

***New York Times*, U.S.:**
"Election Results 2008," 2008.

During the presidential election in 2008, the *New York Times* published a series of visualizations showing votes by counties and state. The maps include data on previous elections back to 1992. For each year, the application allows viewers to select the visual technique used to represent the data. This spread focuses on the graduated dot symbolization. A comparison with the choropleth technique is available on the next page.

http://elections.nytimes.com/2008/results/president/map.html

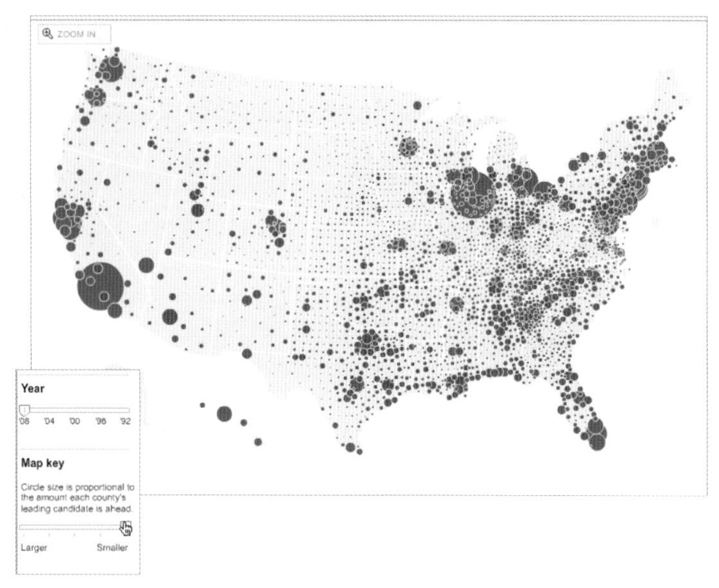
ZOOM IN
Year
'08 '04 '00 '96 '92
Map key
Circle size is proportional to the amount each county's leading candidate is ahead
Larger Smaller

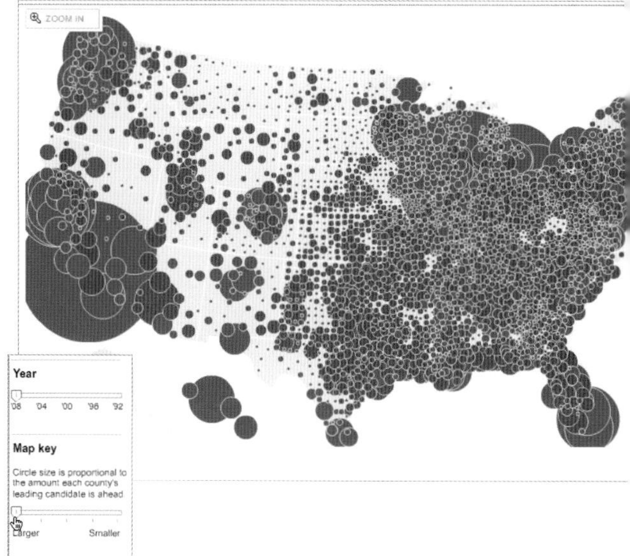
ZOOM IN
Year
'08 '04 '00 '96 '92
Map key
Circle size is proportional to the amount each county's leading candidate is ahead
Larger Smaller

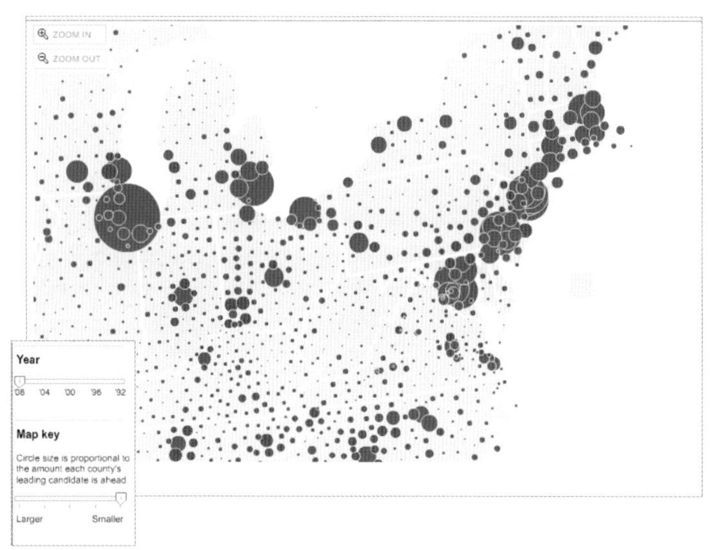
ZOOM IN
ZOOM OUT
Year
'08 '04 '00 '96 '92
Map key
Circle size is proportional to the amount each county's leading candidate is ahead
Larger Smaller

ZOOM IN
ZOOM OUT
Year
'08 '04 '00 '96 '92
Map key
Circle size is proportional to the amount each county's leading candidate is ahead
Larger Smaller

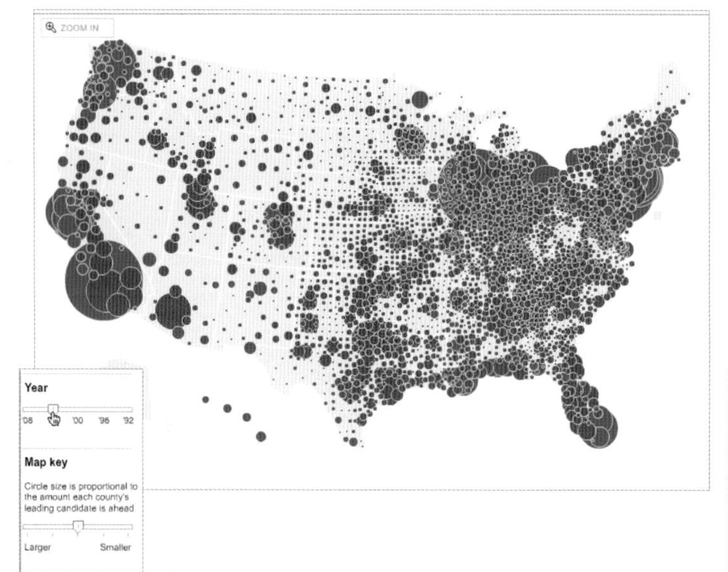
ZOOM IN
Year
'08 '00 '96 '92
Map key
Circle size is proportional to the amount each county's leading candidate is ahead
Larger Smaller

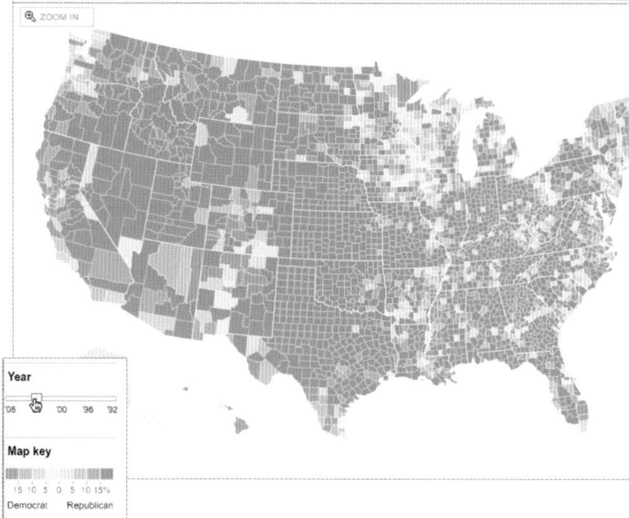
ZOOM IN
Year
'08 '00 '96 '92
Map key
15 10 5 0 5 10 15%
Democrat Republican

These maps are from the same online series shown on the previous page. The maps were published by the *New York Times* during the presidential election in 2008. Color depicts categorical data: the political affiliation of voters, whether Democrat (blue) or Republican (red). The area of circles represents quantitative data, which is proportional to the amount of votes in each county by the leading candidate. The application allows viewers to choose the graduated system providing five ways of scaling circles. Note the differences in perceiving the phenomena with the changes in the circle scales. Finally, compare the bottom row maps and how identical data is depicted using different methods: a graduated symbol map (left) and a choropleth map (right).

CORRECT METHOD: circles scaled proportional to area: calculated according to square roots

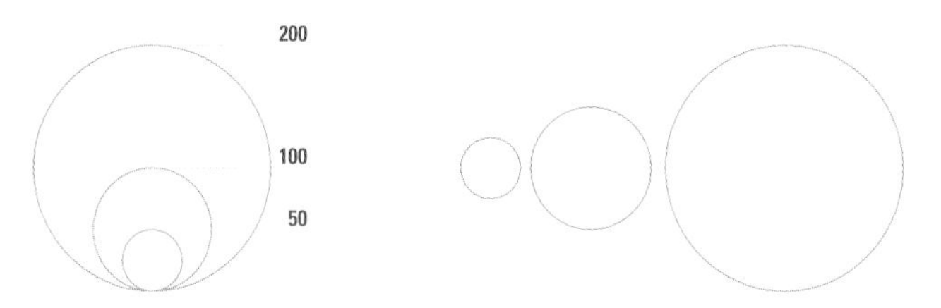

WRONG METHOD: circles scaled proportional to diameter: calculated according to radius

Using the radius of a circle symbol to stand for the statistical amount is erroneous and leads to misrepresentation of the data. Furthermore, it causes misperception of the phenomena, due to the increase in size of symbols as a consequence of the calculation. In sum, the radius of circles or the side lengths of squares should not be used to scale graduated symbols.

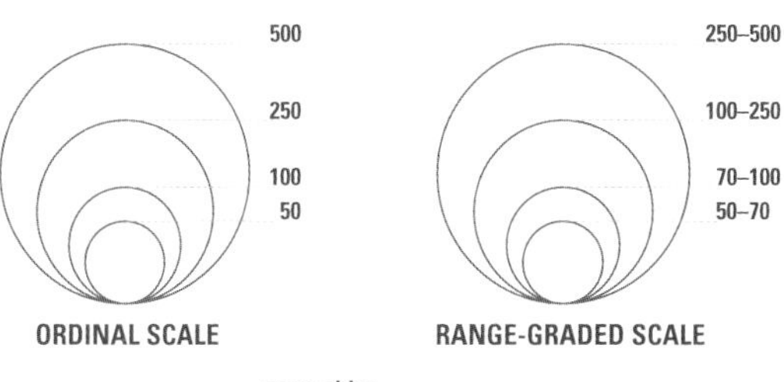

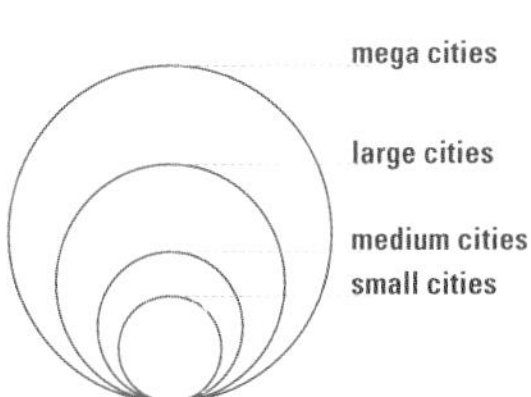

As the identical legends illustrate, we can use graduated symbols to stand for three types of scales: ordinal, range graded, and ratio. Illustration redrawn after Robinson and colleagues.[54]

Making Meaningful Groups

The goal of breaking down quantities into groups (or classes) is to enhance patterns that might otherwise not be revealed in the more detailed representation (unclassed). Closely associated with how we reveal patterns is the other side of any visualization, which is how the viewer detects patterns given our own perceptual limitations. For example, we are unable to distinguish more than seven shades of gray (see the box Magical Number Seven on page 97). Finally, the purpose of the map also helps determine how the breaks and the number of classes are defined.

The methods used for breaking down quantities are especially important and will largely influence the graphical encoding as well as how the visualization will be perceived. Carefully chosen groups will enable identification of meaningful information.

There are three basic methods for defining boundaries between the groups (or classes):

1. **Equal steps. Data are grouped into arbitrary equal divisions that can either be based on equal intervals, such as equal value steps (0–100, 100–200), or equal number of data values, such as on quantiles, where, after ordering values, data are divided by the number of classes into groups.**

2. **Unequal steps. Data are grouped using interval systems toward the upper or lower ends. Mathematical progressions help define the intervals using an arithmetic series (numeric difference) or a geometric series (numeric ratio). The method is used, for example, to depict increasing or decreasing values at either constant or varying rates. The resulting classes will contain members with similar data values.**

3. **Irregular steps. Data are grouped according to internal characteristics of the distribution. One reason for using such variable series is to highlight data values that would not be apparent when using a constant or regular series, while preserving an understanding of the whole distribution. To accomplish such complex tasks, especially when dealing with large datasets, we need to use statistical means involving both graphic and iterative techniques to help in selecting the breaks. Frequency and cumulative graphs are commonly used in those cases.**

CASE STUDY

CHOROPLETH MAPS

Choropleth maps are perhaps the most popular technique for representing statistical data using area symbols. Choropleth maps typically display data that have been aggregated by administrative units (the area symbols), and the values have been normalized (e.g., densities, ratios, averages).

One of the problems with choropleth maps is that the size of the area base for the encoding—the administrative unit—influences the perception of the quantity being represented. To avoid confounding geographic area with data values, it is crucial that normalized data be used instead of absolute data. Densities, ratios, and averages should be calculated prior to encoding.

The visual variables used in choropleth maps to encode quantitative data include color value, color saturation, and texture, or a combination of them. Color hue is often used for differentiating between categorical data in the case of multivariate maps. Color value and saturation are ordered variables, whereas color hue is not. That is the reason color value is usually used in choropleth maps, which represent range-graded data. MacEachren warns, "A common objection by cartographers to maps of quantities produced by noncartographers is that these maps often ignore the importance of the linear order schema and employ a set of eye-catching (but randomly ordered) hues. Sometimes the hues are ordered, but according to wavelength of the hue. Wavelength ordering is not immediately recognized by our visual system, and therefore is unlikely to prompt the appropriate linear order schema on the part of the viewer."[55]

Legends should help viewers recognize the implicit order. For example, do darker colors represent higher quantities? The legend should provide the answer.

The elements to be considered when designing choropleth maps are the size and shape of the area unit, the number of classes, and the method used for classifying the data.

Because visual encoding is uniformly distributed within the regions of choropleth maps, the impression is that the phenomena represented are also uniformly distributed, which most often is not the case. The overall impression of the phenomena will be more meaningful if the statistical areas are of similar shape and small in size. Whenever possible, it is recommended to avoid using areas with large variation in size and shape. The maps by the *New York Times* showing political affiliation during the 2008 presidential election provide good comparison of impressions caused when the data are represented by state and by counties.

As already discussed in the case of graduated symbol maps, the number of classes as well as the way the data are divided into the groups influence the resulting patterns. There is extensive literature devoted to methods used to determine the boundaries of classes, and the box Making Meaningful Groups (page 141) offers a brief summary of most common methods. The distribution of the data will likely provide meaningful information for the number of classes. The methods can be used for defining classes in choropleth, isarithmic, and graduated symbol maps.

Data classification will largely influence which data features are emphasized and which are suppressed. If, on one hand, having a large number of classes provides more detailed results, then, on the other hand, there are limits to how many classes of color value (or texture) we are able to distinguish. There are also differences in how we perceive monochromatic versus color symbolizations. In general, it is safe to constrain the number of classes to a maximum of five to eight classes, because the range fits into a cognitively efficient zone (see the box Magical Number Seven on page 97).

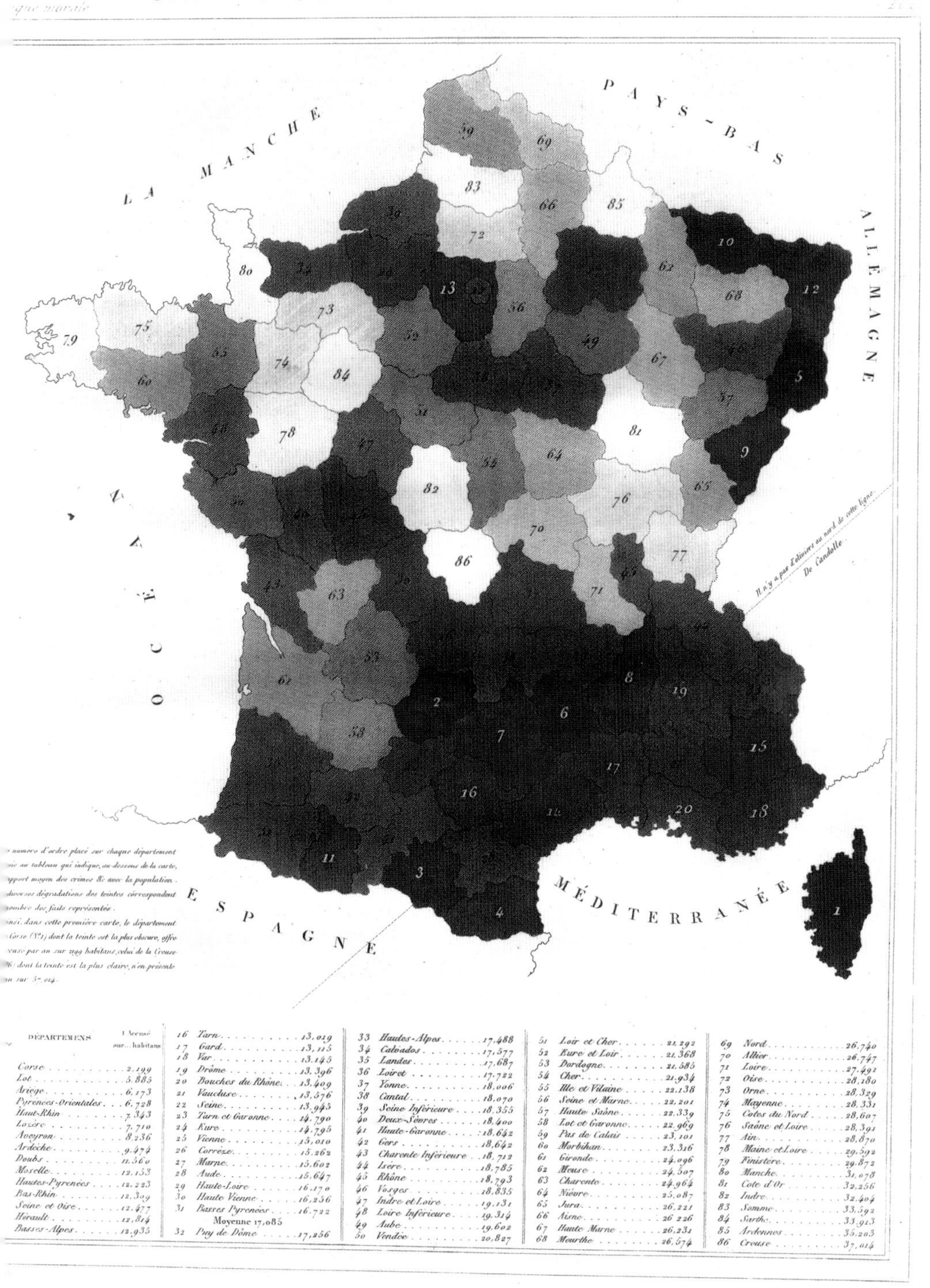

"Crimes contre les personnes" (Crimes Against People) was published in *Essai sur la statistique morale de la France* in 1833. The map depicts crime in France from 1825 to 1830 and was made by André-Michel Guerry, who is considered to have pioneered the mapping of criminal statistics.[56] There are seven shades representing different levels of crime, from dark brown (more crimes) to white (fewer crimes). Each administrative department is ranked, and the map includes the numbers. The list at the bottom provides the absolute numbers of crimes committed in each department. Note that Corsica, which belonged to France at that point in time, had the highest crime rate.

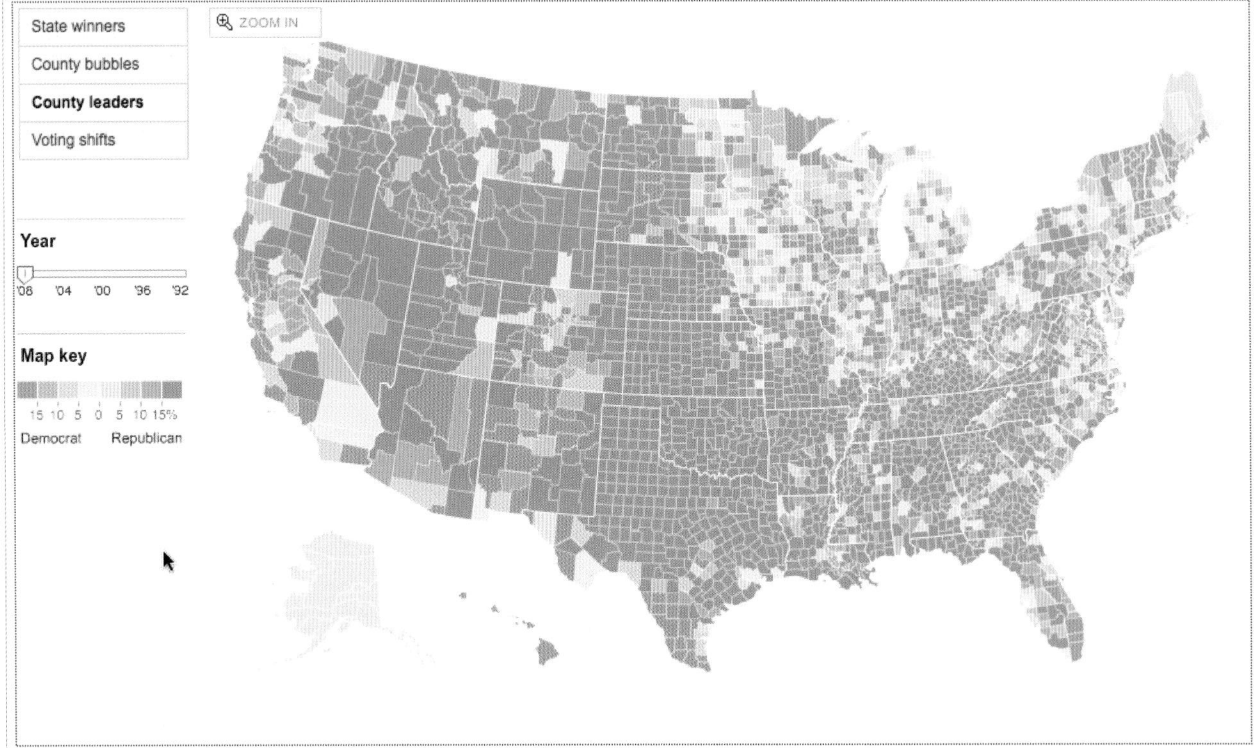

* One electoral vote in Nebraska remains undecided. The state allocates its electoral votes on the basis of the results in each Congressional district. Only 569 votes separate John McCain and Barack Obama in unofficial returns from the 2nd District.

***New York Times*, U.S.: "Election Results 2008," 2008.**

The two choropleth maps depict votes by state (top) and by counties (bottom) during the presidential election in 2008. The maps published by the *New York Times* online belong to the same series already discussed in the section about graduated symbol maps on page 138.

Color hue depicts categorical data: the political affiliation of voters, whether Democrats (blue) or Republicans (red). In the map depicting counties (bottom), color value represents quantitative data, which is proportional to the amount of votes in each county by the leading candidate.

http://elections.nytimes.com/2008/results/president/map.html

Given the relativity of color perception, color should be used with care, especially when encoding quantities. Critical issues to consider when making decisions about palettes include color blindness and perceptual illusions (e.g., light colors are perceived as larger areas than darker colors are). The box Selecting Color Schemes presents a good summary on the perception and the most appropriate scales for use in visualization (see next page).

Because data are encoded within defined contained areas, there is a strong impression of abrupt changes at the boundaries. One attempt at showing smoother transitions is provided by the dasymetric technique. The technique combines methods used in choropleth and isopleth maps, in that it represents areas independent of the statistical units.

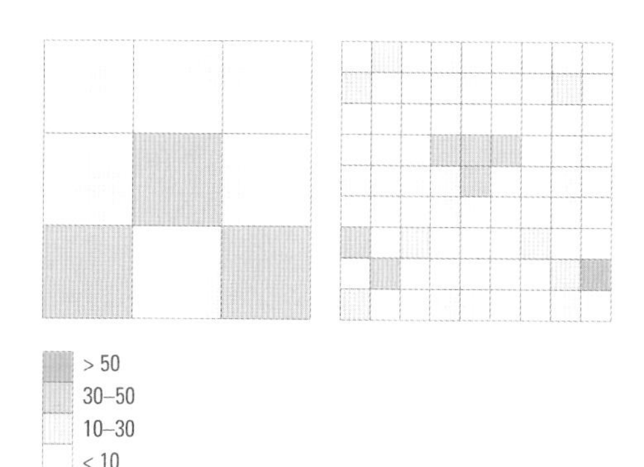

The *New York Times* election 2008 choropleth maps clearly exemplify the influence the sizes of the statistical units have on the representation of the phenomena. As the schematic images above show, representations are more informative when the units are smaller.

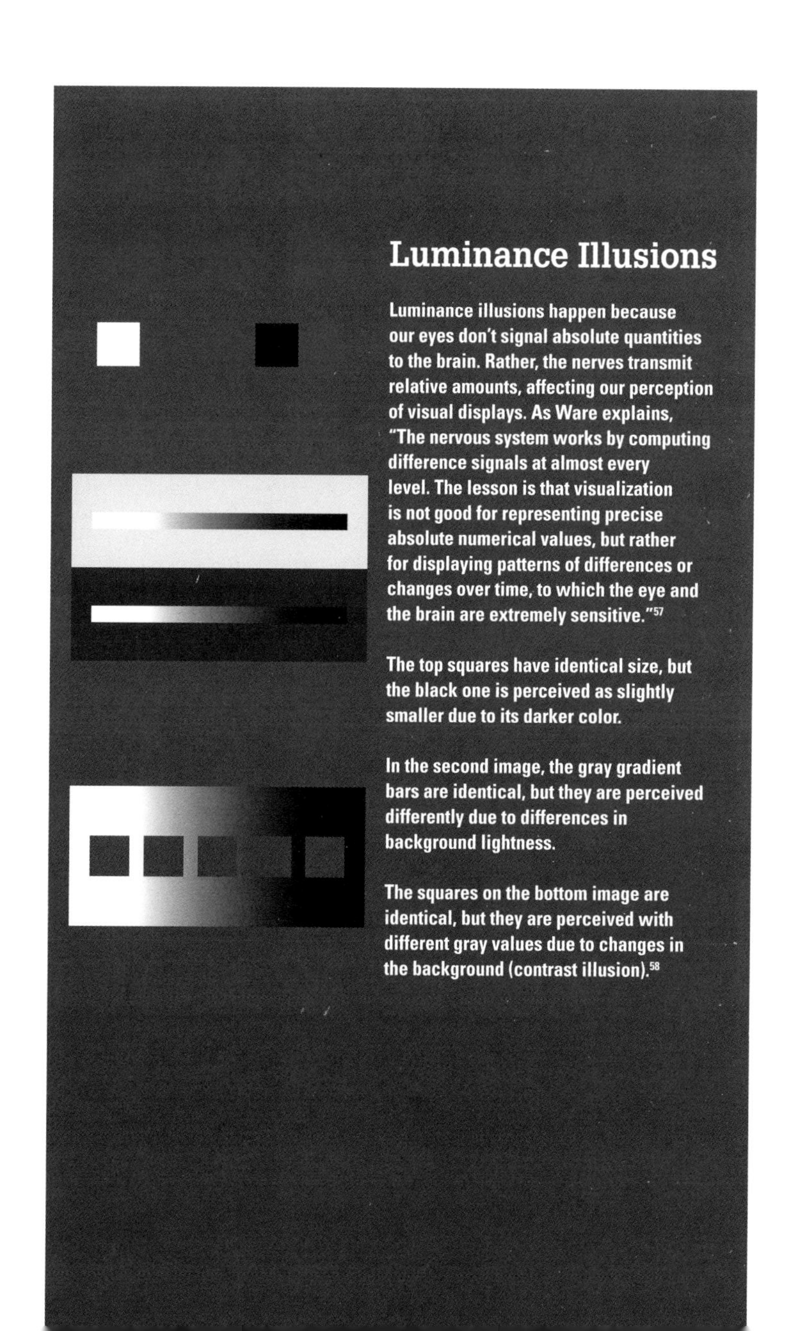

Luminance Illusions

Luminance illusions happen because our eyes don't signal absolute quantities to the brain. Rather, the nerves transmit relative amounts, affecting our perception of visual displays. As Ware explains, "The nervous system works by computing difference signals at almost every level. The lesson is that visualization is not good for representing precise absolute numerical values, but rather for displaying patterns of differences or changes over time, to which the eye and the brain are extremely sensitive."[57]

The top squares have identical size, but the black one is perceived as slightly smaller due to its darker color.

In the second image, the gray gradient bars are identical, but they are perceived differently due to differences in background lightness.

The squares on the bottom image are identical, but they are perceived with different gray values due to changes in the background (contrast illusion).[58]

Selecting Color Schemes

Color has three perceptual dimensions:

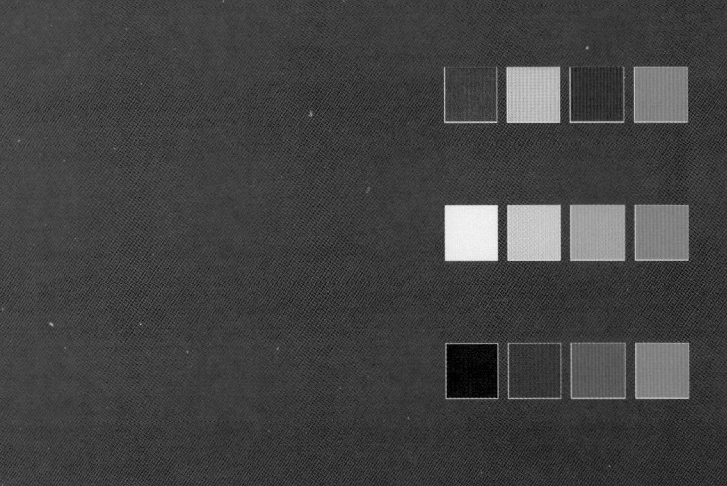

Color hues are what we commonly associate with color names. Color hues are not ordered and allow differentiation only between features, such that yellow is different from blue, green from red, and so on.

Color lightness, also called luminance, is a relative measure and describes the amount of light reflected (or emitted) from an object when compared to what appears white in the scene. Lightness is ranked, and we can talk about a scale from lighter to darker values within a hue.

Color saturation refers to the vividness of a color hue. In the design field, saturation is often called shade or tint. Color saturation varies with color lightness, in that saturations are lower for darker colors. The more desaturated a hue is, the closer it gets to gray—in other words, the closer it gets to a neutral color with no hue.

It is not an easy task selecting effective color schemes for thematic maps and data visualizations in general. This box offers advice from Cynthia Brewer's theories for selecting appropriate color schemes by taking into consideration the nature of the data, as summarized in the graphic typology to the left (drawn after Brewer). More information is available online at the Color Brewer tool, where you can interactively select the number of data classes, with a few other parameters, such as whether the output will be printed (CMYK) or screen based (RGB or HEX), and have color schemes recommended to you:

http://colorbrewer2.org

The number of data classes influences the choice of color schemes; the larger the number of classes, the larger the number of colors needed. The box Magical Number Seven explains the perceptual and cognitive constraints with having more than five to seven classes of objects, and how it might affect legibility as well as memorability of the material in front of us (page 97). Brewer explains, "Many cartographers advise that you use five to seven classes for a choropleth map. Isoline maps, or choropleth maps with very regular spatial patterns, can safely use more data classes because similar colors are seen next to each other, making them easier to distinguish."[59]

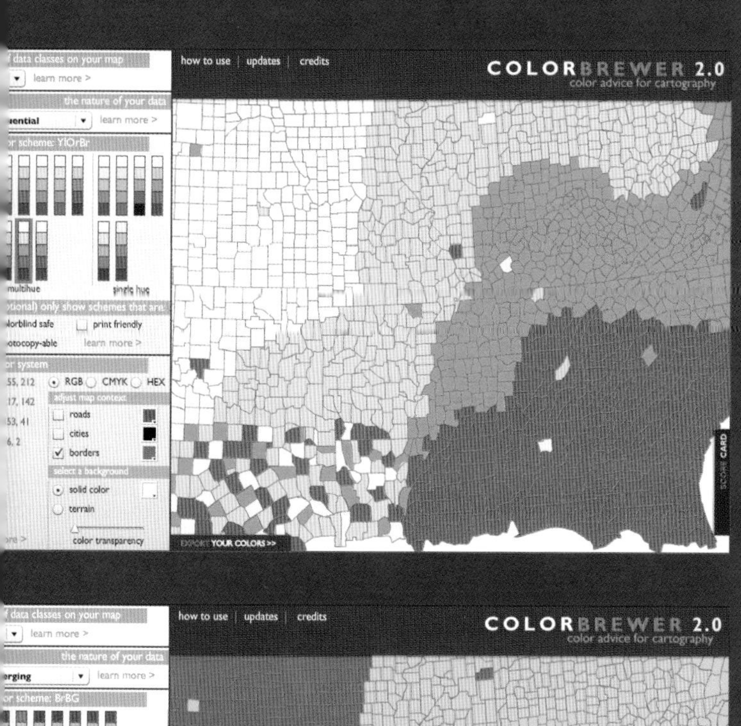

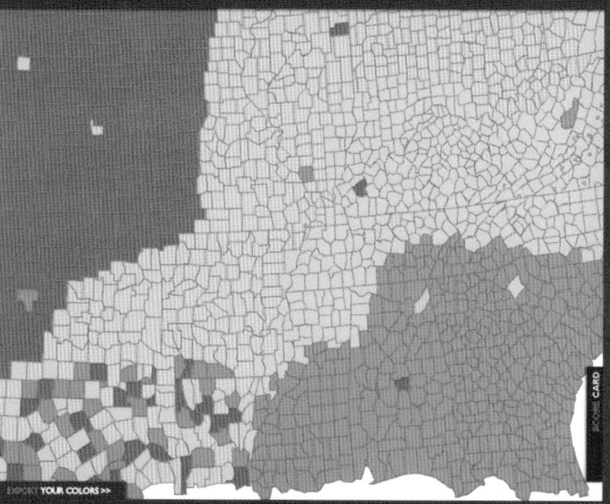

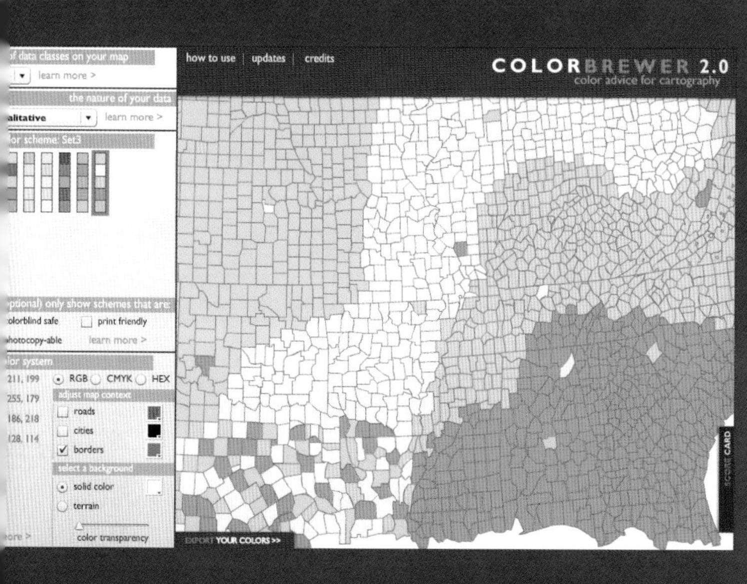

Cynthia Brewer's recommendations for color schemes according to the nature of data are:

"**SEQUENTIAL SCHEMES** are suited to ordered data that progress from low to high. Lightness steps dominate the look of these schemes, with light colors for low data values and dark colors for high data values.

DIVERGING SCHEMES put equal emphasis on mid-range critical values and extremes at both ends of the data range. The critical class or break in the middle of the legend is emphasized with light colors, and low and high extremes are emphasized with dark colors that have contrasting hues.

Diverging schemes are most effective when the class break in the middle of the sequence, or the lightest middle color, is meaningfully related to the mapped data. Use the break or class emphasized by a hue and lightness change to represent a critical value in the data, such as the mean, median, or zero. Colors increase in darkness to represent differences in both directions from this meaningful mid-range value in the data.

QUALITATIVE SCHEMES do not imply magnitude differences between legend classes, and hues are used to create the primary visual differences between classes. Qualitative schemes are best suited to representing nominal or categorical data.

Most of the qualitative schemes rely on differences in hue with only subtle lightness differences between colors. Two exceptions to the use of consistent lightness are

> **PAIRED SCHEME:** This scheme presents a series of lightness pairs for each hue (e.g., light green and dark green). Use this when you have categories that should be visually related, though they are not explicitly ordered. For example, 'forest' and 'woodland' would be suitably represented with dark and light green.
>
> **ACCENT SCHEME:** Use this to accent small areas or important classes with colors that are more saturated/darker/lighter than others in the scheme. Beware of emphasizing unimportant classes when you use qualitative schemes."[60]

We should never forget about devising color blind–safe schemes. Color blindness refers to the inability or limitation to perceive the red-green color direction, and it was discussed in chapter 1 (pages 36–37). A safe strategy is to avoid using only the hue channel to encode information and create schemes that vary slightly in one other channel in addition to hue, such as lightness or saturation.

CASE STUDY

ISOMETRIC AND ISOPLETH MAPS

Isarithmic maps represent real or abstract three-dimensional surfaces by depicting continuous phenomena. There are two kinds of lines of equal value used to demarcate continuous surfaces on the map:

- Isometric lines show distribution of values that can be referenced to points.
- Isopleth lines show distribution of values that cannot be referenced to points.[61]

In isometric maps, the lines depict data values at specific points on a continuous distribution. In other words, the dataset provides data points that define the lines. Topographic maps and temperature maps are good examples of data that are measured at specific locations.

In isopleth maps, the lines depict data that were not measured at a point, but instead are derived values that are calculated in relation to the area of collection. The calculated centroid of each area is considered the data point for the line construction. Isopleth maps representing population density are examples. Maps representing the mean monthly temperatures or average precipitation levels are common examples in which data are derived from observations, though they are slightly different from density maps, in which the attribute value cannot be referenced to points.

In both cases, smooth contours are achieved by the interpolation of data points. When used without the shading, they are called isoline maps. A variation is provided by a planimetric three-dimensional graphic representation of the surfaces.

Edmond Halley's 1701 map of magnetic lines is considered the first map to make use of lines of equal value to encode data (see page 116). The first isopleth maps depicting population densities were created by Danish cartographer N. F. Ravn and published in 1857. Robinson explains, "An isopleth map of population densities employs an involved, graphic, geometric symbolism for describing a three-dimensional surface to show the structure of an imagined 'statistical surface' formed by the variations in ratios of people to areas. An 'ordinary' contour map is in reality a very complicated system of representation, and the concept of a statistical surface of population densities is exceedingly abstract. That the two could be combined by the 1850s, and readily accepted, shows how far thematic mapping had come."[62] The use of isolines to represent population data is less popular today. The majority of isarithmic maps that we encounter nowadays show natural phenomena, such as climate and geology.

The construction of isarithmic maps involves three elements: the location of control points, the interpolation method to connect the location points, and the number of control points.

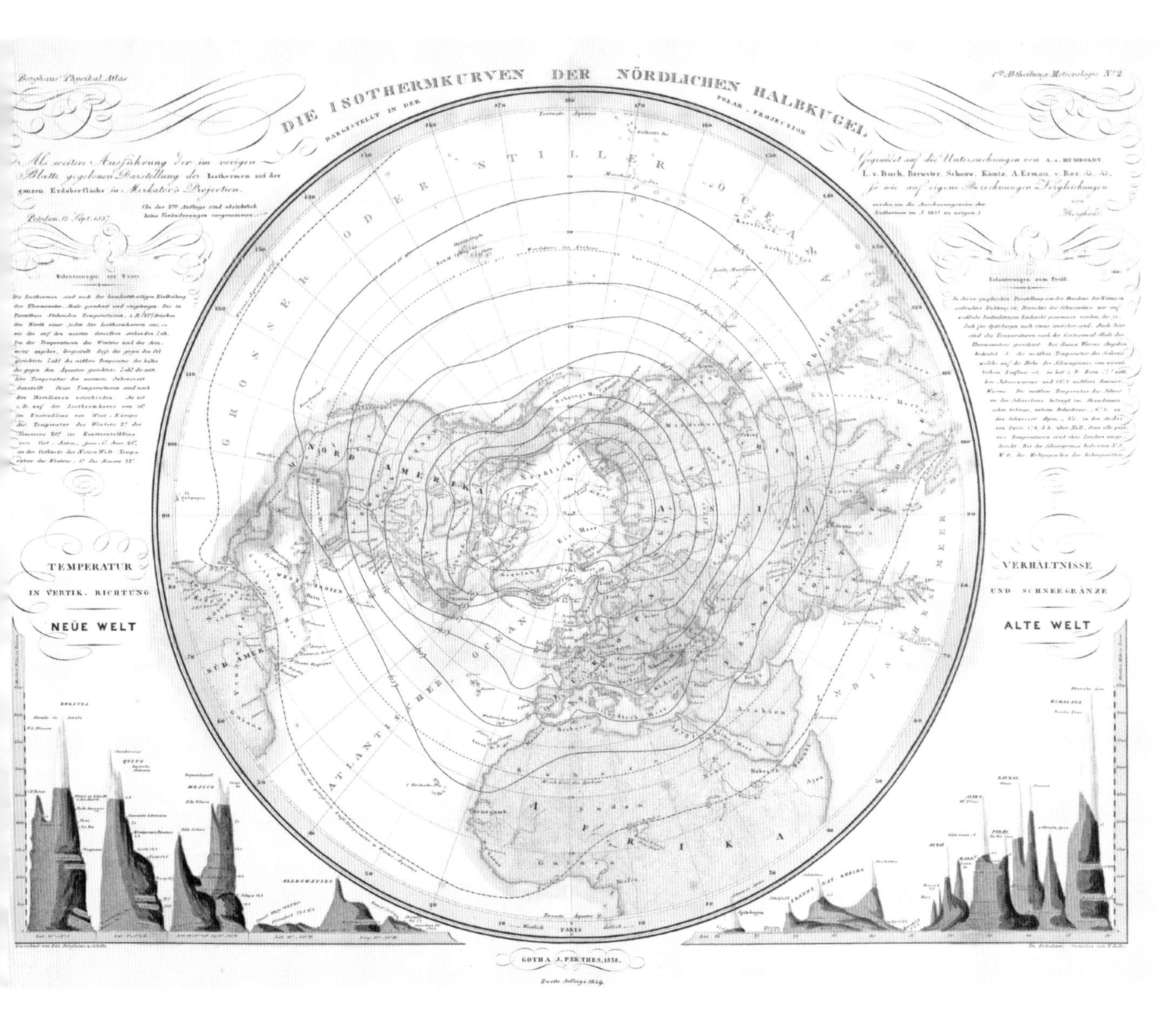

The *Physikalischer Atlas* by Heinrich Karl Wilhelm Berghaus (1797–1884) is considered a monumental achievement in thematic cartography history.[63] The atlas was issued over several years, and the first edition of the bound atlas consists of ninety maps in two volumes, dated 1845 and 1848. This meteorological map is the second map in the atlas. Using a polar projection, Berghaus depicted the mean temperature in the Northern Hemisphere by drawing isotherm lines at 5°C intervals.

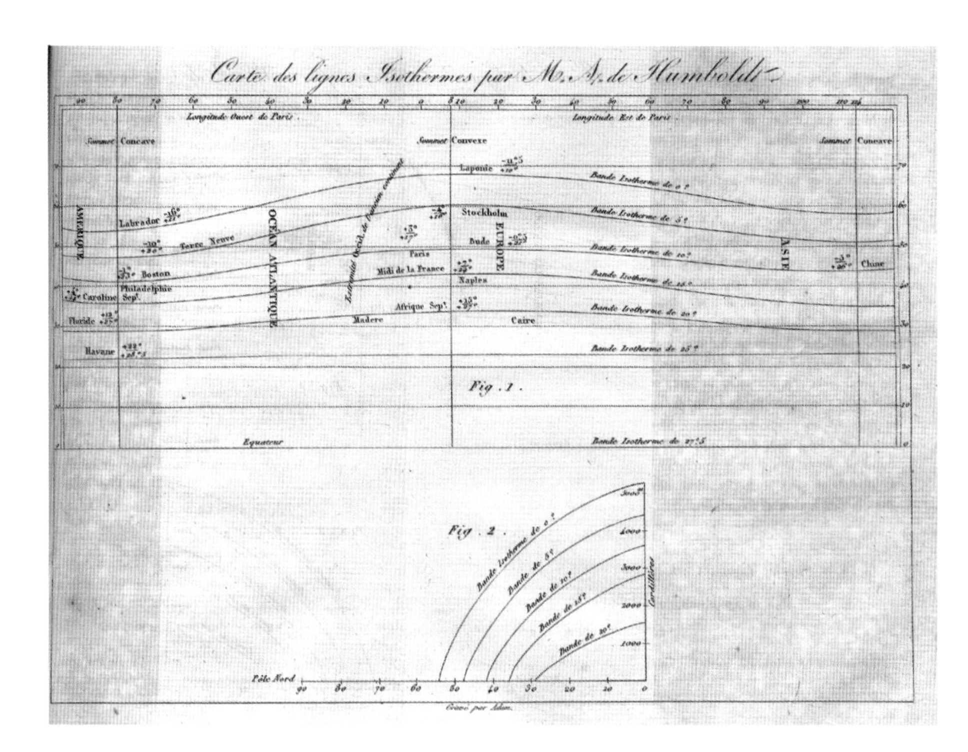

The publication in 1817 of this "Chart of Isothermal Lines" by Alexander von Humboldt played an important role in the widespread use of curves to depict quantitative phenomena in the nineteenth century, even though the first use was by Halley a century earlier. The diagram depicts lines of average temperature in relation to geographical zones defined by the latitude/longitude system. It also coins the term isothermes for the technique.[64]

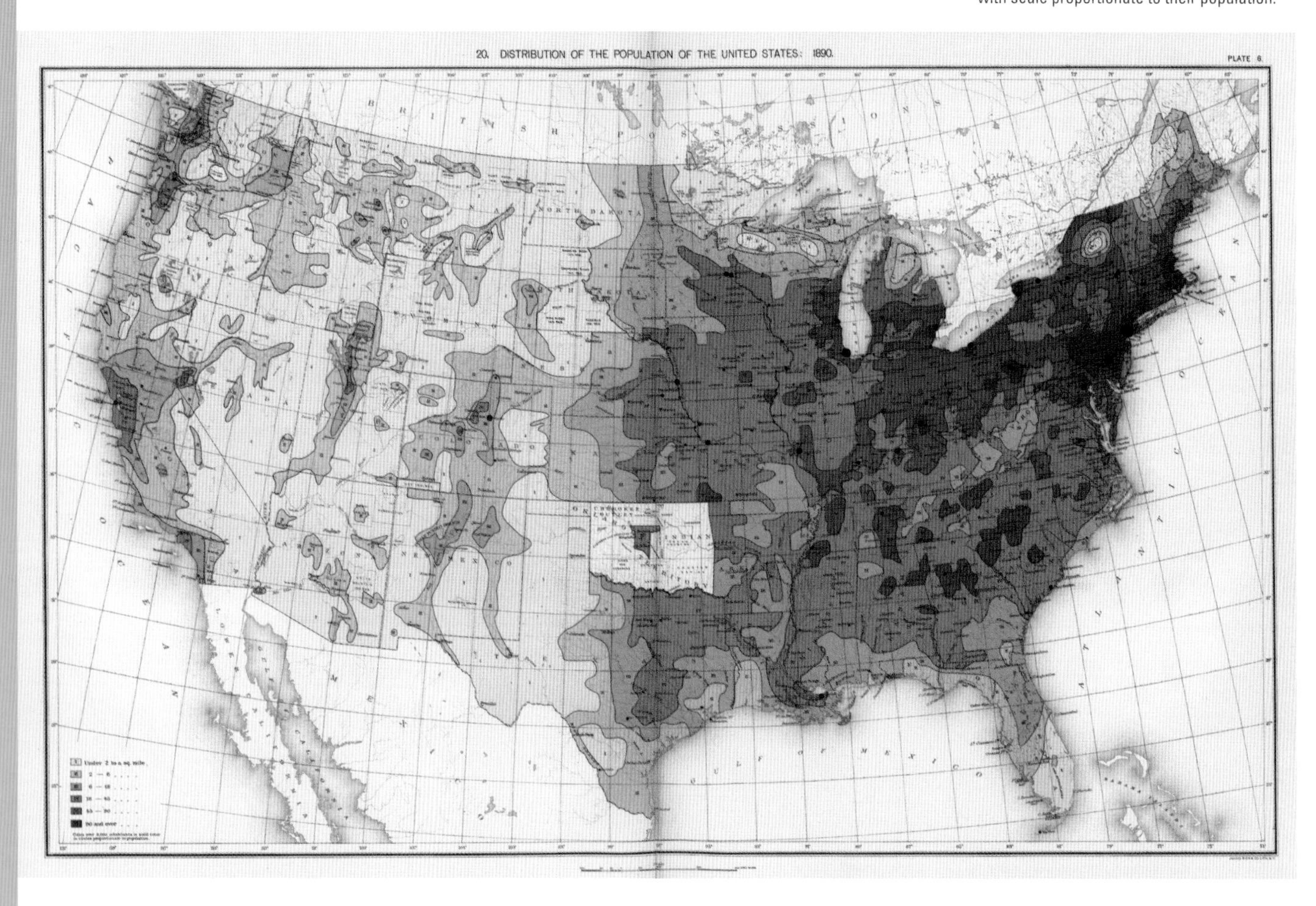

The map shows the distribution of the population of the United States in 1890. It was part of the *Statistical Atlas of the United States* based upon the results of the eleventh census by Henry Gannett, published in 1898. Note the six classes, with darker shades standing for higher density. Cities with over 8,000 inhabitants are represented by black circles with scale proportionate to their population.

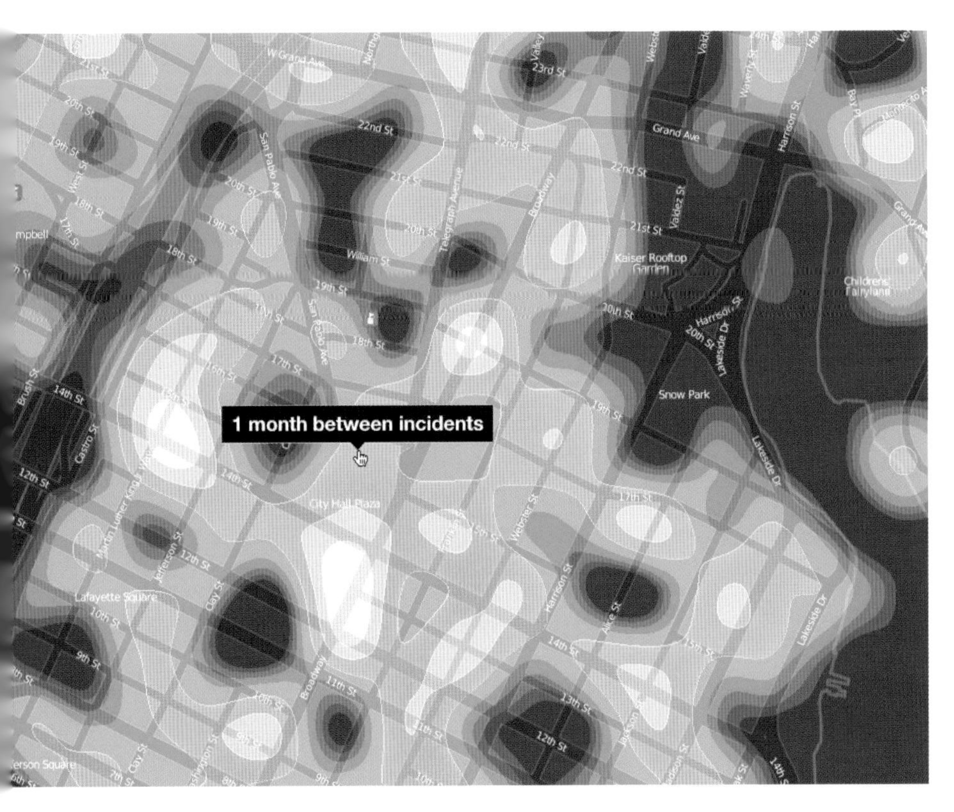

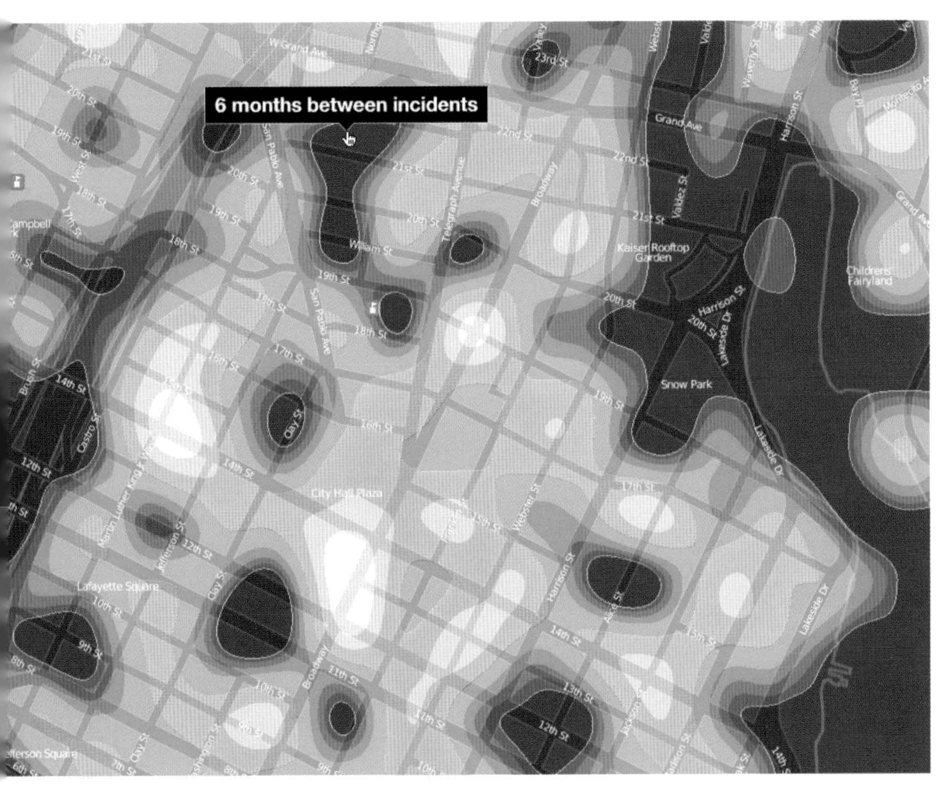

Michal Migurski, Tom Carden, and Eric Rodenbeck (Stamen Design), U.S.: "Oakland Crimespotting," 2008.

Oakland Crimespotting was designed and built by Stamen Design's Michal Migurski, Tom Carden, and Eric Rodenbeck. It is an interactive map showing crimes in Oakland, California. The motivation is stated on the website: "Instead of simply knowing where a crime took place, we would like to investigate questions like: Is there more crime this week than last week? More this month than last? Do robberies tend to happen close to murders? We're interested in everything from complex questions of patterns and trends, to the most local of concerns on a block-by-block basis."[65]

The application is a work in progress since 2008, and the screenshots shown here are not built into the interactive tool available online. On the other hand, they are worth reproducing here, because it is an effective use of isopleth for visually answering some of the questions that motivated the work.

http://oakland.crimespotting.org

CASE STUDY

FLOW AND NETWORK MAPS

Flow and network maps portray linear phenomena that most often involve movement and connection between points: origins and destinations. Maps depicting the flow of migrations in the world or the network of friends on Facebook are examples (see page 50). Most maps encode multivariate data using the visual attributes of line width, line quality, color hue, and spatial properties, the latter of which are provided by the geo-location of the data.

The first known flow maps were made by Harness, who published three of such maps in 1837, mostly depicting the average number of passengers on the Irish railway system. It is unknown whether those became available to other mapmakers, but around the mid-1840s Alphonse Belpaire in Belgium and Charles Joseph Minard in France also began making flow maps. Minard (1781–1870) was a prolific cartographer and produced fifty-one thematic maps mostly focusing on economic geography, of which the majority (forty-two) were flow maps.[66] According to Robinson, "Minard clearly outdid Harness and Belpaire in the number, variety, and sophistication of his thematic maps of movement."[67]

We see a boom in flow and network maps due to the amount of spatio-temporal data currently available. Robinson contends, "Like the dot map and the dasymetric technique, their [flow maps by Minard] sophisticated cartographic methods would have to be reinvented."[68]

This 1855 map by Charles Joseph Minard depicts the approximate amount of cereals that circulated by land and water in France in the year 1853: "*Carte figurative et approximative des quantités de céréales qui ont circulé en 1853 sur les voies d'eau et de fer de l'Empire Français.*" The visual encoding is

1. **Spatial position:** The lines are geo-located according to the given trajectories. A sense of direction is also represented with arrows.
2. **Line width:** The width is proportional to the amount of cereals transported (the quantitative thematic variable). Note that the widths are different for the transport to and from Paris, which are divided by a dotted line. Numeric information is also written within the lines.
3. **Color hue:** Lines are colored according to the means of transport, whether it was via boat (green) or train (red).

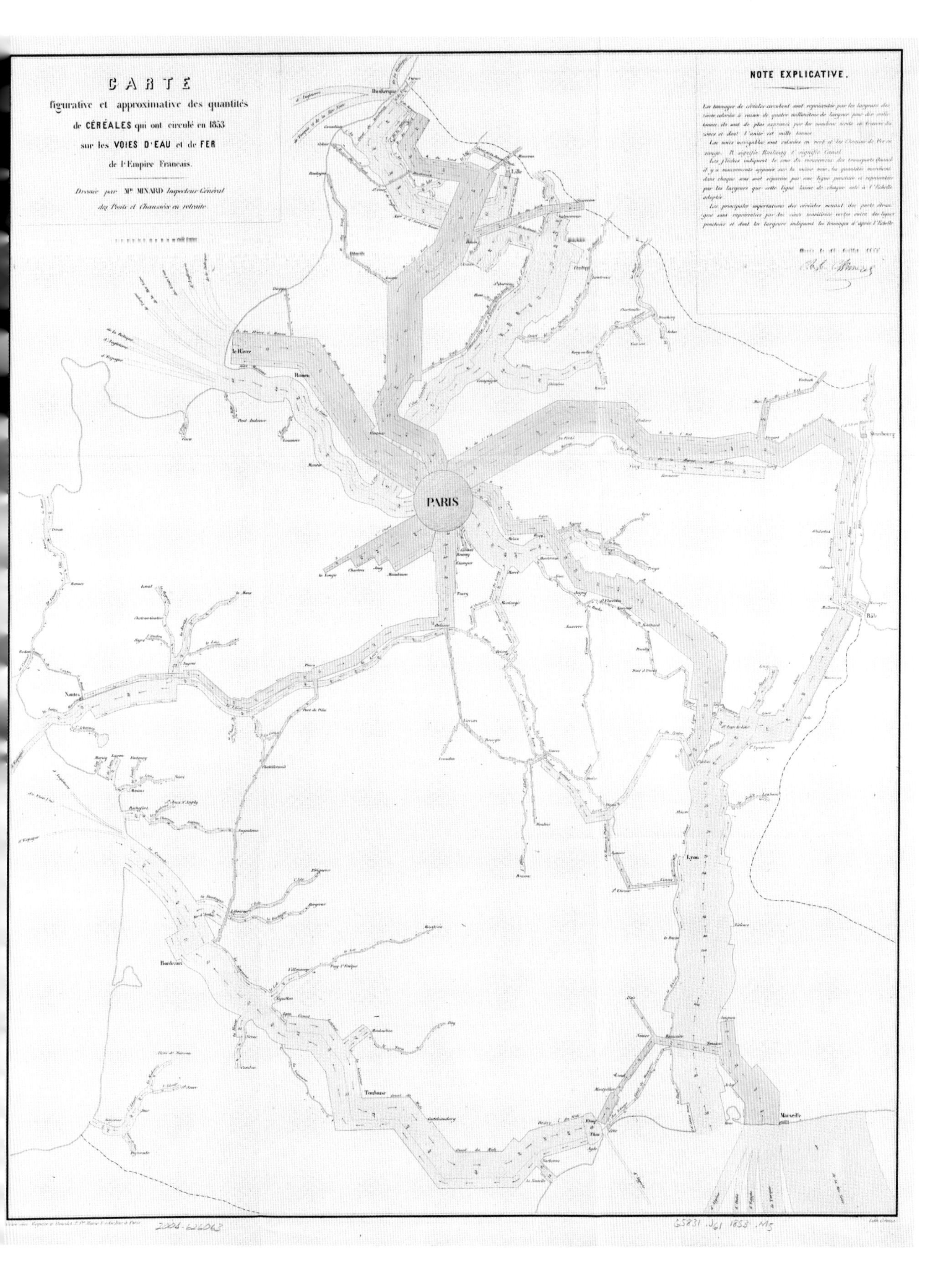
CARTE
figurative et approximative des quantités
de CÉRÉALES qui ont circulé en 1853
sur les VOIES D'EAU et de FER
de l'Empire Francais.
Dressée par Mr MINARD Inspecteur Général
des Ponts et Chaussées en retraite.
NOTE EXPLICATIVE.
PARIS
le Havre
Rouen
Lille
Nantes
Bordeaux
Toulouse
Lyon
Marseille

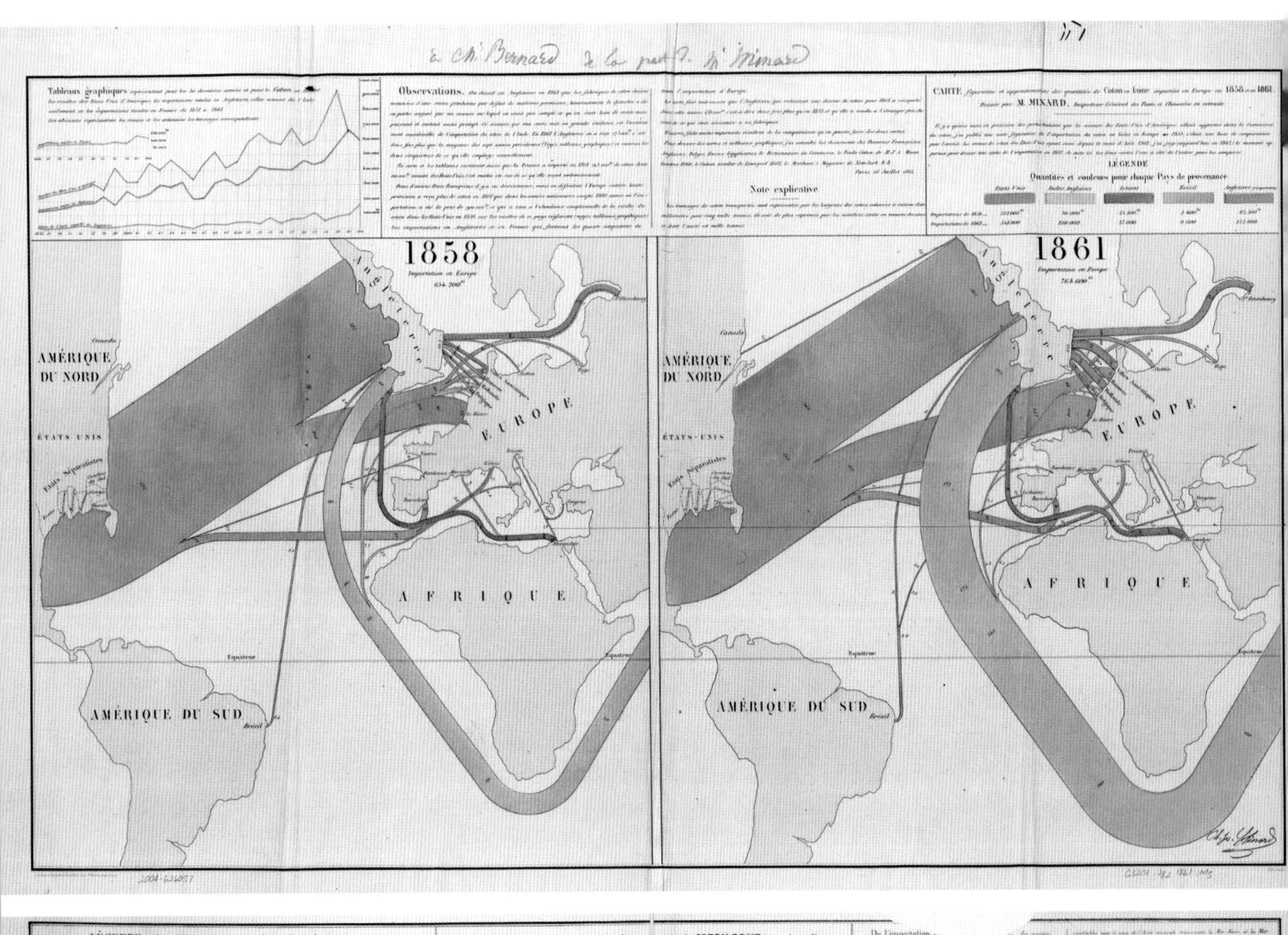

Tableaux graphiques
Observations.
Note explicative
CARTE figurative et approximative des quantités de Coton en laine importées en Europe en 1858 et en 1861.
M. MINARD
LÉGENDE
Quantités et couleurs pour chaque Pays de provenance.
1858
Importation en Europe
1861
Importation en Europe
Angleterre
Canada
AMÉRIQUE DU NORD
ÉTATS UNIS
EUROPE
AFRIQUE
Equateur
AMÉRIQUE DU SUD
Brésil

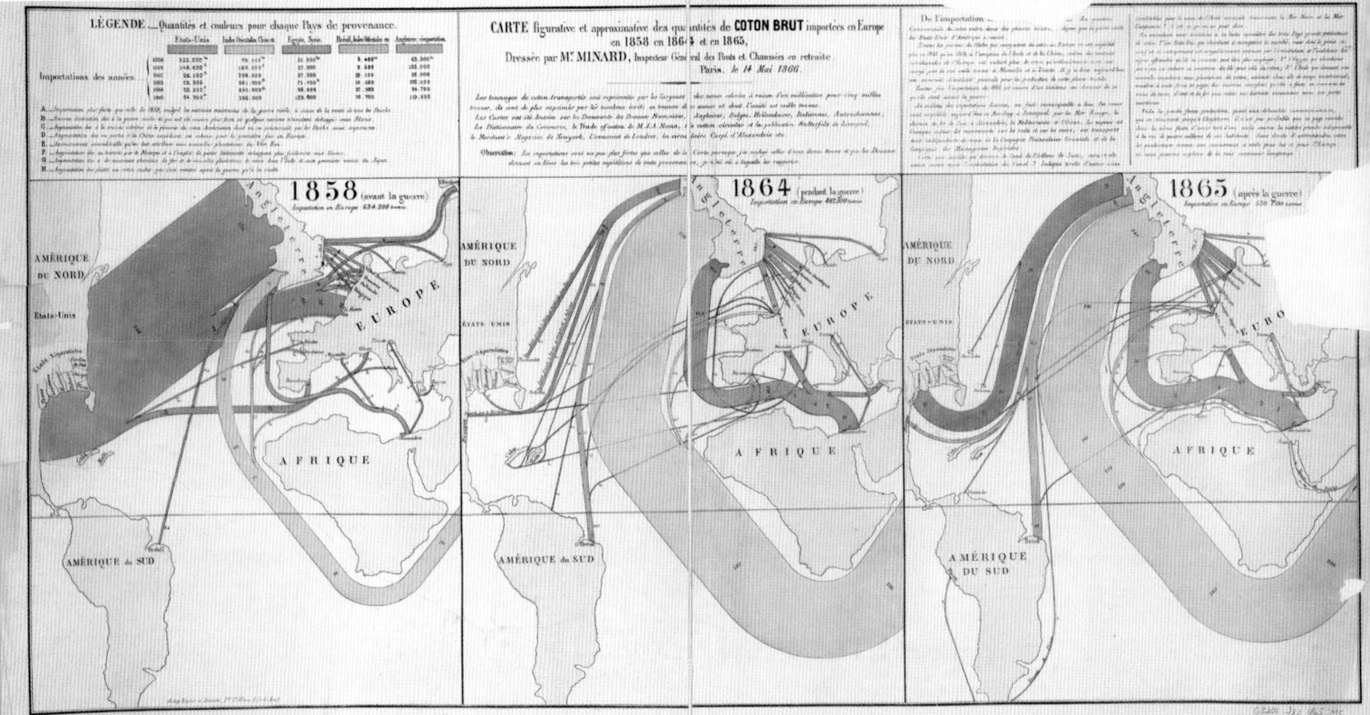

LÉGENDE _ Quantités et couleurs pour chaque Pays de provenance.
Importations des années
CARTE figurative et approximative des quantités de COTON BRUT importées en Europe
en 1858 en 1864 et en 1865,
Dressée par Mr. MINARD, Inspecteur Général des Ponts et Chaussées en retraite.
Paris, le 14 Mai 1866.
1858 (avant la guerre)
1864 (pendant la guerre)
1865 (après la guerre)
AMÉRIQUE DU NORD
Etats-Unis
EUROPE
AFRIQUE
AMÉRIQUE du SUD
AMÉRIQUE DU SUD

Two major challenges of designing flow maps are obfuscating the base map with the bands and avoiding too many overlaps and thus visual clutter. Minard met both challenges when he created flow maps in the nineteenth century. The two series of flow maps depict the approximate amounts of cotton imported by Europe. The map on the top, "Carte figurative et approximative des quantitiés de coton en laine importées en Europe en 1858 et en 1861," was published in 1862 and portrays data for 1858 and 1861. The map at the bottom, "*Carte figurative et approximative des quantités de coton brut importées en Europe en 1858, en 1864 et en 1865,*" was published in 1866 and depicts data for three years: 1858, 1864, and 1985.

The reason for reproducing both maps here is so that we can examine how Minard distorted the base maps in favor of the flows of goods, which is the objective of the maps. If we compare the two series of maps, we will see how the one at the bottom, with increasing flow of goods over the years, depicts a more distorted geography, though distortion happens in the former as well. Robinson explains that Minard "was much more concerned with portraying the basic structure of the distribution than he was with maintaining strict positional accuracy of the geographical base—this from an engineer!"[69]

Another feature still in current practice and worth stressing is how Minard bundled flows with shared destinations so as to avoid visual clutter.

In both maps, each millimeter corresponds to 5,000 tons of cotton. In addition to the visual representation provided by the width of bands, Minard included the absolute numbers next to each band. Color encodes the countries from which cotton is imported. The notes, as usual, present commentary on findings and questions. For example, in the maps on the bottom, Minard discusses how the American Civil War affected the commerce of cotton and the countries that were producers.

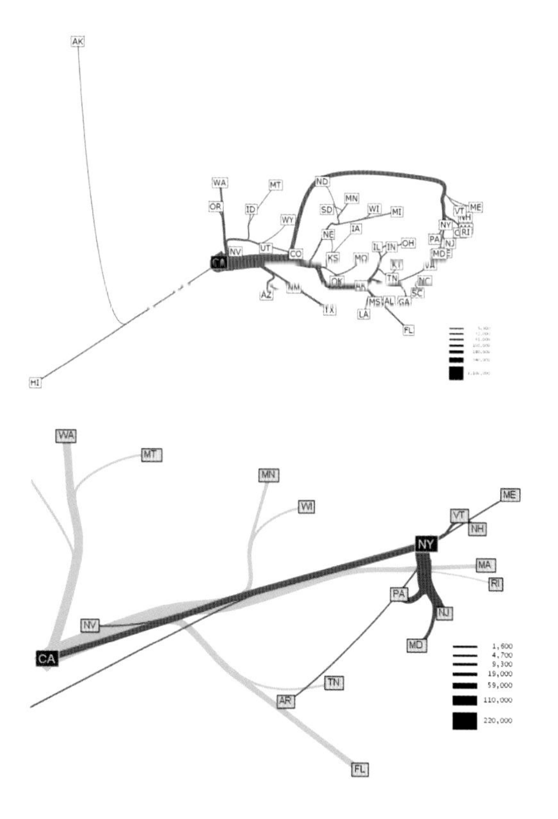

Doantam Phan, Ling Xiao, Ron Yeh, Pat Hanrahan, Terry Winograd (Stanford University), U.S.: "Flow Map Layout," 2005.

Phan and colleagues developed a technique to automatically generate flow maps that uses three lessons learned from Minard: intelligent distortion of spatial positions, intelligent edge routing, and merging of edges with shared destinations.[70] They explain, "Our approach uses hierarchical clustering to create a flow tree that connects a source (the root) to a set of destinations (the leaves). Our algorithm attempts to minimize edge crossings and supports the layering of single-source flow maps to create multiple-source flow maps. We do this by preserving branching substructure across flow maps with different roots that share a common set of nodes."[71]

The top image shows a flow map of migration from California from 1995 to 2000, generated automatically by their system using edge routing but no layout adjustment. The bottom image shows a map of the top ten states that migrate to California and New York, showing that New York attracts more people from the East Coast and California attracts people from more geographic regions.

http://graphics.stanford.edu/papers/flow_map_layout

CASE STUDY

AREA AND DISTANCE CARTOGRAMS

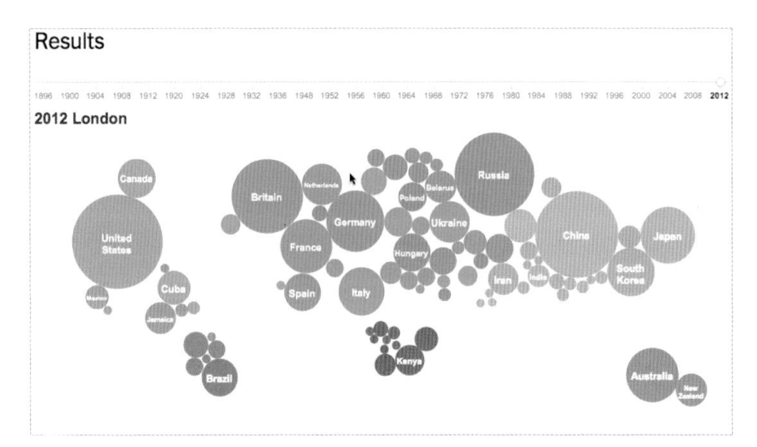

Lee Byron, Amanda Cox, and Matthew Ericso (*New York Times*), U.S.: "A Map of Olympic Medals," 2012.

As opposed to traditional maps, in which space is used to depict space, cartograms distort the shape of geographic regions to encode another variable into the spatial area. There are different types of cartograms, and the one used in "A Map of Olympic Medals" is called a Dorling cartogram. The technique represents geographic space as nonoverlapping circles. The map was designed by Lee Byron, Amanda Cox, and Matthew Ericso, and published as an interactive map at the *New York Times* online in 2012 for occasion of the London Olympic Games. The screenshots show the results for 2012. Size represents the number of medals that countries won in the Olympic Games. Color encodes the continents.

http://london2012.nytimes.com/results

Typically, the spatial variables in the map are used to depict space in the world—the continents, countries, counties, and so on. This was the case in all map forms examined thus far. For example, choropleth maps represent thematic data within the boundaries of the given statistical units. As exemplified by the *New York Times* maps, the uncovered political patterns are closely associated with the administrative units used for the symbolization. Strong arguments have been made that for data involving population, such as in social and economic datasets, a topological mapping of space to space is more appropriate.

Area cartograms were devised with this purpose of revealing spatial-geographic patterns. They use the spatial variables in the map for depicting population data according to a thematic variable. To allow identification of the known geographic spaces, most area cartograms make use of algorithms that retain as closely as possible the geographic space in the transformed map space. The "Twitter Mood" cartogram is an example.

Distance cartograms use the relationships in land distance to depict thematic data in the map. The Travel Time Tube Maps by Tom Carden are good examples (see page 168).

There are different ways to render cartograms based on how space is transformed and the extents to which shape, area, and topology are preserved. "Pulse of the Nation" is an example of a contiguous cartogram. It preserves the topology of the map with the area and the shapes loosely retained. The *New York Times* Olympic medal map is an example of a circular noncontiguous cartogram, where original shapes are exchanged for circular shapes.

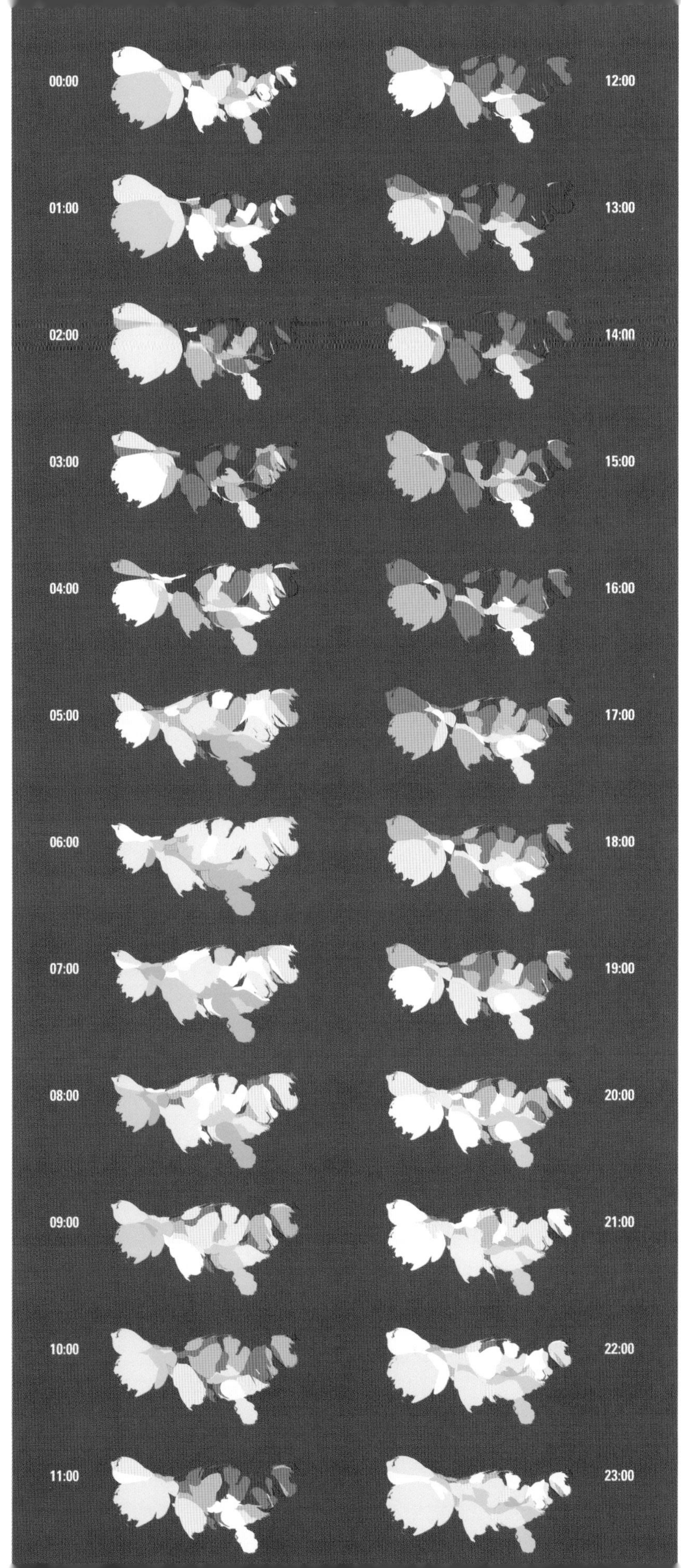

Alan Mislove, Sune Lehmann, Yong-Yeol Ahn, Jukka-Pekka Onnela, and J. Niels Rosenquist, U.S.: "Pulse of the Nation," 2011.

"Pulse of the Nation" examines the U.S. mood throughout the day inferred from more than 300 million tweets collected between September 2006 and August 2009. The mood of each tweet was inferred using ANEW word list.[72] User locations were inferred using the Google Maps API, and mapped into counties using PostGIS and U.S. county maps from the U.S. National Atlas. All times are Eastern Standard Time (EST). Mood colors were selected using Color Brewer[73] (see box Selecting Color Schemes on pages 146–147). The cartograms in this work were generated using the Cart (computer software for making cartograms) developed by Mark E. J. Newman[74] (see Newman's cartogram of the 2012 American presidential election on page 14). The software preserves geographic shape as much as possible. Counties' area sizes are scaled according to the number of tweets that originate in that region. The result is a density-equalizing map. Color encodes mood by means of a color scale ranging from red (unhappy) to yellow (neutral) to green (happy).

It is possible to observe interesting trends such as daily variations, with early mornings and late evenings having the highest level of happy tweets, and geographic variations, with the West Coast showing happier tweets in a pattern that is consistently three hours behind the East Coast. The visualization was created in 2011 by an interdisciplinary research team at Northeastern University and Harvard University: Alan Mislove, Sune Lehmann, Yong-Yeol Ahn, Jukka-Pekka Onnela, and J. Niels Rosenquist.

http://www.ccs.neu.edu/home/amislove/twittermood

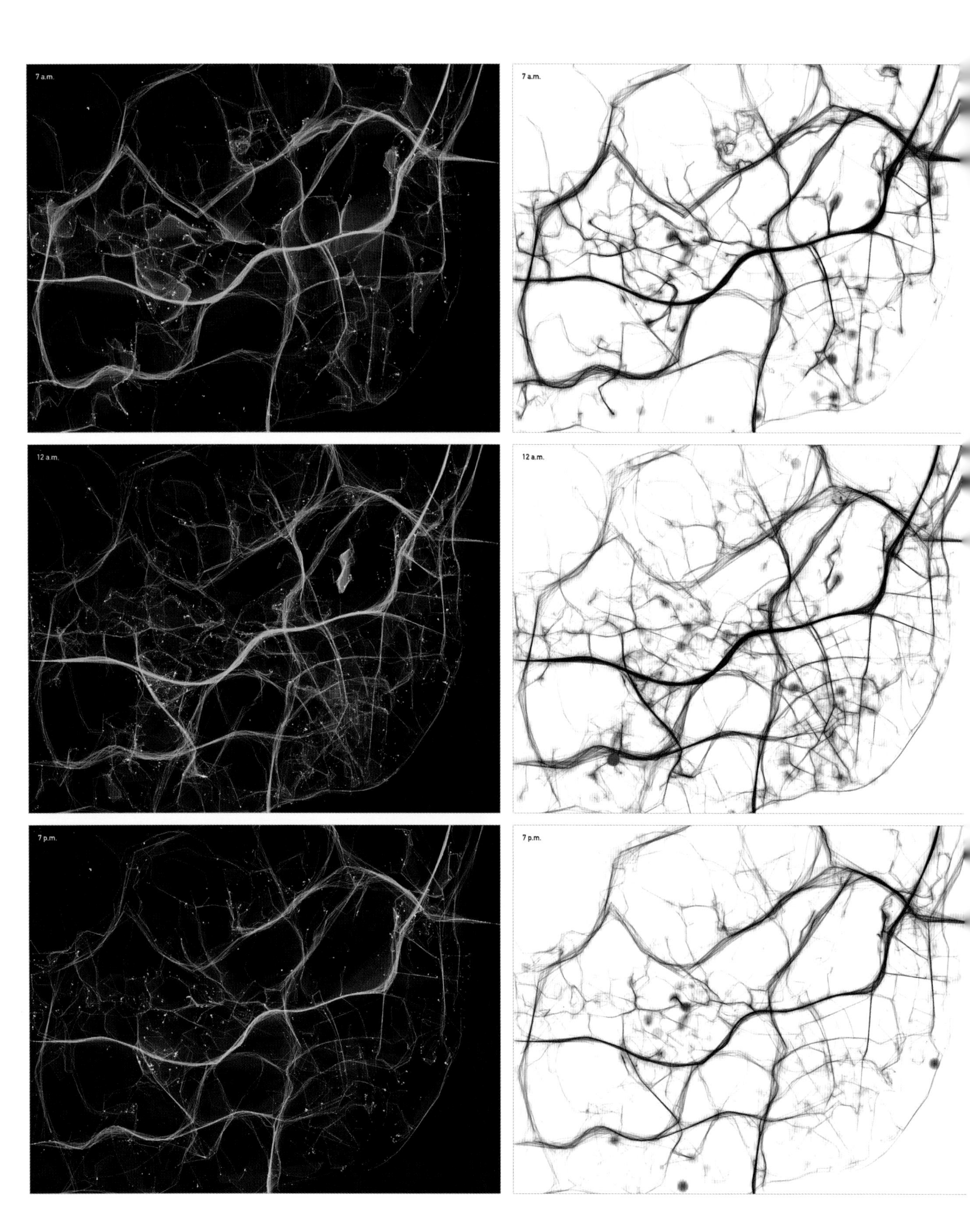
7 a.m.
7 a.m.
12 a.m.
12 a.m.
7 p.m.
7 p.m.

CHAPTER 5

SPATIO-TEMPORAL STRUCTURES

Pedro Cruz, Penousal Machado, and João Bicker (University of Coimbra with MIT CityMotion), Portugal: "Traffic in Lisbon," 2010.

"Traffic in Lisbon" is a series of animations of traffic's evolution in Lisbon during a fictitious twenty-four-hour period (from 0:00 to 23:59). The project maps 1,534 vehicles during October 2009 in Lisbon, leaving route trails and condensed into one single (virtual) day. The two sequences are frames from animations exploring different visual metaphors of the city as an organism with circulatory problems.

In the left sequence, recent paths are color coded according to the vehicle's speed: green and cyan for faster vehicles, yellow and red for slower ones. The accumulation of paths emphasizes main arteries, resulting in thicker lines. The right sequence presents the living organism metaphor by depicting slow vehicles as red circles. Cruz explains, "The superimposition of slow vehicles forms solid red clots in the traffic of Lisbon, depicting it as a living organism with circulatory problems."[15]

http://pmcruz.com/information-visualization/traffic-in-lisbon-condensed-in-one-day

We are surrounded by changes in all dimensions of our existence. All changes require time to become something else, to transform, to remodel, to reorganize, to disappear, and so on. Several fields use time-varying data to understand patterns in natural and social phenomena as well as to help make predictions. Examples range from studies in meteorology and economics to assessment of brain activity.

The chapter focuses on spatio-temporal phenomena and processes inherent to the dimensions of space and time. Data belonging to both space and time are found in diverse domains and include mobility, dispersion, proliferation, and diffusion, to mention a few. Our lives are immersed in time and space, and we constantly reason about both, making decisions about where and when we are, were, or will be. From sketches we draw on napkins to give directions to our friends, to more complex cartographic representations of the

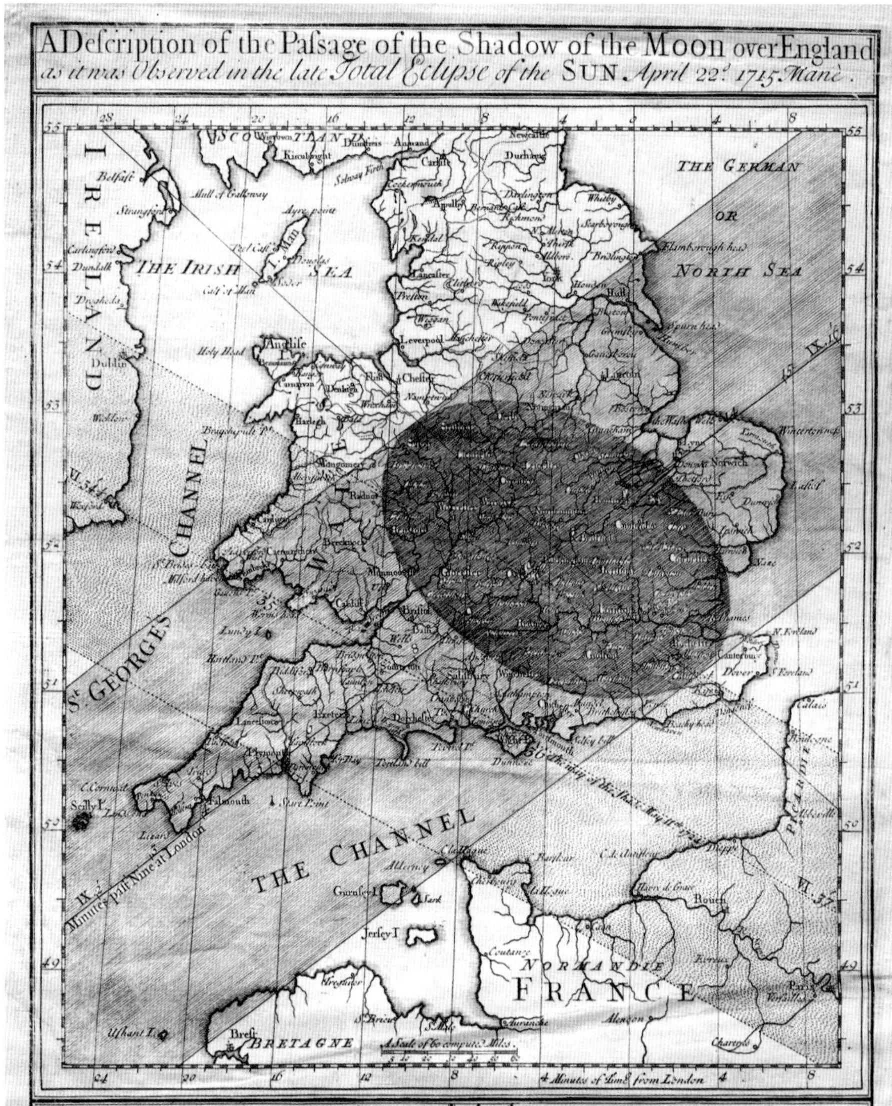

The English astronomer Edmond Halley, known for the comet bearing his name, mapped his prediction of the trajectory of the total eclipse of the Sun in 1715. The map was first published in a leaflet before the eclipse and widely distributed in England. After the event, Halley received observation reports and revised the map in the format that we see here. The map effectively represents a temporal event onto a geographic context: It depicts the passage of the shadow of the Moon across England by graphic means, including the varying duration of the event. Robinson explains, "The use of the shading shows how fertile and imaginative was Halley's grasp of the potentialities of graphic portrayal. The dark ellipse-like figure representing totality was to 'slide' along the shaded path from southwest to northeast, and the relative duration of totality for any place along the path was shown by the width of the ellipse in line with that place."[16]

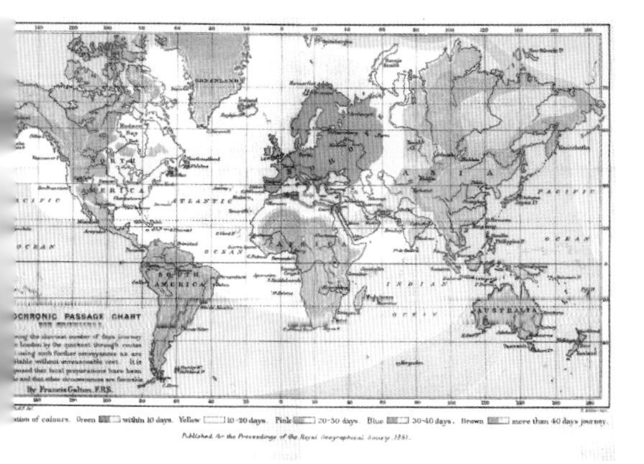

Sir Francis Galton created the "Isochronic Passage Chart for Travellers" for the Royal Geographical Society in 1881. The map uses Mercator projection and shows the number of days it takes to travel from London to other parts of the globe. Galton's source data were timetables of steamship companies and railway systems. Vasiliev explains, "This world map uses isochrones to separate areas that may be reached in a certain number of days. The isochrones themselves are not labeled, but the areas between them are color coded to the legend, each color indicating the number of days required to reach that area from London: yellow for 10–20 days, brown for more than 40 days, and so forth. It is interesting to note that in traveling across the United States to the West Coast, going through Denver and Salt Lake City to San Francisco took 10–20 days whereas travel anywhere north or south of Denver and Salt Lake City took 20–30 days—a direct effect of the railroads and their routes through the Rocky Mountains. On this map, the temporal unit is a 10-day journey 'by the quickest through routes and using such further conveyances as are available without unreasonable cost.' The actual mileage traveled is not necessary; this is a guide to the traveler to help plan the start of a world-wide tour."[17]

real world, we have traditionally used maps as models for spatial reasoning and decision making. Similarly, we have been using maps to represent and help us reason about spatio-temporal phenomena.

Given the dynamic nature of spatio-temporal phenomena, the designer faces several challenges in representing the fluidity of time in space, especially in static form. Geo-visualization is the field involved with designing and developing tools for interactive and dynamic visual analysis of spatial and spatio-temporal data. Interactive tools often make use of multiple linked displays to represent all aspects of spatio-temporal data, in that maps alone usually are not enough and need other visual displays such as statistical graphs to complement the complexities of the phenomena.

Vasiliev explains that time has been used and represented in different ways in different geographies. She identifies four main areas:[1]

- Historical geography: What has happened where in past times.
- Cultural geography: Where events have happened through time.
- Time geography: How much time it took for events to happen in space.
- Quantitative geography encompasses spatial diffusion and time-series analysis: What occurred where in known periods of time.

TYPES OF PHENOMENA

Spatio-temporal phenomena can be organized into three main types:[2]

- Existential changes refer to changes in instant events, such as the appearing or disappearing of objects and/or relationships.
- Spatial changes refer to changes in spatial properties of objects, such as location, size, and shape.
- Thematic changes refer to changes in the values or attributes of space, such as in demographic spatial maps.

When representing objects moving in space across time, it is possible to depict spatio-temporal data values as a trajectory that will show several time points on the map. A historical example is the prediction of the total eclipse of the Sun in 1715 by British astronomer and cartographer Edmond Halley. The *New York Times* employed a similar strategy in the recent interactive map of Hurricane Sandy (see page 164). Another common technique is the flow map, which depicts aggregated moving objects in space, such as in the depiction of migration or transportation of people or goods (see page 152). An extension of this technique is the space–time cube, in which time is represented on the third dimension in addition to the two dimensions of the plane for spatial data. An example is Kraak's space–time cube of Minard's *Napoleon March* graphic.

Unlike objects moving across a territory, it is not possible to represent variations of thematic data of continuous spatial phenomena in one image. Take, for example, changes in demographic values of a territory. There are no changes in the spatial values per se (the territory remains in the same location, with the same borders over time); rather, the changes occur in the thematic values represented by them. As Andrienko explains, "It is impossible to observe changes in spatial distribution of attribute values, or to locate places where the most significant changes occurred, or to perform other tasks requiring an overall view on the whole territory."[3] As reviewed in chapter 4, common ways to depict attributes of space at a point in time include choropleth and dot density maps. Adding other types of visual displays to the geographical representation often helps provide temporal context, such as with complementing maps with statistical graphs. A historical and well-known example is Minard's depiction of Napoleon's 1812–1813 Russian campaign, in which the line graph at the bottom adds context to the spatio-temporal information by showing the temperature faced by the soldiers on their way back to France.

To view thematic data changes over time, we need other techniques, such as multiple maps, animation, or interactive tools. Multiple maps involve sequencing a series of single-date maps. The technique provides a simultaneous view of change and enables comparison of same scale maps evenly spaced in the temporal dimension (see page 128). To detect direction and pace of change, the viewer needs to jump from map to map. Overlay of maps might enhance the perception of change, though this is not always possible when dealing with large amounts of data. Monmonier suggests, "Maps in a temporal series are especially useful for describing the spread or contraction of a distribution."[4]

An animation is a sequence of images representing states of phenomena at successive moments in time. In other words, animation depicts phenomena by mapping the temporal dimension in the data to the physical time we experience in real time. However, animations are poor for comparison tasks, because it is difficult to remember previous states with which to make comparisons. Andrienko and colleagues recommend combining interactive functions to animations to allow comparison and trend detection. Due to phenomena that are either too fast or too slow, the physical time scale might change so as to make the phenomena visible. The movies depicting twenty-four hours of traffic in Lisbon by Pedro Cruz are examples of how spatio-temporal data are mapped into physical time.

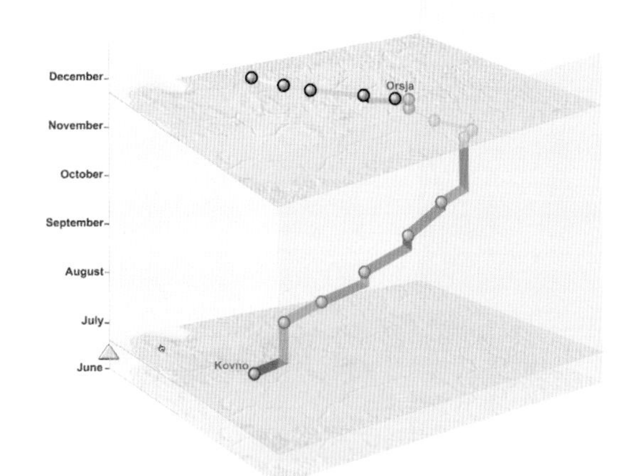

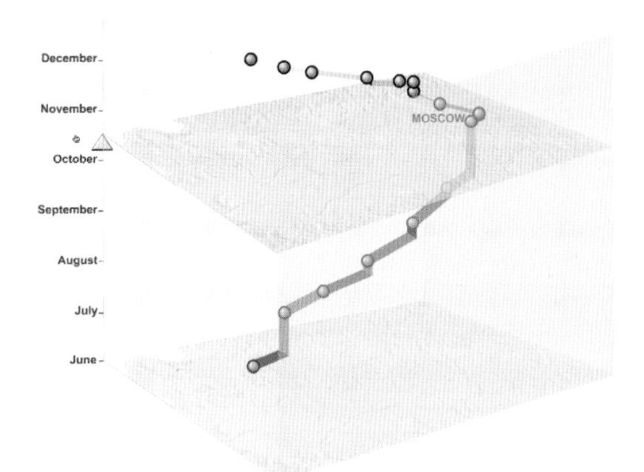

Menno-Jan Kraak, Netherlands: Space–time cube of Minard's "Napoleon March to and from Russia, 1812–1813," 2002.

Menno-Jan Kraak at the International Institute of Geoinformation Sciences and Earth Observation, Netherlands, created this geovisualization of Minard's map of Napoleon's 1812 campaign into Russia (reproduced on the right) to demonstrate "how alternative graphic representations can stimulate the visual thought process."[18] The interactive visualization is a space-time cube in which the *x*– and *y*–axes represent the geography and the *z*–axis represents time. One can navigate in time by moving the cursor in the vertical direction as the screenshots above illustrate.

www.itc.nl/personal/kraak/1812/3dnap.swf

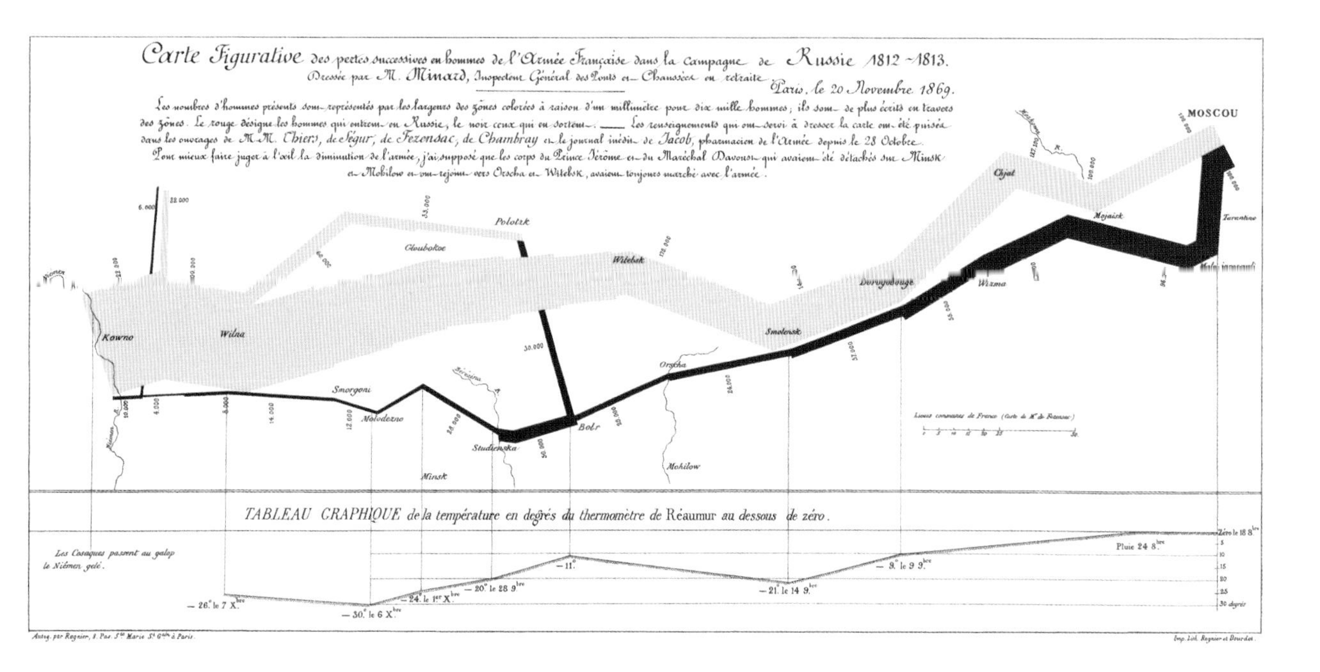

Charles Joseph Minard's 1869 "Napoleon March to and from Russia, 1812–1813" display combines statistical data with a timeline, and spatio-temporal information about the French army. In this multivariate display, the line width represents the number of soldiers marching to and from Russia, with each millimeter standing for 10,000 men. The march starts with 420,000 men in the Polish–Russian border (center left, beige line), reaches Moscow with 100,000 (top right), and ends with 10,000 men (black line). Considering that our visual system is unable to perceive absolute quantities from areas, Minard provides absolute quantities of soldiers along the two lines. Minard removed most cartographic information and kept only geographical landmarks, such as main rivers and cities. The line graph at the bottom represents the temperatures faced by the army on the way back to Poland, which are associated with the line standing for the return trip. Connections between temperatures and the march offer new levels of information: the relationships between deaths and low temperatures (probably also aggravated by fatigue). For example, 22,000 men died crossing the River Berezina due to the extreme low temperatures (–20°C [–4°F]).

Andrienko and colleagues represented the same spatio-temporal data using three different kinds of visual displays: static small multiple maps, animation, and interactive animation. The study found that the types of display affect the analytical and inference processes. People using the multiple maps display were more focused on spatial patterns rather than on events and temporal processes, whereas those using the animation and the interactive display focused more on changes and events rather than on spatial configurations.[5]

TIME

Andrienko and colleague distinguish two temporal aspects that are crucial when dealing with spatio-temporal data: temporal primitives and the structural organization of the temporal dimension.[6] There are two types of primitives: time points (point in time) or time intervals (extent of time). And there are three types of structures: ordered time, branching time, and multiple perspectives. Ordered time is the most commonly used structure and is subdivided into linear and cyclical. Linear time provides a continuous sequence of temporal primitives, from past to future (e.g., timelines), and cyclic time organizes primitives in recurrent finite sets (e.g., times of the day). Branching and multiple perspective times are metaphors for representing alternative scenarios and more than one point of view, respectively. When representing spatio-temporal phenomena, the designer needs to make a series of decisions concerning the visual method, whether the most effective representation would deal with linear time or cyclic time, time points or time intervals, ordered time or branching time, or time with multiple perspectives.

The *New York Times*, U.S.: "Hurricane Sandy," 2012.

When facing potential natural disasters, it is crucial to provide residents with information that help them make decisions that sometimes might even involve life and death, such as in the case of earthquakes, hurricanes, and tsunamis. News weather maps, websites, and television broadcast are common media where we look for information that can help us prepare for such events. The *New York Times*' interactive map provided many features that effectively helped residents on the East Coast prepare for Hurricane Sandy in October 2012. It presented readers with the predicted hurricane path connected with times and storm intensities. The interactive map answers questions related to when, where, and how the storm is forecast to affect residents. A solid line stands for the past path, whereas a dashed line represents future predicted trajectory. The dimension of the impact is represented by a colored surface around the main trajectory. The surface is colored by the hurricane category, further increasing the number of variables represented on the map. In addition, when interacting with the map, the viewer gets information for a particular point in space and time. The map itself carries very little detail, depicting only major cities and state borders. The simplicity of the map facilitates detection and focus on the main issue, which is the spatio-temporal route of the hurricane.

www.nytimes.com/interactive/2012/10/26/us/hurricane-sandy-map.html?hp

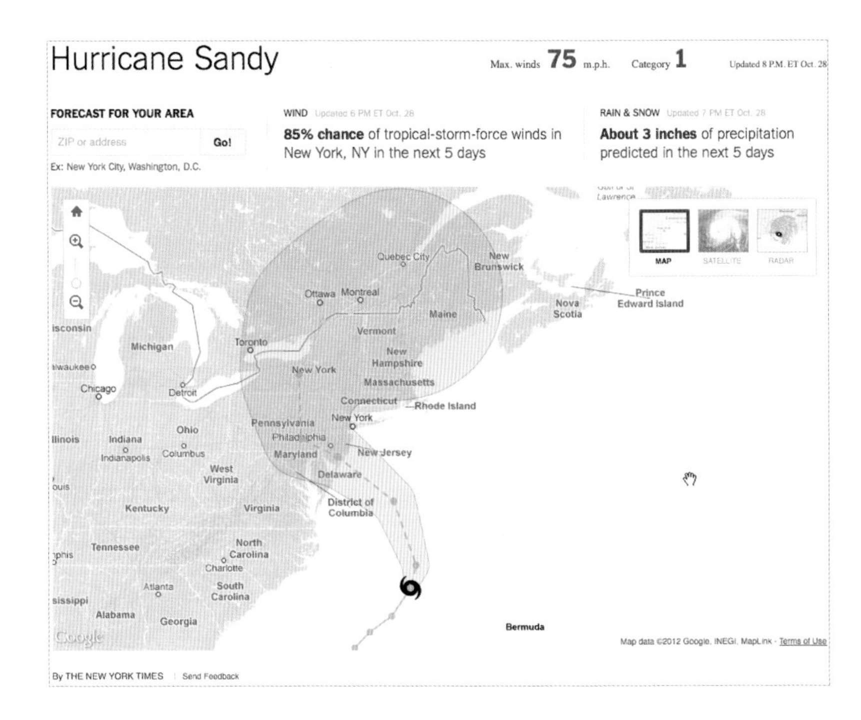

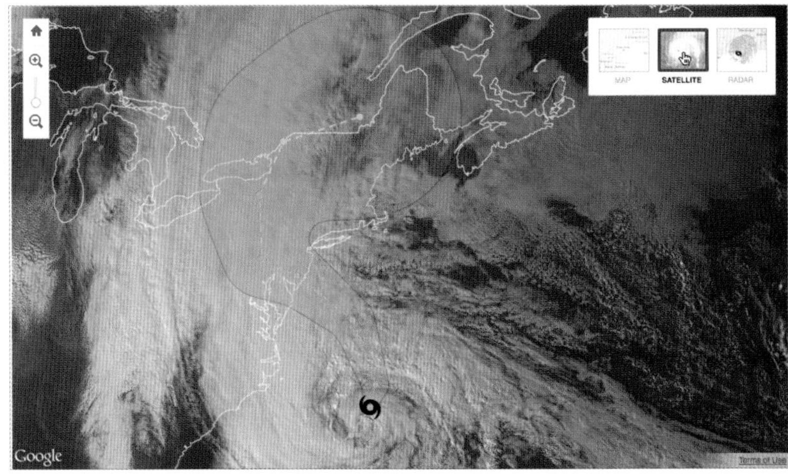

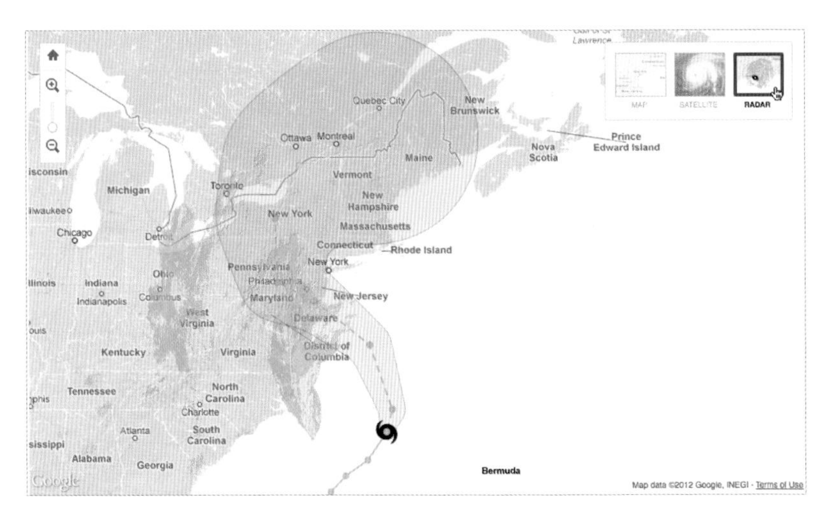

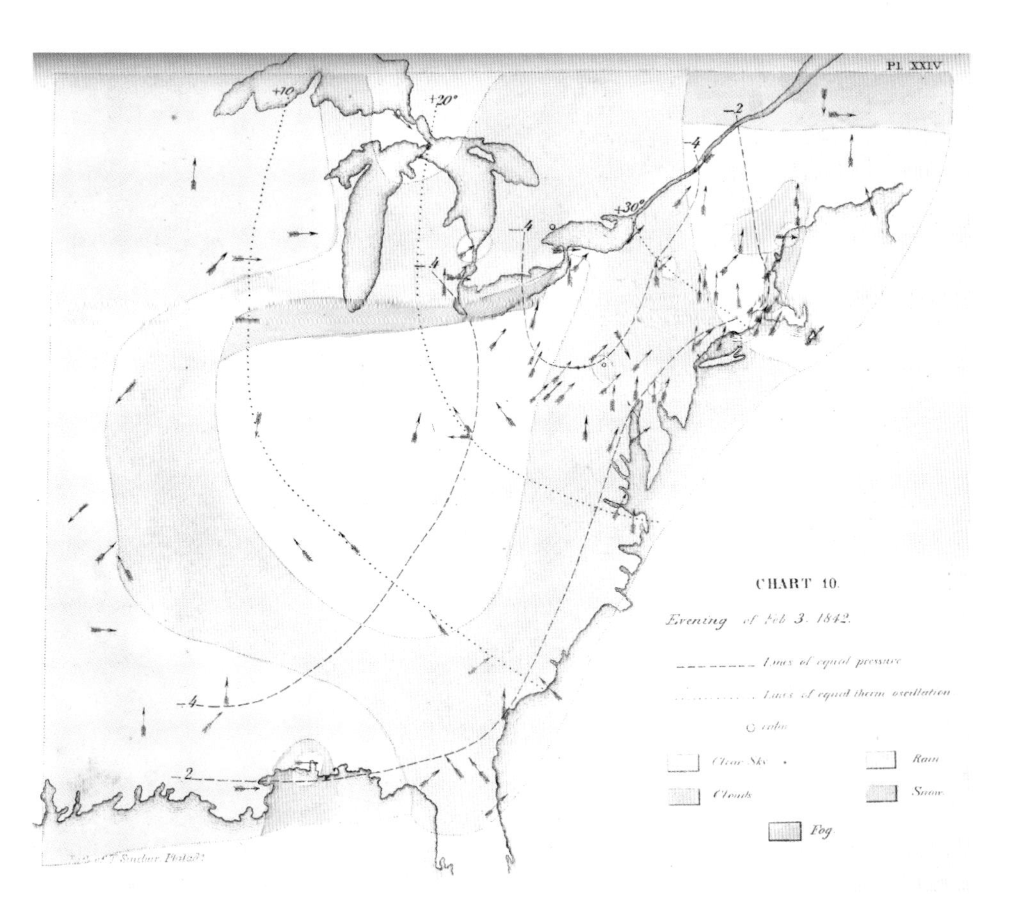

The American mathematician Elias Loomis, known for his textbooks on math, also significantly contributed to meteorology, proposing a system of observers and daily weather maps that resulted in Congress's creation of the Weather Bureau of the United States Signal Service in 1870, today's National Weather Service.

This map is one of thirteen charts published in his article "On Two Storms Which Were Experienced throughout the United States, in the Month of February, 1842." It depicts Loomis's observations on the storms over a wide region in the eastern half of the United States and over several days. Delaney observes, "In two series of sequential maps (dated morning/evening, day), he drew lines of equal deviations in barometric pressure and equal oscillations in temperature, and assigned colors to areas of clear sky, clouds, rain, snow, and even fog. In addition, Loomis used arrows of varying length to indicate wind direction and intensity. In fact, he was anticipating common characteristics of the modern weather map: when the Signal Service's weather maps began appearing in 1871, they were constructed on Loomis's model."[19]

In chapter 2, we saw that time has an inherent semantic structure and a hierarchic granularity that ranges from nanoseconds to hours, days, months, years, millennia, and so on. When structuring and devising measurement systems for time, we have relied traditionally on spatial metaphors as well as on the observation of the motion of celestial objects. As Vasiliev expounds, "The motions of these heavenly bodies, which were used either to be time or to measure time, occurred in space. It was the relationships that these objects had to each other in space—in the sky—that determined what time it was. From the earliest clocks, the measurement of time depended on spatial relations: where the shadow of the sundial's gnomon falls; how much sand passes from one bowl to the other in an hourglass; the amount a candle burned down past hourly markings. Morning begins when the Sun rises, and night when it sets, and these describe the day. The clock face with its numbers and the moving minute and hour hands could be considered a dynamic map of time. We tell what time it is by understanding the spatial relationship between the numbers and where the hands are pointing."[7]

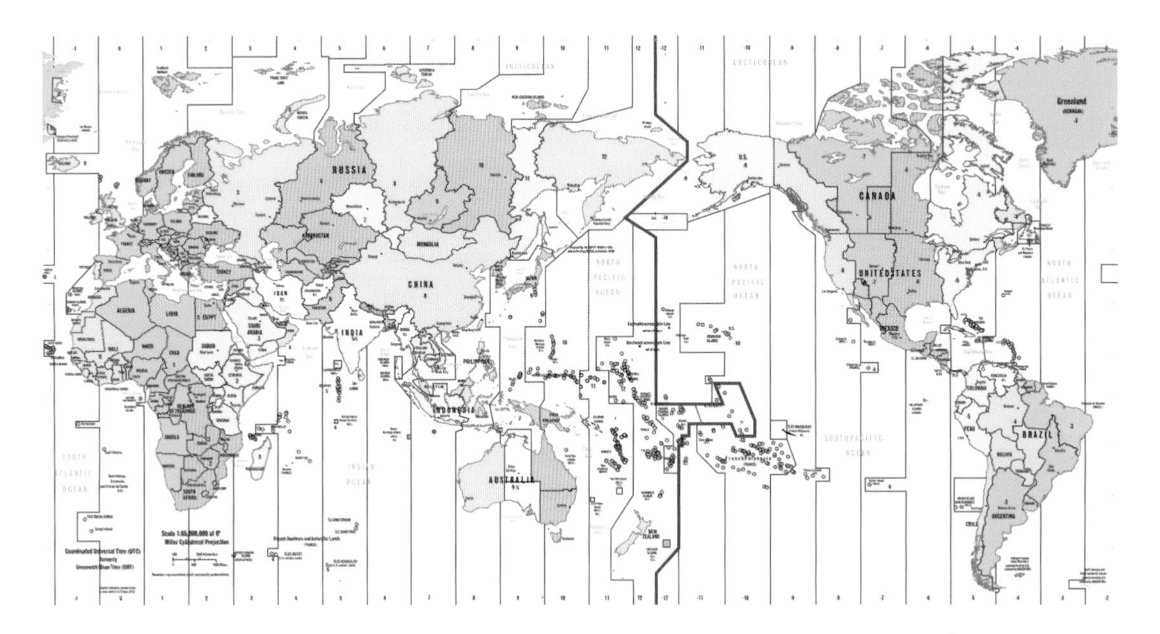

In 1878, Canadian engineer Sir Sanford Fleming proposed a system of worldwide time zones based on lines of longitude by dividing the Earth into 24 time zones (15° wide), with one zone for each hour of the day. The Greenwich Meridian was chosen as the 0° line of longitude, the start point of the system. The endpoint of the system is the 180° line of longitude, that resulted in the creation of the International Date Line. This Pacific-centered map shows the agreed upon time zones in the world for 2012, with the International Date Line represented by the thick red line zigzagging the map vertically.

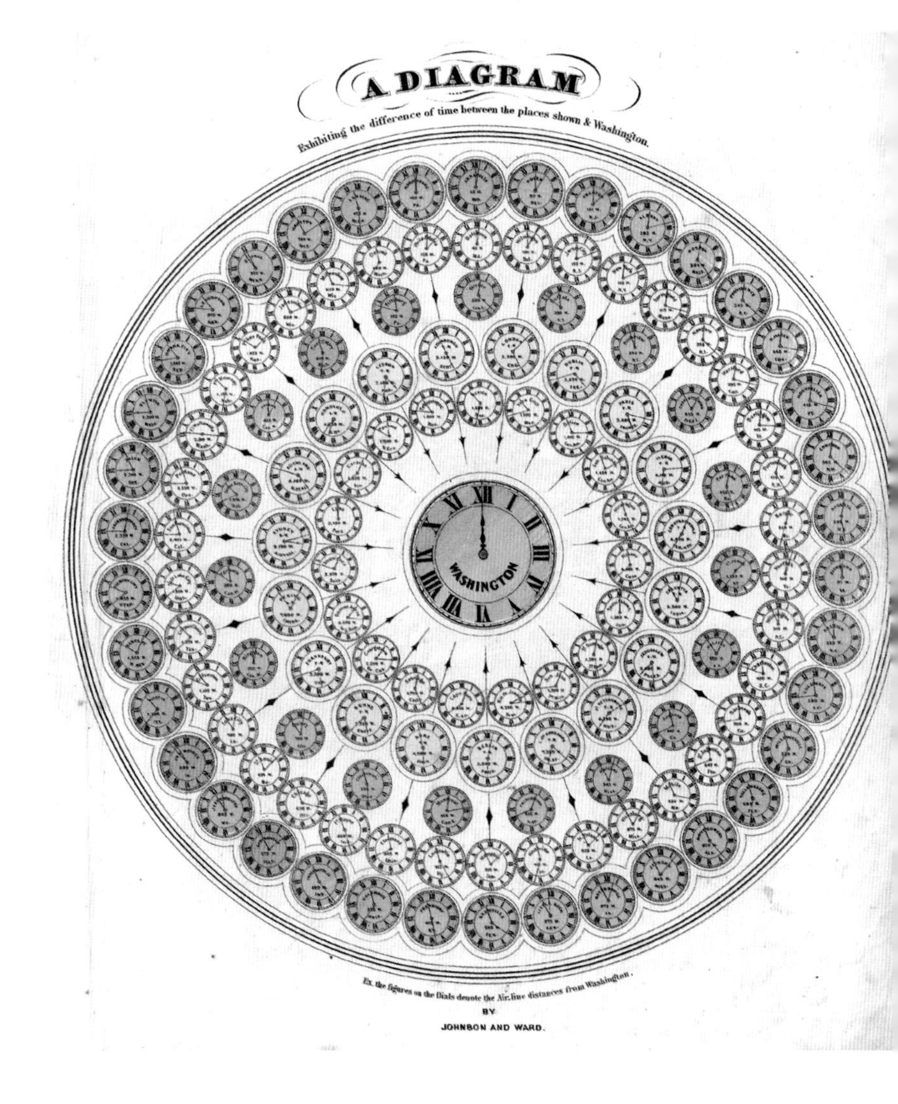

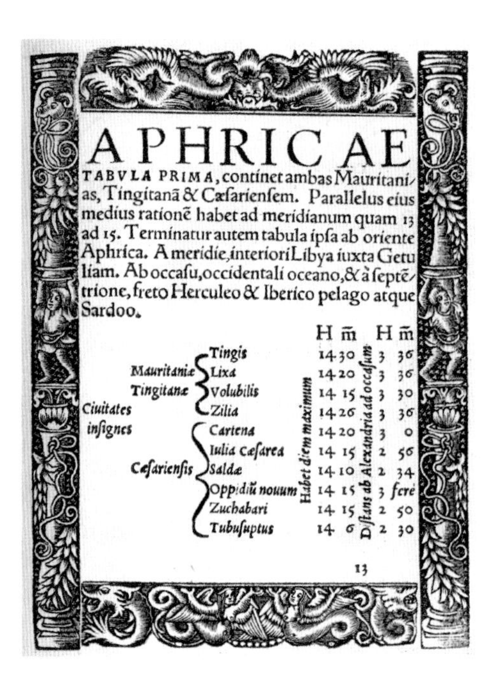

APHRICAE

TABVLA PRIMA, continet ambas Mauritanias, Tingitanã & Cæsariensem. Parallelus eius medius rationẽ habet ad meridianum quam 13 ad 15. Terminatur autem tabula ipsa ab oriente Aphrica. A meridie, interiori Libya iuxta Getuliam. Ab occasu, occidentali oceano, & à septẽtrione, freto Herculeo & Iberico pelago atque Sardoo.

Ciuitates insignes		Habet diem maximum H	m̃	Distans ab Alexandria ad occasum H	m̃
Mauritaniæ Tingitanæ	Tingis	14	30	3	36
	Lixa	14	20	3	36
	Volubilis	14	15	3	30
	Zilia	14	26	3	36
Cæsariensis	Cartena	14	20	3	0
	Iulia Cæsarea	14	15	2	56
	Saldæ	14	10	2	34
	Oppidũ nouum	14	15	3	fere
	Zuchabari	14	15	2	50
	Tubusuptus	14	6	2	30

13

This woodcut table, *Aphricae Tabula I*, was reproduced in Sebastian Münster's 1540 edition of Ptolemy's *Geographia*. Delaney explains, "For each listed North African location, the data in the table show the length of its longest day (in hours and minutes) and its distance (in hours and minutes, hence time) west from Alexandria, Egypt."[20]

Alvin Jewett Johnson designed this world time zones diagram for publication in his *New Illustrated Family Atlas* in 1862. The circular diagram depicts the differences in time between places in the world. It is structured around Washington, DC, which is represented as a clock with the time set at 12. Other major cities in the U.S. and the world surround it with clocks adjusted accordingly.

A familiar example of the spatialization of time is the longitude coordinate system that uses space to organize time. The system both locates places cartographically and measures time as arc distances based on divisions of the globe into 360 degrees, where one hour corresponds to 15 degrees of longitude. The Prime Meridian is the starting line that divides the globe into time zones measured as differences between a particular location and the Coordinated Universal Time (UTC). Vasiliev explains that the longitude system helped standardize time around the globe. "In order to understand the standardization of time worldwide, it is important to map it.... The important progression here is from the acknowledgment that the Sun shines on the Earth's surface in different places at the same time, to the post-Industrial Revolution need to have all humans in any one place observe the same (standard) time and have them understand why time is standard and what the correct time is."[8]

When examining temporal structures in chapter 2, we saw that the Newtonian notion of absolute time was essential to the creation and representation of timelines (see page 88). This is an underlying notion that persists to this day, including visualizations of spatio-temporal data that tend to represent time as ordered. Moreover, the great majority use time points as the primitive in both linear and cyclical ordered temporal structures.

Another temporal feature relevant to the study of spatio-temporal phenomena is that time contains natural cycles and reoccurrences, some more predictable than others. For example, seasons are more predictable than social or economic cycles.[9]

TIME AS DISTANCE METAPHOR

We often use the metaphor of time as distance in our daily lives, such as when we provide temporal measures for giving directions. We say it will take ten minutes to reach the supermarket, it is a three-hour train ride, and so on. There are many instances in which the measure provided by "how long it takes" replaces the spatial distances between places. Isochrone lines and distance cartograms are two common techniques using time distances. Most representations in this category are based on an origin-destination structure, with information centered on a specific spatial point.

Isochronic maps use isolines of equal travel times constructed from a defined location (origin) to represent spatio-temporal phenomena. In other words, the lines, representing temporal distances, are overlaid on a conventional projection base map, where space is kept constant and the time surfaces conform to the temporal distances as represented by the isochrones. Galton's "Isochronic Passage Chart for Travellers" is a historical example of the technique (see page 161).

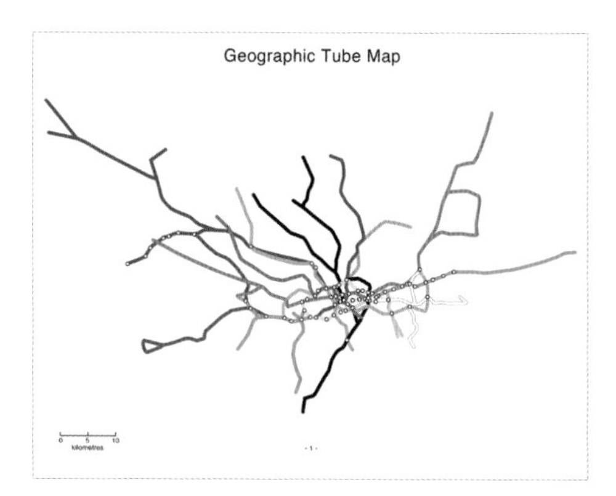

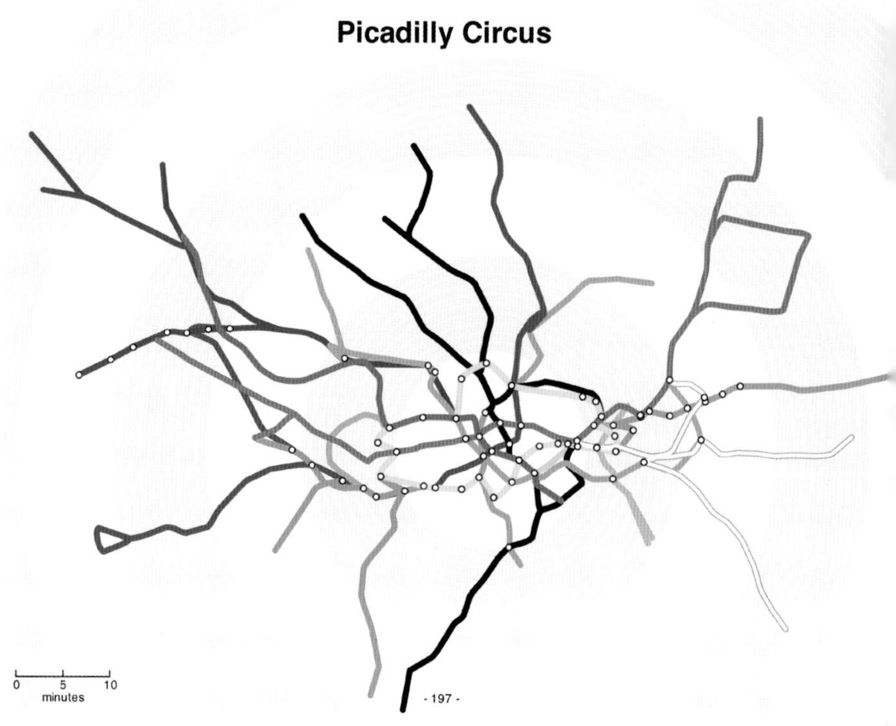

Tom Carden, U.K.:
"Travel Time Tube Map," 2011.

The interactive London Underground map redraws its structure according to the time it takes to travel from a selected departing station. In other words, once a station is selected, it is positioned at the center of a series of concentric circles representing traveling time distances to all other destinations, which are subsequently repositioned. Concentric circles represent ten-minute intervals. To redraw the London Tube map, the software calculates the shortest paths from the origin to the destination stations, with the radius proportional to the time to travel. Tom Carden created this online Java applet in Processing in 2011 as a personal experiment. The top image shows the map rendered according to geographic features, and the other two screenshots show the map centered at Picadilly Circus (left) and at Highgate station in the northern part of London (right).

www.tom-carden.co.uk/p5/tube_map_travel_times/applet

In distance cartograms, a set of concentric circles centered in a specified origin point represents temporal distances, often without a base map, which would be distorted to fit the temporal distances. In other words, it uses temporal distance as a proxy for spatial distance, resulting in distortion of the topology to conform to the temporal measures.

SCALES

Spatio-temporal phenomena exist at different spatial and temporal scales, which significantly affect the extent and amount of detail represented. As seen in chapter 4, maps involve reducing dimensions in order to bring spatial reality to the scale of our human sensory systems. We reduce the three dimensions of space into the two dimensions of maps, and sometimes we reduce even further the three dimensions of space into a one-dimensional element, such as when we represent cities as dots on a map. Similar strategies need to be in place when depicting spatio-temporal phenomena, as MacEachren explains, "Temporally, some geographic space-time processes (e.g., earthquake tremor) are fast enough that we need to slow them down to understand them (as when we 'map' a molecule, cell, or computer chip, for which an increase in scale makes visible a pattern that would otherwise remain hidden).

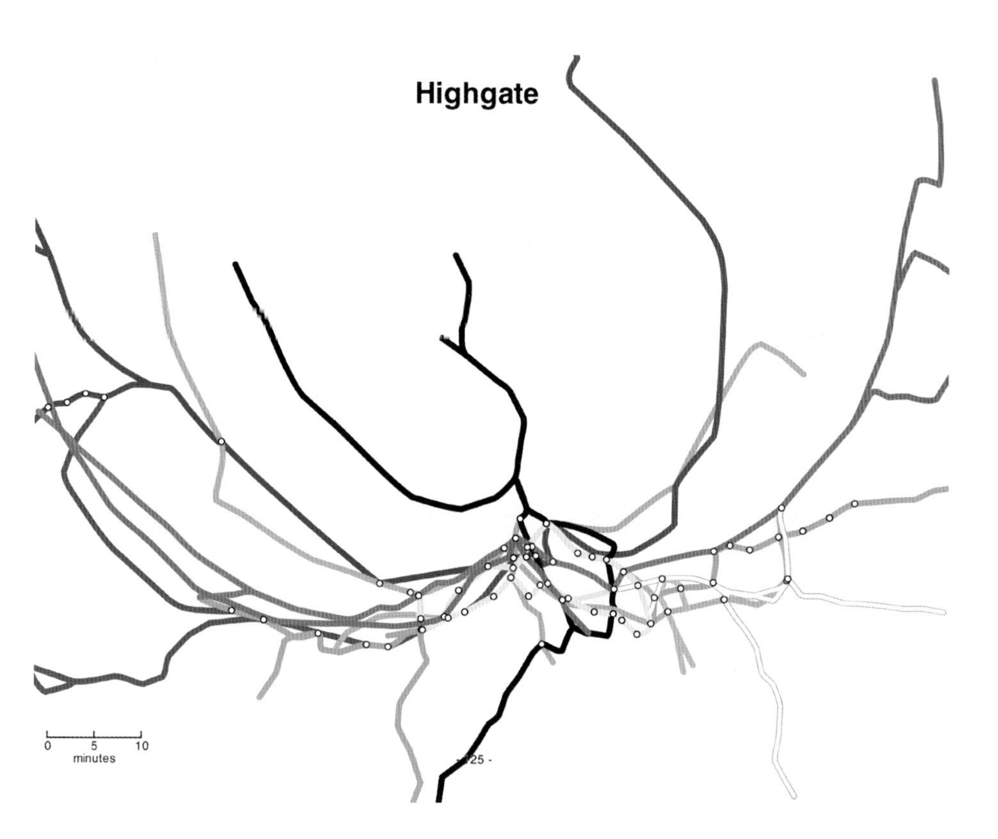

Most temporal geographic phenomena, like spatial ones, have a time span too large to be grasped at once, so therefore we need to compress time as well as space."[10]

We have examined how geographic scale affects the amount of information revealed in maps, where large-scale maps present a larger and more detailed number of features than a small-scale map does (see page 123). Similarly, time can also be scaled at different granularities, affecting the amount of information provided for analysis. Typically, local phenomena are nested within global phenomena, such as the relationships between a local storm and global climate change. The same is true for personal phenomena, in that local phenomena, such as activities within a day, are different when considered within a week (weekdays versus weekends), a year (working versus holidays), or a lifetime. Furthermore, temporal scales involve aggregating time into conceptual units, such as when we use a day for twenty-four hours or divide the week into weekdays and weekends. Decisions will depend on the type of data and the tasks at hand. For example, a multiple map series uses a single granularity, whereas interactive applications tend to offer different scales.

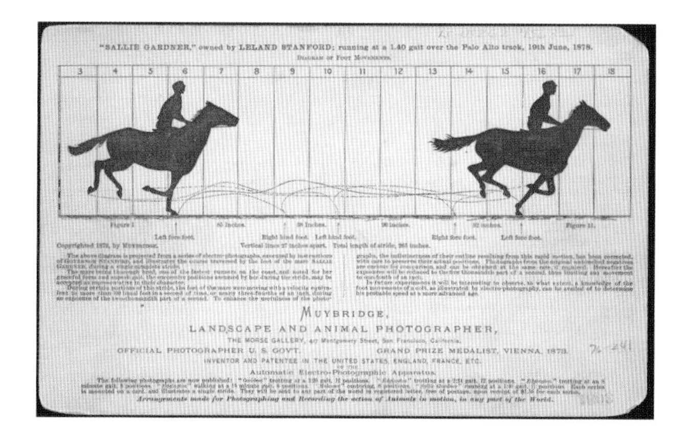

This image was created by Eadweard Muybridge to illustrate a horse in motion running at a 1:40 gait over the Palo Alto track, on 19 June 1878. Muybridge portrays the motion with the aid of a diagram depicting the foot movements between two frames for beginning and end.

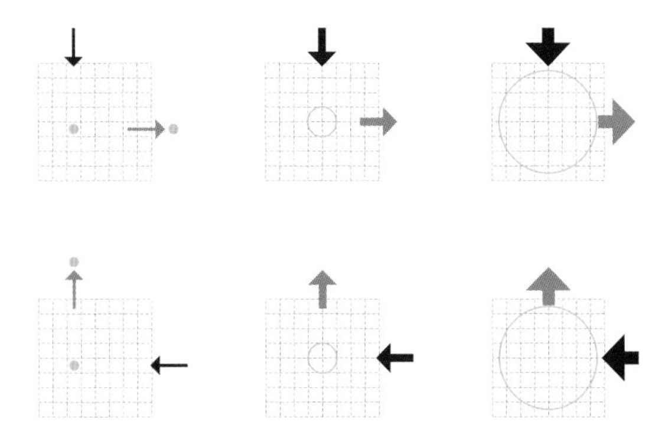

Diagram after Jacques Bertin's information system: question types and reading levels.[21]

Because of the complexities of spatial and temporal dependencies in the representation of phenomena, each scale—spatial and temporal—must match the phenomena under consideration. However, the most adequate or effective scales are not always known beforehand and must be discovered in the process of analysis, which involves trial and error. Interactive visualization tools tend to allow multiscale analysis and the manipulation of both space and time to help discover an appropriate match. As Andrienko and colleagues contend, "Various scales of spatial and temporal phenomena may interact, or phenomena at one scale may emerge from smaller or larger phenomena. This is captured by the notion of a hierarchy of scales, in which smaller phenomena are nested within larger phenomena. Thus, local economies are nested within regional economies; rivers are nested within larger hydrologic systems; and so on. This means that analytical tools must adequately support analyses at multiple scales considering the specifics of space and time."[11]

TYPES OF QUESTIONS

In the seminal book *Semiology of Graphics*, the French cartographer Jacques Bertin identifies two key concepts for visually conveying information: question types and reading levels.[12] Bertin argued that there are as many types of questions as components in the information (data variables). He considered that for each question type there would be three reading levels in the visualization: elementary (datum), intermediate (set of data), and overall (whole dataset).

Following a similar approach, but specifically for spatio-temporal data, Peuquet defined three components: space (where), time (when), and objects (what), allowing three types of questions:[13]

- when + where > what: questions about an object or set of objects at a given location(s) at a given time(s)
- when + what > where: questions about a location or sets of locations for an object(s) at a given time(s)
- where + what > when: questions for a time or set of times for a given object(s) at a given location(s)

Andrienko and colleagues extend the task typology by adding the "identification–comparison" dimension.[14]

There has been an increase in the collection as well as accessibility of spatio-temporal data in recent years due to the various new sensors (GPS, cell phone, etc) and aerial and satellite imagery, which pose new challenges, especially in what concerns techniques for dealing with large amounts of data (big data) as well as dynamic data being sourced in real time. The case studies that follow present projects that address these questions.

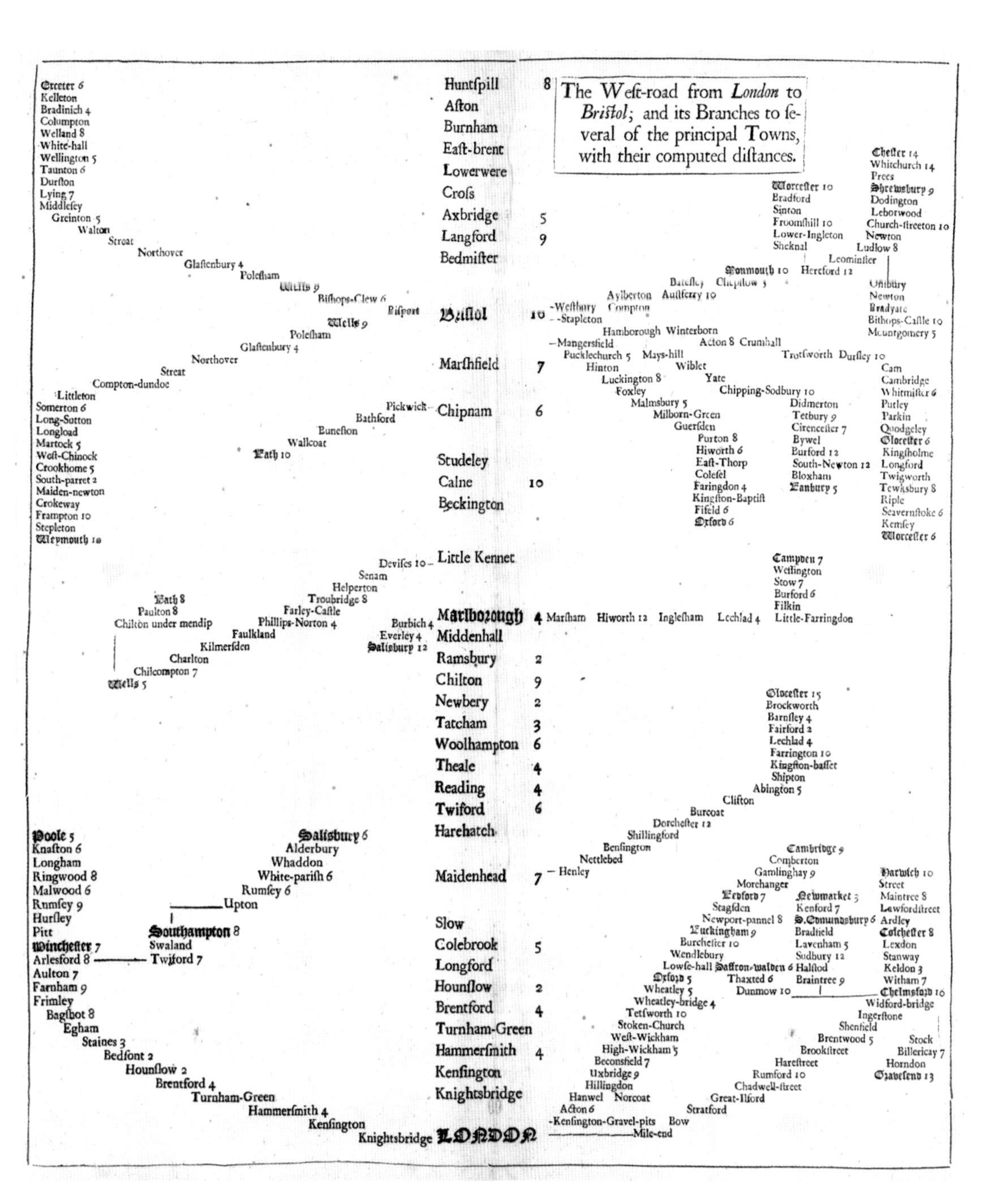

"The West-Road from London to Bristol; and Its Branches to Several of the Principal Towns, with Their Computed Distances" was published in John Speed's *The Theatre of the Empire of Great-Britain* in 1676. Delaney explains how this stripped-down map with relative distances functions, "Here, roads consist of stacks of place names; the title one ("West-Road") runs up the spine of the page from London at the bottom. The names of larger towns are printed in bold, old English typeface letters. In the seventeenth century, one's options for leaving London by foot or horse were few. Heading west on this road towards Bristol—which everyone would know ("you need to take the West Road . . .") —one would expect to arrive in Hammersmith after four miles and reach Brentford via Turnham-Green after four more. (These localities are part of Greater London today.) From Maidenhead and Marlborough, other roads are shown going north. This hybrid approach, similar to a subway map today, has been an effective travel tool for over three hundred years."[22]

CASE STUDY

INFORMATION DIFFUSION
Whisper

Whisper is an interactive application that visualizes the process of information diffusion in social media in real time. It tracks the time, place, and topic of information exchanges in the Twitter micro-blog service. It was designed in 2012 by the international team of Nan Cao, Yu-Ru Lin, Xiaohua Sun, David Lazer, Shixia Liu, and Huamin Qu.

They consider that information spreads from information sources to users, as when users retweet messages, further affecting their followers and ultimately the user's geographic location. Among the relevant features in understanding this process and the effects of information spreading is the role people play in that process, including that of key opinion leaders. Cao and colleagues explain, "Whisper seeks to represent such rich information through a collection of diffusion pathways on which users' retweeting behavior is shown at different levels of granularity. Each pathway is also a timeline whose time span is configurable to enable an exploration of the diffusion processes occurring between two chosen points in time."[23]

The visualization uses the visual metaphor of the sunflower to construct the information space of the narrative, which is then populated by the actors, places, and themes. It uses a single representation with two coordinated views: the dynamic view shows the tweets and retweets generated in real time, and the static view allows exploration of historical data by means of a timeline. There are several dimensions to the data that includes temporal, spatial, spatio-temporal, nominal, and categorical.

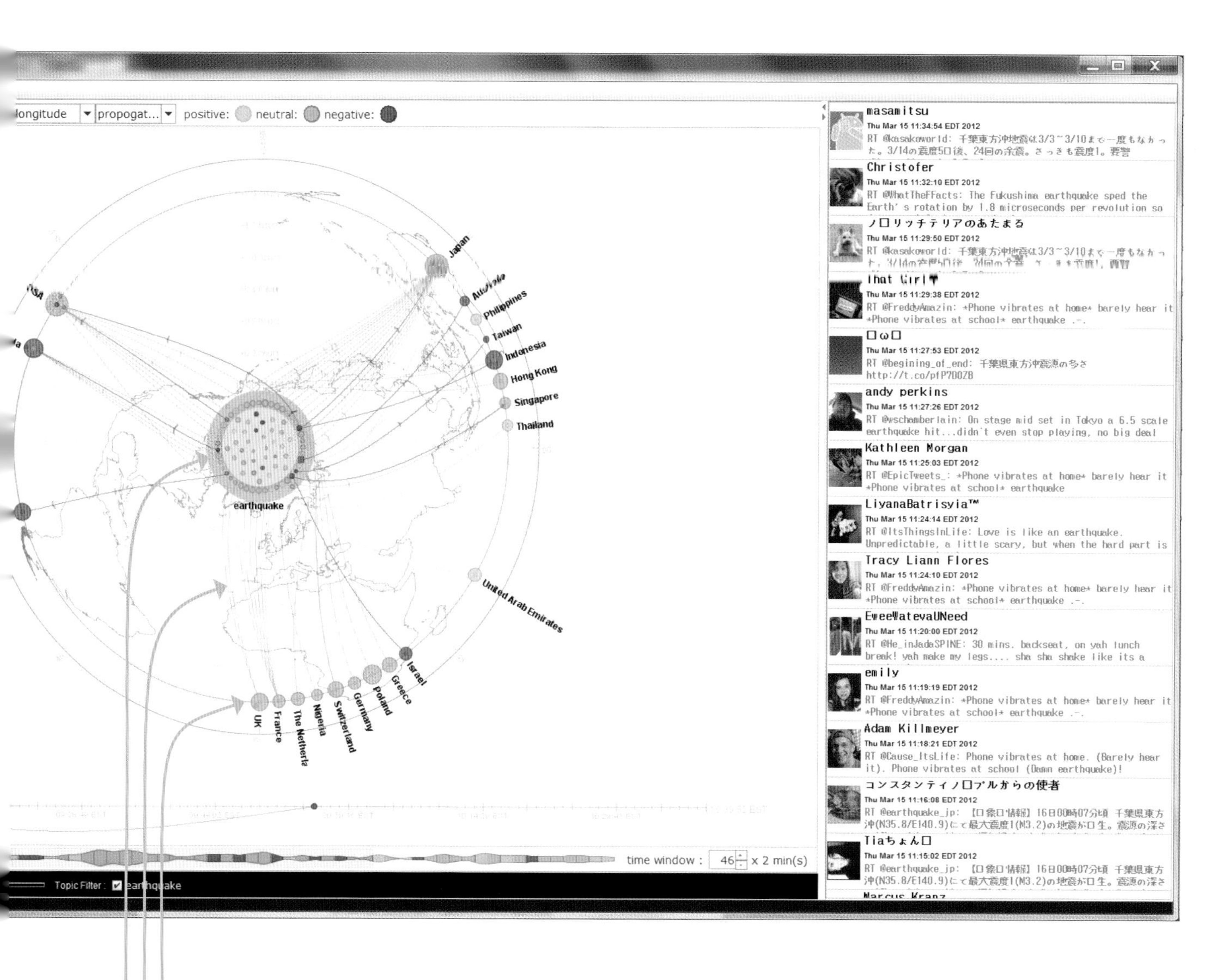

The dynamic view of the visualization is composed of three main elements:

Topic disk: A circular structure holds the tweets. Tweets are placed according to the frequency of retweets in a polar direction, such that once a message is retweeted for the first time, it moves from the center to the periphery of the circle. Tweets that are not retweeted—in other words, those not contributing to any information diffusion—fade out over time, giving place for new tweets.

User group: Retweets are hierarchically grouped by shared topics of interest or shared geographic locations, with the latter geo-located in the map.

Diffusion pathways: The path linking a tweet to the retweet user group provides the diffusion path that is represented as a timeline, with marks standing for retweets over time.

Color hue encodes sentiment on a three-color palette, where red stands for negative, orange for neutral, and green for positive opinions.

Color opacity encodes activeness of tweets or user groups.

Size encodes the expected influence of a tweet, which is calculated by the expected influence of the tweet user based on the number of followers the user has.

Shape encodes the type of user: a square represents users from media outlets or organizations and circles stand for all other users.

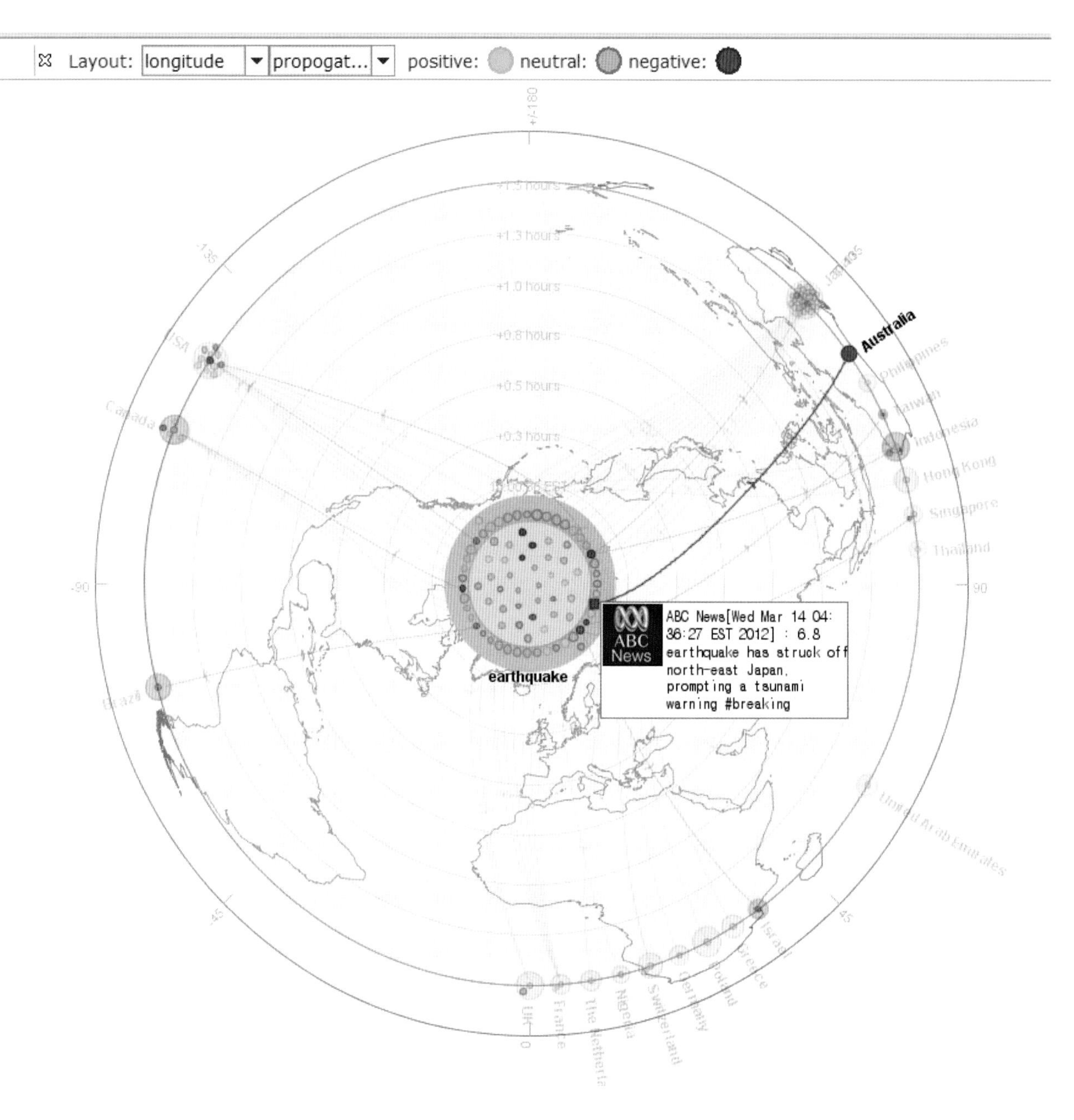

The image shows a diffusion of information on Twitter regarding a 6.8 magnitude earthquake and a series of aftershocks and tsunamis that hit the northern coast of Hokkaido island, Japan in 2012. The event caught global attention because the location was one of the areas in Japan devastated by the 2011 disaster. This image shows that some countries, including Australia, were initially concerned about the Pacificwide tsunami threat triggered from the earthquake. The use of the geographic structure for examining this particular event in Whisper is quite effective.

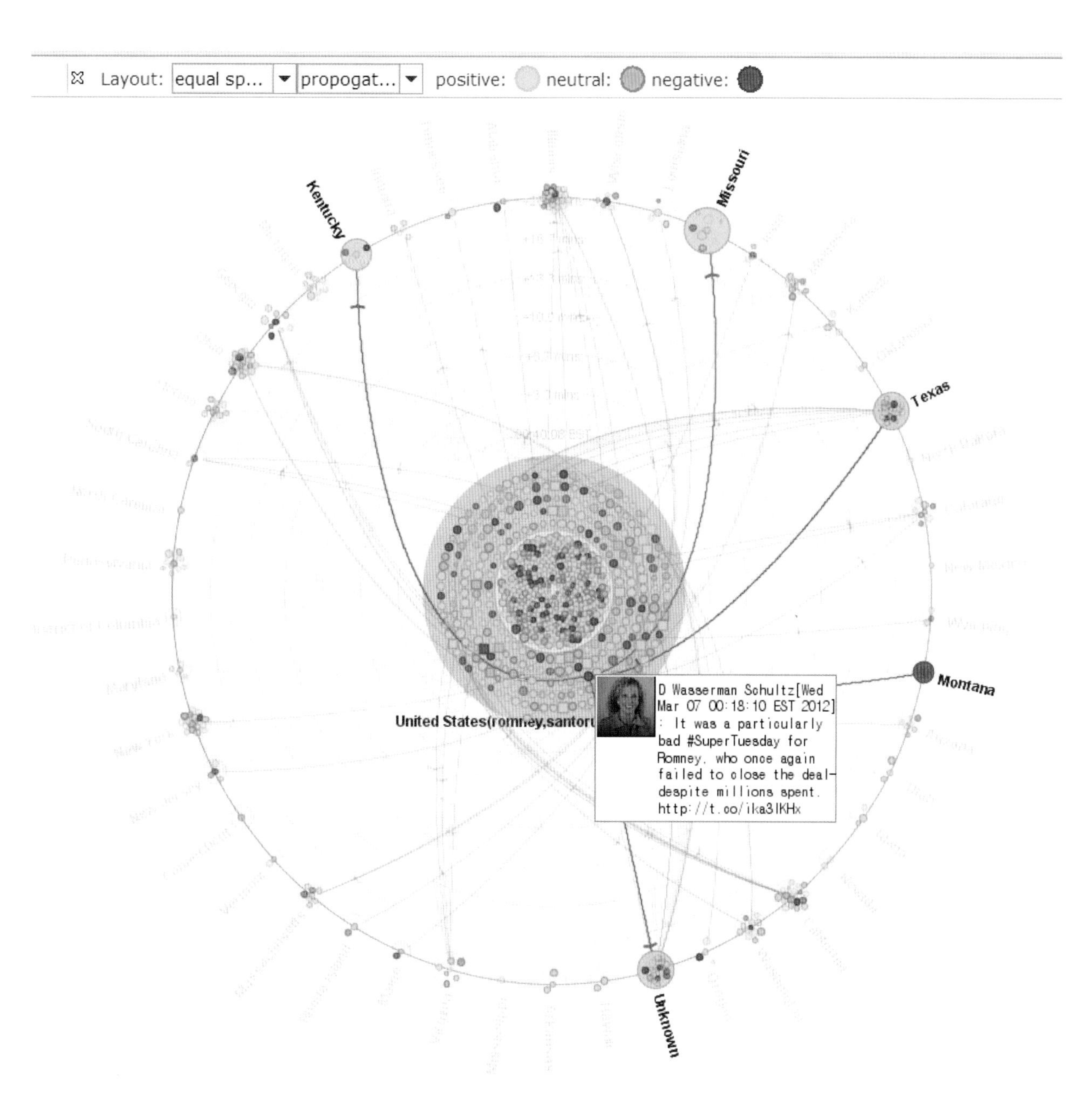

This image depicts the spatial diffusion patterns of the 2012 Republican presidential primaries and caucus results on Super Tuesday. Note spreading of the tweet by opinion leader, Congresswoman Schultz.

CASE STUDY

CHILD DEVELOPMENT
HouseFly and *WordScape*

In order to study child development as it occurs in the home, professors Deb Roy and Rupal Patel began an investigation in their own family with the birth of their first child. They installed a camera and microphone in the ceiling of every room of their house and recorded the majority of their child's waking experience for the first three years of life, resulting in a dataset of 80,000 hours of video and 120,000 hours of audio. HouseFly is a software tool developed to help researchers visualize and browse this massive dataset. Between 2009 and 2010 Philip DeCamp developed the application in collaboration with Deb Roy, director of the Cognitive Machines group at the MIT Media Lab.[24]

Instead of displaying each stream of video separately, HouseFly combines them to create a dynamic, three-dimensional model of the home. The user can navigate to any location in the house at any time and get a better sense of what they would have seen and heard if they had actually been there. Beyond the reconstruction of individual events, HouseFly also incorporates speech transcripts, person tracks, and other forms of retrieving and accessing data in an effort to uncover some of the unseen patterns of everyday life.

What we see in this image is the 3-D synthesized home environment constructed from 11-camera video. HouseFly uses immersive video as a platform for multimodal data visualization. The application allows one to move in space and through time to examine the 80,000 hours of video. At the bottom, the timeline offers another way to navigate the content, including the ability to add notations in time about words of interest in the transcripts of the speech environment of the child.

Twenty minutes of motion by the child (red) and the caregiver (green) are represented as traces rendered in space. To examine the temporal dimension of the motion, one can switch the view to the side and the traces will be ordered vertically, with earlier times at the bottom, allowing a chronological view of interactions (bottom).

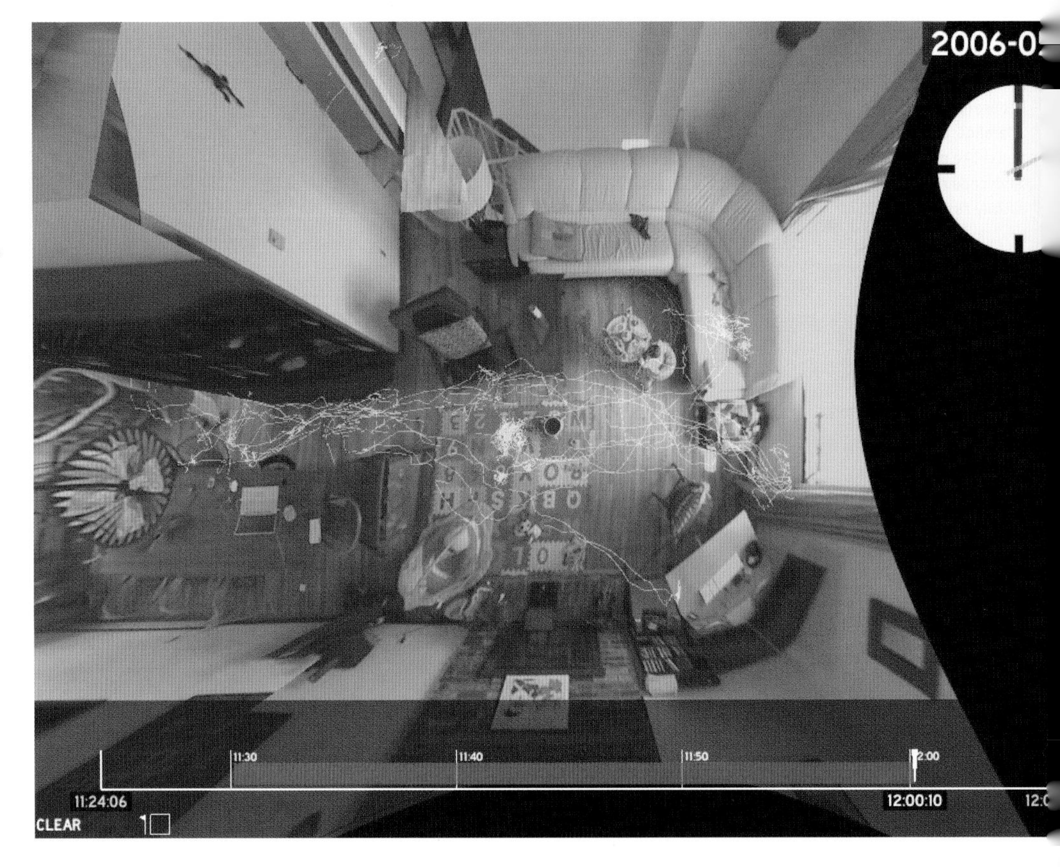

WordScapes are generated by mining the audio data for all utterances of a given word, like "water," tracking the locations of the occupants for twenty seconds around each utterance, and then stacking the resulting tracks like a pile of noodles. The resulting landscape reveals the overall distribution of activity associated with a given word. Some words, like "book," are used most frequently in the child's bedroom, where caregivers often read to the child, while words like "mango" occur almost exclusively in the kitchen. Such analysis may provide insight into how and why different children learn different words more readily than others.

"WATER"

CASE STUDY

MOBILITY

From Mobility Data to Mobility Patterns

Huge amounts of data generated and collected by a wealth of technological infrastructures, such as GPS positioning, and wireless networks have affected research on moving-object data analysis. Access to massive repositories of spatiotemporal data with recorded human mobile activities have opened new frontiers for developing suitable analytical methods and location-aware applications capable of producing useful knowledge.

This case study briefly introduces few visual techniques devised by an interdisciplinary team involved with mobility data mining, knowledge discovery, and visual analytical tools. The project was part of the European Community–funded effort on Geographic Privacy-aware Knowledge Discovery and Delivery–GeoPKDD, with the objective to investigate "how to discover useful knowledge about human movement behavior from mobility data, while preserving the privacy of the people under observation. GeoPKDD aims at improving decision-making in many mobility-related tasks, especially in metropolitan areas."[25]

The main people involved in this particular output are Gennady Andrienko, Natalia Andrienko, Fosca Giannotti, Dino Pedreschi, and Salvatore Rinzivillo.[26] What we see is a small sample of their extensive and pioneer work in the visual analyses of movement data. I strongly recommend their writings, which include discussion of computational methods, not examined here.[27]

The dataset consists of GPS tracks of 17,241 cars collected during one week in Milan, Italy, which resulted in 2,075,216 position records. The work was conducted mostly between 2005 and 2009 with continued ongoing efforts.

Natalia and Gennady Andrienko organize the methods for visually analyzing movement data into four types:[28]

- **Looking at trajectories:** Trajectories are considered as wholes. The focus is on examination of spatial and temporal properties of individual trajectories as well as comparison among trajectories.
- **Looking inside trajectories:** Trajectories are considered at the level of segments and points. The focus is on examination of segment's movement characteristics and the sequences of segments with shared patterns.
- **Bird's-eye view on movement:** Trajectories are viewed as aggregations, not individually. The focus is on examination of the distribution of multiple movements in space and time.
- **Investigating movement in context:** Movement data are examined with other kinds of spatial, temporal, and spatiotemporal data describing context. The focus is on relations of interactions between the moving objects and the environment.

Each series of images illustrates a method type with the exception of movement in context, not reproduced here.

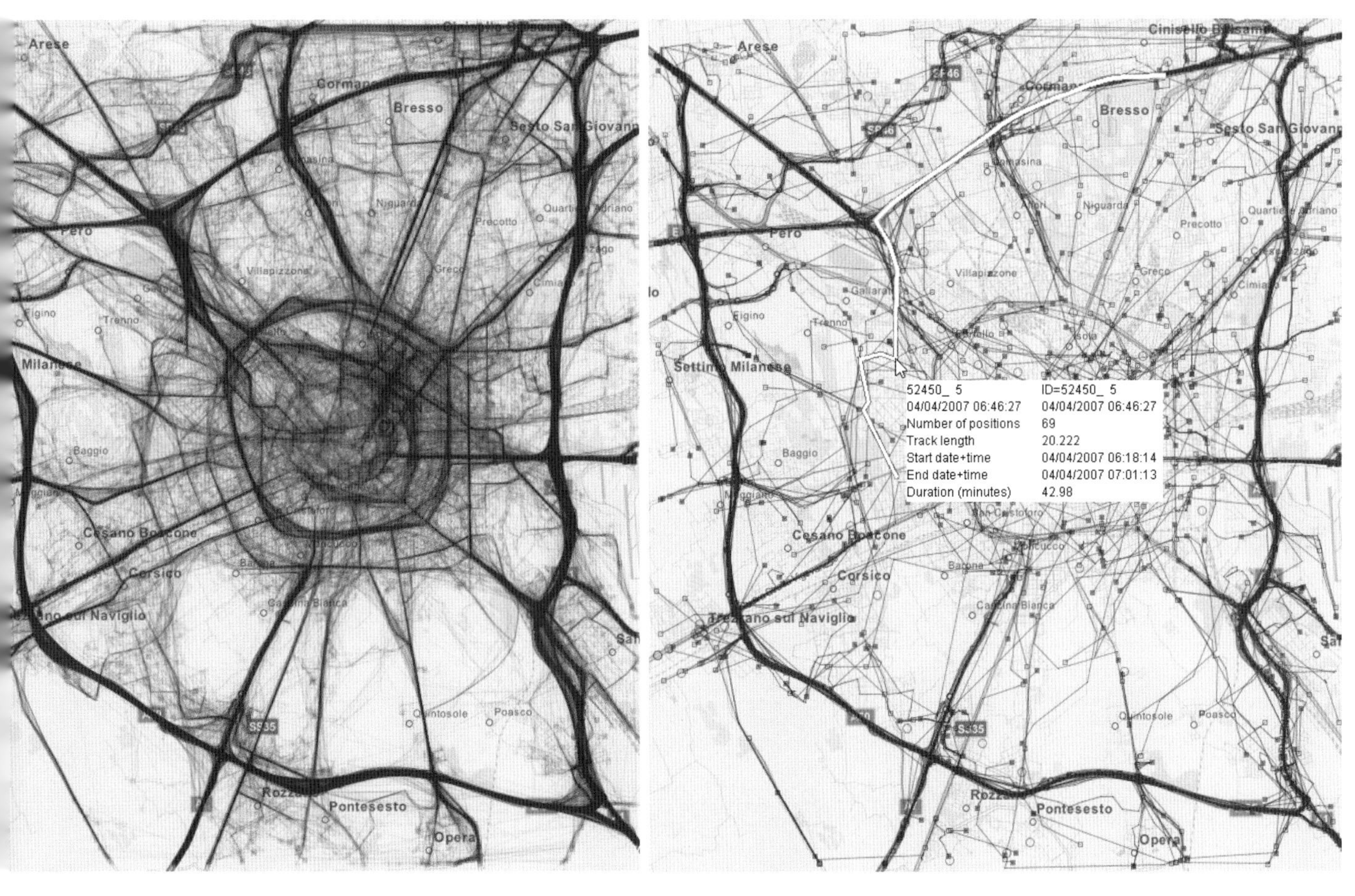

VISUALIZING TRAJECTORIES

This image shows a subset of the Milan dataset consisting of 8,206 trajectories that began on Wednesday, April 4, 2007. To make the map legible, the trajectory lines are drawn with only 5 percent opacity.

The visual analytical tool allows one to interactively manipulate the view as well as apply filters. The image on the right shows the result of using a temporal filter that limits the representation of trajectories within a 30-minute time interval, from 06:30 to 07:00. The same function can be used to generate map animations. The screenshot illustrates that by interacting with the trajectories one can read detailed information about its attributes, such as start and end time, number of positions, length, duration, etc.

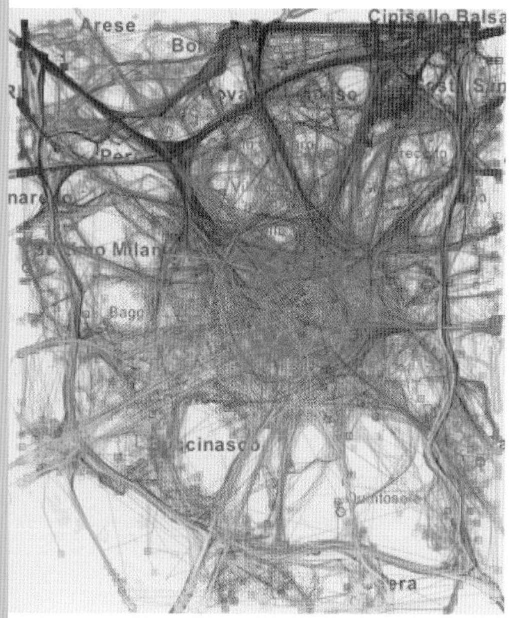

The image shows the result of clustering by "common destinations," which compares the spatial positions of the ends of trajectories. From the 8,206 trajectories, 4,385 have been grouped into 80 density-based clusters and 3,821 treated as noise.

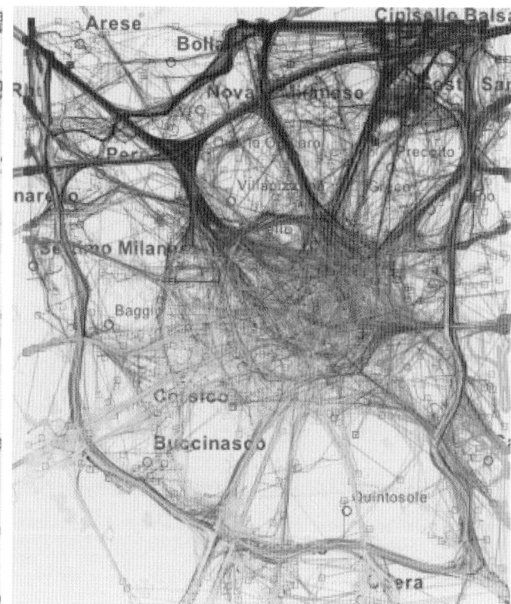

In this image, we see the clusters with the noise removed.

The image shows the biggest cluster, which consists of 590 trajectories that end at the northwest part of Milan.

CLUSTERING TRAJECTORIES

Natalia and Gennady Andrienko explain, "Trajectories of moving objects are quite complex spatiotemporal constructs. Their potentially relevant characteristics include the geometric shape of the path, its position in space, the life span, and the dynamics, i.e. the way in which the spatial location, speed, direction and other point-related attributes of the movement change over time. Clustering of trajectories requires appropriate distance (dissimilarity) functions which can properly deal with these non-trivial properties."[29] To avoid universal functions that would make the visualization hard to interpret, the team has developed a method called "progressive clustering."[30] It is a step-by-step process in which the analyst progressively refines the clustering by modifying the parameters and applying the new settings, thus gradually building understanding of the different aspects of the trajectories. The four images show the result of progressive clustering to the same subset of the Milan data as the images on the previous page.

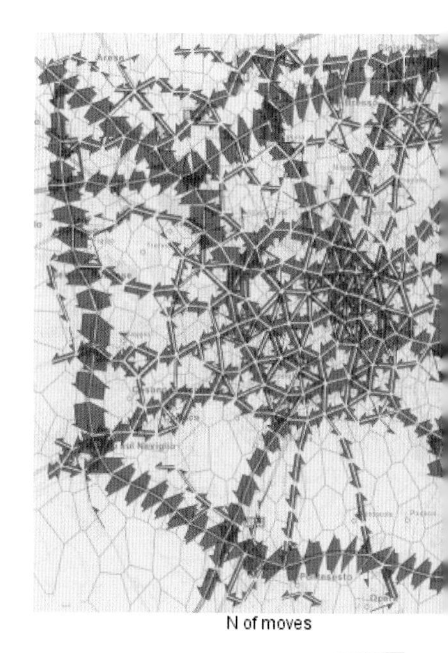

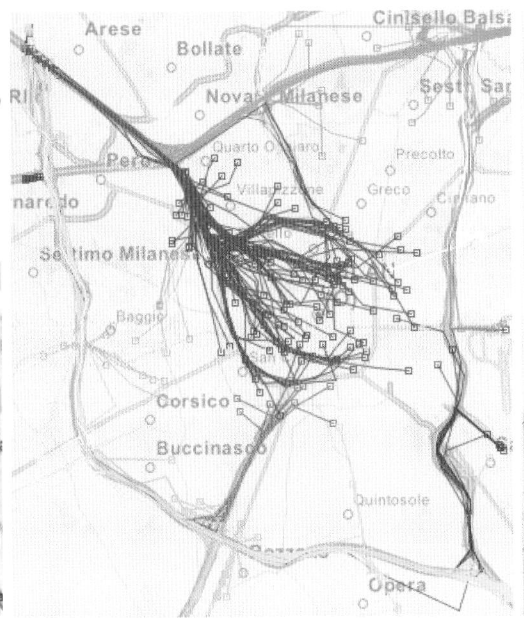

When clustering by "route similarity," which compares the routes followed by the moving objects, the result is a total of eighteen clusters, with the noise hidden. The largest cluster (in red) consists of 116 trajectories going from the city center. The next largest cluster (in orange) consists of 104 trajectories going from the northeast along the northern motorway. The yellow cluster (68 trajectories) depicts trajectories going from the southeast along the motorway on the south and west.

The image shows the Space-Time Cube (STC) representation of the result from clustering by "route similarity" (same clustering as shown in the previous image). STC is a common type of display of movement data that uses a three-dimensional cube, with two dimensions representing space, and one time. STCs were briefly discussed earlier in the chapter (see pages 161–162).

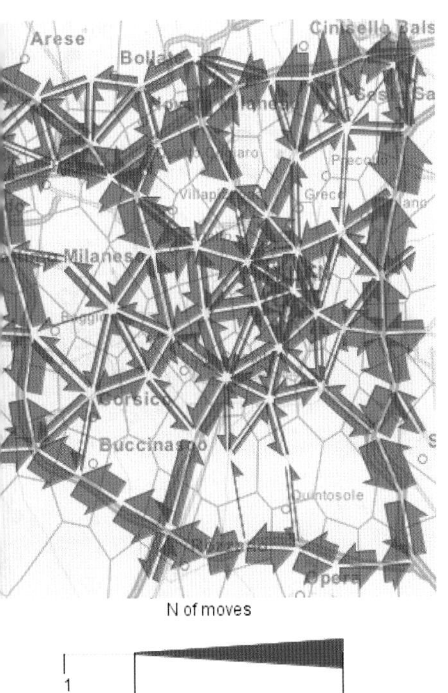

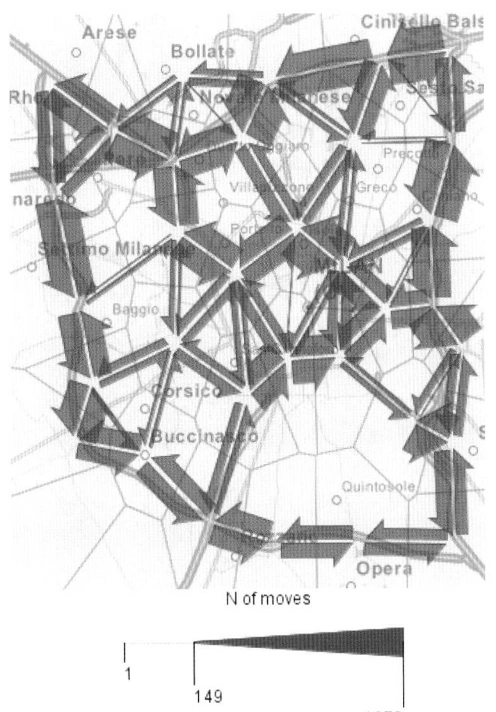

BIRD'S-EYE VIEW OF MOVEMENT DATA

Generalization and aggregation of trajectories enable understanding of the spatial and temporal distribution of multiple movements, which is not possible by looking at individual trajectories. There are different techniques for aggregating movement data, and the most common method examines flows of moving objects by pairs of locations, as those in origin-destination pairs. Given the complexity of the data, and to avoid visual clutter, Andrienko and colleagues have devised a more efficient method that segments trajectories into all visited locations along the path and then aggregate the transitions from all trajectories.[31] The result can be viewed in this sequence of images showing flow maps based on fine, medium and coarse territory divisions. To distinguish flows in different directions, each segment is represented by "half-arrow" symbols. The line widths stand for magnitudes. Details on exact value of magnitudes, as well as other flow-related attributes, are provided by interaction with the segments.

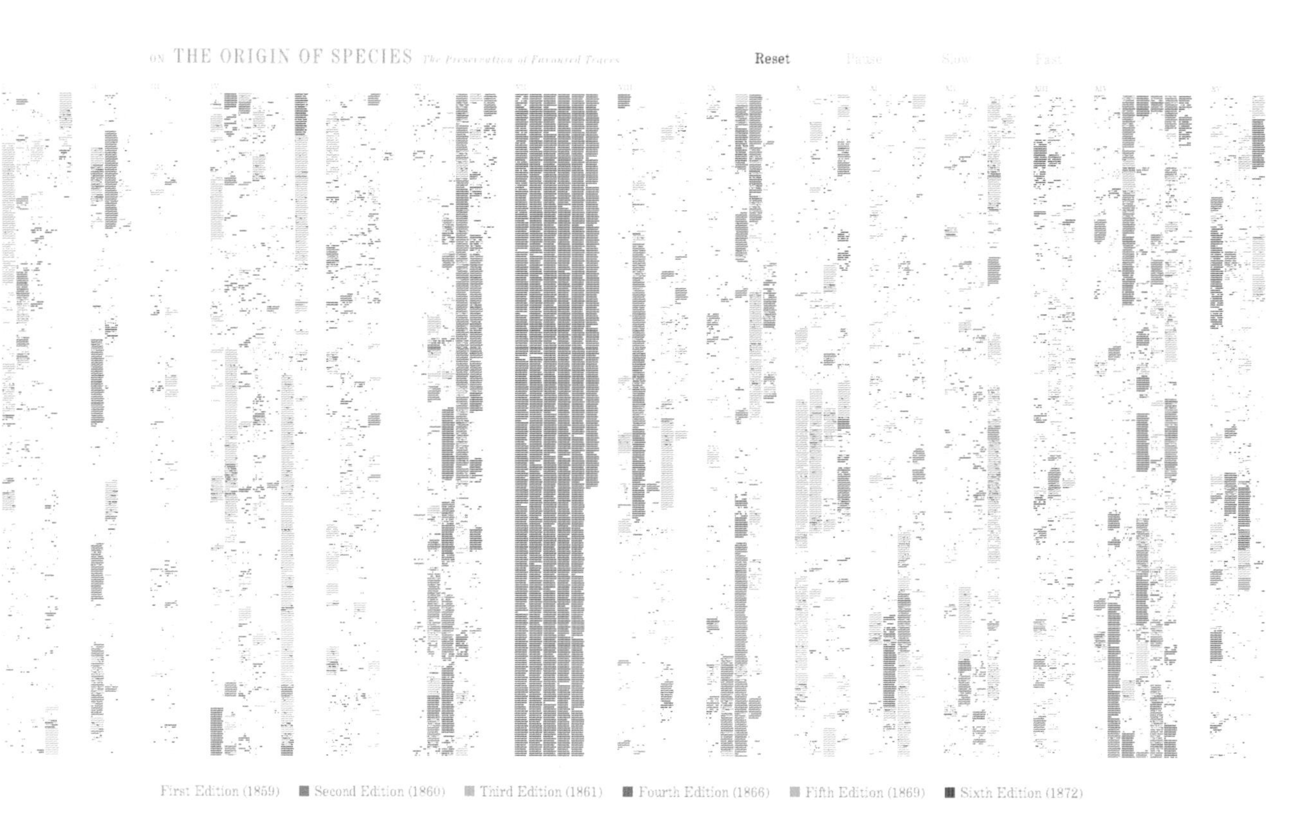
ON THE ORIGIN OF SPECIES The Preservation of Favoured Traces
Reset
Pause
Slow
Fast
First Edition (1859)
Second Edition (1860)
Third Edition (1861)
Fourth Edition (1866)
Fifth Edition (1869)
Sixth Edition (1872)

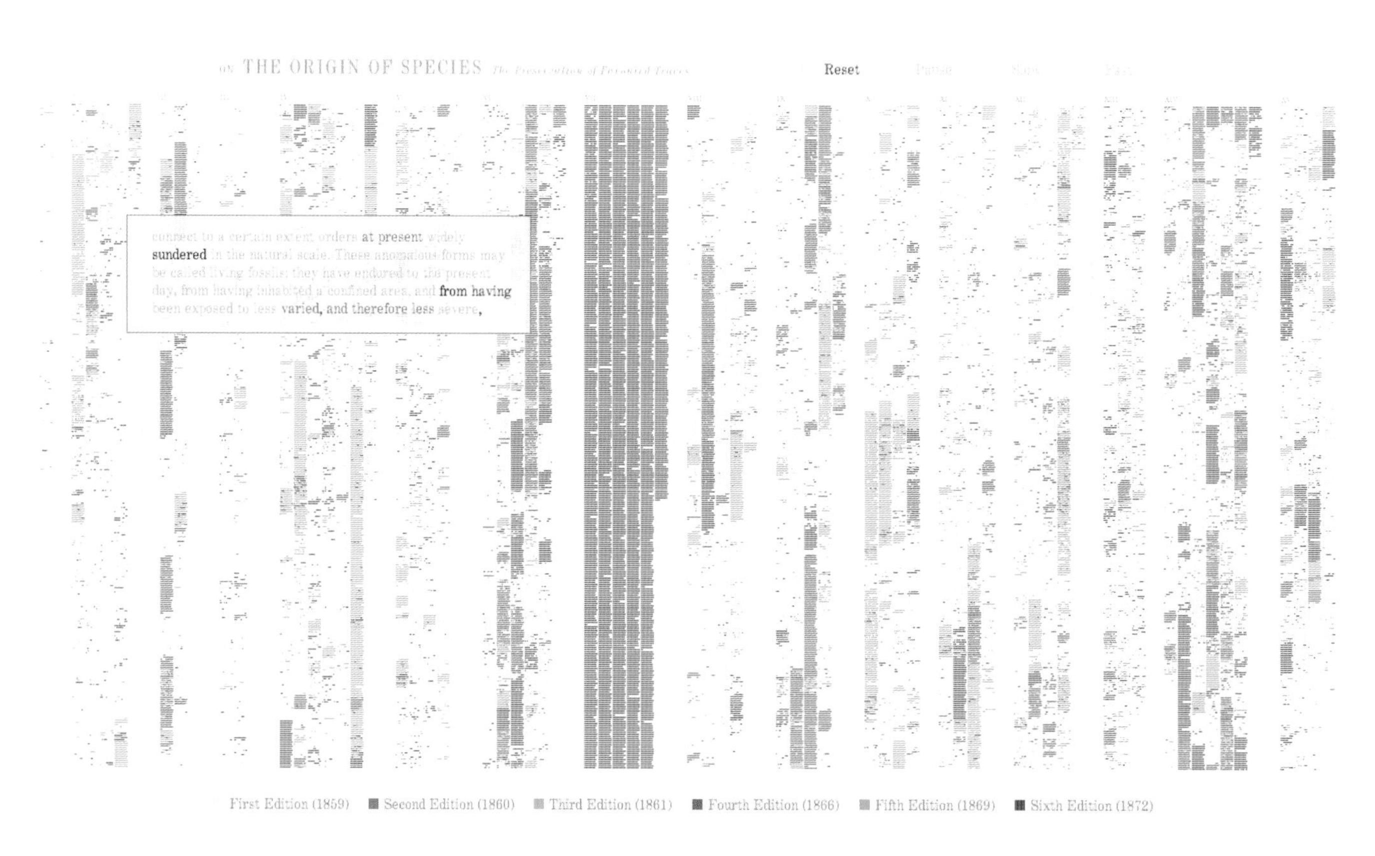
ON THE ORIGIN OF SPECIES The Preservation of Favoured Traces
Reset
Pause
Slow
Fast
connect to a certain extent orders at present widely
sundered in the natural scale. These anomalous forms may
be called living fossils; they have endured to the present
day, from having inhabited a confined area, and from having
been exposed to less varied, and therefore less severe,
First Edition (1859)
Second Edition (1860)
Third Edition (1861)
Fourth Edition (1866)
Fifth Edition (1869)
Sixth Edition (1872)

CHAPTER 6

TEXTUAL STRUCTURES

Ben Fry, U.S.: "On the *Origin of Species*: The Preservation of Favoured Traces," 2009.

The interactive online visualization depicts changes in the six editions of Darwin's *On the Origin of Species*. Each edition is color coded, allowing, for example, at a glance to see how entire volumes were changed over the course of fourteen years. Given the scope of Darwin's work and the limited space we have on the screen, Fry enables one to read text by clicking on the colored blocks. The bottom image shows how the words are also color coded, highlighting changes and refinements in the text over the years. Fry explains, "We often think of scientific ideas, such as Darwin's theory of evolution, as fixed notions that are accepted as finished. In fact, Darwin's *On the Origin of Species* evolved over the course of several editions he wrote, edited, and updated during his lifetime. The first English edition was approximately 150,000 words and the sixth is a much larger 190,000 words. In the changes are refinements and shifts in ideas—whether increasing the weight of a statement, adding details, or even a change in the idea itself."[13] The application was built with Processing, an open source Java-based programming language he developed with collaborator Casey Reas.

http://benfry.com/traces

Recent advances in information storage and computational power have affected and largely facilitated the analysis of natural-language data. Large amounts of historical as well as contemporary documents are available in digital format, opening up new and powerful ways of examining literary data. Furthermore, online social interactions and conversations, mostly textual, are providing new data sources that, coupled with new research questions, are prompting understanding of social phenomena never before possible.

Methods and tools for the visualization of textual data are scarce. Examination of early books on visualization of information, including those by Willard Brinton, Jacques Bertin, and even Edward Tufte, reveal the lacuna. To my knowledge, the first book to dedicate a chapter on document visualization is *Using Vision to Think* by Card

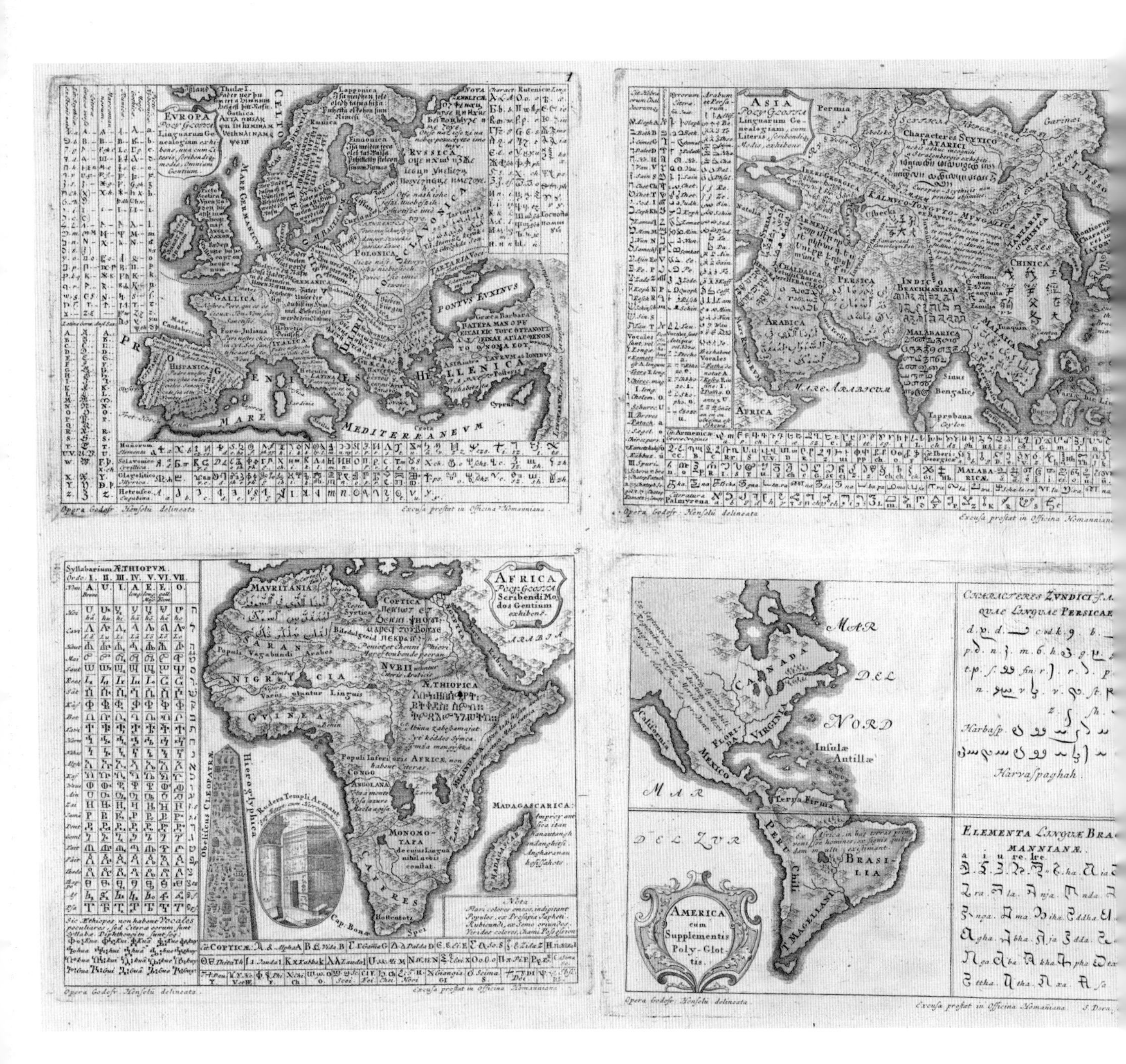

Gottfried Hensel published a series of maps in 1741 in Nürnberg, depicting the use of languages in geographic space. The language usages are demarcated in the map by means of written samples separated by dotted lines. The samples are mostly translations of the first words of the Lord's Prayer into local languages. Robinson speculates that these maps are the first ones to use colors to represent categorical data. He writes, "Hensel's map of Africa uses color to show locations of the descendants of Shem, Ham, and Japheth. His maps may be the first to use color to distinguish areas on a thematic map."[14] The use of colors is explained in the African map on the bottom-right corner as a note in Latin: the colors mark areas settled by descendants of the three sons of Noah: Japhet ("rubicundi," pink), Shem ("oriundos," yellow-orange), and Ham ("virides," olive green).[15]

and colleagues in 1999. The introduction to the chapter "Data Mining: Document Visualization" elucidates the focus: "Emerging technology trends imply that document visualization will be an important visualization application for the future.... These trends [the World Wide Web, digital libraries, communication advances] portend a vast information ecology in which information visualization could have a major role."[1]

Indeed, we see more research directed at parsing large text datasets that includes the emerging field of digital humanities, characterized by interdisciplinary collaborations, and the use of other analytical tools, often in combination with the more traditional interpretative methods of inquiry. In his seminal book *Graphs, Maps, Trees*, Moretti argues for a "distanced reading" of literature that calls for models rather than text. The method proposes processes of reduction and an abstraction of literary corpus instead of the reading of individual works—i.e., a quantitative approach. Moretti contends, "Quantitative research provides a type of data which is ideally independent of interpretations ... and that is of course also its limit: it provides data, not interpretation."[2]

Outside the academic domain, the largest contribution to the visualization field has come from the collaborative team of Fernanda Viégas and Martin Wattenberg, who together have devised and made public several tools available through the IBM website ManyEyes (www-958.ibm.com). For example, *Phrase Net* and *Word Tree* are tools widely used by both the general public and academics (see pages 196–203). When asked about new frontiers in visualization in a 2010 interview, Viégas and Wattenberg argued, "One of the things I think is really promising is visualizing text. That has been mostly ignored so far in terms of information visualization tools, and yet a lot of the richest information we have is in text format."[3]

Nominal Data

Objects, names, and concepts are examples of nominal data. We distinguish nominal datum on the basis of quality: A is different from B. The questions we ask about nominal data are what and where. Nominal data have no implicit quantitative relationship or inherent ordering, and questions such as how much don't apply. Consider the following nominal data: trouser, shirt, banana, fish. We cannot say that trousers are ranked higher than bananas without adding other kinds of information. We can organize the data, but we need to make use of external methods, such as organizing alphabetically, for example.

When we organize nominal data, changes in the data type might happen. For example, if we decide to count how many times each word appears in this book, we would be able to order the words according to their frequency in the text, but what started as nominal data now becomes ordinal data. In other words, ordering or sequencing doesn't apply to nominal data, unless we impose some external order that might change their nature.

Nominal datum can share characteristics that might distinguish it from others, and more important, allow grouping. Bananas and trousers are different kinds of stuff: the first we normally eat, and the latter we normally wear. On the other hand, we can eat bananas and fish as well as group them under a food category, even though one would be a member of a fruit subcategory and the other would not. Because categorization plays a major role in manipulating nominal data, it is often called categorical data.

Nominal data are considered qualitative and are rarely visualized without correlating to other kinds of data. For example, we could rank (ordinal) countries (nominal) according to the amount of exports (quantitative) of bananas (nominal).

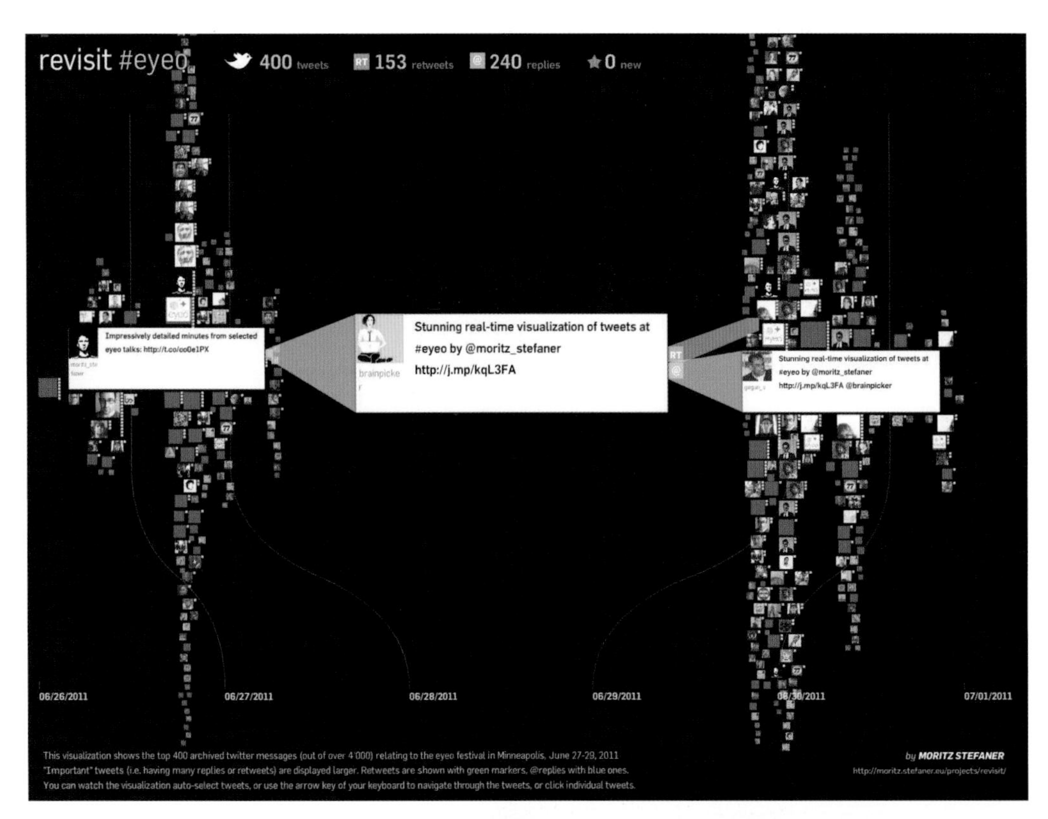

Moritz Stefaner, Germany: "Revisit," 2010.

"Revisit" by Moritz Stefaner (2010) is a real-time visualization of Twitter messages around a specific topic. The system has been used at numerous conferences as a visual backchannel, including SEE Conference, Alphaville, VisWeek, and Eyeo Festival. The interactive application depicts flows of tweets while showing their connections. The network of tweets is organized horizontally by time, with earlier time to the left-hand side. Tweets are connected if they share content, either by the action of retweet (depicted by the blue color) or by @-reply (green). Individual tweets are represented by the squared icon of its author, with its size proportional to its importance, given by frequency of retweets or replies connected to each tweet. As Stefaner explains, "In contrast to other Twitter walls used at public events, it provides a sense of the most important voices and temporal dynamics in the Twitter stream, and reveals the conversational threads established by retweets and @-replies."[16]

http://moritz.stefaner.eu/projects/revisit-twitter-visualization

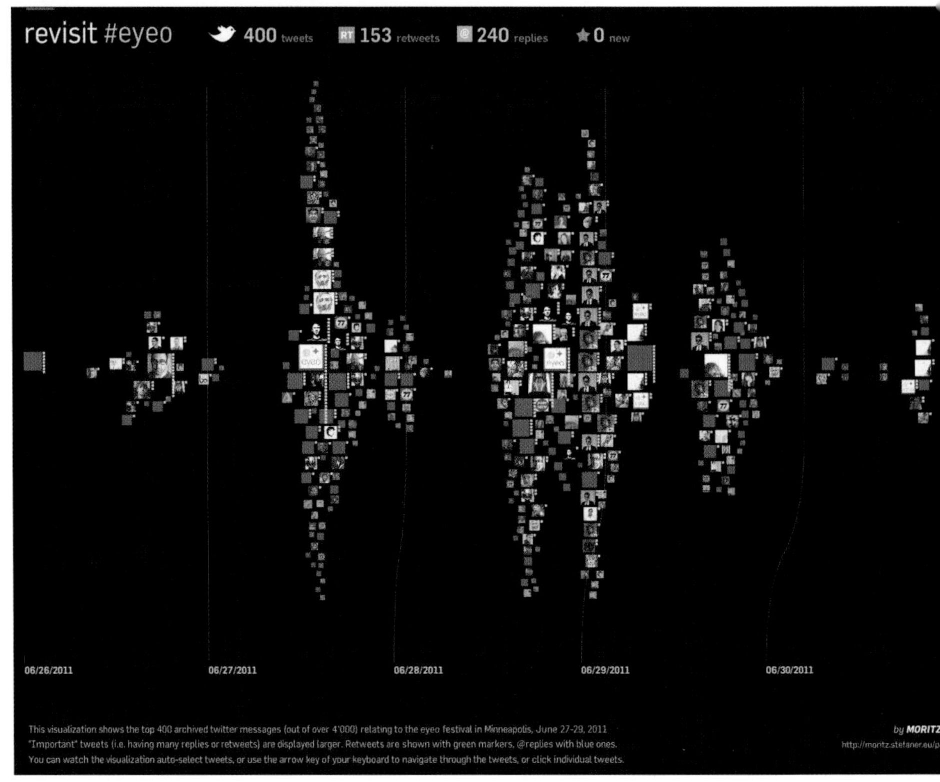

Image from fourteenth-century illuminated manuscript Codex St. Peter perg 92, leaf 11v, depicting Raimundus Lullus and Thomas le Myésier: *Electorium parvum seu breviculum* (after 1321).

TYPES OF VISUALIZATIONS

Most text documents such as books, news articles, tweets, and poems are unstructured data, in that they do not have predefined data models. Searching for words, sentences, and topics in documents might yield the distribution of themes or frequency of words, for example. Data mining and text analytic techniques offer methods to extract patterns and structure that provide meaning to these documents. Ward and colleagues define three levels of text representation that can be used to convert unstructured text into some form of structured data for subsequent generation of visualizations:[4]

- Lexical: Transforms a string of characters into a sequence of atomic entities for further analysis.
- Syntactic: Examines and defines the function of each token. Decisions on which language model and grammars to use will further define the analytical approach.
- Semantic: Extracts the meaning of the structure derived from the syntactic level toward an analytic interpretation of the full text within a specific context.

The goal of most natural-language data analysis is to look for patterns, structures, or relationships within a collection of documents (corpus). Depending on the task of interest (i.e., co-occurrences, relationships, evolution of topics), different types of visualizations are required. Marti Hearst identifies three types of visualizations of textual data:[5]

- Visualizations of connections among entities within and across documents: Applications are in the field of text mining, and as Hearst explains, they aim at "the discovery by computer of new, previously unknown information, by automatically extracting information from different written resources."[6]
- Visualizations of document concordances and word frequencies: Applications are in the field of literature analysis, linguistics, and other fields for which the goal is to understand the properties of language, such as language patterns and structure.
- Visualizations of relationships between words in their usage in language and in lexical ontologies: Applications are mostly in the fields of literary analysis and citation analysis.

VISUAL LANGUAGE AND VERBAL LANGUAGE

Visualization of texts can be divided roughly into two large groups in what concerns the types of structures and visual elements used in the display. One group uses language, per se, as the atomic visual element in displaying linguistic data. The other uses external forms of data structures to visualize textual data, such as when we employ geographical or statistical methods to depict patterns in texts.

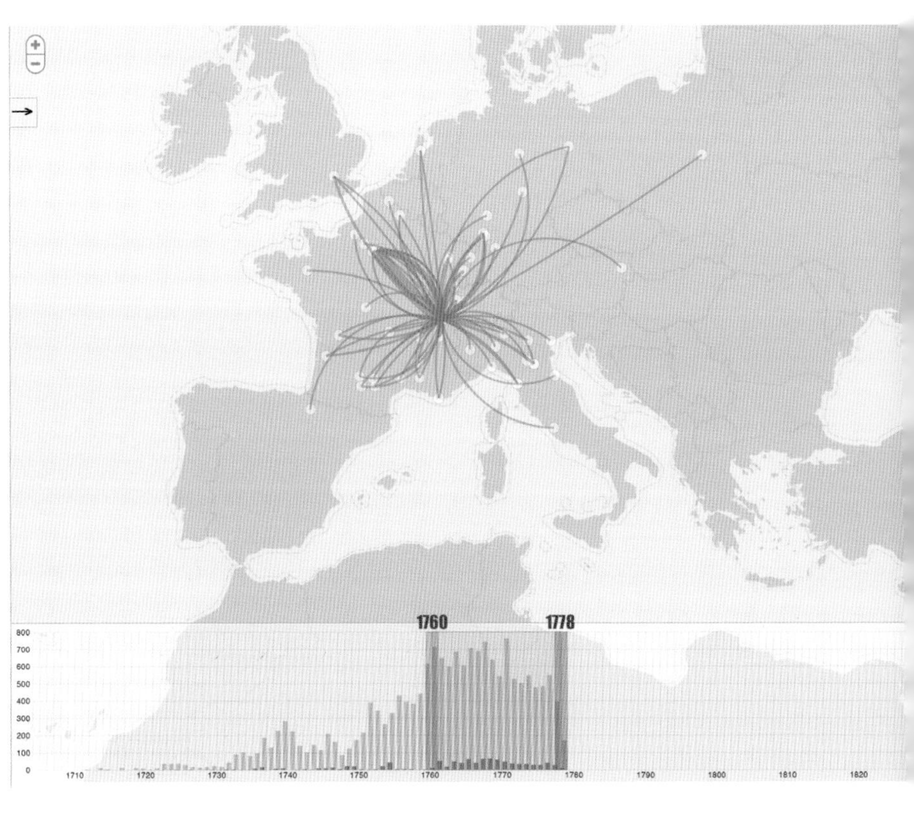

"Mapping the Republic of Letters"team at Stanford University, U.S.: "*Corrispondenza,*" 2010.

Corrispondenza is a geographic correspondence viewer combined with a focusable timeline created at Stanford University for the "Mapping the Republic of Letters" collaborative project in the digital humanities. The goal of the visualization is to depict spatially and temporally the correspondences among early-modern scholars.

The tool uses a timeline depicting two data measures by year: the letters plotted on the map and those not plotted. They explain, "We added to this a feature that shows on the map connections that do not have dates, so, letters that do not appear on the timeline. If there is no date for a letter, there is no place to put it on the timeline. As long as we have a source and a destination, we indicate that line as a gray line that is persistent, i.e. does not change with the change in time period."[17] This feature can be seen in the top image depicting the Franklin letters. The visualization includes both letters that are missing location information, which are represented by gray bars in the timeline, and letters that are missing dates, which appear as gray lines on the map.

The bottom image shows the Voltaire letters. It shows letters without location information. The result is quite dramatic, as it shows that there are many more letters not plotted than those plotted.

https://republicofletters.stanford.edu/tools

Published July 3, 2011

Inaugural Words: 1789 to the Present

A look at the language of presidential inaugural addresses. The most-used words in each address appear in the interactive chart below, sized by number of uses. Words highlighted in yellow were used significantly more in this inaugural address than average. (Related Article)

Full text of the address

2009

Barack Obama

Mr. Obama called on Americans to work together to rebuild a faltering economy. "For everywhere we look, there is work to be done. The state of the economy calls for action, bold and swift, and we will act," he said. He also promised to restore America's place in the world. "Know that America is a friend of each nation and every man, woman, and child who seeks a future of peace and dignity, and that we are ready to lead once more."

nation America people
work generation world common
time seek spirit day American peace crisis hard
greater meet men remain job power moment women
father endure government short hour life hope freedom carried
journey forward force prosperity courage man question future friend
service age history God oath understand ideal pass economy care
promise children Earth stand demand purpose faith hand found interest war call

The *New York Times*, U.S.: "Inaugural Words: 1789 to the Present," 2011.

The visualization "Inaugural Words: 1789 to the Present" was published in 2011 at the *New York Times* online. It looks at the language of presidential inaugural addresses. The most-used words in each address are sized according to the frequency of use, and ordered accordingly. Words that were used significantly more in an address than average appear highlighted in yellow. Selecting a word opens a window with the parts of the transcript where the words were enunciated. In addition, there is an interesting histogram comparing the use of the word with that of other presidents.

www.nytimes.com/interactive/2009/01/17/washington/20090117_ADDRESSES.html

The examination of literary content by means of other data structures, such as maps, is further combined with other literary analytical methods, because they help explain all that texts can offer. Moretti explains, "What do literary maps do … First, they are a good way to prepare a text for analysis. You choose a unit—walks, lawsuits, luxury goods, whatever—find its occurrences, place them in space … or in other words: you reduce the text to a few elements, and abstract them from the narrative flow, and construct a new, artificial object like the maps that I have been discussing. And, with a little luck, these maps will be more than the sum of their parts: they will possess 'emerging' qualities, which were not visible at the lower level."[7] An example is the interdisciplinary and international project in the digital humanities centered at Stanford University, "Mapping the Republic of Letters." Since 2008, the initiative has developed several visual analytical tools that include the use of maps and quantitative approaches to examining the correspondence, travel, and social networks of early-modern scholars in the world. Another example is the quantitative analysis of the frequency and evolution of regular and irregular verbs in English language led by linguist Steve Pinker.[8]

The focus of this chapter is on visualizations that examine linguistic data within a document or corpus by using written language to represent itself—in other words, when a typographic system is the main visual system in conveying information. Though in high demand, due to the growing need to analyze large amounts of

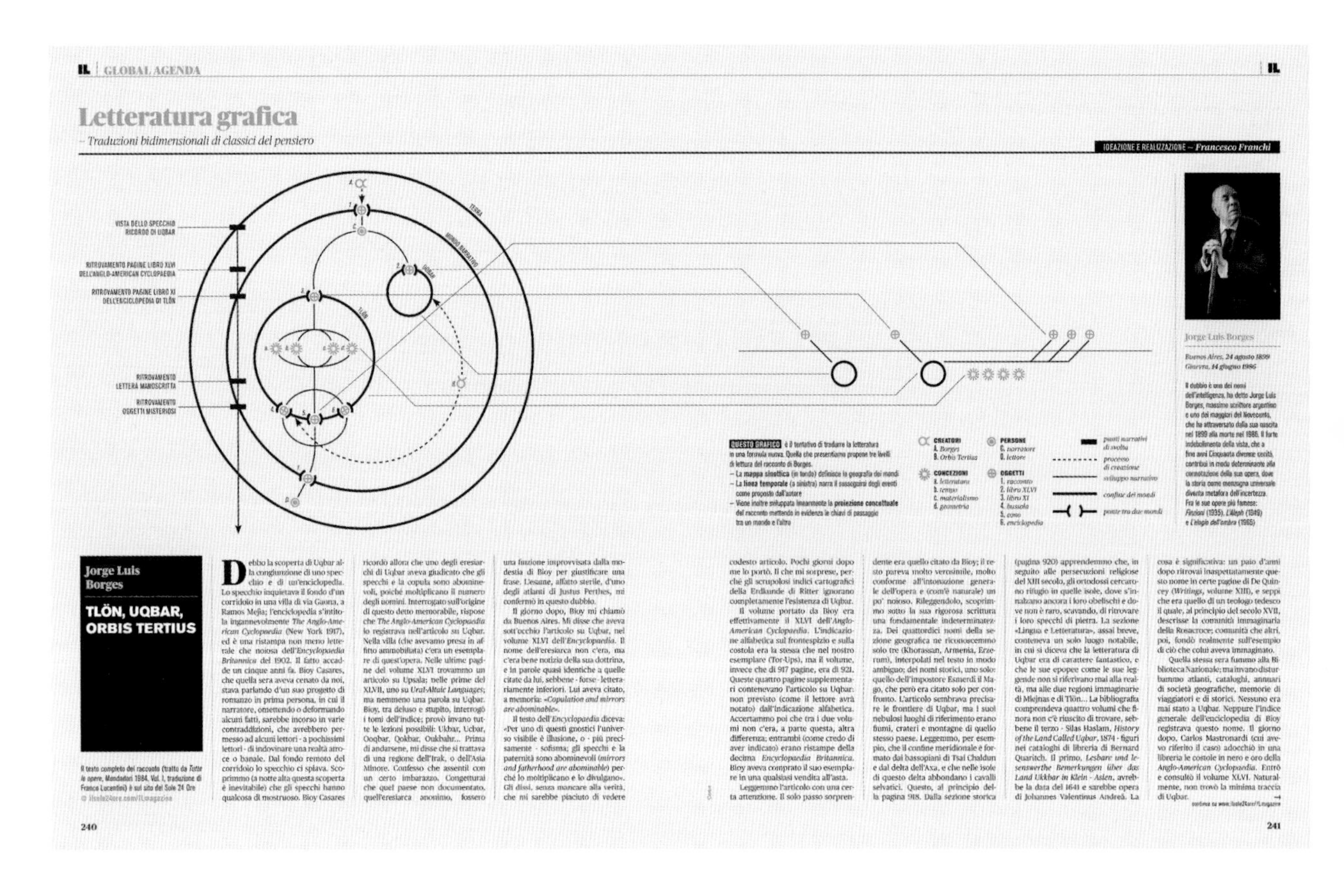
IL | GLOBAL AGENDA

Letteratura grafica

– Traduzioni bidimensionali di classici del pensiero

IDEAZIONE E REALIZZAZIONE – *Francesco Franchi*

Jorge Luis Borges

contribuì in modo determinante alla connotazione della sua opera, dove la storia come menzogna universale diventa metafora dell'incertezza. Fra le sue opere più famose: *Finzioni* (1935), *L'Aleph* (1949) e *L'elogio dell'ombra* (1965)

Jorge Luis Borges

TLÖN, UQBAR, ORBIS TERTIUS

Il testo completo del racconto (tratto da *Tutte le opere*, Mondadori 1984, Vol. I, traduzione di Franco Lucentini) è sul sito del Sole 24 Ore

Debbo la scoperta di Uqbar alla congiunzione di uno specchio e di un'enciclopedia. Lo specchio inquietava il fondo d'un corridoio in una villa di via Gaona, a Ramos Mejía; l'enciclopedia s'intitola ingannevolmente *The Anglo-American Cyclopaedia* (New York 1917), ed è una ristampa non meno letterale che noiosa dell'*Encyclopaedia Britannica* del 1902. Il fatto accadde un cinque anni fa. Bioy Casares, che quella sera aveva cenato da noi, stava parlando d'un suo progetto di romanzo in prima persona, in cui il narratore, omettendo o deformando alcuni fatti, sarebbe incorso in varie contraddizioni, che avrebbero permesso ad alcuni lettori - a pochissimi lettori - di indovinare una realtà atroce o banale. Dal fondo remoto del corridoio lo specchio ci spiava. Scoprimmo (a notte alta questa scoperta è inevitabile) che gli specchi hanno qualcosa di mostruoso. Bioy Casares ricordò allora che uno degli eresiarchi di Uqbar aveva giudicato che gli specchi e la copula sono abominevoli, poiché moltiplicano il numero degli uomini. Interrogato sull'origine di questo detto memorabile, rispose che *The Anglo-American Cyclopaedia* lo registrava nell'articolo su Uqbar. Nella villa (che avevamo presa in affitto ammobiliata) c'era un esemplare di quest'opera. Nelle ultime pagine del volume XLVI trovammo un articolo su Upsala; nelle prime del XLVII, uno su *Ural-Altaic Languages*; ma nemmeno una parola su Uqbar. Bioy, tra deluso e stupito, interrogò i tomi dell'indice; provò invano tutte le lezioni possibili: Ukbar, Ucbar, Ooqbar, Qokbar, Oukbahr... Prima di andarsene, mi disse che si trattava di una regione dell'Irak, o dell'Asia Minore. Confesso che assentii con un certo imbarazzo. Congetturai che quel paese non documentato, quell'eresiarca anonimo, fossero una funzione improvvisata dalla modestia di Bioy per giustificare una frase. L'esame, affatto sterile, d'uno degli atlanti di Justus Perthes, mi confermò in questo dubbio.

Il giorno dopo, Bioy mi chiamò da Buenos Aires. Mi disse che aveva sott'occhio l'articolo su Uqbar, nel volume XLVI dell'*Encyclopaedia*. Il nome dell'eresiarca non c'era, ma c'era bene notizia della sua dottrina, e in parole quasi identiche a quelle citate da lui, sebbene - forse - letterariamente inferiori. Lui aveva citato, a memoria: *«Copulation and mirrors are abominable»*.

Il testo dell'*Encyclopaedia* diceva: «Per uno di questi gnostici l'universo visibile è illusione, o - più precisamente - sofisma; gli specchi e la paternità sono abominevoli (*mirrors and fatherhood are abominable*) perché lo moltiplicano e lo divulgano». Gli dissi, senza mancare alla verità, che mi sarebbe piaciuto di vedere codesto articolo. Pochi giorni dopo me lo portò. Il che mi sorprese, perché gli scrupolosi indici cartografici della Erdkunde di Ritter ignorano completamente l'esistenza di Uqbar.

Il volume portato da Bioy era effettivamente il XLVI dell'*Anglo-American Cyclopaedia*. L'indicazione alfabetica sul frontespizio e sulla costola era la stessa che nel nostro esemplare (Tor-Ups), ma il volume, invece che di 917 pagine, era di 921. Queste quattro pagine supplementari contenevano l'articolo su Uqbar: non previsto (come il lettore avrà notato) dall'indicazione alfabetica. Accertammo poi che tra i due volumi non c'era, a parte questa, altra differenza; entrambi (come credo di aver indicato) erano ristampe della decima *Encyclopaedia Britannica*. Bioy aveva comprato il suo esemplare in una qualsiasi vendita all'asta.

Leggemmo l'articolo con una certa attenzione. Il solo passo sorprendente era quello citato da Bioy; il resto pareva molto verosimile, molto conforme all'intonazione generale dell'opera e (com'è naturale) un po' noioso. Rileggendolo, scoprimmo sotto la sua rigorosa scrittura una fondamentale indeterminatezza. Dei quattordici nomi della sezione geografica ne riconoscemmo solo tre (Khorassan, Armenia, Erzerum), interpolati nel testo in modo ambiguo; dei nomi storici, uno solo: quello dell'impostore Esmerdi il Mago, che però era citato solo per confronto. L'articolo sembrava precisare le frontiere di Uqbar, ma i suoi nebulosi luoghi di riferimento erano fiumi, crateri e montagne di quello stesso paese. Leggemmo, per esempio, che il confine meridionale è formato dai bassopiani di Tsai Chaldun e dal delta dell'Axa, e che nelle isole di questo delta abbondano i cavalli selvatici. Questo, al principio della pagina 918. Dalla sezione storica (pagina 920) apprendemmo che, in seguito alle persecuzioni religiose del XIII secolo, gli ortodossi cercarono rifugio in quelle isole, dove s'innalzano ancora i loro obelischi e dove non è raro, scavando, di ritrovare i loro specchi di pietra. La sezione «Lingua e Letteratura», assai breve, conteneva un solo luogo notabile, in cui si diceva che la letteratura di Uqbar era di carattere fantastico, e che le sue epopee come le sue leggende non si riferivano mai alla realtà, ma alle due regioni immaginarie di Mlejnas e di Tlön... La bibliografia comprendeva quattro volumi che finora non c'è riuscito di trovare, sebbene il terzo - Silas Haslam, *History of the Land Called Uqbar*, 1874 - figuri nei cataloghi di libreria di Bernard Quaritch. Il primo, *Lesbare und lesenswerthe Bemerkungen über das Land Ukkbar in Klein - Asien*, avrebbe la data del 1641 e sarebbe opera di Johannes Valentinus Andreä. La cosa è significativa: un paio d'anni dopo ritrovai inaspettatamente questo nome in certe pagine di De Quincey (*Writings*, volume XIII), e seppi che era quello di un teologo tedesco il quale, al principio del secolo XVII, descrisse la comunità immaginaria della Rosacroce; comunità che altri, poi, fondò realmente sull'esempio di ciò che colui aveva immaginato.

Quella stessa sera fummo alla Biblioteca Nazionale; ma invano disturbammo atlanti, cataloghi, annuari di società geografiche, memorie di viaggiatori e di storici. Nessuno era mai stato a Uqbar. Neppure l'indice generale dell'enciclopedia di Bioy registrava questo nome. Il giorno dopo, Carlos Mastronardi (cui avevo riferito il caso) adocchiò in una libreria le costole in nero e oro della *Anglo-American Cyclopaedia*. Entrò e consultò il volume XLVI. Naturalmente, non trovò la minima traccia di Uqbar. →

240 241

unstructed data available digitally, analytical methods that use a language–typography correspondence are small in number. Hearst contends, "Nominal or categorical variables are difficult to display graphically because they have no inherent ordering. The categorical nature of text, and its very high dimensionality, make it very challenging to display graphically."[9]

Francesco Franchi, Italy: "Jorge Luis Borges," 2008.

The infographic was published in 2008 in "Letteratura Grafica," a column of the Italian monthly newsmagazine *IL–Intelligence in Lifestyle*. It depicts three levels of the Argentinean writer Jorge Luis Borges's oeuvre: geographical (circular part), temporal (left-most text), and conceptual (linearly). Francesco Franchi, the art director, explains, "The column is an attempt to translate some pieces of literature classics in a nonlinear way through two dimensions, graphics and maps. The goal is to produce synoptic maps that allow the relationships between the elements of literary narrative to be seen, and specifically, to show complex relationships in a more easily understood way using linear forms."[18]

HOW WE PROCESS TEXTUAL INFORMATION

Ware explains that, under the dual coding theory, there are two fundamentally different types of information stored in distinct working memory and long-term memory systems: *imagens*, characterized by mental representations of visual information, and *logogens*, denoted by mental representations of language information, except for the sound of words.[10] He further elucidates, "Visual text is processed visually at first, but the information is rapidly transformed into nonvisual association structures of *logogens*. Acoustic verbal stimuli are processed primarily through the auditory system and then fed into the logogen system. Logogens and imagens, although based on separate subsystems, can be strongly interlinked; for example, the word cat and language-based concepts related to cats will be linked to visual information related to the appearance of cats and their environment."[11]

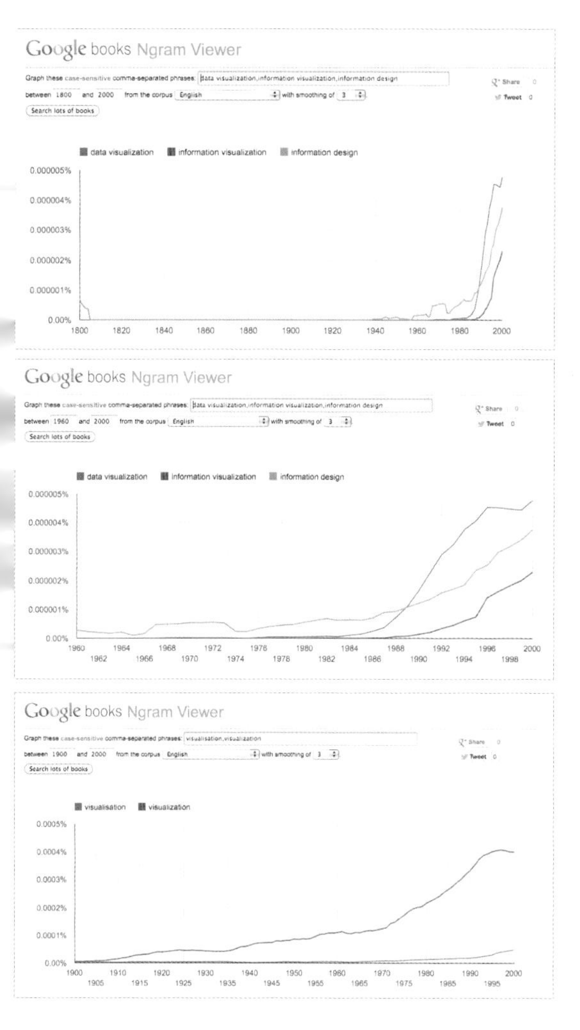

Google Books initiative, U.S.: "Ngram Viewer," 2010.

Devised in 2010 by Google Books initiative, the Ngram Viewer allows anyone to search a word (1-gram) or several words or phrases (n-grams) in a corpus of books and examine usage over time. The top two line graphs show my searches for the usage of the terms "data visualization," "information visualization," and "information design" in the English books corpus. The topmost graph shows usage for the terms between 1800 and 2000, and below it I narrowed the search to start in 1960, because this date shows the beginning of a trend, with a growing usage for the three terms starting in the '90s. In the bottom graph, I compare trends in usage for the two possible spellings of "visualization" and "visualisation" in the same corpus of English books.

In the article "Natural Language Corpus Data," Peter Norvig argues that counting the number of appearances of words is relevant: "Why would I say this data is beautiful, and not merely mundane? Each individual count is mundane. But the aggregation of the counts—billions of counts—is beautiful, because it says so much, not just about the English language, but about the world that speakers inhabit. The data is beautiful because it represents much of what is worth saying."[19]

http://books.google.com/ngrams

Different from images and diagrams, which are understood in parallel, natural languages—whether spoken, written, or signed—are taken serially. There is an inherent temporal nature to language that transforms language into a sequence of mentally recreated dynamic utterances.[12]

PROBLEMS OF USING TYPOGRAPHY AS VISUAL ELEMENTS

There are several problems with using typography as the main visual element in visualizations, especially when using most Western writing systems. Long words occupy more space than small ones do, thus resulting in a misconceived impression of weight, given that we tend to associate size with importance. The issue is even more prominent when other visual variables, such as color and weight, are added to the typographic system, because they influence the perception of hierarchy in the graphic. A similar problem was discussed in relation to choropleth maps and how the sizes of geographic space coupled with the color encoding system mislead the interpretation of information by providing an erroneous impression of importance (see page 142).

On the other hand, when we substitute words by graphical elements other than typography we hide the information that we intend to reveal. The absence of written language in a display depicting linguistic data restricts the possibilities of interpretation of the intended information, especially when reading content is of importance. As explained in the box Nominal Data (see page 187), we understand nominal data through differentiation—in other words, by distinguishing whether two concepts are the same or different. This is one of the reasons behind labels in most graphic displays. For example, in a map with dots representing cities, we are able to differentiate cities by reading their names.

In previous chapters, we examined data structures using typographic elements to depict information in visualizations, and those are affected by the same constraints described here. What follows are three case studies that use typographic systems to depict textual data in informational displays: *Wordle*, *Phrase Net*, and *Word Tree*.

CASE STUDY

Wordle

www.wordle.net

The image and video-sharing online community Flickr devised in 2002 *Tag Cloud*, a tool that serves as both navigation and a graphic depiction of the most popular tags by their users. The method has since gained wide use, not only among tag-based websites, who use it mostly as a tag aggregation tool while affording access to content, but mostly as a means to analyze and graphically present the frequency of words in a corpus. The latter is commonly called a "word cloud."

Both representations encode the variable of word frequency to the visual property of type size. In addition, word clouds tend to include other visual parameters, mostly for aesthetic purposes, such as direction and color. For example, the website *Wordle* invites the user to define visual parameters of the graphic by offering several color schemes, fonts, and two options for word placement: alphabetical (as in all tag clouds) or center line.

Wordle is an online tool for making "word clouds" created by Jonathan Feinberg in 2008. The online Java applet allows anyone to paste a text, choose some visual parameters, and output a word cloud for later use or sharing purposes. Similar to other textual analysis tools, Wordle removes "stop words," or high-frequency words, such as the, it, to, because otherwise the graphic would mostly contain only those. Feinberg warns that word clouds are constrained as a visualization method and points to four major caveats: word sizing is deceptive given that two words with the same frequency will be perceived differently depending on their length (number of letters); color is meaningless, in that it doesn't encode any variable and is used for aesthetic appeal; fonts are fanciful, and favors expressiveness; word count is not specific enough, because "merely counting words does not permit meaningful comparisons of like texts."[20] Yet, it is extremely popular and has been widely used.

Despite the low efficacy, word clouds have become quite popular, especially in education settings. In an investigation about usability of word clouds, Viégas and colleagues contend that learning and memory are two cognitive processes supported by word clouds, despite the fact that most people surveyed did not understand the encoding system (type size) in the graphic. They argue, "The feeling of creativity is central to the experience of using *Wordle*. Even the examples where Wordle aids learning and memory include elements of creation. For people making mementos, creativity is key to the experience; many people relate *Wordle* to scrapbooking. In the classroom, *Wordle* is not just a broadcast medium, but something that students can use themselves. One typically does not think of visualization as a creative outlet, any more than one would think of a microscope as an authoring tool. Rather than a scientific instrument, however, the type of visualization represented by *Wordle* may be more like a camera: a tool that can be used to document and create."[21]

design
visual
information

design
visual
data
information
visualizations

I used the introduction of this book to generate in *Wordle* the word clouds reproduced here. All outputs used options offered in the site: Coolvetica font, Horizontal layout, alphabetical order, and the "kindled" color palette. They differ in relation to the maximum number of words in each layout, that are from top to bottom: three, five, ten, twenty-five, and finally fifty words. The larger the number of words, the harder it is to discern relevant information. Also note the changes in font size and font color among the versions due to the random way the application renders the *word clouds*.

CASE STUDY

Phrase Net

www-958.ibm.com/software/data/cognos/manyeyes/page/Phrase_Net.html

Designers are familiar with the potentials and constraints of using typography, and to what extent rendering type on a surface, be it a book or a screen, affects or affords legibility. As explained previously, there are several issues with using typography in information displays. On the other hand, natural language imposes constraints that need to be respected when the purpose of the visualization is the interpretation of meaning. For example, the ordering of words is relevant, because it indicates certain groupings that affect the semantics of the text. Viégas and Wattenberg further explain, "The conflict between positioning and legibility can lead to displays that are hard to read or where spatial position is essentially random."[22]

Phrase Net is an online visualization that diagrams the relationships between words in a text. The technique was devised by Fernanda Viégas and Martin Wattenberg in 2009 for IBM's site, Many Eyes. The unit of analysis is the phrase, and relationships among words in a phrase are depicted as networks while respecting syntactic ordering. The application examines how pairs of words are combined according to the parameters defined by users. For example, among the connectors in the list we find *and*, *at*, *'s*, and so on. One can also define a connector that might be appropriate to the text at hand. After the extraction of the pairs, the program then renders the result as a network, where the nodes are the words represented by means of typography, and the links are lines depicting the connections based on the selected pattern "A <connector> B." The links are weighted according to in and out connections, with the line weight representing the amount and the arrows pointing to the direction of word ordering. The type size of words represents the total number of occurrences of the term. Type is rendered in a sequential blue color palette, with the shades standing for the ratio of out-degree to in-degree, where dark blue signifies high ratio—in other words, more out-links than in-links.

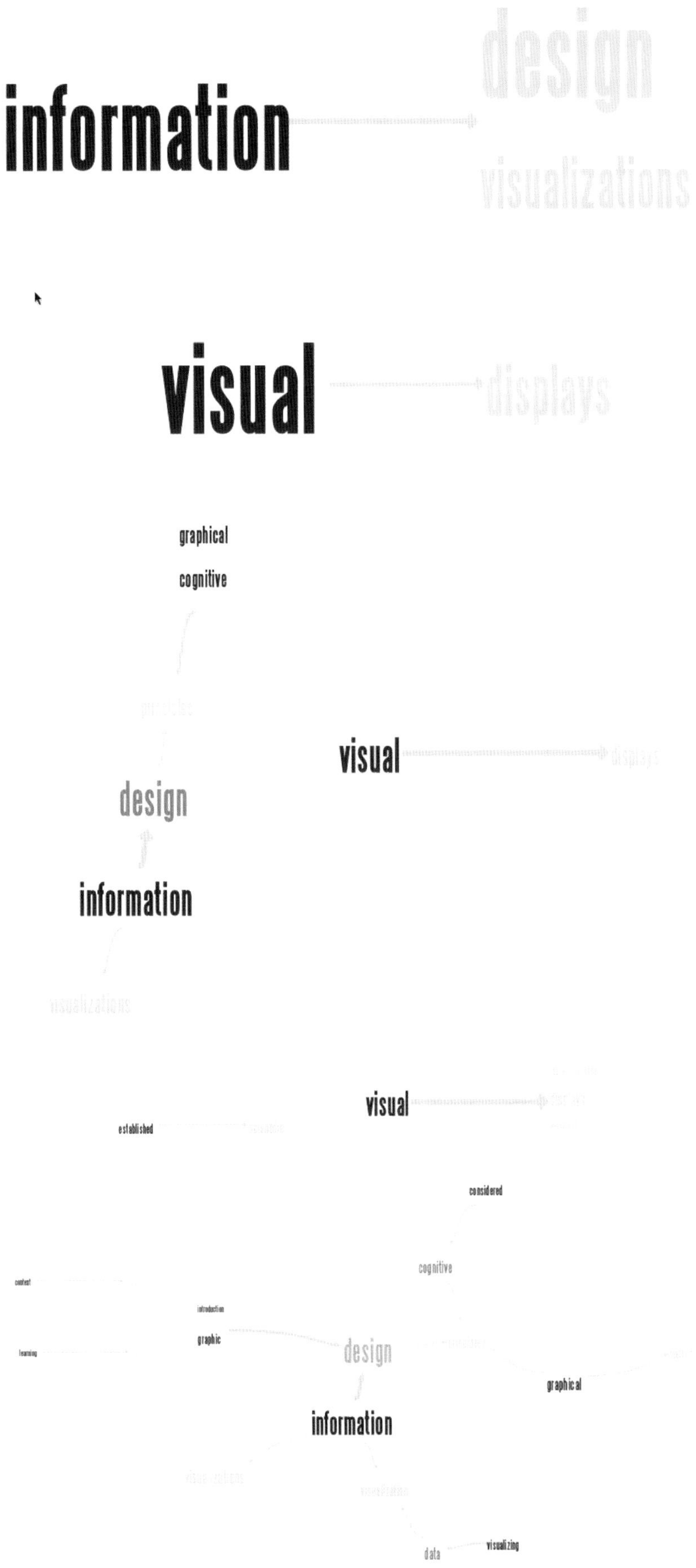

information
design
visualizations

visual
displays

graphical
cognitive
design
visual
displays
information
visualizations

visual
established
considered
cognitive
context
introduction
graphic
learning
design
graphical
information
data
visualizing

I used the introduction of this book to generate the diagrams reproduced here. They examine pairs of words connected by a space between them. From top to bottom the diagrams show the top five, ten, and twenty-five words. In contrast to word clouds, Phrase Net renders relationships between words, including the direction of the connection, that is the word order.

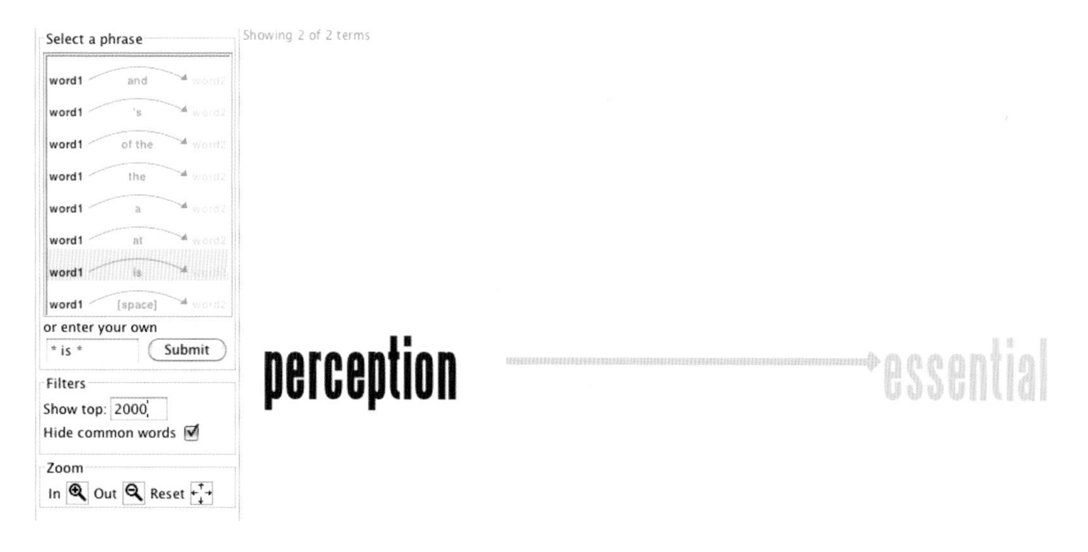

This Phrase Net diagram visualizes 2000 words connected by the verb *is* in the introduction of this book. The result is quite interesting, and something worth remembering: data perception is essential to visualization.

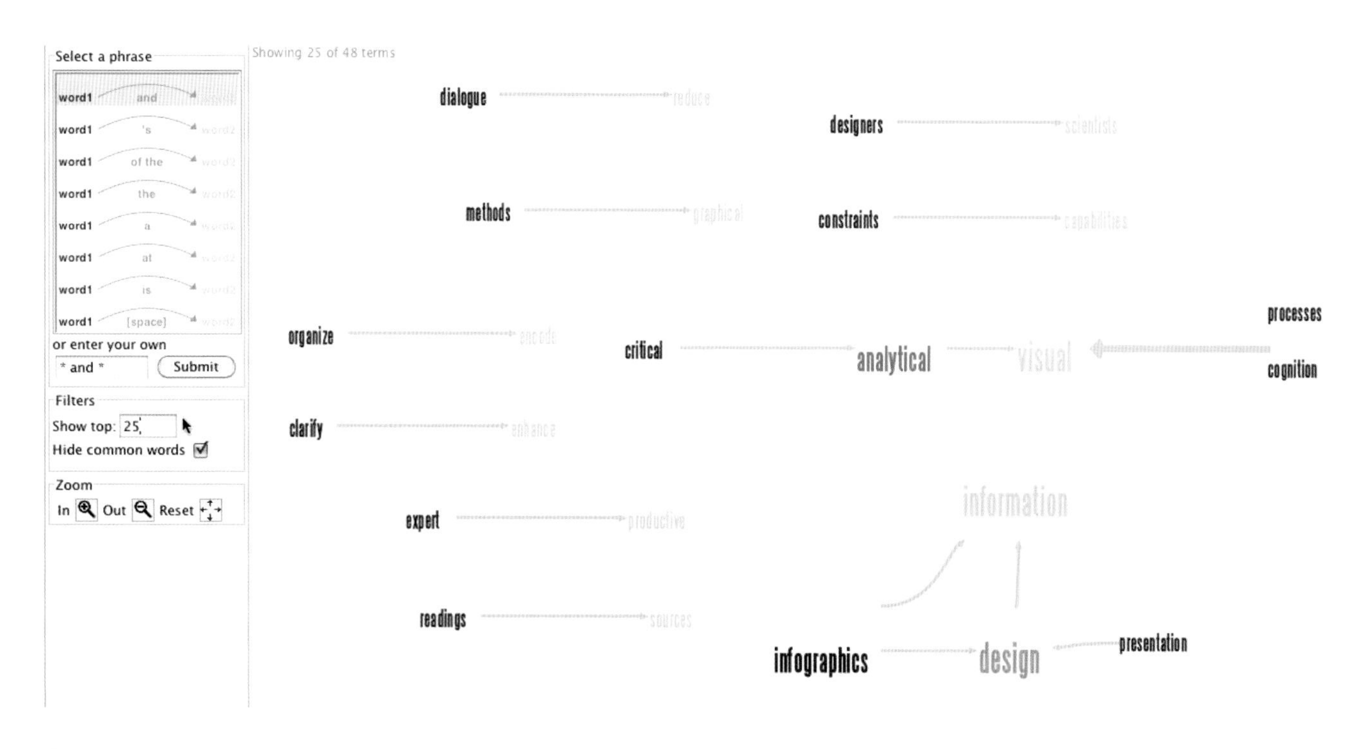

This Phrase Net diagram visualizes twenty-five words connected by the conjunction *and* in the introduction of this book.

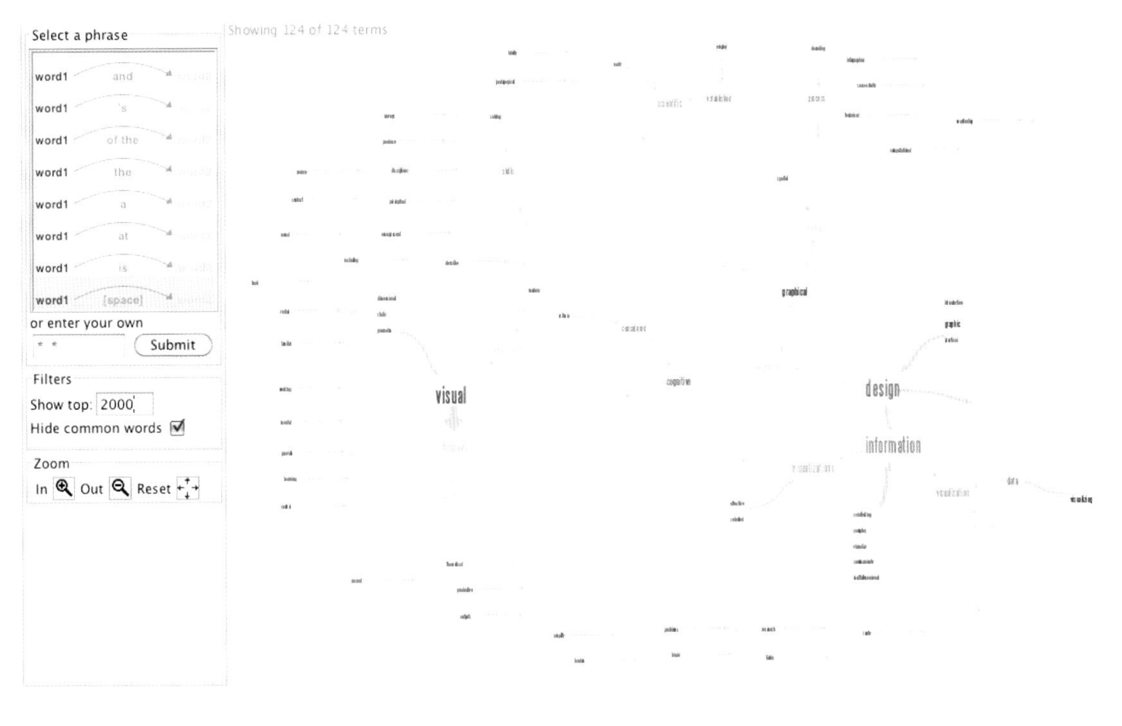

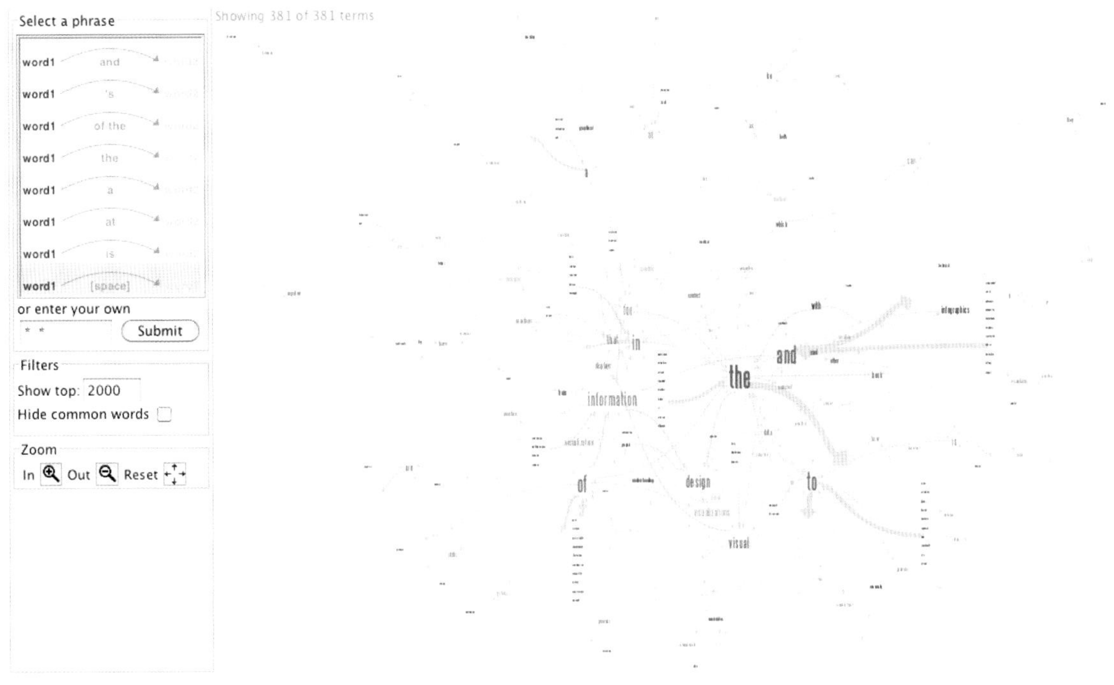

These Phrase Net diagrams visualize the same number of words (2000) connected by a space in the introduction of this book. The one at the bottom was rendered with common words in the representation. As previously discussed in chapter 2, when there are too many connections, occlusions occur and the graph becomes too complicated to be easily understood.

CASE STUDY

Word Tree

www-958.ibm.com/software/data/cognos/manyeyes/page/Word_Tree.html

Word Tree is a visual search tool for unstructured text. The technique was created by Fernanda Viégas and Martin Wattenberg in 2007 for IBM's site, Many Eyes. The visualization starts when we select a word or a phrase as the search term. Then the program looks for all occurrences of the term within the given text. It finally builds a tree structure of the content, with branches rendered until it finds a unique phrase used exactly once. There are three options for arranging the branches: alphabetically, by frequency (largest branches first), and by order of first occurrence, which reflects the original text.

The authors explain that the tool Word Tree is a visual version of a traditional concordance, also known in computer science as the visual version of a suffix tree. Besides preserving the context in which the term occurs, the method also preserves the linear arrangement of the text.

Similar to word clouds, font size represents term occurrence, with the font size proportional to the square root of the frequency of the term. Different from most text visualization methods, Word Tree does not discard stop words or punctuation, because those are considered critical for purposes of context.

I used the introduction of this book to generate these Word Tree diagrams. They show the content structure starting (at the top) and ending (at the bottom) with the adjective *visual*.

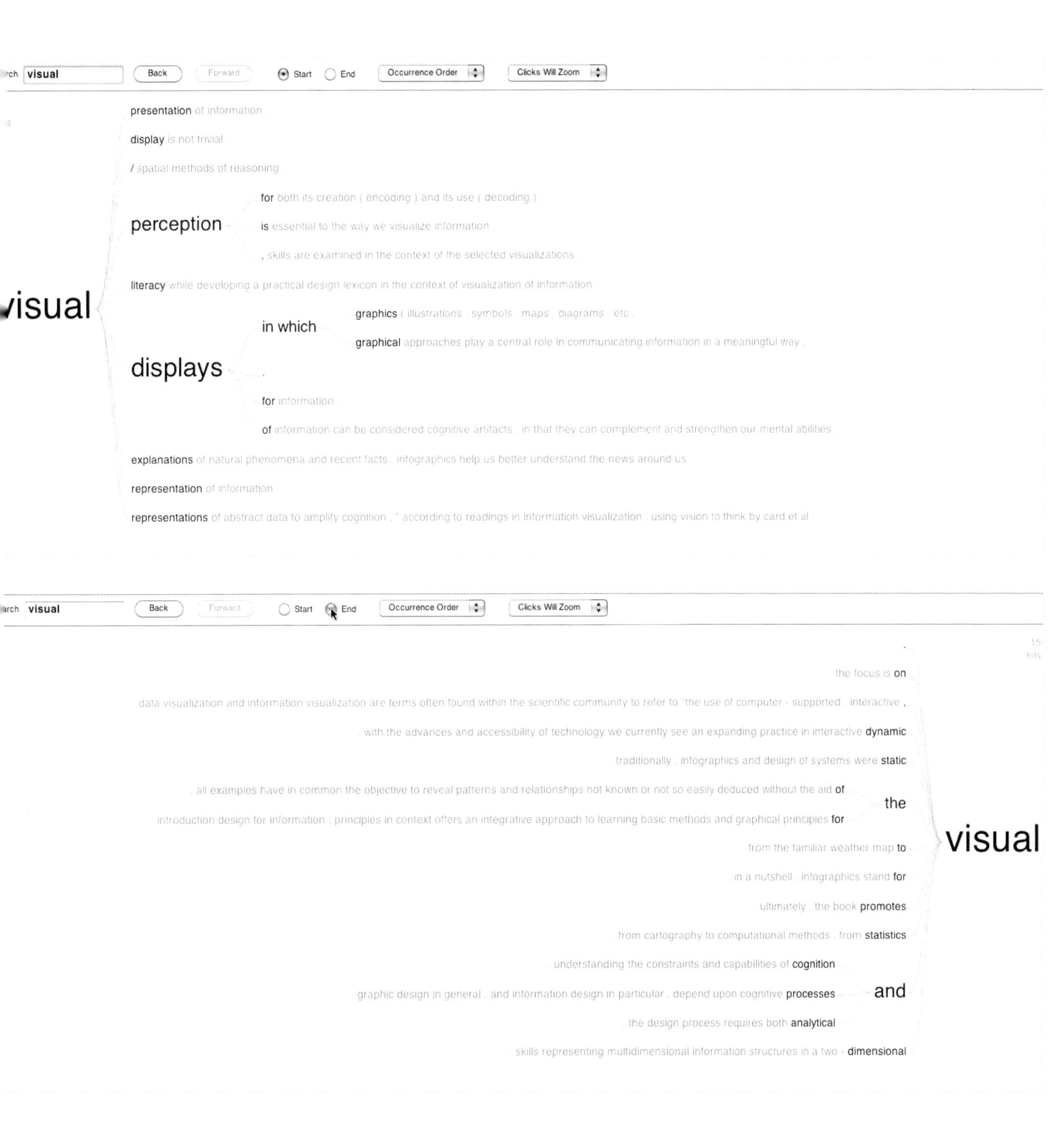

visual
Back
Forward
Start
End
Occurrence Order
Clicks Will Zoom
presentation of information
display is not trivial
/ spatial methods of reasoning
perception
for both its creation (encoding) and its use (decoding)
is essential to the way we visualize information
, skills are examined in the context of the selected visualizations
literacy while developing a practical design lexicon in the context of visualization of information
visual
in which
graphics (illustrations , symbols , maps , diagrams , etc
graphical approaches play a central role in communicating information in a meaningful way
displays
for information
of information can be considered cognitive artifacts , in that they can complement and strengthen our mental abilities
explanations of natural phenomena and recent facts , infographics help us better understand the news around us
representation of information
representations of abstract data to amplify cognition , " according to readings in information visualization : using vision to think by card et al
visual
Back
Forward
Start
End
Occurrence Order
Clicks Will Zoom
15 hits
the focus is on
data visualization and information visualization are terms often found within the scientific community to refer to "the use of computer - supported , interactive ,
with the advances and accessibility of technology we currently see an expanding practice in interactive dynamic
traditionally , infographics and design of systems were static
all examples have in common the objective to reveal patterns and relationships not known or not so easily deduced without the aid of
the
introduction design for information : principles in context offers an integrative approach to learning basic methods and graphical principles for
visual
from the familiar weather map to
in a nutshell , infographics stand for
ultimately , the book promotes
from cartography to computational methods , from statistics
understanding the constraints and capabilities of cognition
graphic design in general , and information design in particular , depend upon cognitive processes
and
the design process requires both analytical
skills representing multidimensional information structures in a two - dimensional

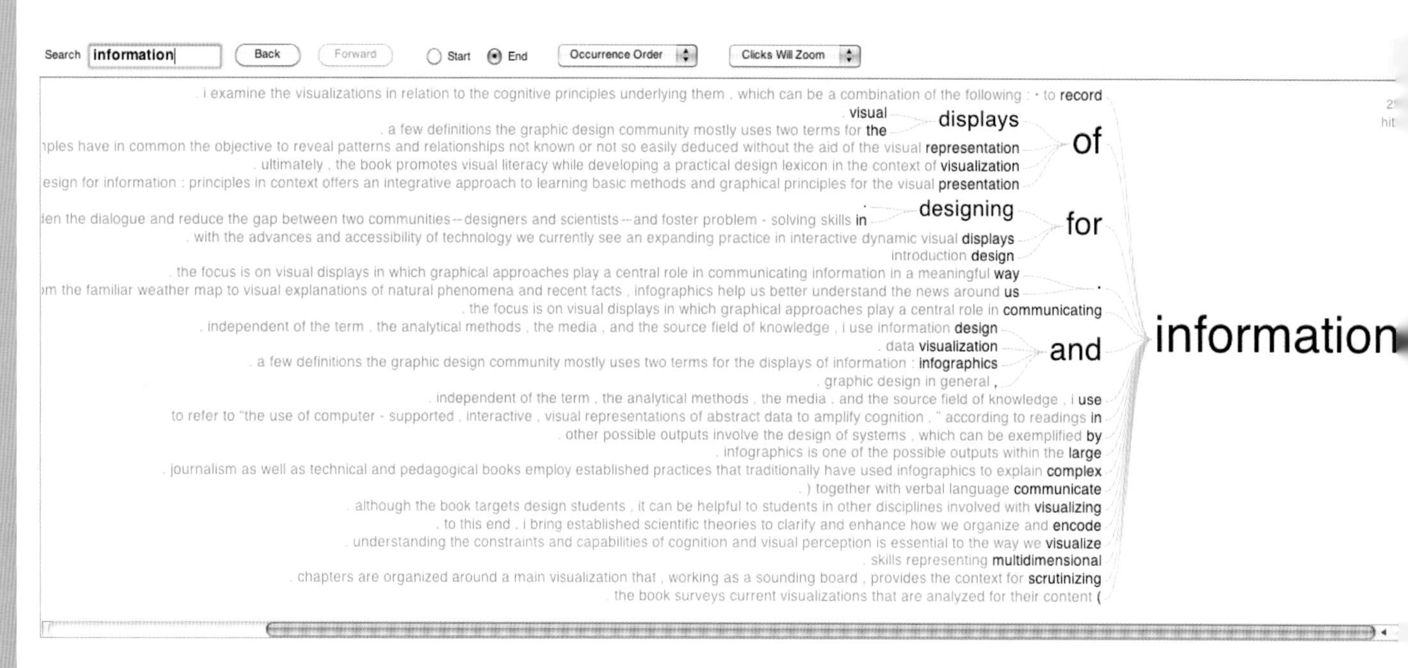

The Word Tree diagrams show content from the introduction of this book. I first searched for the term *information*, and then visualized it at the end (left) and at the beginning of sentences (right). Next, I combined the word *design* to the initial search, and the result is the diagram at the bottom right. The diagram below reveals content structure for occurrences starting with the term *book*.

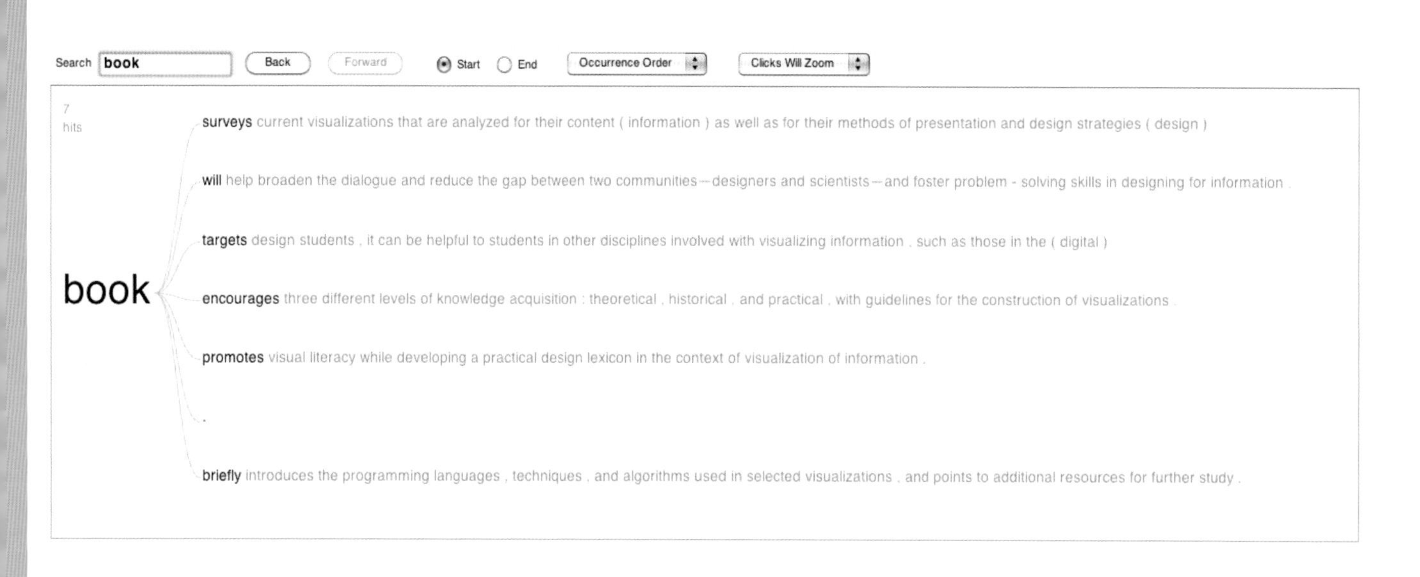

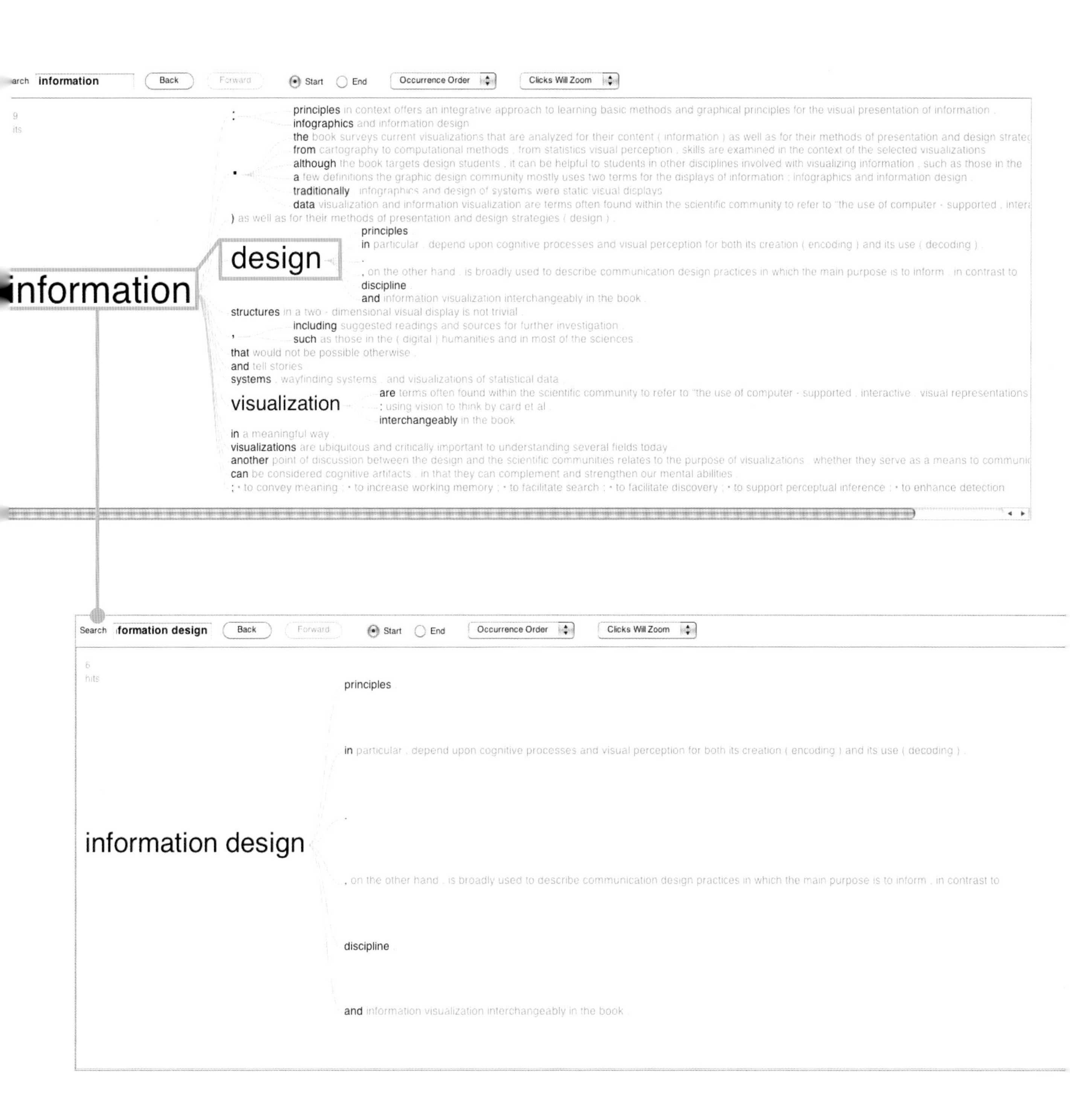

information
Back
Forward
Start
End
Occurrence Order
Clicks Will Zoom
principles in context offers an integrative approach to learning basic methods and graphical principles for the visual presentation of information .
infographics and information design
the book surveys current visualizations that are analyzed for their content (information) as well as for their methods of presentation and design strateg
from cartography to computational methods . from statistics visual perception . skills are examined in the context of the selected visualizations
although the book targets design students . it can be helpful to students in other disciplines involved with visualizing information . such as those in the
a few definitions the graphic design community mostly uses two terms for the displays of information : infographics and information design .
traditionally . infographics and design of systems were static visual displays
data visualization and information visualization are terms often found within the scientific community to refer to "the use of computer - supported , inter
) as well as for their methods of presentation and design strategies (design) .
design
principles
in particular . depend upon cognitive processes and visual perception for both its creation (encoding) and its use (decoding) .
, on the other hand . is broadly used to describe communication design practices in which the main purpose is to inform . in contrast to
discipline
and information visualization interchangeably in the book .
structures in a two - dimensional visual display is not trivial .
including suggested readings and sources for further investigation
such as those in the (digital) humanities and in most of the sciences .
that would not be possible otherwise .
and tell stories
systems . wayfinding systems . and visualizations of statistical data .
visualization
are terms often found within the scientific community to refer to "the use of computer - supported . interactive . visual representations
: using vision to think by card et al .
interchangeably in the book
in a meaningful way
visualizations are ubiquitous and critically important to understanding several fields today
another point of discussion between the design and the scientific communities relates to the purpose of visualizations . whether they serve as a means to communi
can be considered cognitive artifacts . in that they can complement and strengthen our mental abilities
; • to convey meaning ; • to increase working memory ; • to facilitate search ; • to facilitate discovery ; • to support perceptual inference ; • to enhance detection
Search
formation design
Back
Forward
Start
End
Occurrence Order
Clicks Will Zoom
6
hits
information design
principles
in particular . depend upon cognitive processes and visual perception for both its creation (encoding) and its use (decoding) .
, on the other hand . is broadly used to describe communication design practices in which the main purpose is to inform . in contrast to
discipline
and information visualization interchangeably in the book .

APPENDIX

DATA TYPES

It is beyond the scope of this book to go into details about data classification, which is a huge topic. However, we need to have a minimal understanding of the types and attributes of data in order to effectively encode them. Considering that the whole book uses information on data, this appendix offers a description of the terminology used in this book.

The word *data* originates from the plural of the Latin word *datum*, which means "something given," where *something* stands for a piece of information. The piece of information can be anything from a numerical fact to a person or a quantity. The word *data* in this book is used in its plural definition and refers to a collection of observed or measured phenomena of the following types: nominal (some call it categorical), ordinal, and quantitative. What follows is a brief summary of each data type with the operations they afford. There are in-depth studies and classifications of data that are strongly recommended because they can help the designer better understand how to visually encode data; a list is found in the notes.[1]

NOMINAL DATA

Objects, names, and concepts are examples of nominal data. We distinguish nominal datum on the basis of quality: A is different from B. The questions we ask about nominal data are what and where. Nominal data have no implicit quantitative relationship or inherent ordering, and questions such as how much don't apply. Nominal datum can share characteristics that might distinguish it from others, and more important, allow grouping. Because categorization plays a major role in manipulating nominal data, it is often called categorical data. Nominal data are rarely visualized without correlating to other kinds of data and other forms of organization. For example, we could rank (ordinal) countries (nominal) according to the amount of exports (quantitative) of apples (nominal).

Note that the box Nominal Data on page 187 contains the same information described here, but in more detail.

ORDINAL DATA

Ordinal data can be arranged in a given order or rank, such that we can say which comes first or second, which is smaller or larger, and so on. Ordinal data provides the order, but not the degree of differences between the elements. In other words, intervals are not measurable; only the attributes are ordered from lowest to highest. For example, we might know which country ranks first in relation to the amount of apple exports, but not by how much more in relation to the second place.

QUANTITATIVE DATA

Quantitative data can be measured, and as such, data can be numerically manipulated, such as with statistical methods. Numerical data have magnitudes and require that we ask questions of how much. We can count the number of apples produced daily, the average size of the apples, the maximum weight of a box of apples, and so on.

Quantitative data can be transformed into ordinal data by classing it. For example, if we know the population of cities in a region, then we can divide them into ranges and order them by small, medium, and large cities. The box Making Meaningful Groups discusses strategies for classing data (see page 141).

NOTES

INTRODUCTION

1 Card et al. (1999), 7.
2 For further reading on visual displays serving as cognitive artifacts, see Bertin (1967/1983); Card et al. (1999); Norman (1993); Tversky (2001); Ware (2004).
3 Dover in Barber (2005), 174.
4 www.3x4grid.com/about.html (Accessed March 13, 2012).

CHAPTER 1

1 Simon (1962), 468. It is outside the scope of this book to discuss the nature of complex systems; on the other hand, it is a relevant topic considering the kinds of systems that we often encounter with big data.
2 Chen (2006), 89.
3 Cone-trees: Robertson et al. (1991); hyperbolic views: Lamping and Rao (1996), Munzner (1997).
4 Treemaps: Johnson and Shneiderman (1991).
5 Dondis (2000), 85.
6 See: Ware (2004, 2008), Card et al. (1999), MacEachren (2004), Kosslyn (1994).
7 Readings on mnemonic devices: Yates (1966), Foer (2011).
8 Pinker (1990), 104, italics in original.
9 Ware (2004), 20–22.
10 Ibid., 149–150.
11 See: Wertheimer (1950), Arnheim (1974), Ware (2004).
12 Wertheimer (1959).
13 Murdoch (1984), 81.
14 Ware (2013), 20–22.
15 Ibid., 164.
16 Ibid., 159.
17 Murdoch (1984), 47.
18 Ibid., 55.
19 Pietsch (2012), 39.
20 Ibid., 54.
21 Ibid., 102.
22 Ibid., 131.
23 Robertson et al. (1991), 189.
24 B. Johnson and B. Shneiderman (1991).
25 B. Shneiderman: www.cs.umd.edu/hcil/treemap-history. "Treemaps for space-constrained visualization of hierarchies" (Accessed October 23, 2011).
26 Munzner, Tamara (1998).
27 For articles and references for the treemap technique, see the website by Ben Shneiderman: www.cs.umd.edu/hcil/treemap-history/index.shtml (Accessed October 23, 2011).
28 Wattenberg describes his method in the paper "Visualizing the Stock Market" at ACM CHI99: www.research.ibm.com/visual/papers/marketmap-wattenberg.pdf (Accessed December 27, 2011).
29 See Lakoff and Johnson (2003).
30 See Lakoff (1987).
31 See Lakoff (1987, 1993); Tversky (2001).
32 See Kosslyn (1994).
33 See Cleveland (1994); Kosslyn (1994, 2006).
34 Kosslyn (2006), 39.
35 Wong (2010), 74.
36 Ware (2004), 135.
37 Ware (2008), 68.
38 Dynamic treemap layout comparison by Martin Wattenberg and Ben Bederson: www.cs.umd.edu/hcil/treemap-history/java_algorithms/LayoutApplet.html (Accessed December 27, 2011).
39 Bertin (2010), 202.
40 Spence and Wainer in introduction to Playfair (2005), 27.
41 Ware (2004), 136.
42 http://marumushi.com/projects/newsmap (Accessed February 28, 2012).
43 See *The Complete Work of Charles Darwin Online*: http://darwin-online.org.uk (Accessed February 21, 2012).
44 See Balzer and Deussen (2005).

CHAPTER 2

1 Shneiderman et al. (2010), 32.
2 Barabási (eBook version July 2012), 7.
3 Ibid., 10.
4 Newman (2010), 141.
5 Ibid., 2.
6 Albert and Barabási (1999).
7 Milgram and Travers (1969).
8 John Guare (1990).
9 See Bertin's books *Semiology of Graphs* (2010) and *Graphics and Graphic Information Processing* (1981).
10 Shneiderman et al. (2010), 47.
11 SPaTo Visual Explorer is an interactive software tool for the visualization and exploration of complex networks. The method and software were developed by Christian Thiemann in the research group of Dirk Brockmann at Northwestern University, financially supported by the Volkswagen Foundation and the European Commission. www.spato.net (Accessed November 3, 2012).
12 Barabási et al. (2007), 8685.
13 Lombardi in Hobbs (2003), 47.
14 Hobbs (2003), 66.
15 Easley and Kleinberg (2010), 39.
16 For detailed description of the work refer to Henry et al. (2007).
17 Henry et al. (2007), 276.
18 Newman (2010), 127.
19 Josh On: www.theyrule.net/about (Accessed September 28, 2012).
20 Barabási et al. (2007).
21 Notes written by Stefaner in an email message on January 7, 2013.
22 Danny Holten (2006).
23 It appeared in the 1898 Minutes of Proceedings of the Institution of Civil Engineers. Vol. CXXXIV, Session 1897–98, Part IV.
24 www.densitydesign.org/research/fineo (Accessed October 18, 2012).

25 Parallel Sets visualization was first described in Transactions on Visualization and Computer Graphics, Vol. 12, No. 4 (07/08 2006).
26 Broeck et al. (2011), 2.
27 www.gleamviz.org/challenges/ (Accessed February 20, 2013).
28 Thiemann in www.spato.net (Accessed November 3, 2012).

CHAPTER 3

1 Lakoff and Johnson (2003), 59.
2 Ibid., 42.
3 Ibid., 44.
4 Eco in foreword to *Story of Time* (1999), 14.
5 http://aa.usno.navy.mil/faq/docs/calendars.php (Accessed August 21, 2012).
6 Eco in foreword to *Story of Time* (1999), 12.
7 Gould (1988), 10–11.
8 Tversky (2001), 99.
9 Lakoff and Johnson (2003).
10 Tversky (2001), 101.
11 Rosenberg (2007), 71: "In addition to columns for dates and events, these charts add geographic categories, allotting, for example, different columns to different kingdoms and empires. This allows the reader not only to compare systems of dating but histories themselves."
12 Barbeu-Dubourg (1753), "Chronographie ou Description des Temps."
13 Priestley (1764), 6.
14 Ibid., 10.
15 Ibid., 11.
16 Cited in Rosenberg (2007), 61
17 Ibid., note at bottom of page 4.
18 Rosenberg (2007), 62.
19 Ibid., 59.
20 Spence and Wainer in introduction to Playfair (2005), 15.
21 Friendly (2008), 509.
22 Zerubavel (2004), 24.
23 http://whitney.org/Exhibitions/Artport/Commissions/IdeaLine (Accessed August 14, 2012).
24 Wainer (2005), 49.
25 Spence and Wainer in introduction to Playfair (2005), 15.
26 Ibid.
27 Miller (1956), 12–13.
28 Ibid., 7.
29 Ibid., 9.
30 Ibid., 10.
31 Ware (2013), 384.
32 Shelley (2011), 253.
33 Schmidt-Burkhardt (2011), 81.
34 www.wardshelley.com/paintings/pages/description.html (Accessed April 14, 2012).
35 Adams (1878).
36 In app information, IBM: https://itunes.apple.com/us/app/minds-of-modern-mathematics/id432359402?mt=8 (Accessed September 16, 2012).
37 Spence and Wainer in introduction to Playfair (2005), 31.
38 Wattenberg and Viégas (2010).
39 Ibid., 181.
40 Wattenberg (2005), 2.
41 Havre et al. (2000).
42 Byron and Wattenberg (2008).
43 http://fathom.info/fortune500 (Accessed May 22, 2012).
44 Delaney (2012).

CHAPTER 4

1 Map n. 1: *Oxford English Dictionary Online,* 3rd Edition, September 2000; online version March 2012. http://0-www.oed.com.ilsprod.lib.neu.edu/view/Entry/113853. An entry for this word was first included in the *New English Dictionary*, 1905 (Accessed May 26, 2012).
2 Ibid.: "Quotation evidence from 1527, first cited in R. Thorne in R. Hakluyt *Divers Voy* (1582) sig. B4v, 'A little Mappe or Carde of the worlde.'"
3 Robinson (1982), 16.
4 Robinson (1982); Palsky (1998); Friendly (2008).
5 Palsky (1998), 45; Funkhouser (1937); Friendly (2008), 510; Robinson (1982).
6 Robinson et al. (1995), 26–27.
7 Friendly (2008), 517.
8 For a brief account of the International Statistical Congress, see Funkhouser (1937), 310–29.
9 Friendly (2008), 509–10; Palsky (1998), 51.
10 Friendly (2005), 5.
11 See "List of Supported Map Projections": http://webhelp.esri.com/arcgisdesktop/9.3/index.cfm?TopicName=List_of_supported_map_projections and http://webhelp.esri.com/arcgisdesktop/9.3/index.cfm?TopicName=An_overview_of_map_projections (Accessed July 15, 2012).
12 Monmonier (1993), 52.
13 Monmonier (1988), 21; Robinson et al. (1995), 80.
14 Robinson et al. (1995), 78–80.
15 Monmonier (1993), 32.
16 Robinson et al. (1995), 74–78.
17 Monmonier (1996), 14.
18 Monmonier (1993), 52.
19 Ibid., 22.
20 Robinson et al. (1995), 428.
21 Ibid., 331.
22 Some classifications consider four levels of measurement (or data scales), and the one not described here is *interval*, which, in addition to the description of kind and rank, adds information about distance between ranks.
23 Bertin (2010), 285.
24 There are good surveys of systems in the literature, and I especially recommend MacEachren (2004) and Adrienko and Adrienko (2006).
25 Ware (2008), 174–75.
26 Volume is not considered here as basic graphic elements, but could be added to the system depending on the needs. Some visualizations make use of simulated volumes in two-dimensional visual displays.
27 Ware (2004), 20.
28 The third dimension is not considered here, but it doesn't mean that it shouldn't be included, because it might be relevant to certain visualizations.
29 Robinson et al. (1995), 70.
30 Robinson et al. (1995), 61.
31 Delaney (2012), 28.
32 Monmonier (1993), 21.
33 Monmonier (1988), 16.
34 http://prettymaps.stamen.com/201008/about (Accessed July 14, 2012).

35 MacEachren (2004), 303–4.
36 Bertin (1977), 230–1.
37 MacEachren (2004), 279.
38 Stevens (1975), 15.
39 Wilkinson (1999), 103.
40 Kosslyn (1994), 90.
41 For example, ArcGIS: www.esri.com (Accessed July 15, 2012).
42 Robinson et al. (1995), 499.
43 Robinson (1982), 113.
44 Robinson et al. (1995), 500–1.
45 Fry in http://fathom.info/dencity (Accessed June 26, 2012).
46 Fry (2008), 6–15.
47 Koch (2011), 192.
48 The GRO was established by British Parliament in 1836 with the purpose of registering and reporting data on births, marriages, and burials, data historically collected by local parishes. See Koch (2011), 123.
49 Koch (2011), 84.
50 Koch (2011), 201–2.
51 Ibid., 4.
52 Johnson (2007), 197.
53 Robinson (1982), 207.
54 Robinson et al. (1995), 483.
55 MacEachren (2004), 188.
56 Robinson (1982), 166.
57 Ware (2004), 135.
58 Images redrawn after Ware (2004).
59 Brewer, Cynthia A.: www.ColorBrewer2.org (Accessed January 7, 2013).
60 Ibid.
61 Robinson et al. (1995), 508.
62 Robinson (1982), 218.
63 Ibid., 64–67.
64 Ibid., 71–72.
65 http://oakland.crimespotting.org (Accessed July 14, 2012).
66 Robinson (1982), 144–54.
67 Ibid., 150.
68 Ibid., 154.
69 Robinson (1982), 150.
70 Phan et al. (2005), 1.
71 Ibid., 5.
72 M. M. Bradley and P. J. Lang, "Affective Norms for English Words (ANEW): Stimuli, Instruction Manual and Affective Ratings." Technical Report C-1, the Center for Research in Psychophysiology, University of Florida.
73 Color Brewer is an online tool devised by Cynthia Brewer and Mark Harrower at Pennsylvania State University. The tool is discussed in the box "Selecting Color Schemes." URL: www.ColorBrewer2.org (Accessed January 7, 2013).
74 Computer software for making cartograms is available online at www-personal.umich.edu/~mejn/cart (Accessed May 3, 2012).

CHAPTER 5

1 Vasiliev (1997), 10–13.
2 Andrienko et al. (2002), 3.
3 Andrienko et al. (2002), 11.
4 Monmonier (1993), 184.
5 Andrienko et al. (2010), 1588.
6 Ibid., 1582.
7 Vasiliev (1997), 8.
8 Ibid., 28.
9 Andrienko et al. (2010), 1582.
10 MacEachren (2004), 425.
11 Andrienko et al. (2010), 1585.
12 Bertin (2010).
13 Peuquet (1994), 448.
14 Andrienko and Andrienko (2006).
15 Pedro Cruz in a document explaining the project.
16 Robinson (1982), 49–50.
17 Vasiliev (1997), 30–31.
18 Kraak (2003), 390.
19 Delaney (2012), 66.
20 Delaney (2012), 4.
21 Bertin (1981), 13.
22 Delaney (2012), 4.
23 Cao et al. (2012), 2651.
24 Further details can be read at DeCamp's PhD thesis at MIT and by looking at Deb Roy's TED talk at www.ted.com/talks/deb_roy_the_birth_of_a_word.html' (Accessed January 13, 2012).
25 Description obtained from the website on the Geographic Privacy-aware Knowledge Discovery and Delivery—GeoPKDD effort: www.geopkdd.eu (Accessed January 6, 2012).
26 Natalia Andrienko and Gennady Andrienko are at the Fraunhofer Institute IAIS, Germany. Fosca Giannotti is at the KDDLAB and ISTI/CNR, Italy. Dino Pedreschi and Salvatore Rinzivillo are at the KDDLAB and the Pisa University, Italy.
27 Detailed information on computational methods and analytical techniques for dealing with mobility data can be found in numerous articles written by the authors of this mobility project, as well as in two of their published books listed in the bibliography: Andrienko and Andrienko (2006), and Gianotti and Pedreschi (2008).
28 Andrienko and Andrienko (2013), 6.
29 Andrienko and Andrienko (2013), 9.
30 Further details in: S. Rinzivillo et al. (2008).
31 Andrienko and Andrienko (2011).

CHAPTER 6

1 Card et al. (1999), 409.
2 Moretti (2007), 9.
3 In interview with J. Heer, ACM Queue.
4 Ward et al. (2010), 292–293.
5 Hearst (2009), chapter 11.
6 Ibid.
7 Moretti (2007), 53.
8 See Pinker (2011), and articles in *Nature* 449 (2007), and *Science* 331 (2011).
9 Hearst (2009), chapter 11.
10 Ware (2013), 311.
11 Ibid., 311–312.
12 Ibid., 328.
13 http://benfry.com/traces (Accessed June 26, 2012).
14 Robinson (1982), 54.
15 Delaney (2012), 193.
16 http://moritz.stefaner.eu/projects/revisit-twitter-visualization (Accessed September 6, 2012).
17 https://republicofletters.stanford.edu/tools (Accessed August 9, 2012).

18 www.francescofranchi.com/projects/infographics/letteraturagrafica (Accessed February 22, 2012).
19 Peter Norvig, in Beautiful Data (2009), 220.
20 Feinberg in *Beautiful Visualization* (2010), 56.
21 Viégas, Wattenberg, Feinberg (2009), 7.
22 Viégas and Wattenberg (2009), 1.

APPENDIX

1 Further reading on taxonomies of data, see Ware (2004), Card et al. (1999), Shneiderman (1996), and Bertin (2010).

BIBLIOGRAPHY

Adams, Sebastian (1878/2007): *Adam's Chart of History: A Chronology of Ancient, Modern, and Biblical History Timeline.* Green Forest, AR: Master Books.

Andrienko, Natalia; Andrienko, Gennady (2006): *Exploratory Analysis of Spatial and Temporal Data: A Systematic Approach.* Berlin: Springer.

— (2013): "Visual analytics of movement: a rich palette of techniques to enable understanding" in C. Renso, S. Spaccapietra, and E. Zimányi (Eds.) *Mobility Data: Modeling, Management, and Understanding.* Cambridge Press, 2013 (Forthcoming).

Andrienko, N.; Andrienko, G; Gatalsky, P. (2002): "Data and Task Characteristics in Design of Spatio-Temporal Data Visualization Tools" in *Symposium on Geospatial Theory, Processing, and Applications.*

Andrienko, G.; Andrienko, N.; Demsar, U.; Dransch, D.; Dykes, J.; Fabrikant, S. I.; Jern, M; Kraak, M.-J.; Schumann, H. (2010): "Space Time and Visual Analytics" in *International Journal of Geographical Information Science,* Vol. 24, No. 10, 1577–1600.

Andrienko, N.; Andrienko, G. (2011): "Spatial generalization and aggregation of massive movement data" in *IEEE Transactions on Visualization and Computer Graphics,* 17(2), 205–219.

Antonelli, Paola (Ed.) (2008): *Design and the Elastic Mind.* New York, NY: Museum of Modern Art.

Arnheim, Rudolf. (1974): *Art and Visual Perception: A Psychology of the Creative Eye.* Berkeley, CA: University of California Press.

Balzer, M.; Deussen, O.; Lewerentz, C. (2005): "Voronoi Treemaps for the Visualization of Software Metrics" in *SoftVis '05 Proceedings of the 2005 ACM Symposium on Software Visualization.* New York, NY: ACM, 165–215. (Accessed at http://dl.acm.org/citation.cfm?id=1056018.1056041).

Barabási, Albert-László; Albert, Réka (1999): "Emergence of scaling in random networks" in *Science* 286 (5439): 509–512. (DOI:10.1126/science.286.5439.509)

Barabási, Albert-László (2012): eBook *Network Science* (July 2012).

Barber, Peter (2005): *The Map Book.* London, UK: Walker & Company.

Barber, Peter; Harper, Tom (2010): *Magnificent Maps: Power, Propaganda, and Art* by. London, UK: British Library.

Barbeu-Dubourg, J. (1753): *Chronographie, ou Description des Tems.* (Accessed at Bibliothèque Nationale de France: http://gallica.bnf.fr/ark:/12148/bpt6k1314025)

Bertin, Jacques (1983): *Semiology of Graphics: Diagrams, Networks, Maps* (W. J. Berg, Transl.). Madison, WI: University of Wisconsin Press.

— (2010) *Semiology of Graphics: Diagrams, Networks, Maps* (W. J. Berg, translation; H. Wainer, foreword) Redlands, CA: ESRI Press.

— (1981): *Graphics and Graphic Information Processing.* New York, Berlin: Walter de Grutyter.

Bourgoing, Jacqueline (2001): *The Calendar: History, Lore, and Legend.* New York, NY: Harry N. Abrams.

Brewer, Cynthia (2005): *Designing Better Maps: A Guide for GIS Users.* Redlands, CA: ESRI Press.

— (2008): *Designed Maps: A Sourcebook for GIS Users.* Redlands, CA: ESRI Press.

Broeck, W. V.; Gioannini, C.; Gonçalves, B.; Quaggiotto, M.; Colizza, V.; Vespignani, A. (2011): "The GLEaMviz computational tool, a publicly available software to explore realistic epidemic spreading scenarios at the global scale" in *BMC Infectious Diseases* 2011, 11:37. (Accessed at http://www.biomedcentral.com/1471-2334/11/37)

Byron, Lee; Wattenberg, Martin (2008): "Stacked Graphs—Geometry & Aesthetics," *Visualization and Computer Graphics,* IEEE Transactions, Vol. 14, No. 6, 1245–1252. (DOI: 10.1109/TVCG.2008.166)

Cairo, Alberto (2012): *The Functional Art: An Introduction to Information Graphics and Visualization.* Berkeley, CA: New Riders.

— (2011): *Infografía 2.0: Visualización interactiva de información en prensa.* Spain: Alamut.

Caldarelli, Guido; Catanzaro, Michele (2012): *Networks: A Very Short Introduction* (Very Short Introductions) Oxford University Press, USA.

Cao, N.; Lin, Y.-R.; Sun, X.; Lazer, D.; Liu, S.; Qu, H. (2012): "Whisper: Tracing the Spatiotemporal Process of Information Diffusion in Real Time in Visualization and Computer Graphics" in *IEEE Transactions,* Vol. 18, No. 12, 2649–58.

Card, Stuart K.; Mackinlay, Jock; Shneiderman, Ben (Eds.) (1999): *Information Visualization: Using Vision to Think.* San Francisco, CA: Morgan Kaufmann.

Chen, Chaomei (2003): *Mapping Scientific Frontiers: The Quest for Knowledge Visualization.* London, UK: Springer-Verlag.

— (2006): Redlands, CA: *Information Visualization Beyond the Horizon,* Second Edition. London, UK: Springer-Verlag.

Cleveland, William S. (1993): *Visualizing Data.* Murray Hill, NJ: AT&T Bell Laboratories.

— (1994): *The Elements of Graphing Data.* Murray Hill, NJ: AT&T Bell Laboratories.

Delaney, John (2012): *First X, Then Y, Now Z: An Introduction to Landmark Thematic Maps.* Princeton, NJ: Princeton University Library.

Dondis, Donis A. (2000): *A Primer of Visual Literacy.* Cambridge, MA: MIT Press.

Drucker, Joahanna; McVarish, Emily (2009): *Graphic Design History: A Critical Guide.* Upper Saddle River, NJ: Pearson Prentice Hall.

Easley, David; Kleinberg, Jon (2010): *Networks, Crowds, and Markets: Reasoning about a Highly Connected World.* New York, NY: Cambridge University Press. (Accessed via preprint online at http://www.cs.cornell.edu/home/kleinber/networks-book/)

Feinberg, Jonathan (2010): *Wordle* in J. Steele and N. Iliinsky (Eds.) *Beautiful Visualization.* Sebastopol, CA: O'Reilly Media, 37–58.

Ferguson, Stephen (1991): "The 1753 Carte chronographique of Jacques Barbeu-Dubourg" in the *Princeton University Library Chronicle.* (Winter). Précis in Historical Abstracts. (Accessed at author's site http://www.princeton.edu/~ferguson/PULC_1991_duBourg.pdf)

Ferster, Bill (2012): *Interactive Visualization: Insight through Inquiry.* Cambridge, MA: MIT Press.

Few, Stephen (2009): *Now You See It: Simple Visualization Techniques for Quantitative Analysis*. Burlingame, CA: Analytics Press.

— (2006): *Information Dashboard Design: The Effective Visual Communication of Data*. Sebastopol, CA: O'Reilly Media.

— (2004): *Show Me the Numbers: Designing Tables and Graphs to Enlighten*. Burlingame, CA: Analytics Press.

Foer, Joshua (2011): *Moonwalking with Einstein: The Art and Science of Remembering Everything*. London, UK: Penguin Press.

Frangsmyr, T.; Heilbron, J. L.; Rider, R. E. (1990): *The Quantifying Spirit in the Eighteenth Century* (Uppsala Studies in History of Science, 7). Berkeley, CA: University of California Press.

Frascara, Jorge (2001): "Diagramming as a Way of Thinking Ecologically" in *Visible Language*, Vol. 35, No. 2, 165–177.

— (2004): *Communication Design: Principles, Methods, and Practice*. New York, NY: Allworth Press.

Friendly, Michael (2005): "Milestones in the History of Data Visualization: A Case Study in Statistical Historiography" in C. Weihs and W. Gaul (Eds.) *Classification: The Ubiquitous Challenge*. New York, NY: Springer, 34–52. (Accessed at http://www.math.yorku.ca/SCS/Papers/gfkl.pdf)

— (2007): "A Brief History of Data Visualization" in *Handbook of Computational Statistics: Data Visualization*. Springer-Verlag, 1–34. (Accessed at author's site: http://www.datavis.ca/papers)

— (2008): "The Golden Age of Statistical Graphics" in *Statistical Science*, Vol. 23, No. 4, 502–535. (Accessed at author's site http://www.datavis.ca/papers)

Friendly, M.; Denis, D. J. (2001): "Milestones in the History of Thematic Cartography, Statistical Graphics, and Data Visualization." Web document: http://www.datavis.ca/milestones (Accessed October 25, 2011).

Fry, Ben (2008): *Visualizing Data: Exploring and Explaining Data with the Processing Envirnment*. Sebastopol, CA: O'Reilly Media.

Funkhouser, H. Gray (1937): "Historical Development of the Graphical Representation of Statistical Data" in *Osiris*, Vol. 3, 269–404. University of Chicago Press on behalf of the History of Science Society. (Accessed at http://www.jstor.org/stable/301591)

Giannotti, F., Pedreschi, D. (Eds.). (2008): *Mobility, data mining, and privacy: geographic knowledge discovery*. Berlin: Springer Heidelberg.

Goh, K.-I.; Cusick, M. E.; Valle, D.; Childs, B.; Vidal, M.; Barabási, A.-L. (2007): "The human disease network" in *Proceedings of the National Academy of Sciences—PNAS* Vol.104, No.21, 8685–8690.

Gould, Stephen Jay (1988): *Time's Arrow, Time's Cycle: Myth and Metaphor in the Discovery of Geological Time* (Jerusalem—Harvard Lectures). Cambridge, MA: Harvard University Press.

Guare, John (1990): *Six Degrees of Separation*. New York, NY: Random House.

Harley, J. B. (2002): *The New Nature of Maps: Essays in the History of Cartography*. Baltimore, MD: Johns Hopkins University Press.

Havre, Susan L.; Hetzler, B.; Nowell, L. (2000): "Theme River: visualizing theme changes over time" in *Information Visualization, InfoVis 2000*. IEEE Symposium, 115–123. (DOI: 10.1109/INFVIS.2000.885098)

Hearst, Marti (2009): *Search User Interfaces*. New York, NY: Cambridge University Press.

Henry, Nathalie; Goodell, H.; Elmqvist, N.; Fekete, J.-D. (2007): "20 Years of Four HCI Conferences: A Visual Exploration" in *International Journal of Human-Computer Interaction*, Vol. 23, No. 3, 239–285.

Hobbs, Robert Carleton (2004): *Mark Lombardi: Global Networks*. New York, NY: Independent Curators International.

Holten, Danny (2006): "Hierarchical Edge Bundles: Visualization of Adjacency Relations in Hierarchical Data" in *Visualization and Computer Graphics*, IEEE Transactions, Vol. 12, No. 5, 741–748. (DOI: 10.1109/TVCG.2006.147)

Horn, Robert E. (1998): *Visual Language: global communication for the 21st century*. Portland, OR: XPLANE Press.

Iliinsky, Noah; Steele, Julie (2011): *Designing Data Visualizations*. Sebastopol, CA: O'Reilly Media.

Johnson, Brian; Shneiderman, Ben (1991): "Treemaps: A Space-Filling Approach to the Visualization of Hierarchical Information Structures" in *Proceedings of the IEEE Information Visualization '91*, 275–282.

Johnson, Steven (2007): *The Ghost Map: The Story of London's Most Terrifying Epidemic and How It Changed Science, Cities, and the Modern World*. New York, NY: Riverhead Trade.

Kahn, Paul; Lenk, Krzysztof (2001): *Mapping Web Sites*. Hove, UK: RotoVision.

Katz, Joel (2012): *Designing Information: Human Factors and Common Sense in Information Design*. Indianapolis, IN: Wiley.

Kemp, Martin (2001): *Visualizations: The Nature Book of Art and Science*. Berkeley, CA: University of California Press.

Klanten, Robert; Bourquin, N.; Ehmann, S.; van Heerde, F. (Eds) (2009): *Data Flow: Visualising Information in Graphic Design*. Berlin, Germany: Die Gestalten Verlag.

Klapisch-Zuber, Christiane (2003): *L'Arbre des Familles*. Paris, Fr.: Éditions de La Martinière.

Koch, Tom (2011): *Disease Maps: Epidemics on the Ground*. Chicago, IL: University of Chicago Press.

— (2005): *Cartographies of disease: Maps, mapping, and medicine*. Redlands, CA: ESRI Press.

Kosara, Robert; Bendix, F.; Hauser, H. (2006): "Parallel sets: Interactive exploration and visual analysis of categorical data" in *Visualization and Computer Graphics*, IEEE Transactions, Vol. 12 , No. 4, 558–568. (DOI: 10.1109/TVCG.2006.76)

Kosslyn, Stephen M. (1994): *Elements of Graph Design*. New York, NY: W. H. Freeman.

— (2006): *Graph Design for the Eye and the Mind*. New York, NY: Oxford University Press.

Kraak, Menno-Jan (2002) "Geovisualization illustrated" in *ISPRS Journal of Photogrammetry & Remote Sensing*, 57 (2003) 390–399. (DOI:10.1016/S0924-2716(02)00167-3)

Lakoff, George (1987) *Women, fire, and dangerous things: What categories reveal about the mind*. Chicago, IL: University of Chicago Press.

— (1993): "The Contemporary Theory of Metaphor" in A. Ortony (Ed.) *Metaphor and Thought*. New York, NY: Cambridge University Press, 202–251.

— (1994): "What Is Metaphor?" in J. A. Barden and K. J. Holyoak (Eds.) *Analogy, Metaphor, and Reminding*. Norwood, NJ: Ablex Publishing, 203–258.

Lakoff, George; Johnson, Mark. (2003): *Metaphors We Live By*. Chicago, IL: University of Chicago Press.

Lamping, J.; Rao, R. (1996): "The hyperbolic browser: a focus plus context technique for visualizing large hierarchies" in *Journal of Visual Language and Computing*, Vol. 7, No. 1, 33–55.

Larkin, Jill H.; Simon, Herbert A. (1987): "Why a Diagram is (Sometimes) Worth Ten Thousand Words" in *Cognitive Science*, Vol. 11, No.1, 65–99.

Lieberman, E.; Michel, J-B; Jackson, J.; Tang, T.; Nowak, M. (2007): "Quantifying the Evolutionary Dynamics of Language" in *Nature*, Vol. 449, No. 7163 (Oct. 11), 713–716. (DOI: 10.1038/nature06137)

Lima, Manuel (2011): *Visual Complexity: Mapping Patterns of Information.* Princeton, NJ: Princeton Architectural Press.

MacEachren, Alan M. (2004): *How Maps Work: Representation, Visualization, and Design.* New York, NY: The Guilfdor Press.

— (1994): *Some Truth with Maps: A Primer on Symbolization and Design.* Washington, DC: Association of American Geographers.

Malamed, Connie (2009): *Visual Language for Designers.* Beverly, MA: Rockport Publishers.

Marey, E. J. (1885): *La Méthode Graphique dans les Sciences Expérimentales et principalement en physiologie et en médecine,* Paris, France: G. Masson.

Mazza, Riccardo (2009): *Introduction to Information Visualization.* New York, NY: Springer.

Michel, Jean-Baptiste; Shen, Y. K.; Aiden, A. P.; Veres, A.; Gray, M. K.; The Google Books Team; Pickett, J. P.; Hoiberg, D.; Clancy, D.; Norvig, P.; Orwant, J.; Pinker, S.; Nowak, M. A.; Lieberman, A. E. (2011): "Quantitative Analysis of Culture Using Millions of Digitized Books" in *Science*, Vol. 331, No. 6014 (14 Jan. 2011), 176–182.

Miller, George A. (1956): "The Magical Number Seven, Plus or Minus Two: Some Limits on Our Capacity for Processing Information" in *Psychological Review: The Centennial Issue*, Vol. 101, No. 2 (April 1994), 343–352. (Accessed at http://www.psych.utoronto.ca/users/peterson/psy430s2001/Miller%20GA%20Magical%20Seven%20Psych%20Review%201955.pdf)

Monmonier, Mark S.; Schnell, George A. (1977): *Maps, Distortion, and Meaning* (Resource paper: Association of American Geographers, Commission on College Geography; No. 75-4). Association of American Geographers.

— (1988): *Map Appreciation.* Englewood, NJ: Prentice Hall.

— (1993): *Mapping It Out: Expository Cartography for the Humanities and Social Sciences* (Chicago Guides to Writing, Editing, and Publishing). Chicago, IL: University of Chicago Press.

— (1996): *How to Lie with Maps* Second Edition. Chicago, IL: University of Chicago Press.

— (2010): *No Dig, No Fly, No Go: How Maps Restrict and Control.* Chicago, IL: University of Chicago Press.

Moretti, Franco (2007): (1999) *Atlas of the European Novel 1800–1900.* London, UK: Verso.

— *Graphs, Maps, Trees. Abstract Models for Literary History.* London, UK: Verso.

Munzner, Tamara (1997): "H3: Laying out large directed graphs in 3D hyperbolic space" in *Proceeding of the 1997 IEEE Symposium on Information Visualization*, 2–10.

— (1998) "Exploring Large Graphs in 3D Hyperbolic Space"in *IEEE Computer Graphics and Applications*, Vol. 18, No. 4, 18–23.

Murdoch, John E. (1984): *Album of Science: Antiquity and the Middle Ages.* New York, NY: Charles Scribner's Sons.

National Maritime Museum (Compiler) (1999): *Story of Time.* London, U.K.: National Maritime Museum.

Newman, Mark E. J. (2010): *Networks: An Introduction.* New York, NY: Oxford University Press.

Norman, Donald A. (1993): *Things That Makes Us Smart.* Reading, MA: Addison-Wesley.

— (2002): *The Design of Everyday Things.* New York, NY: Basic Books.

— (2010): *Living with Complexity.* Cambridge, MA: MIT Press.

Norvig, Peter (2009): "Natural Language Corpus Data" in Segaran, Toby; Hammerbacher, Jeff (Eds.) *Beautiful Data: The Stories Behind Elegant Data Solutions.* Sebastopol, CA: O'Reilly Media, 219–242.

Palsky, Gilles (1998): "Origine et évolution de la Cartographie Thématique (XVIIe–XIXe siècles)" in *Revista da Faculdade de Letras—Geografia I série*, Vol. XIV, Porto, 39–60.

Pettersson, Rune (2010): "Information Design—Principles and Guidelines" in *Journal of Visual Literacy* Vol. 29, No. 2, 167–182.

Peuquet, Donna J. (1994): "It's about Time: A Conceptual Framework for the Representation of Temporal Dynamics in Geographic Information Systems" in *Annals of the Association of American Geographers*, Vol. 84, No. 3 (Sept. 1994), 441–461. Taylor & Francis, Ltd. on behalf of the Association of American Geographers. (Accessed at http://www.jstor.org/stable/2563777)

Phan, D.; Xiao, L.; Yeh, R.; Hanrahan, P. (2005): "Flow Map Layout" in *Information Visualization, 2005. INFOVIS 2005.* IEEE Symposium, 219–224. (DOI: 10.1109/INFVIS.2005.1532150)

Pietsch, Theodore W. (2012): *Trees of Life: A Visual History of Evolution.* Baltimore, MD: Johns Hopkins University Press.

Pinker, S. (Ed.). (1985). *Visual Cognition.* Cambridge, MA: MIT Press.

— (1990): "A Theory of Graph Comprehension" in Roy Freedle (Ed.) *Artificial Intelligence and the Future of Testing.* Hillsdale, NJ: Lawrence, 73–126.

— (2011): *Words and Rules: The Ingredients of Language.* New York: Harper Perennial.

Playfair, William (2005): *The Commercial and Political Atlas and Statistical Breviary* (Edited and introduced by Howard Wainer, Ian Spence). New York, NY: Cambridge University Press.

Priestley, J. (1764): *A Description of a Chart of Biography.*Warrington. (Accessed at http://archive.org/details/adescriptionach00priegoog)

Rinzivillo, S.; Pedreschi, D.; Nanni, M.; Giannotti, F.; Andrienko, N.; Andrienko, G. (2008): "Visually driven analysis of movement data by progressive clustering" in *Information Visualization*, Vol. 7, No. 3/4, 225–39.

Roam, Dan (2009): *The Back of the Napkin (Expanded Edition): Solving Problems and Selling Ideas with Pictures.* New York, NY: Portfolio Hardcover.

Robertson, G. G.; Mackinlay J. D.; Card S. K. (1991): "Cone trees: Animated 3D visualizations of hierarchical information" in ACM *Proceedings of CHI 1991*, 189–194.

Robinson, Arthur H.; Morrison, J. L.; Muehrcke, P. C.; Kimerling, A. J. (1995): *Elements of Cartography,* Sixth Edition. New York, NY: John Wiley & Sons.

Robinson, Arthur H. (1976): *The Nature of Maps: Essays Toward Understanding Maps and Mapping.* Chicago, IL: University of Chicago Press.

— (1982): *Early Thematic Mapping in the History of Cartography.* Chicago, IL: University of Chicago Press.

— (2010): *The Look of Maps: An Examination of Cartographic Design.* Redlands, CA: ESRI Press.

Reas, Casey; Fry, Ben (2007): *Processing: a programming handbook for visual designers and artists.* Cambridge, MA: MIT Press.

Rosenberg, Daniel (2007): "Joseph Priestley and the Graphic Invention of Modern Time" in *Studies in Eighteenth Century Culture*, Vol. 36, 55–103, Johns Hopkins University Press.

Segaran, T.; Hammerbacher, J. (Eds.) (2009): *Beautiful Data: The Stories Behind Elegant Data Solutions*. Sebastopol, CA: O'Reilly Media.

Schmidt-Burkhardt, Astrit (Ed.) (2011): *Maciunas' Learning Machines*. New York, NY: Springer Vienna.

Shelley, Ward (2011): "Narcotic of the Narrative" in *Leonardo Journal*, Vol. 44, No. 3, 252–255.

Shneiderman, Ben (1996): "The eyes have it: a task by data type taxonomy for information visualizations" in *Proceedings of the IEEE Symposium on Visual Languages* (Sept. 1996), 336–343.

Shneiderman, Ben; Hansen, Derek; Smith, Marc A. (2010): *Analyzing Social Media Networks with NodeXL: Insights from a Connected World*. San Francisco, CA: Morgan Kaufmann.

Schulten, Susan (2012): *Mapping the Nation: History and Cartography in Nineteenth-Century America*. Chicago, IL: University of Chicago Press.

Simon, Herbert A. (1962): "The Architecture of Complexity" in *Proceedings of the American Philosophical Society*, Vol. 106, No. 6, 467–482.

— (1981): *The Sciences of the Artificial*. Cambridge, MA: MIT Press.

Spence, Robert (2007): *Information Visualization Design for Interaction*, Second Edition. Essex, UK: Pearson Education.

Stankowski, Anton. *Visual Presentation of Invisible Processes: How to Illustrate Invisble Processes in Graphic Design*. Teurfen AR, Switzerland: Arthur Nigli.

Steele, Julie; Iliinsky, Noah. (Eds.) (2010): *Beautiful Visualization: Looking at Data through the Eyes of Experts*. Sebastopol, CA: O'Reilly Media.

Stevens, S. S. (1975): *Psychophysics: Introduction to Its Perceptual, Neural, and Social Prospects*. New York, NY: John Wiley & Sons.

Travers, Jeffrey; Milgram, Stanley (1969): "An Experimental Study of the Small World Problem" in *Sociometry*, Vol. 32, No. 4 (Dec. 1969), 425–443.

Tufte, Edward R. (1990): *Envisioning Information*. Cheshire, CT: Graphic Press.

— (1997): *Visual Explanations: Images and Quantities, Evidence and Narrative*. Cheshire, CT: Graphic Press.

— (2001): *The Visual Display of Quantitative Information*. Cheshire, CT: Graphic Press.

— (2006): *Beautiful Evidence*. Cheshire, CT: Graphic Press.

Tversky, Barbara (2001): "Spatial Schemas in Depictions" in Meredith Gattis (Ed.) *Spatial Schemas and Abstract Thought*. Cambridge, MA: MIT Press, 79–112.

Van Ham, Frank; Wattenberg, Martin; Viégas, Fernanda B. (2009): "Mapping Text with Phrase Nets" in *Visualization and Computer Graphics*, IEEE Transactions, Vol. 15, No. 6, 1169–1176. (DOI: 10.1109/TVCG.2009.165)

Vasiliev, I.R. (1997): "Mapping Time" in *Cartographica*, Vol. 34, No. 2, 1–51.

Viégas, Fernanda B.; Wattenberg, Martin; Feinberg, Jonathan (2009): "Participatory Visualization with Wordle" in *Visualization and Computer Graphics*, IEEE Transactions, Vol. 15, No. 6, 1137–1144. (DOI: 10.1109/TVCG.2009.171)

Wainer, Howard (1997): *Visual Revelations*. Mahwah, NJ: Lawrence Erlbaum.

— (2005): *Graphic Discovery: A Trout in the Milk and Other Visual Adventures*. Princeton, NJ: Princeton University Press.

— (2011): *Picturing the Uncertain World: How to Understand, Communicate, and Control Uncertainty through Graphical Display*. Princeton, NJ: Princeton University Press.

Ward, Matthew; Grinstein, G; Kleim, Daniel (2010): *Interactive Data Visualization.: Foundations, Techniques, and Applications*. Natick, MA: A. K. Peters.

Ware, Colin. (2004): *Information Visualization*, Second Edition*: Perception for Design*. San Francisco, CA: Morgan Kaufmann.

— (2008): *Visual Thinking for Design*. Burlington, MA: Morgan Kaufmann.

— (2012): *Information Visualization*, Third Edition: *Perception for Design* (Interactive Technologies). San Francisco, CA: Morgan Kaufmann.

Wattenberg, Martin (1999): "Visualizing the Stock Market" in *CHI EA '99 CHI '99 extended abstracts on Human factors in computing systems*. New York, NY: ACM, 188–189. (Accessed at http://www.research.ibm.com/visual/papers/marketmap-wattenberg.pdf; http://dl.acm.org/citation.cfm?id=632716.632834&coll=DL&dl=GUIDE&CFID=101543275&CFTOKEN=15601080)

— (2005): "Baby Names, Visualization, and Social Data Analysis" in *Proceedings of the 2005 IEEE Symposium on Information Visualization* (INFOVIS '05), 1–7.

Wattenberg, Martin; Viégas, Fernanda (2010): "Beautiful History: Visualizing Wikipedia" in J. Steele and N. Iliinsky (Eds.) *Beautiful Visualization*. Sebastopol, CA: O'Reilly Media, 175–192.

Wattenberg, Martin; Viégas, Fernanda (2008): "The Word Tree, an Interactive Visual Concordance" in *Visualization and Computer Graphics*, IEEE Transactions, Vol. 14, No. 6, 1221–1228. (DOI: 10.1109/TVCG.2008.172)

Wertheimer, Max (1950): "Laws of Organization in Perceptual Forms" in W. E. Ellis (Ed.) *A Source Book of Gestalt Psychology*. New York, NY: The Humanities Press, 71–88.

— (1959): *Productive Thinking*. New York, NY: Harper & Brothers.

Wilkinson, Leland (1999): *The Grammar of Graphics*. New York, NY: Springer-Verlag.

Wong, Dona M. (2010): *The Wall Street Journal Guide to Information Graphics*. W. W. Norton & Company.

Wurman, Richard Saul (2001): *Information Anxiety 2*. Indianapolis, IN.: Que.

Yates, Frances (1966): *The Art of Memory*. Chicago: University of Chicago Press.

Yau, Nathan (2011): *Visualize This: The Flowing Data Guide to Design, Visualization, and Statistics*. Indianapolis, IN: Wiley Publishing.

Zerubavel, Eviatar (1989): *The Seven Day Circle: The History and Meaning of the Week*. Chicago, IL: University of Chicago Press.

— (2004): *Time Maps: Collective Memory and the Social Shape of the Past*. Chicago, IL: University of Chicago Press.

CONTRIBUTORS

I am indebted to all contributors. This book would not exist, if it were not for the generous permission to reproduce their work. The authors are the copyright owners, in some cases together with their affiliated institutions. On a separate table, I acknowledge the sources and permissions for the historical images.

AUTHOR/COPYRIGHT OWNER	YEAR	TITLE	CHAPTER	PAGE
Gregor **Aisch** (visualization), Marcus **Bösch**, Stellen **Leidel** (editors)	2011	**10 Years of Wikipedia**	**3:** Temporal	**113**
Gennady **Andrienko**, Natalia **Andrienko**, Fosca **Giannotti**, Dino **Pedreschi**, Salvatore **Rinzivillo**	2005–09	**Mobility in Milan**	**5:** Spatio-temporal	**180**
Jussi **Ängeslevä**, Ross **Cooper**	2002	**Last Clock**	**3:** Temporal	**82**
Albert-László **Barabási,** Marc **Vidal,** and collaborators	2007	**The Human Disease Network poster**	**2:** Relational	**60**
Bestiario (data visualization company)	2009	**Research Flow**	**3:** Temporal	**106**
	2009	**ReMap**	**1:** Hierarchical	**43**
	2010	**Bioexplora** (biodiversity tree and map)	**1:** Hierarchical	**40**
	2010	**Tessera**	**1:** Hierarchical	**42**
Cynthia **Brewer**, Mark **Harrower** (Pennsylvania State Univ.)		**ColorBrewer 2.0**	**4:** Spatial	**146**
British Broadcasting Corporation (BBC)		**British History Timeline**	**3:** Temporal	**96**
Paul **Butler** for **Facebook**	2010	**Map of friendships in Facebook**	**2:** Relational	**50**
Tom **Carden**	2011	**Travel Time Tube Map**	**5:** Spatio-temporal	**168**
Nan **Cao**, Yu-Ru **Lin**, Xiaohua **Sun**, David **Lazer**, Shixia **Liu**, Huamin **Qu**	2012	**Whisper**	**5:** Spatio-temporal	**172**
Pedro **Cruz**, Penousal **Machado**, João **Bicker** (University of Coimbra, MIT CityMotion Portugal)	2010	**Traffic in Lisbon**	**5:** Spatio-temporal	**158**
Philip **DeCamp,** Deb **Roy**	2009–10	**HouseFly**	**5:** Spatio-temporal	**176**
	2009–10	**Wordscapes**	**5:** Spatio-temporal	**179**
DensityDesign Research Lab (Politecnico di Milano) Paolo **Ciuccarelli** (scientific coordinator), Giorgio **Caviglia**, Michele **Mauri**, Luca **Masud**, Donato **Ricci**	2010	**Fineo**	**2:** Relational	**70**
Paolo **Ciuccarelli** (scientific coordinator), Michele **Mauri** (project leader), Giorgio **Caviglia**, Lorenzo **Fernandez**, Luca **Masud**, Mario **Porpora**, Donato **Ricci**, Gloria **Zavatta** (theme development)	2011	**Milan Expo 2015**	**2:** Relational	**78**
Hugh **Dubberly** (creative direction), Thomas **Gaskin** (design), Patrick **Kessler** (algorithms), William **Drenttel,** Jessica **Helfand** (patent)	2011	**3 x 4 Grid**	Introduction	**15**
Charles and Ray **Eames** (original design) for **IBM**	2012	**iPad app "Minds of Modern Mathematics"**	**3:** Temporal	**103**
Jonathan **Feinberg**	2008	**Wordle**	**6:** Textual	**194**
Eric **Fischer**	2010	**Locals and Tourists**	**4:** Spatial	**136**
Francesco **Franchi** (art director, ***IL–Intelligence in Lifestyle***)	2008	**Jorge Luis Borges**	**6:** Textual	**192**
Francesco **Franchi** (art director, ***IL–Intelligence in Lifestyle***), Laura **Cattaneo** (illustration)	2009	**Green Report and Global Report**	Introduction	**10**
Ben **Fry**	2003	**Isometricblocks**	**2:** Relational	**53**
	2004	**Zip code map**	**4:** Spatial	**134**
	2009	**On the *Origin of Species*: The Preservation of ...**	**6:** Textual	**184**
	2011	**The Fortune 500**	**3:** Temporal	**110**
	2011	**Dencity**	**4:** Spatial	**134**
Google Books initiative	2010	**Ngram Viewer**	**6:** Textual	**193**

AUTHOR/COPYRIGHT OWNER	YEAR	TITLE	CHAPTER	PAGE
Ron **Graham**	1979	**Collaboration Network of Erdös**	2: Relational	52
Menno-Jan **Kraak** (University of Twente / ITC)	2002	**Space-time cube of Minard's "Napoleon March ..."**	5: Spatio-temporal	162
Mark **Lombardi** (image courtesy: Pierogi and Donald Lombardi, photo credit: John Berens)	1999	**World Finance Corporation and Associates ...**	2: Relational	46
Mapping the Republic of Letters team (Stanford University)	2010	**Corrispondenza**	6: Textual	190
Justin **Matejka**, Tovi **Grossman**, George **Fitzmaurice** (Autodesk Research)	2011	**Citeology**	2: Relational	68
Sean **McNaughton** (*National Geographic*), Samuel **Velasco** (5W Infographics)	2010	**Fifty Years of Space Exploration**	3: Temporal	102
Bureau Mijksenaar	2010	**Wayfinding system for Amsterdam RAI**	Introduction	11
Alan **Mislove**, Sune **Lehmann**, Yong-Yeol **Ahn**, Jukka-Pekka **Onnela**, J. Niels **Rosenquist**	2011	**Pulse of the Nation**	4: Spatial	157
Gerson **Mora**, Alberto **Cairo**, Rodrigo **Cunha**, Eliseu **Barreira** (Revista ***Época***, Editora Globo)	2010	**Giant Waves**	Introduction	10
Jacob **Moreno**	1934	**Sociograms**	2: Relational	48
Tamara **Munzner** (first reproduced by IEEE)	1998	**3D Hyperbolic Tree**	1: Hierarchical	29
The New York Times (NYT)	2008	**Mapping the Human "Diseasome"**	2: Relational	61
	2008	**Election Results 2008**	4: Spatial	139
***NYT*:** Matthew **Bloch**, Shan **Carter**, Amanda **Cox**	2008	**All of Inflation's Little Parts**	1: Hierarchical	44
***NYT*:** Matthew **Bloch**, Lee **Byron**, Shan **Carter**, Amanda **Cox**	2008	**The Ebb and Flow of Movies**	3: Temporal	106
***NYT*:** Shan **Carter**, Amanda **Cox**, Kevin **Quealy**, Amy **Schoenfeld**	2008	**How Different Groups Spend Their Day**	3: Temporal	112
***NYT*:** Matthew **Bloch**, Shan **Carter**, Alan **McLean**	2010	**Mapping the 2010 U.S. Census**	4: Spatial	131
NYT	2011	**Inaugural Words: 1789 to the Present**	6: Textual	191
	2012	**Hurricane Sandy**	5: Spatio-temporal	164
***NYT*:** Mike **Bostock**, Shan **Carter**, Amanda **Cox**	2012	**Over the Decades, How States Have Shifted**	2: Relational	73
***NYT*:** Lee **Byron**, Amanda **Cox**, Matthew **Ericso**	2012	**A Map of Olympic Medals**	4: Spatial	156
Mark **Newman** (University of Michigan)	2012	**Presidential Election Cartogram**	Introduction	14
Josh **On**	2004	**They Rule**	2: Relational	59
Doantam **Phan**, Ling **Xiao**, Ron **Yeh**, Pat **Hanrahan**, Terry **Winograd**	2005	**Flow Map Layout**	4: Spatial	155
Pitch Interactive: Wesley **Grubbs** (creative director), N. **Yahnke** (programmer), M. **Balog** (concept artist)	2008	**2008 Presidential Candidate Donations**	2: Relational	72
Pitch Interactive for ***Popular Science*** magazine	2009	***Popular Science* Archive**	3: Temporal	86
Pitch Interactive	2010	**US Federal Contract Spending in 2009 ...**	2: Relational	72
Stefanie **Posavec**, Greg **McInerny**	2009	**(En)tangled Word Bank**	Introduction	16
Nathalie Henry **Riche**, Howard **Goodell**, Niklas **Elmqvist**, Jean-Daniel **Fekete**	2007	**NodeTrix**	2: Relational	54
George **Robertson**, Jock D. **Mackinlay**, Stuart **Card** (Xerox Palo Alto Research Center)	1991	**Cone tree**	1: Hierarchical	29
Ward **Shelley** (courtesy of the artist and Pierogi Gallery)	2011	**Diagram after Alfred Barr**	3: Temporal	99
	2007	**Addendum to Alfred Barr, ver. 2**	3: Temporal	98
		Extra Large Fluxus Diagram	3: Temporal	101
Ben **Shneiderman**, Brian **Johnson** (University of Maryland)	1993	**TreeViz interface**	1: Hierarchical	29
Stamen Design		**Prettymaps**	4: Spatial	123
		Dotspotting	4: Spatial	123
	2008	**Oakland Crimespotting**	4: Spatial	151
Stamen Design for **Facebook**	2012	**Map of the world's friendship in Facebook**	4: Spatial	50
Moritz **Stefaner**	2010	**Revisit**	6: Textual	188
Moritz **Stefaner** (visualization), Martin **Rosvall**, Jevin **West**, Carl **Bergstrom** (Bergstrom Lab, Univ. of Washington)	2009	**well-formed.eigenfactor**	2: Relational	64
Jer **Thorp**	2009	***New York Times* 365/360**	2: Relational	56
Jan Willem **Tulp** (Tulp Interactive)	2011	**Ghost Counties**	Introduction	12

AUTHOR/COPYRIGHT OWNER	YEAR	TITLE	CHAPTER	PAGE
Alessandro **Vespignani**, Vittoria **Colizza** (principal investigators), GLEAMviz research and development team, Nicole Samay (image provider)		**GLEAMViz**	**2**: Relational	**74**
Fernanda **Viégas,** Martin **Wattenberg**	2003	**History Flow**	**3**: Temporal	**105**
Fernanda **Viégas,** Martin **Wattenberg** for **IBM ManyEyes**	2007	**Word Tree**	**6**: Textual	**200**
	2009	**Phrase Net**	**6**: Textual	**196**
Fernanda **Viégas,** Martin **Wattenberg**	2009	**Flickr Flow**	Introduction	**6**
	2012	**Wind Map**	**4**: Spatial	**115**
Martin **Wattenberg** for **SmartMoney.com**	1998	**SmartMoney Map of the Market**	**1**: Hierarchical	**30**
Martin **Wattenberg** for **Whitney Museum of American Art**	2001	**Idea Line**	**3**: Temporal	**87**
Martin **Wattenberg** for Laura **Wattenberg**	2005	**NameVoyager**	**3**: Temporal	**107**
Marcos **Weskamp**	2004	**Newsmap**	**1**: Hierarchical	**38**

HISTORICAL IMAGES

COPYRIGHT OWNER	AUTHOR	YEAR	TITLE	PAGE
Public Domain/Wikimedia Commons	Sebastian C. **Adams**	1871	Synchronological Chart of Universal History	**100**
Public Domain/Wikimedia Commons	Guido of **Arezzo**	1274	Hand of Guido	**20**
Public Domain	Jacques **Barbeu-Dubourg**	1753	Chronographie Universelle	**89**
Container Corporation of America	Herbert **Bayer**	1953	Chronology of Life and Geology	**108**
London Transport Museum	Harry **Beck**	1933	London Tube Map	**9**
Princeton University Library*	Heinrich K. W. **Berghaus**	1845	Meteorological map (The Physikalischer Atlas)	**149**
Princeton University Library*	Traugott **Bromme**	1851	Map depicting volcanic activity around the world	**121**
Public Domain	Émile **Cheysson**	1889	Statistics of the Universal Exhibitions in Paris	**92**
Public Domain/Wikimedia Commons	Denis **Diderot**	1751	Table of "Figurative System of Human Knowledge"	**25**
Public Domain	Pierre Charles **Dupin**	1826	Map of distribution and intensity of illiteracy in France	**117**
Public Domain	Heinrich Gustav Adolf **Engler**	1881	Tree of Relationships of Plants of the Cashew Family	**27**
Public Domain	Leonhard **Euler**	1736	Illustration of the seven bridges in the city of Königsberg	**49**
Public Domain/Wikimedia Commons	Adam **Ferguson**	1780	Timeline "History"	**88**
Public Domain	Charles de **Fourcroy**	1782	Tableau Poléometrique	**33**
Public Domain	Max **Fürbringer**	1888	Phylogenetic Tree of Birds	**28**
Public Domain	Francis **Galton**	1881	Isochronic Passage Chart for Travellers	**161**
LOC Geography and Map Division*	Henry **Gannett**	1898	Distribution of population of the United States in 1890	**150**
Public Domain	Georg August **Goldfuss**	1817	System of Animals	**26**
Princeton University Library*	André-Michel **Guerry**	1833	Crimes contre les personnes	**143**
Public Domain/Wikimedia Commons	Ernst **Haeckel**	1866	Monophyletic Family Tree of Organisms	**26**
Public Domain/Wikimedia Commons		1879	Family Tree of Man	**27**
Public Domain/Wikimedia Commons		c. 1879	Paleontological Tree of Vertebrates	**27**
Princeton University Library*	Edmond **Halley**	1701	A New and Correct Chart Showing the Variations...	**116**
Public Domain		1715	Predicted trajectory of the total eclipse of the Sun	**160**
Princeton University Library*	Gottfried **Hensel**	1741	Use of languages in geographic space	**186**
LOC, Geography and Map Division*	Fletcher W. **Hewes**, Henry **Gannett**	1883	Statistical Atlas of the United States	**14**
Princeton University Library*	Alexander von **Humboldt**	1817	Chart of Isothermal Lines	**150**
Public Domain	Bishop **Isidore of Seville**	7th cent.	"Consanguinity Trees," I, II, III	**24**
Public Domain/Wikimedia Commons	Alvin Jewett **Johnson**	1870	World, Showing the Distribution of the Temperature ...	**125**
Public Domain/Wikimedia Commons		1862	A Diagram Exhibiting the difference of time between ...	**166**

COPYRIGHT OWNER	AUTHOR	YEAR	TITLE	PAGE
Public Domain	Athanasius **Kircher**	1646	Universal Horoscope of the Society of Jesus	**25**
LOC Rare Book Special Collections Div.*	Ramon **Llull**	1515	Tree of Knowledge	**25**
Princeton University Library*	Elias **Loomis**	1842	Map "On Two Storms Which Were Experienced ..."	**165**
Public Domain	Etienne-Jules **Marey**	1885	Paris–Lyon Train Schedule, France	**8**
Public Domain/Wikimedia Commons	Charles **Minard**	1858	Carte figurative ... viandes de boucherie envoyés ...	**138**
LOC, Geography and Map Division*		1855	Carte figurative ... céréales qui ont circulé en 1853 ...	**153**
LOC, Geography and Map Division*		1862	Carte figurative ... coton en laine importées ...	**154**
LOC, Geography and Map Division*		1866	Carte figurative ... coton brut importées en Europe ...	**154**
Public Domain/Wikimedia Commons		1869	Napoleon March to and from Russia, 1812–1813	**163**
Public Domain	Frère de **Montizon**	1830	Map of population in France	**130**
Princeton University Library*	in Sebastian Münster	1540	Aphricae Tabula I	**167**
LOC Prints and Photographs Division*	Eadweard **Muybridge**	1878	Diagram of a horse in motion running at a 1:40 gait	**169**
Princeton University Library*	Florence **Nightingale**	1858	Diagrams representing the relative Mortality from ...	**95**
Public Domain/Wikimedia Commons		1858	Diagram of the Causes of Mortality in the Army in the East	**95**
Public Domain/Wikimedia Commons	John **Ogilby**	1675	The Road from London to the City of Bristol	**8**
Public Domain/Wikimedia Commons	William **Playfair**	1786	Exports and Imports of Scotland to and from different ...	**93**
Public Domain/Wikimedia Commons		1786	Exports and Imports to and from Denmark and Norway ...	**93**
Public Domain/Wikimedia Commons		1801	Extent, population, and revenues of the principal nations ...	**36**
Public Domain/Wikimedia Commons		1805	Chart of Universal Commercial History from the year ...	**93**
Princeton University Library*		1821	Chart Shewing the Value of the Quarter of Wheat in ...	**108**
Princeton University Library*		1824	Linear Chronology, Exhibiting the Revenues, Expenditure ...	**111**
Public Domain/Wikimedia Commons	Joseph **Priestley**	1765	A Specimen of A Chart of Biography	**91**
Public Domain/Wikimedia Commons		1769	A New Chart of History	**90**
Public Domain/Wikimedia Commons	Byrthferth de **Ramsey**	c. 1080	Diagram of the misteries of the Univers	**48**
Public Domain/Wikimedia Commons	John **Snow**	1854	Cholera in the south of London map	**135**
Princeton University Library*	in John Speed	1676	The West-Road from London to Bristol; and Its Branches ...	**171**
Public Domain/Wikimedia Commons	William **Swainson**	1837	Five Natural Orders of Birds" in Natural History of Birds	**26**
LOC Geography and Map Division*	Francis A. **Walker**	1874	Fiscal chart of the United States	**111**
LOC Geography and Map Division*		1874	The Progress of the Nation, 1720–1820 Maps	**128**
The complete works of Charles Darwin Online (permission from J. van Wyhe)*	William **West**	1859	Illustration in Charles Darwin's first edition of *On the Origin of Species*	**40**
Public Domain/Wikimedia Commons	anonymous	c. 1321	Codex St. Peter	**189**
Public Domain/Wikimedia Commons	anonymous	1496	Calendar with the positions of the Sun and Moon	**85**
Public Domain/Wikimedia Commons	anonymous	14th cent.	Calendarium Parisiense	**85**

*Further acknowledgments:

Images credited to **Princeton University Library** belong to the Historic Maps Collection, Department of Rare Books and Special Collections.

Images credited to the **Library of Congress (LOC)** belong to three Divisions: Geography and Map Division, Prints and Photographs Division, Rare Book Special Collections Division.

Illustration from *Origin of Species* was reproduced with permission from John van Wyhe ed. 2002–. **The Complete Work of Charles Darwin Online**. (http://darwin-online.org.uk/)

INDEX

A
accent color schemes, 147
Adams, Sebastian C., 100–101
Aisch, Gregor, 113
Albritton, Dan, 38
"All of Inflation's Little Parts" (*New York Times*), 44–45
Amsterdam RAI, 11
Andrienko, Gennady, 180, 182, 183
Andrienko, Natalia, 180, 182, 183
Ängeslevä, Jussi, 82, 83
Aphricae Tabula I (Sebastian Münster), 167
"Architecture of Complexity, The" (Herbert A. Simon), 17
area cartograms, 156–157
"average air temperatures for different parts of the world" (Alvin Jewett Johnson), 125

B
Balog, Mladen, 72, 86
Balzer, Michael, 45
Barabási, Albert-László, 48, 52, 60
Barbeu-Dubourg, Jacques, 89
Barr, Alfred, 98, 99
Barreira, Eliseu, 10
Bayer, Herbert, 108
Beck, Harry, 9
Bederson, Ben, 32
Belpaire, Alphonse, 152
Bendix, F., 70
Berghaus, Heinrich Karl Wilhelm, 149
Bergson, Henri, 85
Bergstrom, Carl, 64
Bertin, Jacques, 33, 55, 125, 126, 127, 170, 185
Bestiario, 40–41, 42–43, 106
Bicker, João, 158, 159
Bioexplora (Bestiario), 40–41
Bloch, Matthew, 44, 109, 131
Bostock, Mike, 73
Brewer, Cynthia, 146, 147
Brinton, Willard, 185
British History Timeline (BBC), 96
Brockmann, Dirk, 77
Bromme, Traugott, 121
Bureau Mijksenaar, 11
Butler, Paul, 50
Byron, Lee, 109, 156
Byrthferth de Ramsey, 48

C
Cairo, Alberto, 10, 11
Calendarium Parisiense, 85
"Calendar with the positions of the Sun and Moon," 85
Cao, Nan, 172
Carden, Tom, 151, 168
Card, Stuart, 29
"Carte figurative et approximative des quantités de céréales qui ont circulé en 1853 sur les voies d'eau et de fer de l'Empire Français" (Charles Joseph Minard), 152, 153
"Carte figurative et approximative des quantités de coton brut importées en Europe en 1858, en 1864 et en 1865" (Charles Joseph Minard), 154, 155
"Carte figurative et approximative des quantitiés de coton en laine importées en Europe en 1858 et en 1861" (Charles Joseph Minard), 154, 155
"Carte figurative et approximative des quantités de viandes de boucherie envoyés sur pied par les départements et consommés à Paris" (Charles Joseph Minard), 138
Carter, Shan, 44, 73, 109, 112, 131
case studies
- area cartograms, 156–157
- child development, 176–179
- choropleth maps, 142–145
- community structure, 78–81
- distance cartograms, 156–157
- dot distribution maps, 130–137
- Fineo, 70–73
- flow maps, 152–155
- geography-based relational structures, 74–77
- GLEAMviz, 74–77
- graduated symbol maps, 138–141
- information diffusion, 172–175
- information flow in science, 64–69
- isometric maps, 148–151
- isopleth maps, 148–151
- linear structure, 70–73
- mobility, 180–183
- network maps, 152–155
- Phrase Net, 196–199
- representing amounts over time, 104–113
- representing events over time, 98–103
- treemaps, 30–45
- Universal Exposition (2015), 78–81
- Wordle, 194–195
- Word Tree, 200–203

Cattaneo, Laura, 10, 11
Caviglia, Giorgio, 71, 78
"Chart of Biography" (Joseph Priestley), 91, 92
"Chart of Isothermal Lines" (Alexander von Humboldt), 150
"Chart Shewing the Value of the Quarter of Wheat in Shillings & in Days Wages of a Good Mechanic from 1565 to 1821" (William Playfair), 108
Chen, Chaomei, 17
Cheysson, Émile, 92
child development case study, 176–179
"Cholera in the south of London" map (John Snow), 135
choropleth maps, 142–145
"Chronographie Universelle" (Jacques Barbeu-Dubourg), 89
"Chronology of Life and Geology" (Herbert Bayer), 108
"Citeology" (Justin Matejka, Tovi Grossman, and George Fitzmaurice), 68, 69
Ciuccarelli, Paolo, 71, 78
class groupings, 141
closure principal, 33
Codex St. Peter, 189
Colizza, Vittoria, 74
Collaboration Network of Erdös (Ron Graham), 52
color blindness, 36, 37, 147
ColorBrewer tool, 146–147
color hues, 146
color lightness, 146
color saturation, 146
color scheme selection, 146–147
Commercial and Political Atlas of 1786 (William Playfair), 36, 92, 93
"Cone Tree" (George Robertson, Jock D. Mackinlay, and Stuart Card), 29
"Consanguinity Trees" (Bishop Isidore of Seville), 24
Cooper, Ross, 82, 83
"Corrispondenza" (Stanford University), 190
Cox, Amanda, 44, 73, 109, 112, 156
"Crimes Against People" (André-Michel Guerry), 143
Cruz, Pedro, 158, 159
Cunha, Rodrigo, 10, 11

D
data visualization, 13
DeCamp, Philip, 176
"degree of similarities between a number of varieties and species" illustration (William West), 40
Delaunay triangulation, 45, 80
"Dencity" (Ben Fry), 134
DensityDesign Research Lab, 78, 80
"Description of a Chart of Biography, A" (Joseph Priestley), 90

Deussen, Oliver, 45
"Diagram of Stylistic Evolution from 1890 until 1935" (Alfred Barr), 98
"Diagram of the Causes of Mortality in the Army in the East" (Florence Nightingale), 94, 95
"Diagram of the Chronology of Life and Geology" (Herbert Bayer), 108
"Diagram of the misteries of the Univers" (Byrthferth de Ramsey), 48
"Diagrams Representing the Relative Mortality from Zymotic Diseases" (Florence Nightingale), 94
Diderot, Denis, 25
distance cartograms, 156–157
"distribution and intensity of illiteracy in France" (Baron Pierre Charles Dupin), 117
"distribution of population of the United States in 1890" (Henry Gannett), 150
diverging color schemes, 147
dot distribution maps, 130–137
Dotspotting, 122, 123
Dover, Michael, 8
Drenttel, William, 15
Dubberly, Hugh, 15
Dupin, Pierre Charles, 117
Dynamic Treemap Layout Comparison (Martin Wattenberg and Ben Bederson), 32

E

Eames, Charles, 103
Eames, Ray, 103
"Ebb and Flow of Movies: Box Office Receipts 1986–2008" (Matthew Bloch, Lee Byron, Shan Carter, and Amanda Cox), 109
Eco, Umberto, 84, 85
"Election Results 2008" (*New York Times*), 139–141, 144, 145
Elmqvist, Niklas, 54, 55
Engler, Heinrich Gustav Adolf, 27
"(En)tangled Word Bank" (Stefanie Posavec and Greg McInerny), 16, 17
Erdös numbers, 52
Erdös, Paul, 52
Ericso, Matthew, 156
Euler, Leonhard, 48, 49
"Exports and Imports of Scotland from Christmas 1780 to Christmas 1781" (William Playfair), 93
Exports and Imports to and from Denmark and Norway from 1700 to 1780 (William Playfair), 93
"extent, population, and revenues in European countries in 1801" (William Playfair), 36
Extra Large Fluxus Diagram (Ward Shelley), 101

F

"Family Tree of Man" (Ernst Haeckel), 27
Fechner, Gustav T., 129
Feinberg, Jonathan, 194
Fekete, Jean-Daniel, 54, 55
Ferguson, Adam, 88
Fernandez, Lorenzo, 78
"Fifty Years of Space Exploration" (Sean McNaughton and Samuel Velasco), 102–103
"Figurative System of Human Knowledge" (Denis Diderot), 25
Fineo application, 70–73
"Fiscal chart of the United States" (Francis A. Walker), 111
Fischer, Eric, 130, 136–137
Fitzmaurice, George, 68, 69
"Five Natural Orders of Birds" (William Swainson), 26
Fleming, Sir Sanford, 166
"Flickr Flow" (Fernanda Viégas and Martin Wattenberg), 6, 7
"Flow Map Layout" (Doantam Phan, Ling Xiao, Ron Yeh, Pat Hanrahan, Terry Winograd), 155
flows. *See* timelines and flows.
"Fortune 500, The" (Ben Fry), 110
Fourcroy, Charles de, 33
Franchi, Francesco, 10, 11, 192
Fry, Ben, 53, 110, 134, 184, 185
Fürbringer, Max, 28

G

Galton, Sir Francis, 161
Gannett, Henry, 14, 150
Gaskin, Thomas, 15
geography-based relational structures case study, 74–77
Gestalt laws
Closure, 33
Common Fate, 73
Good Continuation, 58
introduction, 22–23
Proximity, 19
Segregation between Figure and Ground, 126
Similarity, 51
"Ghost Counties" (Jan Willem Tulp), 12, 13
Giannotti, Fosca, 180
"Giant Waves" infographic (Gerson Mora, Alberto Cairo, Rodrigo Cunha, and Eliseu Barreira), 10
GLEAMviz software system, 74–77
Goldfuss, Georg August, 26
Goodell, Howard, 54, 55
Gould, Stephen Jay, 86
graduated symbol maps, 138–141
Graham, Ron, 52
"Green Report and Global Report" (Francesco Franchi and Laura Cattaneo), 10
Grossman, Tovi, 68, 69
Grubbs, Wesley, 72, 86
Guare, John, 53
Guerry, André-Michel, 95, 143
Guido of Arezzo, 20

H

Haeckel, Ernst, 26, 27
Halley, Edmond, 116, 117, 148, 150, 160, 161
"Hand of Guido" (Guido of Arezzo), 20
Hanrahan, Pat, 155
Harness, Henry Drury, 152
Hearst, Marti, 189
Heckel, Paul, 104
Helfand, Jessica, 15
Helvig, Christoph, 88–89
Hensel, Gottfried, 186
Hewes, Fletcher W., 14
hierarchical structures. *See also* treemaps.
definition of, 25
Gestalt laws, 22–23
introduction, 17
nested schemes, 18–19
node–link diagrams, 33
perception, 21
preattentive processing, 21–22, 23
spatial encoding, 19–20
stacked schemes, 18
visual hierarchies, 19
visualization, 21–23
"History" (Adam Ferguson), 88
"History Flow" (Fernanda Viégas and Martin Wattenberg), 104–105
Hobbs, Robert, 46
"horse in motion" diagram (Eadweard Muybridge), 169
HouseFly software, 176–178
"How Different Groups Spend Their Day" (Shan Carter, Amanda Cox, Kevin Quealy, and Amy Schoenfeld), 112
"Human Disease Network" poster (Albert-László Barabási, Marc Vidal, et al.), 60–61
Humboldt, Alexander von, 150
"Hurricane Sandy" (*New York Times*), 164

I

"Idea Line" (Martin Wattenberg), 87
"Inaugural Words: 1789 to the Present" (*New York Times*), 191
infographics, 11
information design, 11
information diffusion case study, 172–175
information visualization, 13
"Inquiry into the Cause of the Prevalence of the Yellow Fever in New York" (Valentine Seaman), 135
Inquiry into the Permanent Causes of the Decline and Fall of Powerful and Wealthy Nations of 1805 (William Playfair), 92
Isidore of Seville, 24
"Isochronic Passage Chart for Travellers" (Sir Francis Galton), 161
"Isometricblocks" (Ben Fry), 53
isometric maps, 148–151
isopleth maps, 148–151
Isotype (Otto Neurath), 35

J
Jevons, William Stanley, 104
Johnson, Alvin Jewett, 125, 167
Johnson, Brian, 29
Johnson, Mark, 83, 84, 88
"Jorge Luis Borges" (Francesco Franchi), 192
Just Noticeable Difference (JND), 129
K
Kessler, Patrick, 15
Kircher, Athanasius, 25
Koch, Robert, 135
Koch, Tom, 135
Kosara, Robert, 70
Kosslyn, Stephen M., 36
Kraak, Menno-Jan, 162
L
Lakoff, George, 32, 83, 84, 88
"Last Clock" (Jussi Ängeslevä and Ross Cooper), 82, 83
Lazer, David, 172
"Lecture upon the Study of History" (Joseph Priestley), 92
Liber Etymologiarum (Bishop Isidore of Seville), 24
Lima, Manuel, 43
"Linear Chronology, Exhibiting the Revenues, Expenditure, Debt, Price of Stocks & Bread, from 1770 to 1824" (William Playfair), 111
linear structure case study, 70–73
line graphs, 36
"lines of longitude" map (Sir Sanford Fleming), 166
Lin, Yu-Ru, 172
Liu, Shixia, 172
Llull, Ramon, 25
"Locals and Tourists" (Eric Fischer), 136–137
Lombardi, Mark, 46, 47
"London Tube Map, 1933" (Harry Beck), 9
Loomis, Elias, 165
Lullus, Raimundus, 189
luminance illusions, 145
M
MacEachren, Alan M., 124, 127, 142, 168
Machado, Penousal, 158, 159
Maciunas, George, 101
Mackay, J. Ross, 130
Mackinlay, Jock D., 29
"Magical Number Seven, Plus or Minus Two, The" (George A. Miller), 97
"Map of friendships in Facebook" (Paul Butler), 50
"Map of Olympic Medals, A" (Lee Byron, Amanda Cox, and Matthew Ericso), 156
"Map of the world's friendships in Facebook" (Stamen Design), 50
"Mapping the 2010 U.S. Census" (Matthew Bloch, Shan Carter, and Alan McLean), 131
maps
  area cartograms, 156–157
  azimuthal grids, 118
  azimuthal projection, 121
  choropleth maps, 117
  choropleth maps case study, 142–145
  class groupings, 141
  conal surfaces, 118
  conformal projections, 120
  conic grids, 118
  continuous data, 124
  cylindrical grids, 118
  cylindrical surfaces, 118
  Delboeuf illusion, 129
  dimension data, 124
  discrete data, 124
  distance cartograms, 156–157
  dot distribution maps case study, 130–137
  Ebbinghaus illusion, 129
  equal-area cylindrical projection, 119
  equal-area projection, 120
  flow maps case study, 152–155
  graduated symbol maps case study, 138–141
  graphical methods, 128
  history of, 117
  introduction, 115–116
  isometric maps case study, 148–151
  isopleth maps case study, 148–151
  legends, 125, 132
  line elements, 126
  Mercator projection, 119, 120
  mid-1800s advancements, 117–118
  Mollweide projection, 119
  Muller-Lyer illusion, 129
  network maps case study, 152–155
  nonspatial data, 124, 125
  planar surfaces, 118
  plane chart projection, 121
  plane elements, 126
  Poggendorff illusion, 129
  point elements, 126
  Ponzo Illusion, 129
  projections, 118–121
  Robinson projection, 119, 120, 121
  scale, 121–123
  sinusoidal projection, 119
  thematic data, 124
  thematic maps, 116
  Tissot's indicatrix, 119
  titles, 125
  visual encoding, 124
  visual variables, 126–128
  White's illusion, 129
  Zöllner illusion, 129
Marey, Etienne-Jules, 8, 9
Masud, Luca, 71, 78
Matejka, Justin, 68, 69
Mauri, Michele, 71, 78
McInerny, Greg, 16, 17
McLean, Alan, 131
McNaughton, Sean, 102–103
Mercator, Gerardus, 120
Migurski, Michal, 151
Milan Exposition (2015), 78–81
Milgram, Stanley, 53
Miller, George A., 97
Minard, Charles Joseph, 138, 152, 153, 154, 155, 163
"Minds of Modern Mathematics" (Charles Eames and Ray Eames), 103
mobility case study, 180–183
"Mobility in Milan" (Gennady Andrienko, Natalia Andrienko, Fosca Giannotti, Dino Pedreschi, Salvatore Rinzivillo), 181–183
Monmonier, Mark S., 120, 122, 162
"Monophyletic Family Tree of Organisms" (Ernst Haeckel), 26
Montizon, Frère de, 130
Mora, Gerson, 10, 11
Moreno, Jacob, 48
Moretti, Franco, 187, 191
Münster, Sebastian, 167
Munzner, Tamara, 29
Muybridge, Eadweard, 169
Myésier, Thomas le, 189
N
"NameVoyager" (Martin Wattenberg), 107
"Napoleon March to and from Russia, 1812–1813" (Charles Joseph Minard), 163
"Napoleon March to and from Russia, 1812–1813" (Menno-Jan Kraak), 162
"Narrative Structures" (Mark Lombardi), 46, 47
networks
  adjacency matrix, 55
  basic elements, 49
  circular layouts, 62
  community structure case study, 78–81
  community structure layouts, 63
  components, 52–53
  connectivity, 52–53
  degree distribution, 52
  Eulerian paths, 49
  Fineo case study, 70–73
  force directed layouts, 62
  geography-based layouts, 63
  geography-based relational structures case study, 74–77
  GLEAMviz case study, 74–77
  graph theory, 48–49
  information flow in science case study, 64–69
  introduction, 47–48
  linear layouts, 62
  linear structure case study, 70–73
  links, 49, 51–52
  lists, 55
  maps, 152–155
  matrices, 55, 63
node–link diagrams, 55, 57–58

nodes, 49, 51–52
paths, 52–53
polar layouts, 62
properties, 51–52
radial community structure, 63
radial layouts, 62
Sankey type diagrams, 62
small-world phenomenon, 53
trees, 57
undirected links, 51
Universal Exposition (2015) case study, 78–81
unweighted links, 51
"well-formed.eigenfactor" case study, 64–67
Neurath, Otto, 35
"New and Correct Chart Showing the Variations of the Compass in the Western & Southern Oceans as Observed in the Year 1700, A" (Edmond Halley), 116
"New Chart of History, A" (Joseph Priestley), 90, 92
Newman, Mark E. J., 14, 49, 57, 157
Newman, Mia, 50
Newsmap application, 38–39
"*New York Times* 365/360" (Jer Thorp), 56
"Ngram Viewer" (Google Books), 193
Nightingale, Florence, 94, 95
NodeTrix (Nathalie Henry Riche, Howard Goodell, Niklas Elmqvist, and Jean-Daniel Fekete), 54, 55
nominal data, 187, 193

O

"Oakland Crimespotting" (Michal Migurski, Tom Carden, and Eric Rodenbeck), 151
Ogilby, John, 8
On, Josh, 59
"On the Origin of Species: The Preservation of Favoured Traces" (Ben Fry), 184, 185
"On Two Storms Which Were Experienced throughout the United States, in the Month of February, 1842" (Elias Loomis), 165
"Over the Decades, How States Have Shifted" (Mike Bostock, Shan Carter, and Amanda Cox), 73

P

paired color schemes, 147
"Paleontological Tree of Vertebrates" (Ernst Haeckel), 27
"Paris–Lyon Train Schedule, 1885" (Etienne-Jules Marey), 8, 9
Patel, Rupal, 176
Pedreschi, Dino, 180
Phan, Doantam, 155
Phrase Net, 196–199
"Phylogenetic Tree of Birds" (Max Fürbringer), 28
Physikalischer Atlas, The (Heinrich Karl Wilhelm Berghaus), 149
pie charts, 36
Pinker, Steve, 20, 191
Playfair, William, 36, 92, 93, 94, 96, 104, 108, 111
"*Popular Science Archive*" (Wesley Grubbs, Nicholas Yahnke, Mladen Balog), 86
"population in France" map (Frère de Montizon), 130
Porpora, Mario, 78
Posavec, Stefanie, 16
"predicted trajectory of the total eclipse of the Sun" (Edmond Halley), 160
"Presidential Election Cartogram" (Mark Newman), 14
Prettymaps, 122, 123
Priestley, Joseph, 90–92
Primer of Visual Literacy, A (Dondis), 19
"Progress of the Nation, 1720–1820 Maps, The" (Francis A. Walker), 128
proximity principle, 19
Ptolemy's Geographia (Sebastian Münster), 167
"Pulse of the Nation" (Alan Mislove, Sune Lehmann, Yong-Yeol Ahn, Jukka-Pekka Onnela, and J. Niels Rosenquist), 157

Q

qualitative color schemes, 147
Quealy, Kevin, 112
Qu, Huamin, 172

R

Ravn, N. F., 148
Readings in Information Visualization: Using Vision to Think (Stuart Card, et al.), 13
Reas, Casey, 53
"Redefining Disease, Genes and All" (*New York Times*), 61
"ReMap" (Manuel Lima), 43
"Research Flow" (Bestiario), 106
"Revisit" (Moritz Stefaner), 188
Ricci, Donato, 71, 78
Riche, Nathalie Henry, 54, 55
Rinzivillo, Salvatore, 180
"Road from London to the City of Bristol, 1675" (John Ogilby), 8
Robertson, George, 29
Robinson, Arthur H., 117, 120, 148
Rodenbeck, Eric, 151
Rosenberg, Daniel, 92
Rosvall, Martin, 64
Roy, Deb, 176

S

Sankey diagram, 66, 70, 71
Sankey, Matthew H. P. R., 70
Schoenfeld, Amy, 112
Seaman, Valentine, 135
Semiology of Graphics (Jacques Bertin), 170
sequential color schemes, 147
"seven bridges in the city of Königsberg" (Leonhard Euler), 49
Shelley, Ward, 98–99
Shneiderman, Ben, 29, 30, 47, 63
Simon, Herbert A., 17, 26
skills, 9
SmartMoney Map of the Market, 31–35, 37
Snow, John, 45, 135
sociograms, 48
spatio-temporal structures
child development case study, 176–179
existential changes, 161
information diffusion case study, 172–175
introduction, 159, 161
mobility case study, 180–183
multiple maps display, 163
primitives, 163
question types, 170
reading levels, 170
scales, 168–170
space-time cubes, 161–162, 183
spatial changes, 161
thematic changes, 161
time, 163–167
time as distance metaphor, 167–168
types, 161–163
SPaTo Visual Explorer, 77
Speed, John, 171
Spence, Ian, 36, 93, 104
Statistical Atlas of the United States, 1883 (Fletcher W. Hewes and Henry Gannett), 14
Statistical Breviary (William Playfair), 36
"Statistics of the Universal Exhibitions in Paris" (Émile Cheysson), 92
Stefaner, Moritz, 64, 188
Stein, Gertrude, 85
Stevens, Stanley Smith, 129
Streamgraph method, 109
Sun, Xiaohua, 172
Swainson, William, 26
"Synchronological Chart of Universal History" (Sebastian C. Adams), 100–101
"System of Animals" (Georg August Goldfuss), 26

T

"Tableau Poléometrique" (Charles de Fourcroy), 33
Tallents, Francis, 88–89
"10 Years of Wikipedia" (Gregor Aisch), 113
Tessera (Bestiario), 42–43
textual structures
connection visualizations, 189
document concordance visualizations, 189
introduction, 185, 187
lexical, 189
nominal data, 187, 193
Phrase Net case study, 196–199
processing, 192–193
relationship visualizations, 189
semantic structures, 189
syntactic structures, 189
typography as visual elements, 193
verbal language, 189, 191–192
visualization types, 189
visual language, 189, 191–192

word frequency visualizations, 189
Wordle case study, 194–195
Word Tree case study, 200–203
"They Rule" (Josh On), 59
Thiemann, Christian, 77
Thorp, Jer, 56, 58
"3-D Hyperbolic Tree" (Tamara Munzner), 29
"3 x 4 Grid" (Hugh Dubberly, Thomas Gaskin, and Patrick Kessler), 15
timelines and flows
"amount over time" case study, 104–113
color codes, 95
digital timelines, 96
"events over time" case study, 98–103
flow maps, 152–155
graphical conventions, 95–96
historical time representations, 87
horizontal orientation, 88
introduction, 83–84
Joseph Priestley and, 90–92
line indicators, 95
nonuniform timescales, 96
structure models, 86–87
thematic sections, 95
time indicators, 95
time measurements, 84–85
timescale, 95
uniform timelines, 88–89
vertical orientation, 88
Tissot, Nicolas Auguste, 119
"Traffic in Lisbon" (Pedro Cruz, Penousal Machado, and João Bicker), 158, 159
"Travel Time Tube Map" (Tom Carden), 168
treemaps. *See also* hierarchical structures.
algorithms, 30
"All of Inflation's Little Parts" case study, 44–45
area sizes, 34
artifacts, 32
Ben Shneiderman and, 30
color schemes, 36–37
container schema, 32
creation of, 30
luminance channel, 37
Natural Science Museum of Barcelona case study, 40–41
Newsmap case study, 38–39
part–whole image schema, 32
proportions, 34
SmartMoney Map of the Market case study, 31–35, 37
Tessera case study, 42–43
Voronoi, 44–45
"Tree of Knowledge" (Ramon Llull), 25
"Tree of Relationships of Plants of the Cashew Family Anacardiacae" (Heinrich Gustav Adolf Engler), 27
"TreeViz" (Brian Johnson and Ben Shneiderman), 29
Tufte, Edward, 185
Tulp, Jan Willem, 12, 13
Tversky, Barbara, 88
"2008 Presidential Candidate Donations: Job Titles of Donors" (Wesley Grubbs, Nicholas Yahnke, and Mladen Balog), 72
U
"Universal Commercial History from 1500 BCE to 1805" (William Playfair), 93
Universal Exposition (2015), 78–81
"Universal Horoscope of the Society of Jesus" (Athanasius Kircher), 25
"use of languages in geographic space" (Gottfried Hensel), 196
"US Federal Contract Spending in 2009 vs. Agency Related Media Coverage" (Wesley Grubbs, Nicholas Yahnke, and Mladen Balog), 72
Using Vision to Think (Stuart K. Card, Jock Mackinlay, and Ben Shneiderman), 185, 187
V
Vasiliev, I. R., 161, 165, 167
Velasco, Samuel, 102
Vespignani, Alessandro, 74
Vidal, Marc, 60
Viégas, Fernanda, 6, 7, 104–105, 114, 115, 187, 196
"volcanic activity around the world" (Traugott Braumme), 121
Voronoi diagrams, 44–45, 80, 135
W
Wainer, Howard, 36, 89, 93, 104
Walker, Francis A., 111, 128
Ware, Colin, 21, 22, 36, 37, 126, 145, 192
Wattenberg, Martin, 6, 7, 31, 32, 87, 104–105, 107, 114, 115, 187, 196
"Wayfinding System for Amsterdam RAI," 11
Weber, Ernst H., 129
Weber-Fechner law, 129
"well-formed.eigenfactor" (Moritz Stefaner, Martin Rosvall, Jevin West, and Carl Bergstrom), 64–67
Wertheimer, Max, 23
Weskamp, Marcos, 38, 39
West, Jevin, 64
"West-Road from London to Bristol; and Its Branches to Several of the Principal Towns, with Their Computed Distances, The" (John Speed), 171
West, William, 40
Whisper application, 172–175
"Wind Map" (Fernanda Viégas and Martin Wattenberg), 114, 115
Winograd, Terry, 155
Wordle case study, 194–195
WordScapes, 179
Word Tree search tool, 200–203
World Finance Corporation and Associates, c. 1970–84 (Mark Lombardi), 46, 47
X
Xiao, Ling, 155
Y
Yahnke, Nicholas, 72, 86
Yeh, Ron, 155
Z
Zavatta, Gloria, 78
Zerubavel, Eviatar, 84
"Zip code map" (Ben Fry), 134

ACKNOWLEDGMENTS

I would like to start by acknowledging all of the contributors, each of whom kindly replied to my requests for their projects and who granted the permission for the reproduction of their images. Without their exemplar projects, this book would be much impoverished.

I am also grateful to the many writers who before me had undertaken the task to compile and share their knowledge of the field. They are listed in the bibliography which, while mostly containing the cited sources, also includes a few other books that were relevant to my writing.

The structure of this book was influenced by my experience teaching information design for the past ten years, including productive interaction with my students in the Art and Design department at Northeastern University.

There are many people I would like to thank and without whom I would not have had the strength to finalize such an arduous task that is writing a book, including the selecting and gathering of all of the images. Writing a book is a humbling experience, especially for a designer without training in writing. Designing the book was much easier… I would like to thank the continuous support and love of my parents João Carlos and Yara Meirelles and my brother José Pedro Meirelles. I am grateful for the friendship and encouragement of Luisa Rabbia, Fosca Gianotti and Dino Pedreschi, Alex Flemming, Botond Részegh, Albert-László Barabási, Dagoberto Marques and Andrea Campos, Chris Pullman, Mardges Bacon, Yu-Ru Lin, Fenya Su, Cynthia Baron and Shai Inbar, Danielle Monsiegneur, Ying Dong, Xiaohua Sun, and Ronaldo Menezes. I am indebted to Fernanda Viégas and Martin Wattenberg, who were supportive of my undertaking and generously gave permission to use their Wind Map on the cover. My deepest appreciation goes to Ronald Bruce Smith who was patient, supportive, and caring throughout this burdensome journey.

When I started this enterprise after an invitation over a year ago from Emily Potts at Rockport Publishers, I did not know what it truly encompassed. I still feel that I could have spent a longer period with the research, perhaps even for another couple of years. If, on one hand, the pressure to finalize the book was difficult to handle most of the time, on the other, it helped me focus and accomplish the task. There are certainly lacunae and areas that I might have overlooked in the broad field that the visualization of information covers though which I hope have not lead to errors. However, if you find anything that is incorrect, please get in touch with me, as I would love to hear from you and correct any errors in subsequent reprints of the book: meirelles.isabel@gmail.com.

ABOUT THE AUTHOR

Isabel Meirelles is a designer and educator. Since 2003, she has been teaching classes on information design and motion graphics at Northeastern University, Boston, where she is an associate professor in the Art and Design department, College of Arts, Media, and Design. Her intellectual curiosity lies in the relationships between visual thinking and visual representation, with a research focus on the theoretical and experimental examination of the fundamentals underlying how information is structured, represented, and communicated in different media.

Isabel studied Architecture and Urban Design at Faculdade de Belas Artes in São Paulo, Brazil. She received two master's degrees, one in history and theory of architecture at the Architectural Association School of Architecture in London, and the other in communication design from Dynamic Media Institute, Massachusetts College of Art, Boston.

Isabel's professional experience includes architecture, art, and communication design. She has held positions in São Paulo including chairperson of the Art Education & Public Affairs Department at the MaSP–Museum of Art of São Paulo, the principal art museum in Brazil, and senior design positions at major publishing companies, including one of the largest media holdings in Latin America, Editora Abril. In Boston, Isabel has continued a small design practice that focuses mainly on projects for cultural and nonprofit institutions.

Meirelles is a frequent speaker at national and international conferences dealing with information design, motion graphics, and design education. She co-chairs the Arts Humanities and Complex Networks Leonardo symposium, a parallel event to NetSci–International School and Conference on Network Science. Isabel has published articles in a variety of publications, including *Visible Language* journal and several international conference proceedings, like ACM-SIGGRAPH and the International Information Design Conference in Brazil. She frequently collaborates with colleagues in the sciences and the humanities in interdisciplinary projects involving visualization of information.

www.isabelmeirelles.com